BATTLES
OF
THE 20th CENTURY

BATTLES

— OF —
THE 20th CENTURY

Editors
Chris Bishop & Ian C. Drury

The Military Press
New York

Originally published in Great Britain in 1989 by
The Hamlyn Publishing Group Ltd, Michelin House,
81 Fulham Road, London SW3 6RB, UK

This 1989 edition published by Military Press
Distributed by Crown Publishers, Inc., 225 Park Avenue South,
New York, New York 10003

Printed and bound in Hong Kong

ISBN: 0-517-66221-3

h g f e d c b a

Produced by Aerospace Publishing Ltd
179 Dalling Road,
London W6 0ES

Picture acknowledgements

The publishers would like to thank the following individuals
and organisations for their kind help in supplying
photographs for this book.

Robert Hunt Library: 6, 7, 8, 9, 10, 11, 12, 13, 14, 15, 18, 19,
20, 21, 22, 23, 27, 28, 29, 31, 32, 33, 37, 38, 39, 41, 44, 45,
46, 47, 49, 50, 51, 52, 54, 55, 56, 57, 64, 65, 72, 73, 76, 77,
80, 81, 184, 185, 187, 190, 191, 199
Imperial War Museum: 6, 7, 9, 10, 11, 12, 13, 14, 15, 16, 17,
18, 21, 26, 27, 30, 31, 33, 34, 35, 36, 40, 44, 45, 46, 48, 50,
51, 52, 53, 62, 63, 66, 67, 71, 72, 73, 74, 75, 76, 79, 80, 81,
84, 90, 97, 98, 99, 102, 103, 114, 115, 123, 124, 125, 126, 127,
130, 131, 132, 136, 137, 142, 143, 146, 147, 148, 149, 154, 155,
158, 159, 160, 161, 164, 165, 168, 169, 170, 202, 203
Grumman Aerospace Corporation: 182
US Army Signal Corps: 145, 180
US Air Force: 138, 139, 170, 182, 183, 189, 192, 195, 196, 197
US Army: 169, 180, 181, 188, 189, 193, 194, 195, 201
ECPA: 185
Iraqi Army: 198
COI: 202, 203
Australian War Memorial: 20, 21, 48, 49, 75, 79, 94, 95
RAF Museum: 22
WZ Bilddienst: 7, 17
Bruce Robertson: 45, 46, 48
MacClancy Collection: 8, 10, 11, 12, 13, 19, 20, 23, 32, 37,
41, 44, 45, 47, 49, 52, 57, 60, 61, 62, 63, 68, 69, 70, 71, 72,
74, 75, 76, 77, 78, 82, 83, 84, 85, 86, 87, 90, 91, 94, 96, 97,
98, 99, 104, 105, 106, 107, 116, 117, 118, 119, 120, 121, 122, 123,
128, 129, 132, 133, 142, 143, 144, 145, 146, 147, 152, 153, 154,
155, 156, 157, 162, 164, 165, 168, 169, 170, 172, 173, 175, 177,
181, 191, 192, 193, 194, 195, 196, 197, 198, 200, 201
Heinz J. Novarra: 127
US National Archives: 50, 69, 84, 88, 89, 118, 128, 132, 163,
166, 167
Associated Press: 81, 178, 179, 181, 188, 189, 193, 194, 195,
201
US Navy: 88, 89, 92, 93, 100, 101, 103, 111, 112, 113, 135, 150,
151, 158, 159, 162, 166, 167, 177, 180, 191, 201
US Marine Corps: 110, 111, 134, 135, 170, 177, 192, 193
Robert L. Lawson Collection: 162
Pilot Press: 190, 199
Israeli Government Press Office: 198, 199

Contents

RED SUN RISING: The battle of Tsushima

The Russo-Japanese war established Japan as a world power. It led to the first major sea fights since 1866 and land battles which foreshadowed World War I.

Having gone to war with China in 1894/5 over the question of Japanese influence in Korea, a semi-independent Chinese Vassal Japan emerged with territorial gains, including Port Arthur. Following great political pressure, she was obliged to hand them back, only to see Russia in 1898 lease the territory for herself and then, in a period of bullish expansion, occupy part of Manchuria in 1901 and threaten Korea. Attempts by the Japanese at a negotiated settlement during 1903 met with a contemptuous lack of response and suddenly, patience at an end, the Japanese on 5 February 1904 broke off diplomatic relations with their powerful neighbour. Then, during the night of 8/9 February and with no formal declaration of war, three divisions of Japanese torpedo boats attacked Port Arthur and its neighbour, Dalny. At the latter nothing was found, as it was a very dark night, but the 10 boats approaching Port Arthur found major Russian units at anchor in the roads, incompletely protected by torpedo nets. In a series of attacks between 2300 and 0145, and in the face of wild return fire, 18 torpedoes were launched: five found their marks, requiring the battleships *Tsarevitch* and *Retvizan*, as well as the cruiser *Pallada*, to be grounded. The Japanese main body was in support, standing inshore the following morning to engage the Russians ineffectually for half an hour.

The Port Arthur Squadron

With hostilities to be settled on territory other than that of the antagonists, control of the Yellow Sea was of great importance but, while the Tsarist fleet was twice the size of that of the Japanese, its greatest strength lay far away in the Baltic. The force based primarily on Port Arthur and Vladivostok outnumbered the Japanese in battleships by seven to six, but was greatly deficient in all types of cruiser, destroyer and torpedo boat. Above all, the Japanese possessed concentration, superior dockyard facilities and total belief in the rights of their cause. The excellent discipline of the fleet was a reflection of its great leader, Vice Admiral Heihachiro Togo.

On 9 February superior Japanese forces also overwhelmed the Russian cruiser *Variag* and gunboat *Korietz* in the Korean port of Chemulpo (now Inchon), both being scuttled to avoid capture. Only on 10 February was war officially declared.

Having established an initiative, Togo daringly moved lightly-escorted troop convoys to the mainland. Military success was soon forthcoming and, anxious that the Port Arthur squadron might savage his lines of communication, the Japanese admiral made several unsuccessful attempts to block the port while Japanese army forces began its investment.

A new commander, Admiral Stepan Makarov, put some spirit into the Russian forces, but both sides also indulged in extensive minelaying. On the night of 12/13 April 1904 a scrappy surface action resulted in Russians withdrawing onto a line of mines. Two battleships, the *Petropavlovsk* and *Pobieda*, struck mines, the former sinking rapidly with Makarov among the victims. This great loss was offset materially in the following month, when the Japanese battleships *Hatsuse* and *Yashima* were sunk off Port Arthur on a similarly unsuspected line, the latter capsizing as a result of asymmetric flooding about a centreline bulkhead.

August breakout

By June, the Russian base had come under fire from siege artillery and the squadron, under its new commander Admiral Vilgelm Vitgeft, made a half-hearted attempt to break out to Vladivostok. Beaten back, the squadron was finally ordered out in August by imperial edict. On 10 August it sailed again, Togo allowing it to get well out to sea before attacking. Fire appeared to be concentrated on both flagships, and Vitgeft was killed when the *Tsarevitch*

Pobieda
Pobieda was one of the six battleships in the Russian Pacific Fleet based at Port Arthur. She took part in the first battle with the Japanese fleet in February, and participated in the abortive breakout battle on 10 August. After her return to besieged Port Arthur, she was sunk at her moorings by Japanese army 28-cm howitzers. She was raised after the war, rebuilt and served with the Japanese fleet until 1922.

Oslyabya
Oslyabya led the second division of the Russian fleet at Tsushima and was the first Russian battleship to succumb to Japanese shellfire. Carrying so much coal that her main armour belt was submerged, her waterline was penetrated by a 12-in shell and she capsized. Many of her crew were picked up by the ancient armoured cruiser *Dimitri Donskoi* which made an epic escape to the Korean coast.

Death of a Navy

Japanese crowds wave at one of their battleships (Shikishima or the ill-fated Hatsuse) as she weighs anchor. The battleships were all British built and incorporated the latest developments in warship engineering.

The Russian battleship Tsarevitch *was the flagship of Admiral Vitgeft in the last fight of the Port Arthur Squadron. Alone of the Russian battleships, she escaped to Kiao Chau while the others were herded back to the doomed fortress.*

Port Arthur capitulated on 2 January, 1905. Here, on the evening of 26 May, Togo's fleet steams into the Straits to attack Russia's Baltic Fleet which made an epic 18,000-mile voyage to reach the coast of Japan.

Mikasa
Mikasa flew Togo's flag at Tsushima. She sustained more damage than the other Japanese battleships at Round Island on 10 August and again at Tsushima where she suffered 63 casualties. She was retired in 1923 to become a national monument and is preserved to this day.

Shikishima
Built at the Thames Iron Works between 1897 and 1900, *Shikishima* was one of the six modern battleships under Admiral Togo's command and fought in all three major actions.

was hit heavily. With steering damaged the ship circled wildly and, attempting to follow its leader, the Russian line became disorganized. Togo closed in, attacking from all sides, but had not succeeded in sinking anything when dusk fell and the action (known as the Battle of the Yellow Sea) petered out. The Russian squadron had been badly weakened, however, part escaping back to the prison of Port Arthur but the remainder seeking neutral ports and internment.

Only four days later the small Russian cruiser squadron operating a trade war out of Vladivostok was intercepted off Ulsan and the *Rurik* was sunk. Dispirited, the force played no further effective part in the war.

Unbelievably, it was only in October that a Russian reinforcement fleet sailed from the Baltic under Admiral Zinovy Rozhdestvensky. To make up strength, its modern component was saddled with several old ironclads which proved a hindrance both to progress and, eventually, to battle. The force had reached only as far as Madagascar on 2 January 1905, and here the fleet received the news of Port Arthur's fall and the loss of the remaining ships within.

Interception at Tsushima

Only Vladivostok remained: to reach it, Rozhdestvensky had to navigate the narrow Strait of Tsushima, and it was predictably here that Togo's cruisers intercepted him on 27 May 1905. Radio was used to home in the main body, which made contact at 1340 off Okinoshima.

Almost contemptuously, Togo crossed his opponent's bows from right to left, then turned in succession 16 points towards his enemy, using his great speed advantage to force the head of the Russian line to the eastward. The rate of Japanese fire and the effect of its Shimose explosive was here decisive. Again the Russians lost their admiral, Rozhdestvensky being severely injured when his flagship *Suvarov* was hit heavily. Almost blindly following its instinct for sanctuary the Russian fleet completely circled twice over the next few hours in efforts to get back to its base course.

As the fleet progressed it left behind more casual-

ties – *Oslyabya, Suvarov, Aleksandr III, Borodino* and others. With nightfall, Togo pulled his heavy units back, leaving his destroyers to continue. The dark hours saw three of the old Russian ironclads torpedoed and sunk. With the dawn of 28 May the acting commander, Admiral Nebogatov, soon found himself again surrounded and a few token Japanese shots persuaded him to surrender his remaining ships.

Tsushima was virtual annihilation. For the loss of four destroyers, Togo cost the Russians eight battleships, 11 assorted cruisers and seven destroyers (sunk, captured or interned). The disaster brought about the end of the war within five months and the beginnings of the direct opposition to Tsarist rule that grew ultimately to the revolution of 1917.

Vice-Admiral Heihachiro Togo
Trained at the Royal Navy College at Greenwich, Togo was a coldly thorough commander who led the Japanese fleet to victory in the Russo-Japanese war. Before Tsushima he signalled to the fleet 'Let every man do his utmost' and his victory on 27 May was in similarly Nelsonic tradition.

Battle for Manchuria
Japan's emergence as a world power began with war against China 1894-5, and the subsequent Russian expansion into Manchuria was incompatible with Japan's new ambition.

Aleksandr III was one of the four 'Borodino' class battleships which formed the backbone of Admiral Rozhdestvensky's fleet. Like most of the Russian Warships she went down still firing, taking most of the crew with her.

On board the Orel *after the battle. The dawn of 28 May found this crippled battleship in company with three ancient ironclads commanded by Admiral Nebogatov. They were 300 miles short of Vladivostok and safety.*

Orel *struck her colours on 28 May and was eventually repaired and operated by the Japanese navy. The defeat at Tsushima set the seal on Russia's humiliation in the Pacific and contributed to the political disorders in Russia during 1905.*

7

EN AVANT! The battle of the Frontiers

Wearing colourful uniforms of a bygone era, the French army went to war in 1914 believing that aggressive offensive action was the key to victory.

When the French army went to war in 1914 it gloried in its high morale. It considered itself to be superbly equipped, and it was at long last setting out to avenge the defeats and indignities suffered at German hands in the Franco-Prussian War of 1870. Finally it was setting out to regain the lost provinces of Alsace and Lorraine, ceded to the Germans in 1871. As the marching infantry and the cavalry moved out of their depots they advanced immediately towards these two 'lost' territories with eager anticipation.

They were to be bitterly disappointed, for they were moving into what history was to call the Battle of the Frontiers. In fact there was not one battle but a whole string of them, all ending in French defeats. At the time the French army could do little to analyse why this should have happened, but subsequently the reasons became clear to all who chose to look for them.

In immediate terms the French were defeated because their military leaders did exactly what the German staff planners wanted them to: they advanced towards Alsace and Lorraine on the south-eastern sector of the Franco-German border, while the main German moves were being made away to the north-west in the form of the now-famous Schlieffen Plan. This entailed a massive move by the chief weight of the German army through Belgium, along the Channel coast and down behind Paris to encounter the French army in the rear to pen it up against the

borders. When the French army moved towards the two provinces it was thus doing exactly what the Germans hoped, and by so doing considerably assisted the progress of the Schlieffen Plan.

In August 1914 all was not well with the French army, but at the time this unpalatable fact was ignored. At last the French were advancing to Alsace and Lorraine. The bands played as the infantry in their bright uniforms marched east, accompanied by the cavalry, some still in shiny breastplates as worn at Waterloo over a century before. The Germans simply waited.

Emplaced defences

The Germans knew all about French plans and had arranged their forces accordingly. They made few advances during the early stages, but instead prepared a series of carefully emplaced defences at what they considered to be the right places, and they were not far wrong. The French army advanced on a broad front, and by 20 August the first tentative encounters were under way. The French soldiers usually had to march all the way to the borders, and by the time they got there many were tired. They had to carry much of their personal kit on their backs along with their heavy rifles and at least 100 rounds of ammunition. To this could be added the long and heavy bayonet, at least a part of the day's rations and the long greatcoat, usually worn with the front buttoned open at the bottom. Their enemies were already emplaced and ready, fresh and just as eager as the French to start the forthcoming battles.

The French were arranged in five armies from Lille in the north to Mulhouse in the south. Each army had at least two corps, and such was the confidence of the French that these corps usually advanced to the designated frontier positions side-by-side. They were in for a shock because, once the French scouting parties had discovered the main

French Cuirassier, field service dress 1914

Life all European armies, the French army retained heavy cavalry regiments trained to fight with lance and sabre. The *cuirassiers* took to the field in 1914 in uniforms little different from those worn under Napoleon although the glittering breastplate and helmet were concealed with khaki covers.

The Schlieffen Plan
The French attack on the Franco-German border played into the hands of the Germans, who planned a massive battle of encirclement. Sweeping through Belgium, they intended to pass west of Paris before turning south-west and trapping the French armies against the German frontier.

Marching to the front
The French authorities anticipated that 13 per cent of their reservists would fail to return to the colours but in fact over 99 per cent of French soldiers answered the call. It was time to avenge the humiliation of 1870.

The Schlieffen Plan unfolds

Breastplates glittering in the August sunshine, French cuirassiers head for the German frontier. However, cavalry reconnaissance completely failed to identify the direction of the main German thrust and French armies headed into the trap.

The French Commander-in-Chief, General Joffre, reviews Foch's XX Corps, one of the most hard-fighting French formations. On 20 August Foch's corps conducted a tenacious defensive battle at Morhange, 20 miles SW of Metz.

A battery of the famous French 'Soixante-Quinze' 75-mm field guns in action. Firing 15 accurately aimed shells a minute over a very flat trajectory, they were ideal weapons for the open warfare of August to October 1914.

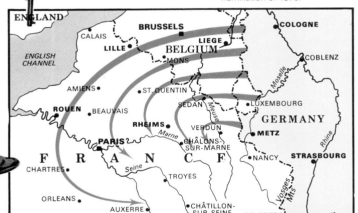

in the mayhem of the advance of the mass of the German army through Belgium and across the northern French plains. The Schlieffen Plan was grinding its way towards Paris and the nation seemed to be in great danger. But the Battle of the Marne lay ahead, and with it the failure of the German plans that led to four years of trench warfare.

The Battle of the Frontiers is now generally seen as a prelude of what was to come after 1914, but at the time it was a disaster for the French. Their long-held theories were seen to be of little worth, and they had to revise their strategies and tactics drastically to suit the 'new' conditions. It also cost them the cream of their armies: the men who fell in the Battle of the Frontiers were the best that the French had. To this day the memorial plaque in the Officer Training College at St Cyr bears the title for the dead of the first year of the war as 'The Class of 1914'. Those officers could never be replaced, and with them perished tens of thousands of the best regular troops that the French army had trained. From then on the war was to be fought with a largely conscript force used en masse in such a way that the casualties of the Battle of the Frontiers were later to be regarded as nothing unusual.

German positions, the massed French formations simply advanced towards them and there followed what can only be termed a series of massacres (rather than battles) as the French were cut down in their tracks.

Over open fields

Much of the damage was done as a result of infantry encounters in which rifles and machine-guns in carefully concealed German positions fired directly into the advancing French ranks. As the French advanced over open fields still covered with the year's harvest, the German machine-gunners could pick them off easily, for the brightly-coloured French uniforms stood out well against the background. The unfortunate French cavalry never got near enough to their destroyers to use their lances and sabres, for a single machine-gun was enough to reduce a squadron to a few uncomprehending men and terrified horses. The French foot soldiers fell in droves, often without firing a shot, still carrying their bayonet-laden rifles pointing to the east as they fell. The French artillery fared little better. The 75s were supposed to be used well forward with their direct fire supporting the all-important advance. What had not been foreseen was that although the

Execution of a German spy
Spy-phobia was rampant in all the belligerent nations in 1914 and anyone with a foreign name was suspect. In England the First Sea Lord, Prince Louis of Battenberg, was compelled to resign despite a lifetime's dedicated service.

75s could fire 15 rounds per minute, ammunition had been allocated for a fire rate of only 2.75 rounds per minute. But the 75s did have their successes, for the fighting was not all one-sided. In some places impetuous German officers led their units forward into the fray only to be caught in the open as the French had been, and in some places the piles of German corpses were as high as those of the French.

Where the French suffered most severely was in their overall lack of heavy artillery. In a sharp foretaste of things to come, German artillery spotter aircraft often flew over the advancing French columns to direct the fire of the heavier batteries onto the unsuspecting troops, who were killed even before they had joined the battle. It was all too much. The French colonial troops were among the first to break. They were always among the first to move into battle and they accordingly suffered the worst that the Germans could direct against them. The rout of the colonial troops started a general retreat from the frontiers, but at the time this fact was lost

French Infantryman, field service dress 1914

A pale green uniform had been approved in 1912 but it was not adopted and in 1914 the French infantry fought in much the same uniform as they had worn in 1870. The red képi was usually covered with a pale blue/grey cover and in 1915 the army changed the whole uniform to *horizon bleu*.

8-mm Lebel rifle

Named after its inventor, Lt. Col. Nicholas Lebel, the French infantry's rifle had been the first gun using smokeless powder to enter service. By 1914 the German and British armies had adopted more modern weapons, and features like the Lebel's tubular magazine were outmoded.

French dragoon machine-gun team
The German armies on the frontier were supposed to remain stationary while those in the north outflanked the French. However, they actually launched offensives of their own and here a French cavalry regiment awaits the onslaught in hastily dug positions.

Specification
Fusil Lebel mle 1886/93
Calibre: 8 mm (0.315 in)
Length: overall 1.303 m (51.3 in); barrel 0.798 m (31.4 in)
Weight: 4.245 kg (9.35 lb)
Muzzle velocity: 725 m (2,379 ft) per second
Magazine: 8-round tubular

German infantry lie prone in open ground near the French frontier. The four French armies deployed between Verdun and Epinal made no headway and Lanzerac's 5th Army on the left flank began to detect the great German outflanking march.

French attacks were pressed home with suicidal courage but they met the same fate as the Sudanese at Omdurman. The fields were strewn with red-trousered bodies and the heavy officer casualties weakened French tactical leadership.

Moltke's generals reported a series of victories but the German C-in-C remained anxious. Where were the captured guns and hordes of prisoners? August 1914 only brought in a few prisoners like the men seen here. The French army was not beaten.

MONS: The BEF makes its stand

Sunday, 23 August 1914: the German 1st Army's remorseless advance is suddenly stopped near the small town of Mons. Blocking the way are 4 British divisions.

The British Expeditionary Force of two infantry corps and a cavalry division under Major General Sir Edmund Allenby had begun to embark at Dublin and Southampton on 12 August 1914. It crossed the Channel that night, spent a few days in tented reception camps near Boulogne, Le Havre and Rouen, travelled by train as far as Le Cateau and then spent the next five days marching into Belgium along rough pavé roads and in sweltering temperatures. It was a journey which had at first exacted a price in blistered feet and sweating exhaustion (especially among the newly-recalled reservists) but which by the evening of 22 August had brought them to a satisfactory state of physical and morale fitness.

The British army was, of course, a joke. German comic papers had long portrayed its soldiers as figures of fun in their short scarlet tunics and small caps set at an angle on their heads, or with bearskins with the chin-straps under their lip, and the first sight of them on that fateful morning did little to dispel the impression. Hauptmann Walter Bloem, commanding a fusilier company of the 12th Brandenburger Grenadiers and part of General Alexander von Kluck's First Army was approaching a group of farm buildings on the outskirts of Tertre, just north of the canal which runs from Condé sur l'Escaut eastwards to the small town of Mons, when he turned a corner and saw in front of him a group of fine-looking horses, all saddled up.

He had hardly given orders for their capture when 'a man appeared not five paces away from behind the

horses – a man in a grey-brown uniform, no, in a grey-brown golfing-suit with a flat-topped cloth cap. Could this be a soldier?' Surely not!

But it was. It was an officer from A Squadron, 19th Hussars, the cavalry regiment attached to the 5th Division of the British Expeditionary Force (BEF), and behind this reconnaissance patrol on the far side of the 20-m (66-ft) wide canal, waited the infantry of one of the 5th Division's brigades, the 14th. Other brigades flanked this on each side; on

Entraining for the front, August 1914
Bavarian infantry set off enthusiastically for the war. They were confident of beating the French again, and the Kaiser spoke for most Germans when he described Britain's soldiery as 'a contemptible little army'. They were soon to be disillusioned.

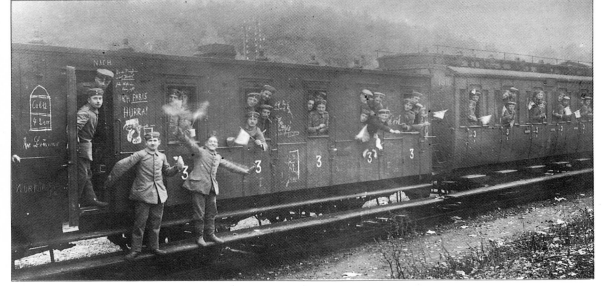

British heavy artillery heads for the front
British and German infantry divisions both included 72 field guns and howitzers but the British had only a single battery of these 60-pdrs, the Germans had two or three batteries of 15-cm heavy guns.

the west to just past Condé sur l'Escaut, and on the east to the Mons salient, where they linked with the left-hand brigade of the 3rd Division, these two divisions comprising the British II Corps under command of General Sir Horace Smith-Dorrien. The divisions of I Corps under General Sir Douglas Haig then continued the line eastwards towards the left flank of Lanzerac's army.

Quiet Sunday morning

The morning of 23rd August brought sights of ordinary small-town and village life continuing unconcernedly among the narrow streets and lanes, between the numberless slag heaps and pit heads of this small coal-mining community. Church bells rang, sombre-coated villagers responded to their summons, a small train filled with holiday-makers chuffed away towards the coast, the scent of newly-ground coffee was everywhere; and the sudden explosion of a shell in the outskirts of Mons itself, among the Royal Fusiliers, was so unexpected that the whole world seemed to hold its breath in astonishment.

But not for long. As the sound and smoke died away, the rifles came up and the appearance of a German cavalry patrol opposite caught no-one unawares except themselves; the first volley of the Fusiliers emptied all their saddles, and very shortly afterwards Oberleutnant von Arnim of the Death's Head Hussars was brought in swearing profusely with a smashed knee.

By now the whole of the British line was alert and waiting, though hardly for what next happened. Before their astonished eyes the woods, hedges and

Keep the Right Flank Strong

German troops smile for the camera as they flood across the Belgian border. The dying words of von Schlieffen had been to 'keep the right flank strong' and in 1914 the BEF found itself straight in the path of this mighty right hook.

Aftermath of one of the mounted actions of the 1914 campaign: British cavalrymen escort captured men from the German 'Death's Head' Hussars. The British cavalry screen helped disguise the weakness of the BEF's position.

The Belgian field army provided valuable aid to the fortresses of Liége and Namur but retreated to the shelter of Antwerp on 20 August. Here, a Belgian dog-drawn machine-gun detachment rests by the roadside.

buildings stretching before them, 1.6 km (1 mile) away across the canal and the flat water-meadows beyond, began erupting solid columns of grey-uniformed men, moving unhurriedly towards them in a solid mass like a football crowd after a match.

Enemy in sight

Watching the grey ocean lapping across the fields, one British officer asked another to pinch him in case he was dreaming, and his wonder was palpable as along 26 km (16 miles) of dead straight canal the British infantry waited while thousands of men walked with apparent innocence and unconcern towards almost certain death. At least 12,000 Lee-Enfield rifles, each held by a soldier expert in the famous British 'rapid fire', augmented by 24 Vickers machie-guns, waited behind the embankment of the canal; and it would seem that hardly one of them was fired until the German front ranks had come within 550 m (600 yards), the range over which the Lee-Enfield fired a flat trajectory.

When fire was opened, the slaughter was immediate – and horrific.

Within minutes whole German battalions were wiped out, junior officers found themselves the only officers left to a regiment bereft of all warrant or non-commissioned ranks and the majority of the men.

Artillery superiority

But there were only 75,000 men in the BEF – and that number, however well trained, cannot hold up 200,000 men indefinitely except in circumstances of severe geographic confinement, which did not apply at Mons.

German artillery brought up during the late morning blew gaps in the British line, and the Royal Fusiliers and the 4th Middlesex, holding the sides of the narrow Mons salient, were in an especially dangerous situation once the guns registered on the town. And all the while more of von Kluck's battalions were flooding down the roads leading to the

battle, widening the front until it overlapped the British line and threatened the flanks.

By 2100 it was evident that the British had been left on their own, and despite justifiable feelings of confidence throughout all ranks in their ability to beat the enemy, they must now retreat. During that night the tired, frustrated and puzzled men of the BEF began the march back which would end on the Marne.

But they had fought the Battle of Mons, and it would live in history for all time. And they left behind them a confused and depressed enemy. That night Bloem wrote in his diary '. . . the men all chilled to the bone, almost too exhausted to move and with the depressing consciousness of defeat weighing heavily upon them. A bad defeat, there can be no gainsaying it . . . we had been badly beaten, and by the English – by the English we had so laughed at a few hours before.'

The combination of British infantry training and the SMLE had shot them flat.

British cavalry covering the retreat from Mons
The British cavalry performed very well in 1914. The bitter lessons of the Boer war had been well learned and British horsemen were adept at fighting dismounted with the same SMLE (Short, Magazine, Lee-Enfield) rifle as the infantry.

NCO, German 15th Lancer Regiment

The German lancers did not abandon the traditional cut of their uniform with the introduction of field grey in 1910. The German army of 1914 included 3 Guard and 16 line lancer regiments. Those on the Western Front in 1914 suffered severe losses from the pace of the advance and in inadequate supply of horse fodder.

'Old Contemptibles'
The British army was little over 100,000 strong; small change by European standards. But man for man it was the finest army in the world: all volunteers and trained to a peak of perfection that continental conscripts could never hope to attain.

German Maxim gun detachment
The Germans were so astonished at the BEF's firepower that they assumed the British were equipped with extra machine-guns. In fact both armies had a pair of machine-guns attached to each infantry battalion.

British infantrymen were able to fire 15 aimed rounds a minute. The range and accuracy of British rifle fire surprised the Germans who were frequently caught in close formation. Their leading companies fell flat, never to rise again.

A casualty receives oxygen in a German aid post. The German 1st Army's attack could have been more successful had von Kluck been allowed to swing farther north but fortunately for the BEF, von Bülow ordered him to remain in close contact.

German field guns march steadily westwards in the searing August heatwave. The BEF abandoned its positions during the night after Sir John French discovered the French army on his flank was falling back.

MIRACLE OF THE MARNE

The Schlieffen Plan was now at crisis point. Two German armies were approaching Paris and the French government had abandoned the capital.

By the end of August 1914 government officials were packing their bags in Paris, ready to abandon the capital in the face of the remorseless German advance. The British commander, Field Marshal Sir John French, was casting nervous glances towards the Channel ports as the British Expeditionary Force continued its retreat and adjacent French armies trudged dejectedly westwards. The Kaiser's armies seemed poised on the brink of victory.

From the other side of the hill, the picture looked equally gloomy. The breathtaking pace of the German advance had exhausted every soldier from the humblest rifleman to the army commanders. The troops on the right wing of the German front line

British cavalry enter the gap
The gap between the German 1st and 2nd Armies was detected from the air but the BEF advanced with extreme caution. Magazine-loading rifles and machine-guns made even a small rearguard a tough proposition.

Gone to ground
By early September most of the battalions of the BEF had lost between half and three-quarters of their strength. Scattered parties of exhausted troops were all that remained of the 1,000-strong battalions which had crossed the Channel a month earlier.

had been marching over 32 km (20 miles) a day for many days, infantry battalions losing about half their men in the process. The army was dependent on horse transport and a desperate shortage of horse fodder was rapidly immobilizing both the cavalry and the artillery. Commanders found their reconnaissance information drying up and their heavy guns falling farther and farther behind.

In the first days of September, General Alexander von Kluck's 1st Army ceased heading directly for Paris and veered south, towards the River Marne. General Joseph Galliéni, the fiery governor of Paris, pressed for an Allied counterattack to catch the Germans in the flank. This was agreed, and on 5/6 September the British and French forces turned on their pursuers.

Despite its ponderous size, the Imperial German army did not have the manpower to cover the whole front. The sort of shoulder-to-shoulder advance along the entire 565 km (350 miles) between Dunkirk and Verdun envisaged in the original Schlieffen Plan was hopelessly unrealistic and gaps had repeatedly appeared between the German armies. General Max von Hausen's 3rd Army made frantic alterations of course to cover the flanks of the leading formations, but when the Allied counterattack materialized there was a 50-km (30-mile) gap yawning between the 1st and 2nd Armies, covered only by a flimsy cavalry screen.

During 6 September the BEF advanced some 13 km (8 miles) to the River Grand Morin, while the French 9th Army under General Ferdinand Foch was still severely pressed to hold its ground. Irrepressible as ever, Foch signalled to Joffre: 'My centre is giving ground, my right retiring; situation excellent, I am attacking.' To his left the 6th Army under General Michel Maunoury ran into heavy opposition and urgently needed a fresh division which had just arrived in Paris. Railway transport was sufficient to bring up only half the troops but Galliéni improvised a transport column by mobilizing some 600 Parisian taxis and their drivers to ferry the troops to the front.

Towards the Marne

By 8 September the BEF was confronted by hastily improvised German defences along the Petit Morin. The Black Watch stormed across near Bellot and pressed on to capture the village of Sablonnaires. The Guards and 2nd Worcesters captured the bridge near Bécherelle and before long the cavalry was over and riding in pursuit of the retreating Germans. Further westwards, a village curiously called Gibralter was held in strength. Concealed machine-gun posts stopped the British advance in its tracks. Eventually the East Surreys worked their way around the flank and the Germans fell back. When the day ended in a dramatic thunderstorm, II Corps under General Sir Horace Smith-Dorrien was within a mile of the Marne and 4th Division at Jouarre, where the Marne is joined by the Petit Morin.

9 September was the decisive day of the battle. The Germans seemed set to defend the Marne, a

The End of the Schlieffen Plan

Under a blazing sun, a column of German infantry marches determinedly onwards. The Schlieffen Plan never honestly addressed how the infantry were supposed to maintain the superhuman pace demanded.

The mental pressure on the commanders was intensified in 1914 by the inadequate means of communication. The armies numbered millions but generals were still dependent on mounted couriers and carrier pigeons.

German troops dig in while awaiting a French attack. The retreat to the Aisne established the basic line of the front which was to remain little altered until 1918. Both sides tried to outflank in the north until they reached the Channel.

German Machine-Gun Corps, 1914

From their formation in 1901 until early 1915 the men of the German Machine Gun Corps wore this distinctive uniform. Thereafter they adopted the uniform of whichever branch of the army they were attached to.

Fighting shoulder-to-shoulder
Behind a scattered line of skirmishers the infantry were still deployed shoulder-to-shoulder in 1914. A close line was good for tactical control and concentrated firepower but proved horribly vulnerable unless dug in.

London Motor Buses rush to the front
The French ferried vital troops to the Battle of the Marne in 600 Paris taxis. Meanwhile the BEF used limited numbers of London buses, hastily painted khaki, to carry men to the front.

Indian infantry digging in
As the battle of the Marne petered out the BEF was reinforced by the Indian Corps which was to remain on the Western Front until late 1915. It played a vital role in stopping the German attack on Ypres at the end of October.

French *Spahi* and his mount
The Spahis, formed in 1834, were native troops from France's North African colonies. Large elements of the Army of North Africa were deployed to France and they rendered sterling service throughout the war.

wide river with few bridges and with ample cover on the eastern bank, but as the BEF renewed its attack at 0500 signs of retreat were soon detected. Unknown to the Allies, the German high command was transfixed by events in Poland and East Prussia, where a gigantic Russian army was marching onto German soil. The German headquarters was over 160 km (100 miles) behind the battlefront, and General Helmuth von Moltke took the fateful decision to dispatch a staff officer to assess the situation in France and direct the movements of the German armies while he grappled with the crisis in the east. German strategy now lay in the hands of a solitary colonel.

Armed with the authority of the Chief of the General Staff, Colonel Richard Hentsch drove 645 km (400 miles) along roads choked with transport columns to reach the headquarters of General Karl von Bülow's 2nd Army on the night of 8 September. His journey had not inspired confidence, and he found von Bülow already contemplating retreat to conform with the 1st Army's retrograde movements to its right. On 9 September, while von Moltke resumed planning the advance on Paris, Hentsch had already ordered a strategic withdrawal.

The battle turned into a series of bitter rearguard actions as Allied troops pressed after the Germans, General Joseph Joffre observing 'victory is now in the legs of the infantry'. Unfortunately, those legs were already very tired and although the BEF managed to pursue their opponents some 16 km (10 miles) on September 10, they could not maintain the pace. To add to the frustration of the Allied commanders, autumnal weather arrived early; torrential rain waterlogged the roads and ground fog severely hampered aerial reconnaissance.

The battle of the Marne petered out by 12 September as the Germans halted just west of the River Aisne. They had gambled on winning the war in a single knock-out blow, but this had failed. Both sides paused to reorganize, and the front lines rapidly extended until they ran from the Channel to the Swiss frontier. Here they would stay for four years of unprecedented carnage.

A British Vickers gun opens fire as the BEF follows up the retreating Germans. The first British troops crossed the Aisne on 12 September but the newly created German 7th Army rapidly blocked the gap and the German retreat was over.

As both sides tried to sweep around the northern flank the British and German forces fought over the flat, low-lying Belgian countryside which would later be the scene for some of the most bitter battles of the war.

The first Indian troops to see action were the 129th Baluchis seen here on Messines Ridge. This was finally lost at the end of October after Germany flung in wave after wave of half-trained youths: der Kindermord von Ypern.

TANNENBERG: Teutonic vengeance

While Germany invaded France, only light forces remained to defend the east against Russia.

German planning made the defeat of France its primary objective after adoption of the Schlieffen Plan in 1905. Forces in the east would be on the defensive until a quick victory over the French allowed the transfer of forces. East Prussia was held by the 8th Army of four corps (I, XVII and XX Corps, and I Reserve Corps), a reserve division, several Landwehr (territorial) brigades and a cavalry division, commanded by General Max von Prittwitz, with General Graf von Waldersee as his chief-of-staff. Additional Landwehr units were in the garrisons of Königsberg and the Vistula fortresses.

On 7 August the German Chief-of-Staff, General Helmuth von Moltke, in accordance with the Schlieffen Plan, ordered Prittwitz to avoid encirclement and to retreat behind the Vistula if necessary. However, von Prittwitz's deputy chief-of-operations, Colonel Max von Hoffman, preferred the aggressive approach of Schlieffen himself: 'Throw everything at the first Russian army to come within reach.'

The Russian North West Front (army group) under General Yakov Zhilinsky, attacking East Prussia, consisted of the 2nd Army based in Warsaw and the 1st Army at Kovno. The commanders were, respectively, Generals Aleksandr Samsonov and Pavel Rennenkampf. Their personal animosity hindered co-operation. Rennenkampf was to march on Königsberg through the Insterburg Gap, surround the fortress, and turn south to assist the northward drive of Samsonov. Rennenkampf, however, had only 6 infantry and 5 cavalry divisions available, although two divisions from the 2nd Army were subsequently transferred to him.

Samsonov had nine infantry and three cavalry divisions (excluding the two infantry divisions transferred to Rennenkampf). His army would advance into East Prussia between Soldau and Johannisburg, towards Allenstein and the Vistula. The 2nd Army, however, mobilized a considerable distance away from the frontier. August 23 was set as the date for both armies to be ready to cross the border.

French appeal

On 14 August the French appealed to Russia for immediate help, so on 17 August the 1st Army crossed the German frontier. Samsonov was not able to cross the border in force until 21 August and on that day von Prittwitz, acting on von Waldersee's advice (he had been a veteran *Kriegspieler* or war-gamer, and had fought the battle out on a map many times) sent von Moltke a pessimistic appraisal of the situation and considered a retreat to the Vistula. Soon afterwards, however, von Hoffman presented his commander with a new plan. This was the one von Hoffman had preferred from the start, a shift for

German 77-mm field gun
The German artillery had little technical superiority over the Russian guns but it was handled far better and generally had far more ammunition. The Russian army had had the money to buy more field guns but had spent most of it on fortresses which proved of little value.

The eyes of the German army
Unlike the constricted Western Front, the armies in the Eastern theatre had room to manoeuvre. However, commanders on both sides found it difficult to control their enormous armies deployed on such daunting frontages.

The destruction of the 2nd Army

Since the disaster of 1905 the Russian army had been derided in the German press as 'The Rubber Lion' but it bounced back with impressive power in 1914. The speed of Russian mobilisation astonished and alarmed the Germans.

When German cavalry patrols discovered the two huge Russian armies pouring over the Prussian border, von Prittwitz began to prepare to retreat to the Vistula. Von Moltke panicked and sent 5 divisions, earmarked for France, hurrying east.

A German field kitchen is passed by a squadron of lancers. The Schlieffen Plan allowed for the Russians overrunning East Prussia, but on the day von Moltke refused to countenance losing so much Prussian soil to enemy invasion.

a decisive blow against Samsonov. Von Prittwitz approved the plan, apparently abandoning any thoughts of retreat.

Berlin was not aware of these developments, however. Von Moltke feared losing East Prussia, even though the original Schlieffen Plan had allowed for that to happen. Von Moltke made a vital decision: he ordered five divisions (four infantry and one cavalry) to be pulled out of the German right wing along the Marne in France, decisively weakening the German drive on Paris. He also sacked von Prittwitz and von Waldersee, replacing them with General Paul von Beckendorff und von Hindenburg and Generalmajor Erich Ludendorff. These two men (the first called from retirement and the second from a staff position in France) would become leaders of the German army and nation as a result of their action. Arriving on the scene, they despatched von Prittwitz and von Waldersee to the rear and ignominy. Ludendorff, however, knew von Hoffman personally and realized that his plan was excellent, so it remained in effect.

Samsonov was driving northwards by forced marches, and by 25 August his five corps were on a 100-km (62-mile) front, only 15 km (9.5 miles) from Allenstein.

Between 21 and 25 August, however, the Germans had used their excellent rail system to shift their forces facing Rennenkampf (except for some Landwehr and the 1st Cavalry Division) to attack Samsonov in the south. XX Corps and the 3rd Reserve Division had fallen back before Samsonov and were now south of Allenstein. I Corps arrived on the right, while XVII and I Reserve Corps railed in on the left. On 25 August intercepted Russian radio messages showed that Rennenkampf would present no threat to the German rear. Samsonov pressed forward, right into the German trap.

The trap is sprung

The Germans began their encirclement. On 26 August, von François took the village of Seeben on the Russian left. North-east of Allenstein, XVII and I Reserve Corps routed the Russian VI Corps. On 27 August François broke through the Russian left and

The German redeployment
The German forces opposite Rennenkampf's 1st Army were rapidly shifted south by rail to overwhelm Samsonov and his hapless 2nd Army. It was a classic use of interior lines aided by the catastrophic incompetence of the Russian commanders.

captured Neidenburg, closing the ring. The three Russian centre corps (XIII, XV, and XXIII) were surrounded. By 29 August the Russians had been compressed into a pocket. On 30 August Samsonov ordered a breakout to the south. XV Corps took Neidenburg briefly, but the encirclement held, the pocket collapsed and Samsonov shot himself.

Some 90,000 Russians were taken prisoner along with 500 guns. Total Russian losses probably exceeded 120,000. Three corps had been annihilated and two others badly mauled. German losses in the whole campaign were not more than 10,000.

Von Hindenburg and Ludendorff then turned on Rennenkampf. The Battle of the Masurian Lakes was a German victory, but the Russians avoided encirclement. By 14 September the Russian 1st Army had withdrawn across the border.

The Battle of Tannenberg is significant because it demonstrated how a numerically inferior defender can use interior lines and mobility to defeat an attacker. It also showed the crucial importance of planning in modern war. The Germans additionally gained vital advantages from aerial reconnaissance and radio interception.

The sweet taste of victory
Clausewitz had laid down that a good defence should be a 'shield of well directed blows' The aggressive tactics of the outnumbered German forces paid off better than anyone dared hope.

German troops receiving cholera vaccination
Medical facilities in World War I were better than in previous European wars although the sheer size of the armies made the casualty's lot as unenviable as ever. The campaign of 1914 was one of the first in which more casualties were inflicted on the battlefield than by sickness.

Rapid re-deployment via the excellent German railway system did not spare German infantrymen from some heroic marching in August 1914. Here, troops fling themselves down by the roadside to catch a brief rest before the next move.

The 2nd Army surrendered after failing to escape encirclement. Here, some of the 90,000 Russian prisoners of war trudge into captivity bringing their machine-guns with them. Samsonov walked into a wood and blew out his brains with his pistol.

German troops camped on the Russian border, autumn 1914. Rennenkampf escaped the fate of Samsonov but his army suffered heavy losses as it retreated east. In the first few months of the war, Russia lost over 250,000 men.

CORONEL AND THE FALKLANDS

'I must plough the seas of the world doing as much mischief as I can till my ammunition is exhausted or until a foe far superior in power succeeds in catching me.'

Germany's interests in the Far East at the beginning of this century were serviced from an enclave at Tsingtao. This was also the base for their East Asiatic Squadron, a crack German Naval force under the command of Vizeadmiral Graf von Spee. It was clear that Tsingtao could not be held when war broke out, so von Spee's squadron had already dispersed in August 1914.

By October the 11,400 ton armoured cruisers *Scharnhorst* and *Gneisenau* had been joined off the coast of Chile by the light cruisers *Leipzig*, *Nürnberg* and *Dresden*. Meeting a British squadron under Rear Admiral Sir Christopher Cradock off Coronel, the crack German crews administered the first serious defeat of the Royal Navy in centuries. The armoured cruisers *Good Hope* and *Monmouth* went down with all their (largely reservist) crews.

Von Spee seemed far from elated by his success. Though he had suffered no significant damage he had expended almost half of his major-calibre ammunition. There was little prospect of obtaining more, he was 16000 km (10,000 miles) from home and he was all too aware that the world's greatest sea-

power, stung by its reverse, would be seeking him out to redress the score.

Possibly a quick break round the Horn and into the vastness of the South Atlantic would have spelled success at this point, but again von Spee seemed to be afflicted by indecision, hanging around at the isolated island of Mas-a-Fuera and then an anchorage on the desolate Chilean coast, north of the Magellan Strait.

Though summer in these latitudes, the weather was atrocious and the squadron did not round the Horn until the night of 1/2 December. Early on the morning of 2 December a British sailing vessel, laden with coal, was sighted. Ever mindful of his long run home, von Spee took her into sheltered

HMS *Invincible*: victor of the Falklands
Flying the flag of Vice-Admiral Sturdee, HMS *Invincible* was faster than any vessel in the German squadron and von Spee had no answer to her 12-in guns. After an unhurried passage to the South Atlantic, it was more by luck than judgement that Sturdee caught von Spee so quickly.

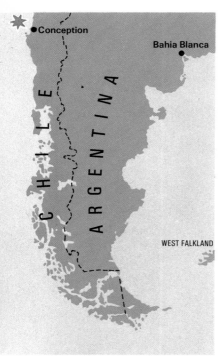

Coronel and the Falklands
Von Spee's squadron was sailing south along the coast of Chile when it encountered Cradock's ill-fated vessels. After the victory von Spee dallied a while then made his fatal decision to attack the Falklands.

***Dresden* caught at Mas a Fuera**
SMS *Dresden* was the only German warship to survive the battle of the Falkland Islands. Afterwards she showed none of the enterprise which had characterized von Spee and his captains. She hid among remote Chilean islands where she was trapped and destroyed several months later.

SMS *Scharnhorst*, Spee's flagship
Scharnhorst and her sister-ship *Gneisenau* were tough, powerfully armed cruisers but no match for a battle-cruiser. Their fate was obvious by midday, 8 October, but they fought to the last. *Scharnhorst* went down still firing and there were no survivors.

'A gallant and honourable foe'

Von Spee vanished into the Pacific at the beginning of the war and Royal Navy units around the world were alerted to deal with him. HMS Cumberland, *a sister of HMS* Monmouth, *operated off the coast of West Africa.*

Von Spee knew his heavy cruisers consumed too much coal to become effective raiders so he kept them together, hoping to beat the first Allied squadron he met. He detached one light cruiser, Emden, *to raid into the Indian Ocean.*

The East Asiatic Squadron anchored off Valparaiso, 13 November 1914. Scharnhorst and Gneisenau are in the left background with Nürnberg lying astern. The other warships are Chilean: (left to right) Esmeralda, O'Higgins and Blanco Encalada.

waters and spent three days transferring her cargo. 8 December dawned bright and clear. It found the *Gneisenau*, supported by the *Nürnberg*, following the coast of East Falkland toward Stanley; von Spee was hull-down to the south. Main batteries were being trained on the radio station when suddenly the great splashes of a two-gun, major-calibre salvo erupted in the morning sun. It was followed by a second, close enough to put fragments on to the *Gneisenau*'s upper deck. Standing farther out, the two German ships eventually rounded the bluff that screened the harbour. At 0940 could be seen a great smoke cloud and tall, tripod masts. These could mean only British capital ships. Von Spee had wasted too much time.

After the disaster at Coronel the British Admiralty had moved rapidly, despatching three battle-cruisers from the Grand Fleet strength. Two of them, HMS *Invincible* and *Inflexible*, had just arrived with four cruisers and were still coaling. Fortunately for Vice-Admiral Sturdee, in command, the old battleship HMS *Canopus* had been beached as a static harbour defence and had bought time for the disadvantaged force by firing indirectly on the *Gneisenau*.

Escape to the East

The *Gneisenau* and *Nürnberg* closed on von Spee and the whole squadron made all haste away to the south-east in loose formation. None could make designed speed through foul hulls and machinery problems. Even before they were over the horizon the Germans could see the first British ships leaving Stanley. Visibility was perfect, the day was young and Nemesis was but a matter of time.

The *Leipzig* began to lag, but urgency was maintained by the constant sight of the pursuers who, in no hurry, overhauled them inexorably under a dense cloud of funnel smoke. At 1247 came the ranging 304.8-mm (12-in) salvo from the leading battle-cruiser, the *Invincible*. By 1300 the Germans were surrounded by splashes yet still unable to reply. At

1320, still without significant damage, von Spee detached his light cruisers to shift for themselves but could see their British counterparts peel off in pursuit while his own ships were still suffering at the hands of the two battle-cruisers. He needed to close the range so turned abruptly and, at 1330, got to within his 12000-m (13,125-yard) maximum. Opening fire the *Scharnhorst* rapidly hit the *Invincible*, but the British reply was merely to sheer further off and continue the bombardment. The British were obviously content to stay at long range and expend as much ammunition as it took, even though the *Gneisenau* was having a light time with her big adversary, the *Inflexible*, blinded by her leader's smoke.

Long periods elapsed with no firing on either side, as each manoeuvred for advantage. By 1500 the weather was deteriorating and the British obviously went for a decision. The range fell to 10975 m (12,000 yards) which, while allowing von Spee's ships to use their secondary 150-mm (5.9-in) guns, began to prove decisive. The *Scharnhorst* was burning heavily forward and had lost her third funnel. As her shooting began to fall off the *Gneisenau* also started to list. Ignoring a call to surrender, von Spee's ship suddenly ceased fire 'like a light blown out' and foundered at 1617. There were no survivors.

The *Gneisenau* fought on, though. Through the mist of drizzling rain now falling, she could see her two opponents had been joined by a four-funnelled armoured cruiser, HMS *Carnarvon*. The murk offered no sanctuary from punishment. Reportedly hit by over 50 large-calibre rounds, the *Gneisenau* had her foremost funnel leaning drunkenly against the second, her foremast was missing and she was faltering to a stop in a cloud of her own smoke. Ammunition had run out and a British battle-cruiser closed the range and put 15 deliberate rounds into the wreck. The survivors formed up on deck, gave three cheers for the Kaiser and abandoned ship; only 200 were saved from the freezing water.

Of the light cruisers, only the *Dresden* was to

SMS *Dresden* at Valparaiso
After Coronel von Spee put in at Valparaiso. The German community treated him to a hero's welcome but, invited to drink to 'the damnation of the Royal Navy', Spee replied: 'I drink to the memory of a gallant and honourable foe.'

escape for a further brief existence. Coronel had been terribly avenged but, besides proving the obvious supremacy of the battle-cruiser over the armoured cruiser, the Falklands battle demonstrated also the toughness of German ships, the surprising range of their armament and the fighting spirit of their crews.

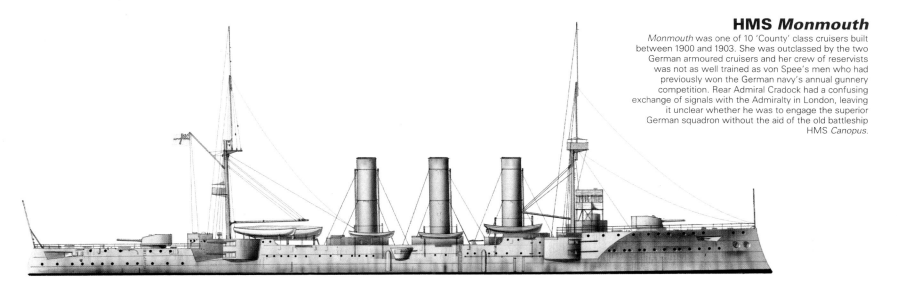

HMS *Monmouth*

Monmouth was one of 10 'County' class cruisers built between 1900 and 1903. She was outclassed by the two German armoured cruisers and her crew of reservists was not as well trained as von Spee's men who had previously won the German navy's annual gunnery competition. Rear Admiral Cradock had a confusing exchange of signals with the Admiralty in London, leaving it unclear whether he was to engage the superior German squadron without the aid of the old battleship HMS *Canopus*.

Although it was summer in the southern hemisphere, the East Asiatic Squadron had to plough through heavy seas as it rounded the Horn. Had he not delayed so long in Chilean waters, von Spee would have found Port Stanley undefended.

Photographed from Invincible's *maintop,* Inflexible *fires a salvo from her 12-in guns at about 13.00 on 8 December 1914. Visibility was unusually good so there was nowhere for the slower and weaker German cruisers to hide.*

After Gneisenau *sank, both British battle-cruisers lowered their boats and steamed slowly over the spot to pick up the survivors. Out of her complement of 765 only 200 were picked out of the freezing water.*

THE GAS ATTACK AT YPRES

German scientists believed poison gas could unlock the western front. By using it in France they opened a Pandora's box of industrial horror.

Highlander, winter 1914/1915

The Belgian town of Ypres, or 'Wipers' to a generation of British soldiers, was the scene of heavy fighting from September to November 1914 as the British and French armies blocked a series of German attacks. Allied counter-attacks made equally little headway and the front lines began to acquire a permanence that contemporary weapons and tactics were unable to break.

Early in April 1915 the BEF took over from the French a further 8 km (5 miles) of front lying between the Menin road and the road between Ypres and Poelcappelle. The British front now stretched for 48 km (30 miles) to Guinchy in the south, and a pause followed as the British and German soldiers fortified their positions and their commanders pondered how to achieve a breakthrough.

The British broke the calm on 17 April by a well-staged attack on Hill 60, a man-made hillock piled up during the building of the Ypres-Comines railway which overlooked British positions in the Ypres salient, allowing the Germans to observe troop movements and enfilade the defences. Engineers and miners from the Monmouthshires dug six tunnels underneath the German positions and packed them with high explosive. In a monstrous explosion at 0700 the defences vanished in a fountain of earth and storming parties rushed forward to occupy the cratered summit. The Germans launched fierce local counter-attacks for the next 36 hours, regaining part of the hill, but accepted defeat by 21 April.

Large cylinders were found in the shattered German front line and an unpleasant smell lingered over the battlefield, but in the chaotic rhythm of attack and counter-attack no-one paid them much attention. The next afternoon a strange yellow-green cloud issued from the German trenches north of Ypres opposite a French colonial division. Wafted by a steady breeze, it engulfed the French positions with immediate and dire effect: men choked, gasping for air, and died coughing up the bloody remnants of their lungs which were dissolving in hydrochloric acid. Chlorine gas had made its foul debut in the Great War.

The gas opened a 7.25-km (4.5-mile) hole in the Allied front line, but the Germans had not anticipated success on such a scale and did not have enough troops immediately available to exploit the gap. They were halted near Mouse Trap Farm by a few companies of Canadian troops and, by 23 April, although a 4-km (2.5-mile) dent had appeared in the north of the salient, the line was holding.

The period 24/30 April became known as the Battle of St Julien as the German offensive was resumed. The Canadian line south of Poelcappelle was attacked with a second gas cloud at 0500 on 24 April, canisters of chlorine gas having been placed every few yards along a 1000-m frontage. Incredibly, the

Five Highland regiments continued to wear the kilt in World War I. The fur coat is typical of the non-regulation kit which appeared during the first winter of the war when troops simply wore anything which would keep them warm.

Waiting for the Boche
French infantry in the new, 1915 pattern uniform, await the next German attack. The jaunty red trousers were replaced by an all-over uniform of pale blue (*horizon bleu*). To reduce head injuries from shrapnel a helmet was gradually introduced during 1915.

Canadians stood their ground, some of them making improvised gas masks by urinating on handkerchiefs which they clasped to their mouths. But the Germans were supported by a murderous artillery barrage and they broke through again; the Allied line being forced back between St Julien and Fortuin.

In the first days of May the British fell back to shorten the line. A third major gas attack failed when British artillery laid down a heavy barrage behind the gas cloud, pinning the German attackers in their trenches. On May 4 the Germans continued to shell parts of the old British front line, unaware that

the defenders had slipped away in the night. On May 5 the gas cylinders were employed again opposite Hill 60: the summit was recaptured and was to remain in German hands until June 1917.

The axis of the German attack switched to Frezenberg ridge during the second week of May. Remorseless shelling reduced the primitive defences to shapeless piles of earth, but the fact remained that a determined group of men with magazine rifles was very difficult to dislodge without overwhelming numbers.

The Germans launched one last major attack on May 24. They generated a gas cloud 7.25 km wide,

The industrial battlefield

The first battle for Ypres occurred in the autumn of 1914. This road-block was hastily prepared as the Germans threatened to capture the city. The successful defence created a salient around Ypres which was fought over until 1918.

German troops move along a communication trench in early 1915. The Germans waited for favourable wind conditions for three weeks before finally launching their offensive at Ypres.

A battery of German howitzers arrives opposite Ypres. They ceased fire on the afternoon of 22 April to allow the gas cloud to roll undisturbed over the French lines. German gunners knew gas had worked when French artillery fire stopped abruptly.

Out of the trenches
A group of German soldiers return to billets behind the line, spring 1915. All except the commander have a cover on their *pickelhaube* helmets and several carry extra ammunition. During 1915 many German troops were withdrawn to fight on the Eastern Front.

.303 Ross Rifle

Many of the Canadian troops who fought at Ypres were equipped with the Ross rifle. A highly accurate target rifle, the Ross was too delicate to cope with combat conditions and jammed frequently. Those who could, acquired Lee-Enfields and Field Marshal Haig ordered the withdrawal of the Ross rifle in 1916.

Specification
Rifle, Ross, Mk 3
Calibre: 7.7 mm (o.303 in)
Length: overall 1.285 m (50.6 in); barrel 0.765 m (30.15 in)
Weight: 4.48 kg (9.875 lb)
Muzzle velocity: 792 m (2,600 ft) per second
Magazine: 5-round box

the effects of which were felt 32 km (20 miles) behind the British front line, but the weapon had lost its novelty: alert to the wind direction the British were ready and the assaulting troops were mown down by emplaced machine-guns and pre-registered artillery fire. The tortured rubble of Mouse Trap Farm finally fell into German hands but no important ground was lost. The Ypres offensive was over.

The five weeks of fighting at Ypres cost the British forces nearly 60,000 casualties and the Germans over 35,000. Field Marshal Sir John French used the BEF's shortage of heavy shell to try to unseat Field Marshal Kitchener as the UK's primary war-

lord, and the ensuing press campaign helped bring down the government. Factory workers' lunchtime drinking was held to blame and restrictions on the sale of alcohol were imposed. They were in force until August 1988, an eccentric legacy of the battle of Ypres.

German signalling post
German signallers set up a signal lamp in a communication trench. They have abandoned their *pickelhaube* helmets for the more comfortable forage cap and the absence of personal weapons argues they are in a rear area.

At Ypres the Allied soldiers breathed through urine-soaked handkerchiefs to protect themselves against the chlorine gas. Here, men of the Indian Corps demonstrate an early type of gas mask which did not prove very successful.

Walking wounded head for the dressing station. British attempts to break the German line failed completely, and Sir John French unofficially told The Times that a shortage of artillery shells was hampering British attacks.

Wearing primitive gas masks these British soldiers stand ready to signal 'SOS' and trigger an immediate artillery barrage in front of the British trenches. The Germans abandoned their attack on Ypres in May.

GALLIPOLI: The gamble fails

Now that the Western Front appeared to be deadlocked, the search resumed for an alternative strategy. Winston Churchill believed he had the answer.

Allied action against Turkey was first suggested in November 1914 when Winston Churchill, the First Lord of the Admiralty, urged a joint land and sea assault to capture Constantinople. While the fighting raged in France, the Admiralty continued to examine alternative routes to attack Germany: Admiral of the Fleet Lord Fisher passionately advocated a landing on Germany's Baltic coast, while Churchill bombarded the cabinet with equally fantastic schemes. Anything was better, they argued, than the apparent stalemate in France and the North Sea. A plea from the Russians for some operation against Turkey to relieve the pressure on their army in the Caucasus was the final catalyst.

Churchill's optimism and eloquence triumphed in January 1915. His plan was for a force of obsolete battleships to steam into the Dardanelles, pulverize the Turkish forts and drop their anchors off the Turkish capital, there to dictate peace terms. Wiser heads were turned by the spectacular results of such a coup and practical considerations were brushed aside. On 19 February, 16 British and four French battleships bombarded the forts guarding the entrance to the Dardanelles. Blustery weather prevented another attack for several days but at length the outer forts were reduced to rubble and Churchill's confidence knew no bounds. By 10 March he had the War Council discussing the terms of a Turkish armistice and future strategy once Constantinople had fallen.

Unfortunately the naval forces had already been checked. The narrow channels farther up the straits

Turkish soldier 1914-1918

The disastrous collapse of the Turkish army during the Balkan wars of 1912-13 led the British to underestimate Turkish military strength in 1914. Aided by a German military mission, the Turkish army was reorganised. Senior leadership remained weak but the bravery of the individual Turkish solder was to be a conspicuous feature of the Gallipoli campaign. The khaki service dress was introduced in 1909 together with the peakless cloth hat. Officers wore a grey fur cap.

British heavy artillery
A British 60-pdr in action at Cape Helles. Only eight were operational by July and all but one broke down by August. Attacks by German submarines severely reduced the amount of naval fire support available.

The SMLE (Short, Magazine, Lee-Enfield) was adopted by the British army in 1903 to replace the Lee-Metford which had a short barrel life when using cordite propellant. The SMLE was the finest bolt-action combat rifle ever produced and served the British army well in both world wars.

were mined and casualties mounted rapidly. Elderly battleships had no resistance to underwater attack and one after another they succumbed to the mines. *Bouvet*'s magazine exploded, blowing her and her company to pieces in a single, awesome explosion. Attempts to lift the mines using civilian trawlers failed miserably, and the fleet withdrew to lick its wounds and think again.

The idea of a land attack on Constantinople had won favour in London before the naval assault had failed. By 24 February Field Marshal Lord Kitch-

ener had announced that if the fleet failed, 'The Army ought to see the business through'. Tragically, the whole operation might have succeeded if a landing had been immediately executed but the 28th Division, earmarked for the assault, was retained in France. By the time the landings began, the Turkish defences were well prepared.

At dawn on 25 April 1915 the first waves of Allied troops landed on the foot of the Gallipoli peninsula. The force included the first two divisions of the Australia-New Zealand Army Corps (ANZACS) who

Lee-Enfield .303 rifle

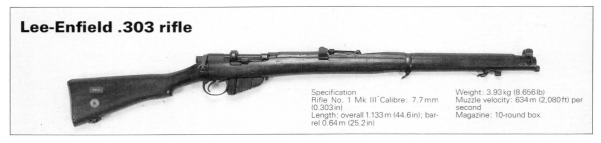

Specification	
Rifle No. 1 Mk III Calibre: 7.7 mm (0.303 in)	Weight: 3.93 kg (8.656 lb)
Length: overall 1.133 m (44.6 in); barrel 0.64 m (25.2 in)	Muzzle velocity: 634 m (2,080 ft) per second
	Magazine: 10-round box

Defeat at the Dardanelles

British troops sailed for the Dardanelles with few maps of the area, little information on the Turkish forces and no idea of the strength of the defences. In fact the Turks had six divisions, one more than the Allies.

Bouvet was one of the old battleships destroyed on the Turkish minefields during the abortive attempts to force the straits by naval power alone. The attack in March nearly succeeded but Admiral de Robeck refused to try again.

The fighting quality of the Anzac troops was conspicuous in a campaign notable for bravery on both sides. Unfortunately, as on the Western Front, a single machine-gun which survived the bombardment could stop an attack dead.

© Richard Natkiel

rapidly established a reputation as some of the finest troops in the world. But there was no joint operations staff and no one with experience of amphibious operations on such a massive scale. Chaos ensued, with some units meeting only token opposition and simply sitting on their beach while other formations were being slaughtered in a nearby cove. The Allies clung to the coast by their fingernails for three days before launching an all-out attack on 28 April. It made no headway but a vigorous Turkish counter-attack was repulsed with equally heavy casualties. Intensive fighting continued into May, but the expeditionary force remained firmly locked into two beachheads, Anzac Cove and Cape Helles.

Political repurcussions

The recriminations began in the War Council. Fisher left and Churchill was forced to resign. The naval contingent was reduced after a destroyer and *U-51* sank three battleships during May. Meanwhile Kitchener circulated a memorandum warning that British prestige would be severely weakened if the

General Birdwood's dug-out at Anzac Cove
The labyrinth of dug-outs sometimes led to confusion. Officers from both sides were discussing a truce here on 22 May when an Australian soldier burst in and demanded 'Have any of you bastards got my kettle?'

Anzac Cove and Cape Helles
The landings on 25 April won only two small bridgeheads and subsequent attempts to widen them collapsed with heavy losses. The second major amphibious assault captured Suvla Bay and linked up with 'Anzac Cove'. The fatal pause after the naval attacks gave the Turks time to prepare their defences.

land forces were to withdraw.

Fresh troops were poured into Gallipoli and expended in vain attempts to dislodge the Turks. Attacks were pressed home with heroic disregard for personal safety, but no amount of bravery or ANZAC ingenuity could break through the stubborn Turkish defence. It was soon remarked that the ideal army would consist of Australian officers, British NCOs and Turkish privates.

In early August the expedition summoned its remaining strength and launched a last, desperate offensive to break the deadlock. As usual the troops responded magnificently, but despite superhuman efforts sustained for nearly a week the front line scarcely advanced. Some 40,000 Allied troops died; the Warwicks, Gloucesters and Worcesters lost every single officer; and General Baldwin and his

entire staff were killed. General Sir William Birdwood's corps suffered 50 per cent casualties.

As summer gave way to autumn the tempo of the fighting slackened. Kitchener was deeply reluctant to grasp the nettle, but few ministers or commanders had any faith left in the expedition. Towards the end of November the decision was taken to evacuate. To retreat in the face of a vigilant and professional army is one of the most difficult operations of war and further heavy losses were anticipated. However, thanks to first class staff work, Birdwood and Admiral Sir Roger Keyes executed a faultless manoeuvre and brought the last troops off by January in the only successful operation of the campaign, a cruel and ironic footnote to a conflict which cost the lives of over 200,000 men on each side.

While his comrades doze in the August heat one Irish Fusilier in the 10th Division teases the Turks. The trenches were only a few yards apart in places and many troops were unable to move during daylight because of enemy sniper fire.

Preparation for the evacuation under way at 'W' Beach, Cape Helles, 7 January 1916. 19,000 men had already left and a Turkish attack the following day was repelled with very heavy losses. Here, a Turkish shell falls short into the sea.

Burning stores illuminate the shore as the evacuation nears completion. It was expected that the Turks would interfere causing heavy losses, but professional staffwork brought the troops off before the Turks realised it.

OPERATION GERICHT:
The inferno of Verdun

Left: *Mort Homme*
When the Germans widened their attack to include the left bank of the Meuse the most bitter fighting occurred on the appropriately named hill *le Mort Homme*. Its commanding view of the surrounding battlefield made it vital for both sides.

Mort pour la Patrie
The constant shelling frequently disinterred chunks of previous months' casualties making Verdun one of the most obscene battlefields of all time. Nearly a million men died here and many of their remains now lie in a giant *ossuaire*, open to view.

Gericht: Judgement day for the French and German armies. The German offensive at Verdun was not designed to conquer territory, just to bleed France white.

On 21 February 1916 1,400 German guns delivered a hammerblow to the French front line before the ancient fortress city of Verdun. Two million shells rained down on just 13 km (8 miles) of front, pulverizing the French trenches, in the process burying or killing most of the defenders. The most horrific battle of World War I had begun.

The German army had remained on the defensive in the west throughout 1915 while defeating Serbia and driving the Russians out of Poland. Now it was the turn of France. Unlike Hindenburg and Ludendorff, General Erich von Falkenhayn recognized that the West was the decisive theatre and a victory there would end the war.

Von Falkenhayn prepared his offensive meticulously but with no starry-eyed visions of the offensive. He sought not to conquer great swathes of French territory but to seize ground which the French army would be compelled to take back or die in the attempt. He calculated that no French government could countenance the loss of the famous fortress as the damage to national morale would be unbearable. Taking Verdun would trigger a headlong French counter-offensive in which Germany would reap all the tactical advantages of the defence and 'the forces of France would bleed to death'.

The monstrous German barrage of 21 February included two 380-mm naval guns which bombarded targets far behind the lines, while 13 'Big Bertha' 420-mm howitzers pounded French strongpoints to

oblivion: the sheer concussion from their firing broke windows two miles away. The hurricane swept away the French front line but a handful of desperate men was still alive at 5 p.m. when the German infantry went over the top. Isolated parties of Colonel Emile Driant's 56e and 59e Chasseurs à Pied clung to the remains of their positions in the face of concentrated trench mortar and flamethrower attack.

Driant's epic last stand in the Bois des Caures delayed the entire German offensive by 24 hours. On the night of 22 February as snow squalls blanketed much of the tortured earth, the Germans had still failed to break into the French defences. But it could not last, and on 24 February the Germans reached the second line which was a defensive position only in name. It fell in three hours.

The front line trenches were all gone, but to the French public and the world at large, the real strength of Verdun was the chain of concrete forts sunk into the hills surrounding the city. Nestled deep into the earth, their ferro-concrete armour rendered them impervious to bombardment and their turret-mounted weapons dominated the ground for miles around. Or at least, they had. In fact, most of their guns had been removed to supplement France's meagre supply of mobile heavy artillery elsewhere. There had seemed little point leaving valuable weapons in forts which, although useful, were obsolete by 1914 and were out of range of the front line.

Lack of guns was not the forts' only problem. They were under the strict control of the governor of Verdun, not the local corps commander who had once been refused access to Fort Douaumont because he had no written permission to enter. He assumed they were fully manned, unaware that the bulk of the garrisons had been sent into the trenches in 1915 and all that remained were 56 Territorial

Ils ne passeront pas

German infantry head for the Crown Prince's army, January 1916. They were infiltrated to the front line at night and concealed in giant underground bunkers so the French did not detect the build-up of men on the Verdun front.

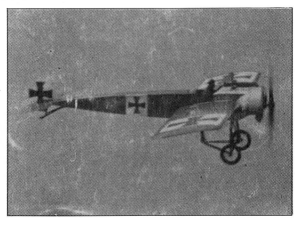

Verdun marked the first serious battle for air superiority. It was essential to prevent French aircraft detecting the German preparations and the Germans concentrated their Fokker E III fighters to maintain an aerial blockade above their lines.

The holocaust begins: the pentagonal shape of Fort Douaumont is almost obliterated by the German bombardment. To the front and rear of the fort can be seen trenches occupied by the surviving French infantry. Many were buried alive.

gunners. Probed by a single German infantry company on 24 February, Douamont was captured immediately, a body blow to French morale.

Von Falkenhayn's chilling calculation was now put to the test. Its defences penetrated and vulnerable, according to the text book, the French army should have retreated from the right bank of the Meuse. The woods and hills of the left bank offered every defensive advantage and no German offensive could have continued there. But it was not to be. The French cabinet would not countenance General Joseph Joffre ordering a retreat; instead, the commander of the 2nd Army, General Henri Pétain, was ordered to assume command of the whole Verdun sector. There would be no retreat.

When the summons to GHQ arrived, Pétain was nowhere to be found at his headquarters. Fortunately his ADC knew the habits of his boss and located the 60-year-old general in the Hotel Terminus of the Gard du Nord. Pétain received the news at 0300, grunted and returned to his mistress.

Always a man to lead from the front, Pétain contracted double pneumonia during a long cold journey around his new command. Yet he swiftly imposed order on chaos and breathed new life into the defences. He personally co-ordinated the artillery fireplan and ensured that the logistic artery, the road from Bar-le-Duc dubbed 'la voie sacrée', remained open. As the French defence stiffened, von Falkenhayn was obliged to extend the frontage of his attack and fight west of the Meuse where French artillery enfiladed his narrow thrust towards Verdun.

The second phase of the German offensive opened on 6 March, again in sporadic snow showers. An horrific struggle ensued for the ominously named hill le Mort Homme, and the fighting along the Verdun front assumed a nightmarish quality which has never been surpassed. Massive artillery barrages overlapped and overran, firing without respite. On the receiving end of this supernatural fury, the infantrymen of both sides cowered in the mud, seldom catching a glimpse of an enemy soldier. April brought warmer weather and added fresh horror. As each shell disinterred lumps of rotting flesh, the stench grew unbearable. Both armies rotated troops through the Verdun front, feeding themselves into the meat grinder. Von Falkenhayn's theory had backfired, for it was not just the French army which was being bled white.

After three months of bitter fighting, the battle for Verdun intensified and Fort Vaux was captured after desperate resistance was cut short by lack of water. On 21 June the Germans came close to breaking through to the city after a barrage of new phosgene poison gas shells, but at horrific cost the French line held. The opening of the British offensive on the Somme in July effectively ended the German offensive and sealed von Falkenhayn's failure. Both armies had suffered some 300,000 casualties and the psychological effects on the survivors percolated both armies, sapping the will to fight on.

The horror of Verdun had not finished: for the rest of the year, the French army conducted a series of counterattacks which gradually regained the lost ground now hallowed with the lives of so many soldiers. Douaumont and Vaux were recaptured, and a judiciously executed assault in December brought to prominence a new French commander, Robert Nivelle. By succeeding where so many had failed, he claimed he had found the formula to crack the Western Front. 1917 would be the year of decision.

42 cm howitzer 'Big Bertha' These were the biggest guns used during World War I. Thirteen of them were employed to pulverize the French positions in February. When they fired, the sheer concussion broke windows two miles away and a shell weighing nearly a ton arced into the sky. The German artillery dominated the battlefield in February but enough French guns had arrived by March to inflict equal damage on the German infantry. Some of the 'Big Berthas' were eventually attacked by long range French 155 mm guns.

Nothing beside remains After months of non-stop shelling this is the western end of Fort Douaumont. Today the tortured earth is covered with conifers but underneath you can still see the lunar landscape for which the infantry fought and died.

One of the North African divisions on its way to Verdun. The French colonial troops were ferocious soldiers but the 37th Division was thrown in piecemeal to stem the initial attack. Shattered by murderous bombardment it was routed.

On 8 May a fire started in Douaumont, possibly by troops brewing coffee on cordite cases. Some flamethrower tanks were ignited exploding a magazine: 650 German troops died and most are still there, walled up in one of the casements.

Practically the whole French army was rotated through Verdun and the losses touched every village in France. One lesson was learned: the ability of forts to withstand almost any attack. It was to be the origin of the Maginot Line.

Officers and men of the 13th Royal Fusiliers near Albert, 7 July 1916, display their collection of German booty after their successful attack on La Boiselle. The German picklehaube helmet worn by several of the men was a particularly prized souvenir – so prized that the Germans took to leaving booby-trapped picklehaubes in dug-outs that they were evacuating. Note also the Luger pistol displayed in the back row on the right, and the picklehaube cover belonging to the 190th Regiment worn by the man with the captured pipe.

THE SOMME: Death of a generation

1 July 1916: after a week long bombardment of the German frontline, nearly 100,000 British soldiers rose from their trenches and marched into No Man's Land.

In December 1915 Sir Douglas Haig agreed to General Joseph Joffre's demands for an Allied attack on a 95-km (60-mile) front along the Somme. But on 21 February 1916 General Erich von Falkenhayn struck with unimagined ferocity at Verdun and began a meat-grinder of a battle into which France fed the best of her armies. The Somme became a British battle.

The army assembled for the Somme battle was unique, the product of the 'New Armies' concept and as such a volunteer force entirely different from the regular British army which had vanished in the battles of 1915. The men were the finest recruits an army could desire but the British army simply did not have the officer and NCO cadres available to provide anything more than basic training. However, the British army had at last assembled a massive gunline and planned a week-long preliminary bombardment: a tactical luxury undreamed of in 1915 and one which engendered an infectious spirit of confidence.

The bombardment begins

The bombardment began on 24 June, and observers watched the German front disappear under fountains of earth and dust. Some 1.7 million rounds were fired at General Otto von Below's six front-line divisions, who waited out the storm in their underground galleries. The Germans had burrowed deep in the chalky soil, and for all its fury the British barrage had but one large-calibre gun per 55 m (60 yards) of front.

The shelling ended after a furious crescendo at 07.30 on 1 July. Wave after wave of British infantry rose from their trenches and walked forward. But they advanced to their deaths: the German machine-gun nests had survived and so had much of the wire. The British army suffered the highest losses it had ever taken in a single day: 57,000 casualties – a figure which still dominates the UK's insular attitude to the 'Great War'. It was a catastrophe never repeated in World War I, and only exceeded by the surrender of Singapore in 1942 as the worst day in the history of the British armed forces.

The first real success on the Somme was achieved on 14 July, when at 03.30 General Sir Henry Rawlinson mounted a brilliant attack with seven divisions. The Germans were caught by surprise and their front was ruptured for a few tantalizing hours: there was even a small mounted cavalry action in the evening. The British came agonisingly close to capturing High Wood, but the German reserves plugged the gap and the Somme offensive became a remorseless battle of attrition. British attack was succeeded by German counter-attack, but neither side was able to establish mastery. The South African Brigade took Delville Wood on 15 July, but suffered 75 per cent casualties in the next three days as the full weight of German artillery blasted the position in support of desperate enemy counter-attacks.

Gough and Birdwood mounted an assault on Pozières Ridge on 23-27 July. The ANZAC Corps captured its part of the ridge but suffered 23,000 casualties in the process. On 28 July the last survivors of the Brandenburg Grenadiers were driven out of the rubble of Longueval. Fighting raged throughout August and on 3 September the ANZACs took Mouquet farm which overlooked the German lines, providing a view several miles beyond Bapaume.

The French I Corps advanced 3.2 km (2 miles) on 3 September, and on the next day the whole French 10th Army attacked on a 16-km (10-mile) front between Barleux and Chilly, capturing the latter along with 5,000 prisoners and nearly 100 machine-guns. By mid-September almost all the forward crest of the main ridge between Delville Wood and Mouquet farm was in British hands. Bapaume beckoned.

A three-day bombardment preceeded another major British attack on 15 September, which included for the first time tanks, totalling 32. Flers fell early in the morning to New Zealand troops supported by armour, an airman reporting that 'A tank is walking up the High Street of Flers with the British Army cheering behind.' High Wood, once again, provided the toughest resistance. The 47th Division was beaten off in the morning, but in the afternoon mounted a second attack which finally ejected the Bavarian defenders. The attack on 15 September was a marked contrast to the shambles of 1 July: three heavily fortified villages had been taken along with 4,000 prisoners and an advance of about 1.6-km (1-mile) made along a 9.5-km (6-mile) front.

Fall of Thiepval

The fine summer deteriorated into a wet autumn. Thiepval fell at long last on 27 September, but operations in October were bedevilled by incessant rain. The mud was as bad as it ever would be at Ypres in 1917, and the Germans could be forgiven for thinking that the battle was over at last. However, drier and cooler weather in early November was the cue for the last phase of the Somme battle, launched against the salient around Beaumont Hamel. The British attack in the Gommecourt-Thiepval sector on 1 July had been a disastrous failure and the front line had never really moved. Consequently, the assault could be mounted from the original British frontline rather than over ground torn up by months of shelling. Seven divisions of General Sir Hubert Gough's 5th Army attacked on 13 November, aided by a dense fog. The 51st Highland Division stormed the underground labyrinth of Beaumont-Hamel, and when the action finished on 21 November the battle of the Somme was over.

British dressing station
On 1 July the British Army suffered over 37,000 wounded which hopelessly overloaded the medical system. In the subsequent fighting the lot of the wounded continued to be grim indeed with the whole battle area dominated by artillery and machine gun fire.

Maxim MG 08 machine-gun

The slaughter of British infantry on 1 July was largely due to about 100 German machine-gun posts. The gunners reached their parapet before the assaulting infantry and shot every attack to a standstill. The machine-gunners were the elite of the German Army and remained the linchpin of their defence on the Western Front until the end of the war.

The territorial gains were unspectacular: along a 48-km (30-mile) front the greatest penetration was about 11.25 km (7 miles) deep and had no strategic significance. The British Empire had sustained 450,000 casualties and the French suffered about 150,000. German losses exceeded 600,000, Hentig describing the Somme as 'the muddy grave of the German Field Army'.

The Somme was not a unique battle. The British

Seven miles in five months

The British barrage was largely provided by 18 pdr field guns which were too light to destroy the German positions. Despite the experience at Gallipoli, the barrage on the German frontline was still lifted too early.

As the British infantry left their trenches, the Germans raced up from their underground bunkers. The British were still in No Man's Land when the machine-guns opened fire, mowing down wave after wave of the attacking troops.

The attack by 29th Division was compromised by the premature explosion of a mine under the Hawthorn redoubt, ten minutes before zero hour. All along the line the German artillery, which was presumed to be knocked out, sprang back into life.

Master of the battlefield
Tear gas and chlorine gas shells were widely used during the battle of the Somme. Because of their vital role, machine-gunners tended to be better protected than other troops; the German machine-gun teams even had oxygen tanks in their positions to last out the longest gas barrage.

German dead at Beaumont-Hamel, November 1916
One of the classic photographs of the Great War says more than words ever can about the horror of industrial warfare. Britain lost a generation in 1916 but so did Germany and her casualty list was already approaching a million dead. Germany's warlords now faced strong pressure for a compromise peace in 1917.

British Officer, July 1916

The dramatic expansion of the British Army since 1914 created a chronic shortage of skilled officers and NCOs to lead the huge, volunteer force. The courage displayed by the junior officers was exemplary but their tactical ability was strongly criticised in German reports.

Specification
sMG08
Calibre: 7.92 mm (0.312 in)
Lengths: gun 1.175 m (46.26 in), barrel 719 mm (28.3 in)
Weights: gun complete with spares 62 kg (136.7 lb), sledge mount 37.65 kg (83.0 lb)
Muzzle velocity: 900 m (2.953 ft) per second
Rate of fire: 300-450 rpm
Feed: 250 ground fabric belt

'The monstrous anger of the guns'
One of the mainstays of the German heavy batteries was the 21 cm howitzer. Although the British lagged behind in the provision of heavy guns, the volume of British fire revealed to the Germans that they were facing an industrial power greater than their own.

Standing guard, July 1916
The British did not do all the attacking on the Somme. Ordered to defend every inch of their positions, the Germans constantly mounted ferocious counter-attacks to throw the British back to their start line. This policy of 'no retreat' proved very costly indeed.

army simply suffered the sort of casualties already experienced by the French, Germans, Russians and Austrians. Indeed, it has been observed that the first day of the Somme was the 132nd day of the holocaust at Verdun. For the Germans the revelation of the UK's industrial muscle came as an unpleasant surprise and it began to dawn on some of her leaders that the odds against them were lengthening.

Despite the failure of the first assault a second major attack was launched on July 14. It was a measure of GHQ's optimism that 5 divisions of cavalry were massed behind the front ready to pursue the beaten enemy.

Haig now resigned himself to a battle of attrition, not a breakthrough. After heavy fighting in August a major assault on Flers took place on 15 September supported by 32 tanks. It was the first tank action in history.

Haig continued the battle into the autumn despite heavy rain which made the ground unspeakably difficult. The last big push was not until November. Both sides had suffered about 600,000 casualties and the front line had barely moved.

THE BRUSILOV OFFENSIVE: Russia's last victory

Austro-Hungarian infantryman 1916

Two years of total war left Russia and Austria-Hungary teetering on the brink of collapse. No-one expected a Russian attack in June 1916.

The Brusilov offensive is named after the Russian general, Aleksei Brusilov, whose indomitable energy and military skill was a sharp contrast to the fumbling ineptitude of many other Russian commanders. He staged his attack in June 1916, two months after a Russian offensive north of the Pripet marshes had been slaughtered with machine-like efficiency by the armies of Generals Scholz and Hutier. For the loss of some 20,000 men, the Germans inflicted nearly 150,000 casualties on the hapless Russian soldiery and it was widely assumed that the Russians would not be able to mount another offensive until the autumn.

Brusilov recognized that attacking armies sowed the seeds of their defeat the moment they began to prepare their offensive. Defenders invariably detected the build-up of enemy forces on their front and rushed reinforcements to the threatened point. The result was, at best, a battle of attrition and, at worst, the sort of butchery which destroyed the Russian northern armies in March 1916.

Brusilov spent no time on the normal preliminaries to an offensive. The Austrian armies facing him observed no massing of artillery batteries, no new encampments behind the lines, no guns zeroing in on their command posts and communications trenches. From the River Pripet to the Dniestr valley and the Romanian border, there was no sign of the impending storm. But underground, in some places only 75 m (82 yards) from the Austro-Hungarian front line, fresh Russian troops were patiently sitting in newly dug bunkers. Arriving under cover of darkness they stayed below ground during the day, waiting for the signal.

On 4 June the Russian artillery opened fire along the entire 320-km (200-mile) front of Brusilov's South Western Army Group. Twenty-four hours later it stopped as suddenly as it had begun: Russian infantry boiled up out of the ground and swept across no man's land. The Austrian front line was engulfed. In some places the defenders were caught in their bunkers. In the north the Austro-Hungarian 4th Army collapsed overnight. Army headquarters was overrun by Russian troops and Lutsk abandoned as the Austro-Hungarian soldiers surrendered in droves. In the south the Russian attack met with even greater success, with units of the Austro-

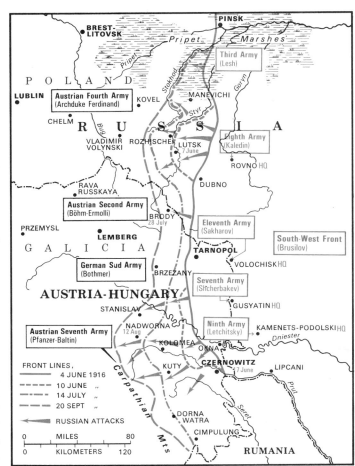

By 1916 the Austro-Hungarian army consisted mainly of half-trained conscripts led by inadequate numbers of hastily trained officers. The bluish grey service dress illustrated here was introduced in 1909 but from 1915 onwards Austrian troops began to wear German-supplied field grey.

Austrian howitzer in action, June 1916
Like their Russian opposite numbers, Austrian gunners were frequently short of ammunition. When Brusilov launched his surprise attack many Austrian batteries were overrun as the infantry in front of them fled or surrendered.

Hapsburg humiliation

Austrian troops in Lemburg. From Galicia to the Carpathian mountains the fighting had swung to and fro in 1915. However, the Austro-Hungarian army had conquered Serbia and beaten off every Italian attack along the Isonzo.

An Austro-Hungarian machine-gun team in action. There was little co-ordination between the German and Austro-Hungarian war efforts and, without informing their ally, the Austrians stripped the Eastern Front of their best troops to attack Italy.

The Austro-Hungarian armies on the Eastern Front relaxed in the belief that the Russians would not be able to launch another offensive until the autumn. They also believed the main strength of the Russian army to be in Poland opposite the Germans.

Russian heavy artillery, winter 1915
Those heavy guns which could be made mobile were employed to bombard the enemy trenches but they were always short of ammunition. In the army there were grave doubts about the Tsar's leadership by 1916 and a yawning gulf between the Russian people and the westernized elite running the war.

Left: Heading for the rear
Speaking 28 different languages, the Austro-Hungarian army was a fragile institution. After the regular officers and NCOs had been killed standards slipped rapidly. German army units had to be attached to stiffen Austro-Hungarian resistance.

Below: Soldiers of the Tsar
The stoic endurance of the Russian soldier was never more sorely tried than in the Great War. Short of food, ammunition and even rifles, Russian troops fought doggedly even into 1917. The Brusilov offensive showed what they could achieve when properly led.

Hungarian 7th Army simply disintegrating under the pressure. In five days of battle over 70,000 prisoners were taken.

Brusilov had achieved surprise by not massing guns, supplies and ammunition along his front line. After 10 days of battle the offensive faltered for the lack of reserves, transport and ammunition: the Austro-Hungarian armies were given a breathing space. German reinforcements were rushed south but not in sufficient numbers to win back the lost ground, a counter-attack by three divisions under von der Marwitz recouping only a few miles south of Kovel.

Brusilov received little support from other army groups. General Evert botched an attack on 13 June, leaving the best of two Guards divisions hanging on the German wire at Baronovichi. Another attack in the same sector on 3 July met with an equally bloody repulse. Brusilov managed to resume the attack in late July and scored further successes against the Austro-Hungarians. There was then another pause to allow the batteries to replenish their ammunition and then a third push on August 7. A fourth attack was mounted in September in support of the Romanians, who had foolishly entered the war on the Allied side on 27 August.

Brusilov's attacks were successively weaker as he ran out of reserves and ammunition, and as the enemy defences were stiffened with German divisions. But the Austro-Hungarian army had been routed with the loss of over 500,000 prisoners, 1,300 machine guns and 400 field pieces. It was a blow from which Austro-Hungarian military power never recovered.

The Brusilov offensive was the swan song of the Tsarist army, the last victory of Imperial Russian forces before the revolution of February 1917. In just over two years of war the Russian army had sustained 4.5 million casualties and (like the Austrian, French, Italian and Turkish forces) it had had enough. With political incompetence on a heroic scale, Tsar Nicholas II had mismanaged the war, the economy and the government. Even his generals were planning a coup when he abdicated and plunged his country into anarchy and revolution. Brusilov, his most capable general, joined the Bolsheviks in the ensuing civil war.

An Austrian battery belonging to the 4th Army in southern Poland. Between 4 and 6 June this army disintegrated. The headquarters of Archduke Ferdinand was overrun on 7 June, and a 50-mile gap appeared in the Austrian front.

The Russian army had already sustained over 4 million battle casualties by June 1916. Sickness and disease were rife in the army as the supplies of food and medicine dwindled. Here lie some of the last Russian troops to die advancing.

Austrian infantry await a gas attack on the Italian front. By the end of 1916 Archduke Charles tried to sue for peace but no-one would listen. Although weakened, the Austrian army could still take the offensive against Italy the following year.

JUTLAND: Clash of the dreadnoughts

31 May 1916: After two years of frustration the Royal Navy finally intercepts the German High Seas Fleet.

Following the usual pattern of German planning, Vizeadmiral Franz von Hipper's Scouting Divisions of battle-cruisers and light forces were directed to leave the River Jade early on 31 May 1916, to proceed up the west coast of the Jutland peninsula and make a demonstration in the Skagerrak. This was calculated to attract the British battle-cruiser force, which would then be cut off from its base by the High Seas Fleet, now under Vizeadmiral Reinhard Scheer.

British radio intercepts worked well, with Vice Admiral Sir David Beatty's Battle-Cruiser Fleet and Admiral Sir John Jellicoe's Grand Fleet actually sailing before the enemy late on 30 May and heading eastward to rendezvous west of the Skagerrak. However, by transferring ashore the call sign of Scheer's flagship, SMS *Friedrich der Grosse*, the Germans successfully misled the British into believing that the High Seas Fleet was still at Wilhelmshaven. Jellicoe therefore followed Beatty at easy steam and at a distance that was to prove crucial. Both Beatty and von Hipper expected to meet his opposite number unsupported. Each was to be surprised.

At 1410 on 31 May the light cruiser HMS *Galatea*, one of Beatty's scouting line, encountered elements of von Hipper's light forces, which had stopped a neutral. A skirmish immediately ensued and both battle-cruiser groups made for the scene. Beatty was backed by four of the fast new 'Queen Elizabeth' class battleships of Rear Admiral Hugh Evan-Thomas's 5th Battle Squadron. Contact was established at 1530 in calm conditions with good, if patchy, visibility. The seaplane carrier HMS *Engadine*, in company, made history by getting aircraft aloft for reconnaissance though, in truth, their contribution was minimal.

Von Hipper made off to the south, directly for Scheer, Beatty in company as planned. From 1548 both sides were engaged at about 13700 m (15,000 yards). It was a disastrous phase, both HMS *Indefatigable* (at 1602) and HMS *Queen Mary* (at 1626) blowing up after receiving heavy hits and HMS *Lion* (at 1600) nearly suffering the same fate when the roof was blown off her Q turret. This was despite Evan-Thomas's great 381-mm (15-in) guns coming into the action at 1606.

Between the warring lines of battle-cruisers, the light forces were involved in their own dispute but, fortunately, Commodore W. E. Goodenough's 2nd

Royal Sovereign fires a 15-in broadside
The 'Royal Sovereign' class were the last 'super-dreadnoughts' to join the Grand Fleet. HMS *Revenge* and *Royal Oak* were completed in time to serve at Jutland. The Germans lagged far behind in dreadnought construction and completed only two 38-cm gunned ships by 1918.

Light Cruiser Squadron stayed out ahead and was able to give warning that it was running into the whole High Seas Fleet, the head of whose line was sighted at 1628 only 11000 m (12,000 yards) away. Beatty held on until 1640 to confirm and then hauled around 16 points on to a north-westerly course, his duty now quite clearly to entice the enemy back on to the advancing, but still unsuspected, Grand Fleet. In view of the already late hour the gap between Beatty and Jellicoe was to cause decisive delay.

For an hour during this run to the north, the British were able to punish von Hipper heavily, though beyond the range of Scheer. The German battle-cruisers were obliged to open the range only, suddenly, to see a further battle-cruiser squadron to the northeast, i.e. on their starboard bow. This was Rear Admiral the Hon R.L.A. Hood's 3rd Battle-Cruiser Squadron, and Beatty bore eastward to make for it. This had the effect of pushing von Hipper's force to the east to conform and, as they were

leading Scheer, the whole German line was forced around. The manoeuvre was invaluable to Jellicoe, just out of sight, whose fleet was still cruising in six columns, waiting to deploy but lacking information. Armoured cruisers, which should have provided this, had not sufficient speed to get far enough ahead.

The cautious Jellicoe then deployed on his port wing column which, though it put his most powerful ships at the head of the battleline, delayed action even further. By 1825 the heads of the deploying columns were roughly parallel and some 11000 m apart. Visibility was restricted by the funnel smoke of both Beatty's ships and Rear Admiral Sir Robert Arbuthnot's armoured cruisers (1st Cruiser Squad-

'Helgoland' class battleship

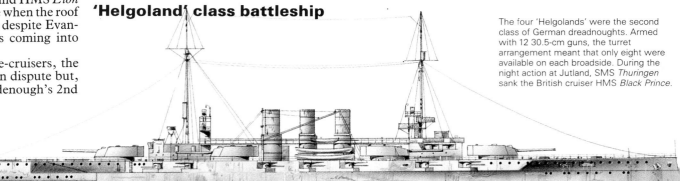

The four 'Helgolands' were the second class of German dreadnoughts. Armed with 12 30.5-cm guns, the turret arrangement meant that only eight were available on each broadside. During the night action at Jutland, SMS *Thuringen* sank the British cruiser HMS *Black Prince*.

'There seems to be something wrong with our bloody ships today'

Beatty's flagship HMS Lion *leads the 1st Battle-Cruiser Squadron in pursuit of the German battle-cruisers. The Germans drew off, trying to lure Beatty's ships into action with the whole High Seas Fleet.*

HMS Iron Duke *was Admiral Jellicoe's flagship at Jutland. Displacing 25,000 tons and armed with 10 13.5-in guns, she fired a heavier broadside than contemporary German dreadnoughts but her armour protection was lighter.*

Lion *at 16.00: seconds later she received a hit from* Lutzow *which blew the roof off Q turret. All the guncrew were killed, but Major Harvey RM won a posthumous VC for flooding the magazine and saving the ship.*

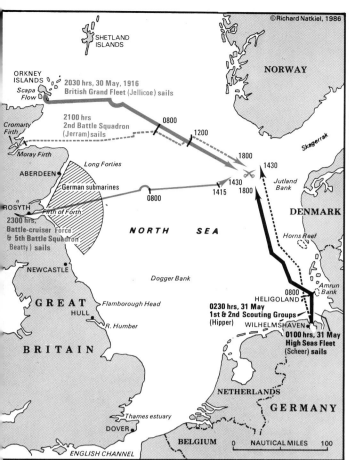

© Richard Natkiel, 1986

SHETLAND ISLANDS

NORWAY

ORKNEY ISLANDS
Scapa Flow
2030 hrs, 30 May, 1916
British Grand Fleet (Jellicoe) sails

0800

1200

Cromarty Firth

2100 hrs
2nd Battle Squadron
(Jerram) sails

Moray Firth

Long Forties

1430   1800

ABERDEEN

German submarines

0800   1415   1430   1800

Skagerrak

Jutland Bank

DENMARK

ROSYTH
Firth of Forth

2300 hrs,
Battle-cruiser Force
& 5th Battle Squadron
(Beatty) sails

NORTH SEA

Horns Reef

NEWCASTLE

Dogger Bank

Amrun Bank

HELIGOLAND

0800

GREAT
BRITAIN
HULL   Flamborough Head

R. Humber

0230 hrs, 31 May
1st & 2nd Scouting Groups
(Hipper)
WILHELMSHAVEN

0100 hrs, 31 May
High Seas Fleet
(Scheer) sails

NETHERLANDS

GERMANY

DOVER

BELGIUM   0   NAUTICAL MILES   100

ENGLISH CHANNEL

Jutland
The Royal Navy was in the fortunate position of being able to read the German naval code, so the Grand Fleet actually left port before the Germans. The planned U-boat ambush never took place because delays in launching the operation meant the submarines had had to turn for home by 31 May.

Above German battle-cruiser SMS *Moltke*
In the first 12 minutes of Jutland, *Moltke* scored nine hits on the British battle-cruiser HMS *Tiger*. None of Beatty's squadron managed to score a direct hit on her but she did take four hits from the massive 15-in guns of the 5th Battle Squadron.

Seydlitz limps home, 1 June 1916
Hit by 21 heavy shells and one torpedo, the crippled battle-cruiser SMS *Seydlitz* made her way alone through the British fleet during the night. She was seen by at least one British dreadnought but not recognised and by dawn she reached the Horns Reef and safety.

ron) passing between the lines, the latter losing HMS *Defence* (blown-up) and HMS *Warrior* (fatally damaged) in doing so.

Even though Hood's flagship HMS *Invincible* was also shattered by a magazine explosion, Jellicoe realized every admiral's dream in crossing the German 'T'. From a 9-km (6-mile) crescent of British battleships, the head of the enemy line took a fearful pounding but, quite suddenly, disappeared as Scheer coolly carried out a manoeuvre oft-practised in peacetime, a 16-point turn together, covered by a mass smoke-screen. It was 1845.

The High Seas Fleet was now on course for Wilhelmshaven and home. Jellicoe's goal was to interpose the Grand Fleet. Both headed roughly southward with light forces forming a visual link. At 1910 Scheer made another turn together to cross the British wake. Misjudging it, he ran again into the main battle line. Only by flinging Hipper forward in the famous battle-cruiser 'death ride' was the German commander able to extricate himself by a third turnabout manoeuvre. By 1940, with just a half hour to sunset, the last big guns fell silent.

As the Grand Fleet was not trained in night fighting, Jellicoe would not risk it and proposed to resume the battle at dawn. Available intelligence regarding Scheer's night intentions was poorly interpreted and his repeated efforts to pass through the Grand Fleet's wake were not reported to Jellicoe. The massed flotillas trailing the British battle squadrons were finally forced aside about midnight in some vicious clashes and Scheer broke through to safety. At 0300 on 1 June Jellicoe turned back, his quarry acknowledged to be beyond reach.

Jutland was over and the controversies began. Materially the Germans could claim a victory, sinking 111,000 tons for the loss of 6,200. British gunnery had been superior, scoring over 100 major-calibre hits to about 64, but projectiles had often broken up on impact and the German ships had also proved to be better at absorbing punishment. It had not been the Trafalgar that had been sought but, even so, it advanced the enemy's cause at sea not one jot.

'Queen Elizabeth' class battleship

The five 'Queen Elizabeths' were members of one of the most successful classes of British battleships. Four of them fought at Jutland as the 5th Battle Squadron which had been temporarily assigned to Vice Admiral Beatty.

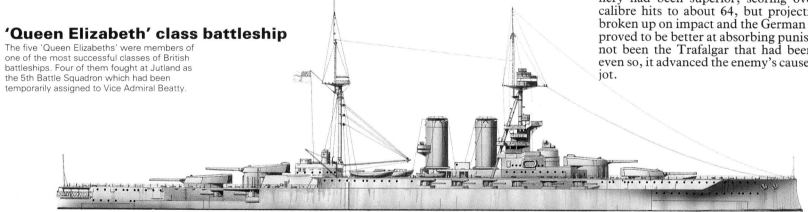

Two other British battle-cruisers were not so lucky: HMS Indefatigable *exploded after a hit from SMS Von der Tann and at 16.26 HMS* Queen Mary's *forward magazine detonated after a hit from SMS Derfflinger. As she rolled over she was torn apart.*

SMS Nassau *opens fire with her midships 28-cm guns. By the time the main battle lines met visibility was very poor and the British had only a fleeting opportunity to engage the German battleships before they fled into the murk.*

On 1 June 1916 the Royal Navy was still master of the seas: the German battle fleet would not be fit for action for many months. This is the forecastle of HMS Chester *which had scouted ahead of Hood's battle-cruisers and suffered heavy damage.*

'WE HAVE THE FORMULA': The Nivelle offensive

April 1917: General Robert Nivelle promises France immediate victory from his new offensive.

Seldom in history has a battle received so much advance publicity as the 2nd Battle of the Aisne. Its instigator was a charismatic French leader, General Robert Nivelle, who had succeeded General Joseph Joffre in December 1916, largely because he promised his government a victory whereas the old Commander-in-Chief could only offer yet more bloody battles of attrition. Nivelle also swayed David Lloyd George, who had at last succeeded in manoeuvring Asquith from office as British Prime Minister.

Lloyd George despaired of success on the Western Front and wanted to sack his Commander-in-Chief Field Marshal Sir Douglas Haig, but the Frenchman strongly impressed him with his arguments for a new style of offensive which he promised would smash the German front in 48 hours. Nivelle spoke perfect English: indeed, he was far more fluent than Haig, who tended to converse in a series of strangulated grunts. The decision was made: Nivelle would lead the Allied armies to victory in spring 1917.

Devious tactics at an Allied strategic planning conference enabled Lloyd George to place Haig and the BEF under Nivelle's command, but Haig's apoplectic reaction diluted the instructions to 'co-operation' rather than subordination. However, the damage was done and relations between the French and British military leaders became distinctly chilly.

Nivelle was a first-class divisional commander who believed he had found the key to unlock the Western Front. A lightning artillery barrage, rather than the week-long bombardments usually employed, would preceed an attack on the widest possible frontage. A creeping barrage of shells would slowly roll over the German positions followed closely by waves of infantry. Provided the infantry kept to the timetable by which the guns shifted their fire, the enemy would be broken. Nivelle promised victory and as a sop to the doubting Thomases, vowed that he would break off the attack if he had not broken through in the two days he allowed.

Planning for the attack was still in progress when the Germans confounded everyone by retreating as much as 80 km (50 miles) in places. They fell back to a prepared line of fortifications, the *Siegfried-Stellung*, mistakenly called the 'Hindenburg Line' by the Allies. The German leaders knew they could not win the war in the West, so their army was to occupy a defensive belt where it could hold off the Allies while unrestricted submarine warfare destroyed the Allied economies. The land the Germans abandoned

French light machine-gunner

Like the Germans, the French had developed new and more flexible infantry tactics during the holocaust at Verdun. Grenades, rifle-grenades and light machine-guns gave infantry platoons much greater firepower. This *poilu* is armed with the Chauchat machine-gun, widely used in the Nivelle offensive.

Tirailleurs Algerians parade at Aix during April 1917. The NCO on the left sports pre-war summer uniform of blue jacket and white trousers although the rest of the unit wear the drab khaki adopted by units of the French colonial army at the beginning of the war.

was despoiled in the most barbaric manner: not merely devastated in a military sense with booby-traps and poisoned water supplies. The lowliest tree was cut down, and even if a house was not levelled, mirrors were smashed and furniture vandalized. It was Prussian 'frightfulness' at its most repugnant and Crown Prince Rupprecht of Bavaria wanted to resign in protest.

The retreat left Nivelle no other target for his offensive but the Chemin des Dames. The offensive had been so widely discussed in France and even neutral countries that the Germans already had a fair idea of what to expect before they captured some of Nivelle's orders on the body of a dead staff officer. Ensconced in excellent defensive positions, they awaited the French attack with confidence.

The bombardment began on 5 April, but torrential rain forced the attack to be postponed several times. When the French infantry finally rose from their trenches on 16 April they were scythed down in tangled heaps by concealed machine-gun posts which had survived the bombardment. Worse, battery after battery of German artillery suddenly sprang into life to deluge the would-be attackers with an endless rain of shells. The French I Colonial Corps suffered over 60 per cent losses on the first day. Only in a few places did the French penetrate the German front line to gain a total of 11,000 prisoners, and in sleet and driving rain the first German counter-attacks were delivered, snatching back much of the ground won at such French cost.

Bitter fighting over the next four days pushed the Germans out of the Aisne valley but there was no sign of the promised breakthrough. Nivelle quietly lowered his sights and renewed the attack to capture the rest of the Chemin des Dames ridge, but he was summoned to Paris. The cabinet had not forgotten his promise of a 48-hour victory or nothing and he was packed off to command French forces in North Africa. Some 165,000 French soldiers had given their lives and many of the survivors believed it had all been for nothing. On 29 April French army units started to mutiny.

French army mutinies

Raised hopes so cruelly dashed, combined with the appalling toll of nearly three years of war, had at last broken the back of the French army. The situation was exacerbated by Nivelle's opponents, who exaggerated French losses and overlooked the fact that over 100,000 Germans also perished in the campaign. Even when the defence held, there were no cheap victories on the Western Front.

General Henri Pétain, hero of Verdun, was called upon to salvage the French army from its slough of despair. The mutinies were mainly sit-down strikes in the rear areas, although the numbers of loyal troops holding the front were dangerously low. Pétain investigated and dealt with many grievances, increased leave and managed to restore discipline, but the French army would never be the same again. Meanwhile at Ypres, the British army continued its offensive known to history as Passchendaele. Had it faltered and Prince Rupprecht been allowed to launch his planned attack on the French, the course of the war might have been very different.

The breaking of an army

French soldiers march to the front for Nivelle's offensive. Their target was predictable, their enemy reinforced by troops released from Russia and the defences strengthened with new concrete emplacements.

French gunners in action, April 1917: the plan was a lightning bombardment ahead of the infantry attack, but repeated delays were caused by bad weather. This gave the Germans every warning of the time and place of the offensive.

German troops load one of their 25-cm trench mortars which were an important part of the German front-line defences. With their very high trajectory, they were able to lob their bombs right into a trench or shellhole where infantry were sheltering.

On the Aisne front, April 1917
French soldiers in action during Nivelle's ill-starred offensive known as the 2nd Battle of the Aisne. Nivelle sent his men into battle saying 'L'heure est venue! Confiance! Courage! Vive la France!' Within hours it was obvious that his plan had failed.

Un chien de guerre and his master
Dogs were used to deliver messages since they presented a smaller target than a battalion runner and were potentially quicker. They were also used as guard dogs in the front-line trenches to detect enemy trench raiders at night.

Left: French 370-mm howitzer
Nivelle's conspicuous successes at Verdun had depended on a short but powerful bombardment and a creeping barrage of shells moving slowly ahead of the infantry. For his attack on the Chemin des Dames he had some monstrous firepower but the German defences were amongst the strongest on the Western Front.

Aerial view of the battlefield east of Reims where a secondary attack was launched to support the main offensive. From an altitude of 600m (nearly 2,000 feet), the remains of a wood are visible on the heavily cratered ground.

The French medical services were woefully unprepared for the attack. The probable number of casualties had been hopelessly underestimated and troops saw their wounded friends lying about, untreated for days. This had a very poor effect on morale.

Nivelle offered the French soldier final victory but failed to deliver. Fortunately for the Allies, the widespread mutinies which followed went undetected by the Germans.

THE FIRST BATTLE OF THE ATLANTIC:
The U-boat campaign 1914-18

Britain's global empire depended on sea-borne trade and the Atlantic became a battlefield dominated by the submarine.

Over centuries of maritime struggle, the British had learned that the convoying of trade in war was essential to minimize losses. During the century of comparative peace preceding 1914, however, first-hand experience was forgotten while the revolution of steampower at sea had convinced many eminent theorists, such as Sir Julian Corbett, that when no longer bound by the vagaries of wind, merchantmen would prove almost impossible for enemy commerce-destroyers to find. It would, therefore, be better to allow them to sail independently, policing only those areas near terminal ports where traffic inevitably increased in density. The view was shared by the British Admiralty, which emphasized the lower utilization of ships, saturation of port facilities and a shortage of suitable escorts, all destroyers being required for service in the Grand Fleet.

Neither the British nor the Germans had realized before World War I that it would be the submarine rather than the cruiser that would be most effective against commerce. Before the war Winston Churchill understood the threat that submarines posed to warships, but could never contemplate their use against merchantmen 'by a civilised Power'. Jackie Fisher, the more realistic First Sea Lord, had pointed out that submarines had neither facility nor crew to spare – they could either release ships or sink them. The UK, meanwhile, imported nearly two-thirds of her food and maintained stockpiles of raw materials that would last only four to six weeks.

While many merchantmen were quickly armed with one or two old guns for self defence, convoy or escort was considered only for those of high value, e.g. carrying troops, ammunition, oil or refrigerated

Inside a British submarine
Submariners of all navies had been looked down on by senior officers. Neither side fully appreciated the potential of the submarine in 1914 and the operational radius of the U-boats came of much as a surprise to their owners as to the Royal Navy. Crewing these tiny vessels was a hazardous and gruelling experience.

'U-23' class submarine

U-23 and *U-41* joined the German navy from late 1914 to early 1915. With a range of over 8,000 miles they could prey on Allied merchant shipping all around the coast of the UK and France. Crewed by 37 men, these craft displaced 685 tons surfaced and were armed with an 8.8-cm gun and four 500-mm torpedo tubes.

Under the Waves

U.8 is sunk by Royal Navy 'Tribal' class destroyers in March 1915, soon after British waters were declared an unrestricted war zone. Such early British successes were more than matched by U-Boat inflicted losses to the British fleet.

Early anti-submarine measures included the setting up of an 'Auxiliary Patrol' of hundreds of trawlers, drifters and small craft around the British coast. This trawler crew is receiving instruction in the use of newly issued Ross rifles.

In spite of continually developing anti-submarine tactics, ships continued to be lost right up to the end of the war. This is the steam ship City of Glasgow, *torpedoed and sunk in the Irish Sea in September 1918.*

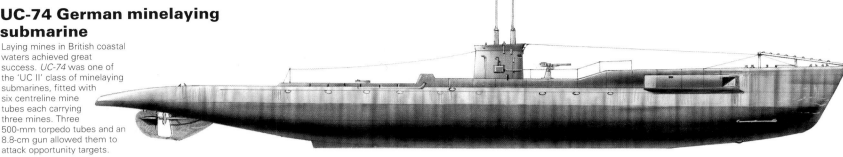

UC-74 German minelaying submarine

Laying mines in British coastal waters achieved great success. *UC-74* was one of the 'UC II' class of minelaying submarines, fitted with six centreline mine tubes each carrying three mines. Three 500-mm torpedo tubes and an 8.8-cm gun allowed them to attack opportunity targets.

food. Only 28 U-boats were initially available, and these operated within the prize rules by surfacing, searching and allowing abandonment before sinking. The process was slow, and a defensively-armed ship had the submarine at a great disadvantage.

Despite only 10 British ships, totalling 20,000 grt, being sunk by submarine during the first six months of war, the U-boats' potential was realized by the Germans and, in February 1915, all waters surrounding the British Isles were declared a war zone in which any ship, including neutrals, could be sunk on sight with Germany claiming the right to dispense with 'customary preliminaries'. It was a licence for an unrestricted U-boat campaign.

Losses increased alarmingly, but the destruction without warning of passenger vessels attracted worldwide opprobrium which even the Germans found difficult to withstand. Many still-neutral American lives were lost in the *Lusitania* in May and the *Arabic* in August, the resultant outcry obliging the Germans to re-impose restrictions on their submarines from 30 August. Despite boats being transferred to the less-controversial Mediterranean and becoming more involved in minelaying, they still succeeded in destroying some 750,000 grt during the whole of 1915. Even so, total losses were still outstripped by new construction and a measure of complacency continued.

Escort problem

Escorts still had no effective means of tackling a submarine once submerged, though they posed a much reduced threat once forced down. The policy of policing areas of high traffic density, however, was a failure as the mere presence of escorts acted as a signpost for a submarine.

The year 1916 saw revised rules of engagement for U-boats, and a growing relaxation in earlier restraint on their use. Some 2.3 million grt of shipping, British and neutral, were lost with an ominous increase from October onward. Admiral Sir John Jellicoe gave a clear and early warning of the trend but, as late as January 1917, the Admiralty still refused to recommend convoys 'in any area where submarine attack is a possibility' on the understandable but scientifically unfounded fear that they would be easier to detect and destroy.

The German Chief of Naval Staff, Grossadmiral Henning von Holtzendorff, was again enthusiastically urging an unrestricted submarine campaign to resolve the course of the war. On 1 February 1917 his views were implemented: within three months 1.8

million grt were destroyed and a further 275,000 damaged, 90 per cent by U-boats. Shipbuilding could not keep pace and neutrals were refusing to sail. A reluctant Admiralty's hand was forced by the direct intervention of the Prime Minister, David Lloyd George, and experimental convoys run on the North Atlantic route. Not only did the loss rate tumble but it was soon realized that, say, 20 ships in company were far less likely to be detected than 20 'independents' and, due to the continuing shortage of escorts, it was customary to make the greater part of an ocean passage without them.

Techniques involved forming the convoy on a broad front but shallow depth, minimizing the target for any submarine that succeeded in gaining an attacking position.

By night, unpredictable changes of course could lose a U-boat seeking to overtake the convoy by running on the surface. Anti-submarine ships no longer had to scour empty ocean for their quarry as the latter was obliged to come to the fixed point of the convoy, though the timely arrival of the convoy took precedence over sinking submarines. Finally, the value of aerial reconnaissance was discovered, the mere presence of an aircraft being sufficient to force a U-boat down, effectively putting it out of the hunt.

At the height of the submarine offensive, a merchantman in British waters had a one-in-four chance of being sunk. By mid-1918, with a complete convoy system in operation, the overall loss rate fell to just one in 120.

The Wolf's lair at Ostend
Coastal submarines based at Ostend and Zeebrugge wrought havoc off the British east coast, especially among the fishing fleets which were still largely sail-powered. The ports were an optimistic objective of the British offensive at Ypres in 1917. This UB-type boat was scuttled at the end of the war.

UC-5 at Temple Pier after her capture
The UC boats were minelayers which preyed on the UK's teeming coastal traffic. Their mines inflicted serious damage but it was a dangerous business, several UC boats being blown up by their own mines. Navigation in narrow channels was never easy and *UC-5* was captured after stranding herself.

PC boats were purpose-built patrol vessels disguised as merchantmen and armed with one 4-inch and two 12-pounder guns. Like the larger Q-ships, they were intended to lure U-boats to the surface where they could be engaged with guns.

A 'U-93' class boat stops a merchantman on the high seas. Early U-boats carried few torpedoes and had limited capability, but by this late stage in the war the underwater raiders carried 16 large torpedoes and had a powerful gun armament.

A U-boat surrenders at Harwich in 1918. Most of the High Seas fleet mutinied and gave up at the end of the war, though one officer crewed boat set out to penetrate Scapa Flow and became the only U-boat to be sunk by shore batteries.

THE THIRD BATTLE OF YPRES: Slaughter at Passchendaele

By early 1917 the Germans had defeated every Allied army opposed to them, except the British. But Field Marshal Haig was undaunted. The BEF would attack again on the Ypres front.

Sixty years after it ended, the 3rd Battle of Ypres still casts a dark shadow over British attitudes to the Great War. It is remembered as Passchendaele, a name which evokes ghastly images of British soldiers dying in a nightmarish landscape of mud and slime. Nearly 300,000 British troops died in Field Marshal Sir Douglas Haig's remorseless offensive which was already the subject of bitter controversy before it finished. David Lloyd George was one of the first, and certainly not the last, to condemn it as futile butchery.

Haig planned 1917 as a year of attrition which would pave the way for a decisive victory over Germany in 1918. History proved him correct; but the doggedness with which he pursued the attrition battle into the autumn has left an indelible question mark over his generalship. The strategic objective was to break through towards the Flemish coast and capture the German naval bases at Zeebrugge and Ostend. The other objective was based on simple calculation: the Allies had 14 million soldiers and the Central Powers had 9 million, while the Allies also had another 9 million men in reserve and the Central Powers only 3 million. If the Germans could be worn down in a major battle in 1917, Haig's reasoning dictated, their army would break under the pressure and the war would be over.

The holocaust at Verdun, followed by General Robert Nivelle's disastrous offensive, broke the back of the French army, leaving the British to bear the burden of the Western Front. Haig's army was a very different one to the Kitchener volunteer force of 1916: while it lacked the passionate enthusiasm of the army which attacked the Somme, it was a far more professional organization which deserved a better fate.

The bombardment opened on 18 July: 3,091 guns, one for every 6 yards of front, firing 4.25 million shells. It was the heaviest barrage yet seen in the war. With mind-numbing force it blasted the German front line into oblivion, but it also pulverized the drainage system throughout this low-lying area. The infantry went over the top on 31 July at 0315. The rain which was to figure so powerfully in the battle began that morning, an incessant downpour that filled the shell craters and would not drain away.

The first day of 3rd Ypres made so little progress that General Sir Hubert Gough, commanding the 5th Army, wanted to call it off. But after a necessary

Hauling up an 18-pdr gun, 9 August 1917
The rain which was to cause so much misery during the Ypres offensive began on July 31. The ground turned into a sticky ooze which sucked down men, horses and guns. It dried out during September but returned with a vengeance for the rest of the battle.

Bloody Wipers

British infantry in the front line at Ypres before Messines. A preliminary set-piece attack in June was very successful but there followed a six-week delay before the main assault was launched along the Ypres front.

A British 6-in howitzer in action during August. The unseasonal rain and the new structure of the German defences defeated the British attacks in that month. Many cabinet ministers wanted Haig's offensive stopped and a new effort made in Italy.

German counter-attacks continued to regain captured parts of their line. During July the Germans introduced a new poison gas: dichlorethyl sulphide (mustard gas). In 10 days they fired a million shells containing 2,500 tons of gas into the British lines.

Hanging on the old barbed wire
Two German soldiers discovered hanging in the British wire after a night raid on the Ypres front. In the six weeks between Messines and the attack at Ypres the Germans detected the British preparations and improved their defences. Trench raids enabled them to identify new units in the British lines.

Sergeant, British Machine-Gun Corps,1917

Each British division included a battalion of 48 Vickers machine-guns manned by men of the Machine-Gun Corps. On his sleeve this sergeant wears the proficiency badge awarded to soldiers for their expertise with the weapon. The Vickers was an outstandingly reliable weapon and continued in British service into the 1960s.

British heavy artillery in action, October 1917
The heavy guns of the Royal Garrison Artillery were the only weapons capable of shattering the German strongpoints. The gas masks protect the gunners from the fumes but they could be firing phosgene gas shells which came into regular use during the Battle of Ypres.

pause Haig resumed the offensive on 16 August in the Battle of Langemarck. The weather cleared up but the Germans fought with great tenacity from a network of ferro-concrete strongpoints impervious to anything but a direct hit from a heavy gun. The assaulting troops vainly tried to bypass them and bomb their rear entrances, but interlocking machine-guns and concentrated shelling smashed every attack.

The second phase began on 14 September, when General Sir Herbert Plumer's 2nd Army began a five-day bombardment of the high ground crossed by the Menin road. The subsequent assault gained its limited objective and at the end of the month a third major attack captured Polygon Wood. But now the rain returned with a vengeance.

Passchendaele is a village between Ypres and Roulers, standing on a low ridge which Haig insisted on capturing in the autumn. He believed that another fierce battle, although costly, would cripple the German army and despite bad weather and the already terrible condition of the ground, the orders were issued. Throughout October Haig fed his men into a meat grinder of a battle: craters filled lip-to-lip with fetid mud and slime were captured and recaptured. The incessant shelling continually disinterred the bodies of the dead, and the salient's hellish appearance was seared into the memories of the survivors.

The numbers game

Passchendaele was finally captured on 6 November, and the battle was halted four days later. In the numbers game, the British forces had sustained nearly 300,000 casualties and the Germans about 250,000. British losses were felt more keenly, as up to this point in the war the British Empire had suffered far fewer casualties than any other major power. This contributed heavily to the bitter memory of 3rd Ypres.

The Germans, who had begun the battle confident of holding the line, had certainly managed to retain most of the ground. But their losses were irreplaceable, and civilian support for continuing the war collapsed in the summer of 1917. The Reichstag voted for peace and only ruthless political control by the army leadership keeping Germany fighting. The 3rd Battle of Ypres maintained the military pressure on Germany at a time of increasing internal chaos. By 1918 the German leaders knew they had to end the war quickly before they had their own Bolshevik revolution.

British prisoners of war
Haig's ambitious plans for 1917 involved breaking the German front line and advancing to capture the submarine bases at Ostend and Zeebrugge. But the line held and the only British soldiers to march eastwards were men taken prisoner.

A machine-gun section passes through Ypres in early October. After the successes of September Haig was determined to take the remaining part of the ridge before winter. But the state of the ground had to be seen to be believed.

A 9.2-in howitzer fires in support of the infantry attacking Passchendaele. The light railway to the right was used to bring up its ammunition. Each shell threw up a fountain of water when it landed and the quagmire grew steadily worse.

Dead and wounded Australians and Germans in the aftermath of an attack on 12 October. Haig's final objective was taken on 6 November but this last phase of the battle was unsurpassed in its horror. Passchendaele overshadowed the rest of the battle.

BREAKTHROUGH IN ITALY:
The rout of Caporetto

02.00, 25 October 1917: the Italian frontline is enveloped in fog and rain. It is suddenly struck by a hurricane artillery bombardment. The Battle of Caporetto has begun.

The poor reputation of Italian troops in the English-speaking world dates from the Battle of Caporetto, which began in October 1917. In little over two weeks the Italian army lost 40,000 men killed or wounded, 293,000 captured and 400,000 deserted. The extent of the catastrophe astonished the Germans and Austro-Hungarians as much as it appalled the UK and France. Italian military power had received a mortal blow.

Italy's entry into the Great War was a masterpiece of manipulation by her diplomats but a questionable decision by her political leaders. In 1882 Italy signed a pact with Germany and Austria-Hungary and as late as the spring of 1914 Italian officials were in

Berlin arranging the transport of an Italian army to the Rhine to join a German invasion of France. However, the Germans were by this time highly dubious about Italy's intentions and her prompt declaration of neutrality in 1914 was not a great surprise.

The Allies and the Central Powers fell over themselves to induce Italy to join the war on their side. The most important bribe was the Italian-speaking territory currently under Austro-Hungarian control: under intense German pressure, Austria-Hungary was ready to concede most of Trentino by April 1915. But a week earlier, Italy had signed a secret treaty in London, agreeing to declare war on Austria-Hungary in exchange for outrageously large proportions of Austrian territory: some parts of Dalmatia she was promised were 90 per cent Slovak-speaking.

The Italian economy had not yet recovered from the war with Turkey three years earlier, her army was short of equipment and her industry strike-

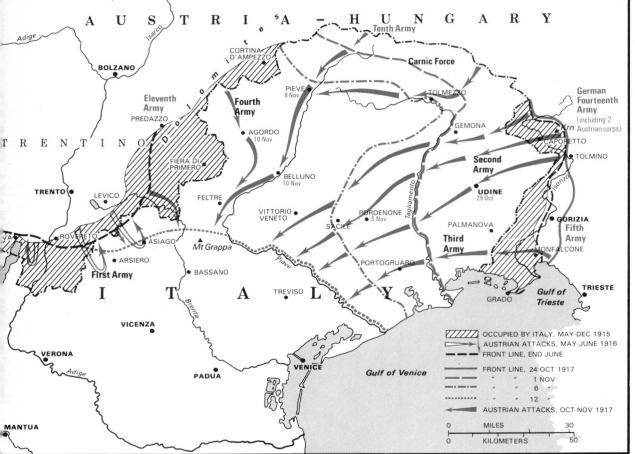

Italian death battalion pioneer

Armour plate re-appeared in World War I. Worn by snipers or engineers, it was heavy but effective. This Italian pioneer wears mail protection around his head since the rocky terrain threw up lethal stone fragments whenever a shell burst. He carries an automatic pistol and sharpened entrenching tool for close combat.

The Race to the Piave

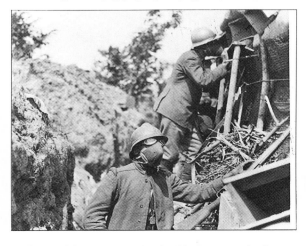

Italian soldiers were to be doubly hampered when the Austrian and German forces attacked. The bombardment included new gas shells against which Italian issue gas masks were unable to offer protection.

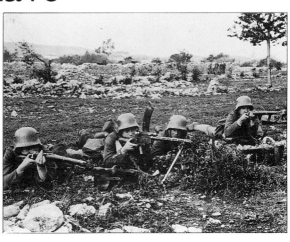

German troops, newly arrived on the Italian front, practise their new tactics two weeks before the offensive begins. Note the platoon commander with binoculars and the pair of Madsen light machine-guns with their large curved magazines.

Austrian officers examine some of the Italian dead on the eastern edge of the front. Had Conrad's troops in the mountains joined the offensive from the beginning, the main Italian armies might well have been encircled in a repeat of Tannenberg.

bound. Nevertheless, Italian soldiers went to war with a will. The border with Austria-Hungary was one long mountainous fortress and some of the least promising ground ever attacked during World War I. The valley of the Isonzo, a river running from north to south into the Adriatic, was the least disagreeable target and became the scene of 11 major battles beginning on 23 June 1915.

The First Battle of the Isonzo set the pattern for the others: Italian infantry made gallant efforts to break into the enemy front line but the co-ordination of the artillery bombardment with the infantry assault was very poor. In addition to the hostile nature of the terrain, where the sharp rocks shed lethal splinters every time a shell burst, there was the problem of the enemy. The Austro-Hungarian army was a heterogeneous mass of rival nationalities whose leaders were jockeying for power within the empire: however, the one thing that united most citizens of the empire was a hatred of Italy and even the most unenthusiastic Ruthenian conscript was delighted to have an Italian in his sights.

Battles on the Isonzo

The 11 battles of the Isonzo slowly ground up the Italian army. Halfway through the series, in June 1916, an Austrian offensive into the southern Trentino broke the Italian front line, inflicting heavy losses, and ended only when the Brusilov offensive drew off all Austro-Hungarian reserves. But the Italian commander, General Luigi Cadorna, was undaunted. The most remorseless conductor of the attrition battle in World War I, he continued his Isonzo offensives beyond the point where even Haig might have drawn the line. By 1917 the Italian army had suffered nearly 1 million casualties and was exhausted.

General Erich Ludendorff willingly provided Austria-Hungary with German divisions for an offensive in 1917: Germany could spare them from the Russian front, and Ludendorff knew that the young Emperor Karl would sue for peace if Austria-Hungary had to fight on much longer. The attack began on 25 October 1917 in rain, fog and snow. The Italians were doubly blinded by liberal use of gas shells and the defences collapsed. One of General Otto von Below's divisions advanced 22.5 km (14 miles) in the first 24 hours and for the next few days the front was wide open. Some Italian units fought rearguard actions while others marched into captivity in formed ranks. Most slipped away to the rear.

Unfortunately, the Austrian and German forces had little cavalry available to exploit their victory, and the pursuit placed enormous strain on their hard-marching infantry. Their triumphal forward progress ended on the River Piave as the Italian line was bolstered by British and French troops hastily dispatched from the Western Front. Caporetto was an exceptional feat of arms for von Below's German 14th Army, which had mounted one of the most aggressive and well-led offensives of the war. Sadly, it was destined to be the penultimate victory of the old Austro-Hungarian army which was in a desperate condition and doomed to suffer a Caporetto of its own within the year.

Trench bombers
Grenades, often called bombs in World War I, played a critical role in storming enemy trenches. These Austrian 'bombers' carry their rifles slung and a sackful of stick grenades. It will be their job to bomb their way along the Italian trenches.

Austro-Hungarian infantry
Wearing 'coalscuttle' helmets, the Austrian infantry looked very like their German allies by late 1917 but they still carried Mannlicher rifles. Here, they practice rapidly advancing from their trenches to catch the enemy before he recovers from the bombardment.

Left: Heading for the Piave
German infantry rest during the headlong pursuit into Italy. The German commanders led from the front at Caporetto, one corps commander, Berrer, was killed at the head of his troops by an Italian shell.

French troops arrive in Italy
A French 155-mm gun in action on the Italian Front. Six French and five British divisions were rushed by rail to shore up the Italian front although the offensive had run out of steam by mid-November when they arrived.

Wrecked Italian ammunition wagons on the Udine road. The town fell on 29 October, just four days after the offensive began. The Italians tried to rally on the river Tagliamento but a brilliantly executed German attack secured a bridgehead on 2 November.

Some of the 300,000 Italian soldiers who surrendered during the Caporetto offensive. Whole units marched into the POW cages shouting 'evviva la Austria'. In addition to the prisoners, the Austrians and Germans captured over 2,500 guns.

Austro-Hungarian troops reach the Piave, the final limit of their advance. By overrunning so much territory the Central Powers captured vast quantities of food, horses and military supplies that their shattered economies were unable to supply.

TO THE GREEN FIELDS BEYOND: The battle of Cambrai

Tanks had not been a success on the Somme or at Passchendaele. On 20 November 1917 the Tank Corps was given one last chance.

At 0620 on 20 November 1917, a British gun in the Cambrai sector fired a single shell into the German lines. It was the signal for a 1,000-gun barrage which fell on the German front line, causing most of the defenders to retreat to their bunkers to await the infantry assault. They did not have long to wait.

Immediately the guns began their shelling, 378 tanks rolled forward over the firm ground with infantry advancing behind. The German wire was new and glinted ominously in the dawn light, but the tanks crushed their way through, opening lanes for the infantry to follow. Reaching the deep and wide trenches of the German front line, the tanks dropped fascines (large bundles of brushwood) to fill the gap, then lurched their way across. Some turned and raked the inside of the German trenches with their machine-guns before rumbling on to the German second line.

Morale effect

The morale effect of these lumbering monsters was dramatic, and in many places the German infantry simply abandoned their positions and scattered. In one day, more ground was gained than in the three-month holocaust of 3rd Ypres. The Cambrai attack was planned by Brigadier General Elles, commanding the Tank Corps, assisted by Brigadier General Tudor, a divisional artillery commander who first suggested the omission of the preliminary bombardment. The idea was to show what tanks could achieve on favourable ground, but it grew in scale from a large raid to a full-scale assault with 19 infantry and 5 cavalry divisions.

The Cambrai attack was originally planned for September, but Field Marshal Sir Douglas Haig's remorseless offensive at Ypres sucked in all available reserves and by the time the attack took place, Passchendaele and the rout in Italy had left General Sir J. H. G. Byng's 3rd Army with no troops spare to exploit the incredible success of the first day.

The tanks which broke the 'Hindenburg Line' were hot, cramped, mechanically unreliable and only thinly armoured. Some 179 tanks were out of action after the first 24 hours of fighting, 65 of them knocked out by enemy fire and the rest bogged or broken down. They were a revolutionary weapon, but essentially a war-engine for siege warfare rather than a mobile fighting platform. They fought in sections of three, one up and two back about 90 m (100 yards) apart: four sections made a tank company which had several infantry companies fighting in support. The infantry were divided into three groups: trench clearers to work directly with the

MG 08/15 light machine-gun
The Germans employed new infantry tactics in their counter-attack at Cambrai: techniques with which they would break the British front wide open in 1918. The MG 08/15 was a lightened version of their standard machine-gun and provided mobile firepower for the assault troops.

Breaking the Hindenburg Line

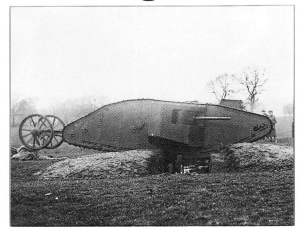

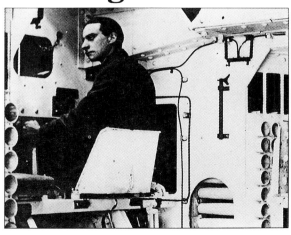

The first prototype tank on test, January 1916. The 28-ton vehicle managed all the obstacles and impressed all observers. Unfortunately, the tanks were never used en masse *during the next 18 months. Cambrai was their last chance.*

Inside a British tank in action the temperature could reach 125 degrees Fahrenheit. The eight-man crew were crammed inside with no hope of escape if their vehicle was hit or caught fire. The noise drowned out all but the loudest shout.

This medieval-style face protection was designed to defend the tank crew against metal splinters. When a round struck the armour but failed to penetrate, it could shower the crew with steel shards which spalled from the inside.

tanks; trench stops to block the enemy trenches at certain points; and trench supports to garrison captured enemy positions.

The attack failed in only one place on the first day. The shattered rubble that was once the village of Flesquières held out, one German artillery battery knocking out one by one the tanks which breasted the slope. The 51st Highland Division was attacking this sector and its commanding officer, Major General Harper, had refused to train his men in the new tactics or, in fact, co-operate in any way with the tank assault, which he described as 'a fantastic and most unmilitary scheme'. Thus there was no infantry at hand to help the tanks and the ruined village was not taken until the second day: the delay allowed the Germans to reinforce the ridge surmounted by Bourlon Wood, and with this commanding ground in their hands they could prevent a full scale breakthrough.

British attacks continued for a week, each supported by smaller numbers of tanks and each meeting tougher resistance. The Germans rushed up reinforcements (including troops released from the Russian front) and launched a full-scale counter-offensive on 30 November using infiltration tactics and a heavy barrage of gas and high explosive. Their assault troops received close support from armoured ground-attack aircraft and the southern shoulder of the Cambrai salient was soon penetrated several miles, parts of the original British front line falling into enemy hands. In the north the Germans had to attack over much more open ground and were pinned down by artillery fire before they could break into the British defences.

In the first days of December the whole battlefield vanished in a blinding snowstorm which effectively terminated the battle. The great tank attack had been a splendid success, and could have led to a large-scale breakthrough had the reserves been available. Continuing the offensive in the absence of reserves proved a costly mistake as the tanks broke down and the Germans were able to stage their counter-attack. In fact both sides had developed the weapons and tactics to crack the Western Front wide open.

Full recoil: a German 7.7-cm gun in action
With their high velocity and flat trajectory, German 7.7-cm field guns were one of the most effective anti-tank weapons available to the defenders. At Flesquières one battery of field guns knocked out every tank sent against it.

Close quarter battle
After the glorious success of the first day, Cambrai began to revert to the familiar rhythm of attack and counter-attack. Key sections of the German defences were retaken in savage local assaults. Here British and German bodies lie side by side in a shell hole.

A tank rears up over the parapet. The Germans had widened their trenches to stop tanks crossing but the medieval solution of fascines enabled them to get across. In a few hours, the German defences were smashed.

The German counter-attack on 30 November succeeded brilliantly and in some sectors, drove the British back over their old front line. Here a lightened version of the MG 08 Maxim gun provides the shock troops with mobile fire support.

The British carried out a planned withdrawal on the night of 4 December but the orders never reached the Tank Corps. Many damaged tanks fells into German hands, to be repaired and used against their former owners the following March.

Gordon Highlanders are shown during the fighting on the Somme crossings, 24 March 1918. The series of German offensives that began on 21 March 1918 led to the end of trench warfare. Accustomed to fighting offensive battles from a trench system, it came as a profound shock to the British Army to fight a defensive action in the open. Flush with troops released from the Eastern Front, the Germans enjoyed a temporary advantage in manpower. It was their last chance to win the war before their economy collapsed completely and the Allies' superior resources made defeat inevitable.

BREAKTHROUGH IN FRANCE:
Ludendorff's offensive

No previous attack had broken through on the Western Front but Ludendorff believed he had the answer.

By December 1917 the German High Command knew that time was running out. The German economy was in ruins, the army tiring and Germany's enemies now included the United States of America. However, although its resources dwarfed those of all other belligerents, the USA would take time to recruit, train and deploy an army from the other side of the Atlantic. Russia had signed a humiliating peace treaty at Brest-Litovsk, freeing the bulk of Germany's armies from the Eastern Front. General Erich Ludendorff, by now the *de facto* master of Germany, saw a window of opportunity and prepared the German army for one last Herculean effort to win the war.

Divide and conquer

Ludendorff was a good Clausewitzian: he knew that whatever ground was captured, it was the enemy's army which mattered. Destroy the main army and everything else follows. Accordingly, he prepared to launch his offensive at the southern end of the British line, in order to divide the Allied forces and defeat them piecemeal. The new tactics had been developed in 1917. Cambrai had demonstrated the potential of infiltration attacks with more flexible infantry units; and at Caporetto and Riga, unregistered artillery fire using a high proportion of gas and smoke shell had achieved spectacular success.

Bruchmüller, General Oscar von Hutier's artillery commander at Riga, was brought west to work the same magic against the British.

The British troops destined to bear the brunt of Ludendorff's offensive were mainly disillusioned survivors of the Somme and 3rd Ypres mingled with fresh conscripts. Their stoical endurance was incredible but they were too long in the tooth to indulge in reckless heroics. Every unit was badly understrength since David Lloyd George had retained 450,000 reserves in England to prevent Field Marshal Sir Douglas Haig from launching another

offensive. Unfortunately this forced troops already in France to spend longer in the line and, to avoid reducing the number of divisions, infantry brigades were reduced from four to three battalions. Old associations were broken up and troops found themselves fighting alongside strangers. The army had not settled into the new order when the hammer blow fell.

To break the British front, Ludendorff recruited special assault divisions, the elite of the German army. They spent the winter away from the front, rehearsing their tactics in which light mortars,

German light mortar detachment
These man-portable mortars played a key part in breaking through the British defences. Up with the leading troops they were used to bombard pockets of resistance and were far more responsive and flexible than the old systems of calling down artillery fire.

Blind leading the blind: Béthune, April 1918
Wounded soldiers shuffle into an advanced dressing station at Béthune. They have been on the receiving end of German gas shells carrying a type of tear gas. The Germans also made extensive use of mustard gas shells while the Allies relied mainly on chlorine and phosgene.

Right: Waiting for the barrage to finish
The German troops taking part in the first day of the offensive had five hours to wait before going over the top. They carry gas masks since nearly a third of the shells hitting the British lines contained gas.

The Kaiser's Battle

German 21-cm howitzers in action, 21 March 1918. The thick fog on the first day of the offensive saved the German infantry from British machine-gun fire but the German artillery could not monitor the infantry's progress and the barrage had to be fired blind.

The Germans broke through the southern end of the British 5th Army. By the end of the first day, the leading German troops were into open country and had captured more ground in 24 hours than the British took on the Somme in four months.

German infantry advance, rifles slung and grenades ready to bomb their way along the British trenches. Most of the British 3rd Army front held because their positions were constructed. 5th Army's incomplete defences had recently been taken over from the French.

German infantryman, March 1918

By 1918 the appearance of the German infantry had changed dramatically. The 'coalscuttle' helmet appeared during mid-1916 and the tall leather boots have been replaced by cloth puttees as used by the British and French. Although he clutches his rifle, his main weapons are the grenades carried in the sacks slung over his shoulders.

flamethrowers and machine-guns mounted on sledges would accompany the leading troops. To communicate with the artillery in the rear, the *Stosstruppen* would use pre-arranged rocket signals on an unprecedented scale.

Bruchmüller's bombardment began before dawn on 21 March 1918: 6,473 guns pounded British positions on a 65-km (40-mile) front held by the 5th Army and part of the 3rd Army. For nearly 5 hours every trench, every HQ, every battery and every supply dump was battered with a mixture of explosive, gas and smoke. Their vision already impaired by gas masks, the survivors were further blinded by a thick fog which lasted into the morning. At 0935 3,500 mortars in the German trenches joined in with rapid fire, and a few minutes later the first stormtroopers were racing through the British front line.

General Sir Hubert Gough's 5th Army collapsed. The front was broken everywhere, leaving isolated posts to fight on or surrender; most gave in after putting up token resistance against hopeless odds. A few went down heroically, but they were fighting the

Cavalry wait their moment
The Germans had very few cavalry to exploit their breakthrough in 1918 whereas the British did at least have some mounted troops who could rapidly plug gaps in the line. These Germans still carry lances which will never be used but the infantry pattern belt equipment shows they are ready to fight on foot.

German follow-up troops as the cutting edge of Ludendorff's army was already deep in the British rear. In the next few days the 5th Army retreated to the line of the Somme, while the 3rd Army found itself fighting for its life.

The agony of the 5th Army continued until early April as the Allied line was smashed back over the old Somme battlefield. The German offensive eventually ceased after the front-line troops had completely outrun their transport and artillery. Ludendorff's next blow fell on a 20-km (12.5-mile) front from Armentières to the La Bassée canal: by a stroke of luck for the Germans the Allied line in the centre of the attack was held by the Portuguese 2nd Division, which was in the process of withdrawing into reserve. On 9 April the stormtroops once again came racing into the Allied lines moments behind a rolling artillery barrage and the hapless Portuguese broke on contact.

On 10 April the German attack broadened to include part of General Sir Herbert Plumer's 2nd Army, but this fell back to the outskirts of Ypres, Plumer ruthlessly shortening his line to release reserves. The apparently inexorable German advance led the infamously taciturn Haig to issue his order of the day: 'There is no course open to us but to fight it out. Every position must be held to the last man. With our backs to the wall and believing in the justice of our cause each man must fight on to the end.'

The Germans managed to sustain their offensive until the end of April, but although they gained more ground and nearly took Amiens, they failed to break the Allied armies. In the first 10 days, Ludendorff had inflicted more casualties on the British than Montgomery's forces were to suffer in the entire campaign in North West Europe in 1944-45. By the end of April both the British and German forces had lost over 200,000 men but it was not over yet: Ludendorff's gamble would be played out to the bitter end.

Junkers JI 'Mobelwagen' ground attack aircraft
Dubbed 'furniture van', the J I two-seater was one of several German ground-attack aircraft which played a major role in the 1918 fighting. Vital areas protected by armour plate, it had twin forward-firing machine-guns and another gun operated by the observer, and carried 20 small bombs.

Once in open country the German trench mortars and light machine-guns gave the German infantry much greater integral firepower than their predecessors in 1914. But as the offensive progressed, German casualties began to match those of the British.

The British fell back over the old Somme battlefield, abandoning the ground that so many men had died to capture. The troops were mixed up in the retreat, isolated groups from different battalions fighting together to stem the German advance.

The first Whippet light tanks in action, 26 March 1918 at Maillet Mailly. The first phase of Ludendorff's offensive was completed in early April but Germany's desperate last throw was not finished yet.

THE SECOND BATTLE OF THE MARNE: Germany falters

27 May 1918: The German army makes its supreme effort to break through the Allied lines and snatch victory in the west.

General Erich Ludendorff's stunning victory over the British in March 1918 was followed by an equally impressive attack on the Aisne. This was also designed to draw in the Allied reserves until the moment was ripe for the knock-out blow codenamed 'Hagen', an attack on the Ypres sector which would drive the British back to the Channel ports. To pave the way, 44 German divisions were launched against the French, firstly on the Chemin des Dames west of Reims and then towards Paris between Noyon and Montdidier. The aim was to create panic in the French capital and compel Foch to withdraw his reserves from the British front to defend Paris.

The attack on the Chemin des Dames was executed faultlessly, the measures taken to conceal the arrival of 4,000 guns and 30 new divisions having been elaborate and largely successful. The British IX Corps (under the command of the French 6th Army) detected the German preparations but its

reports were ignored. Only a few hours before the attack did the French realize the danger, but by then it was too late: at 0100 on 27 May Bruchmüller's most savage bombardment pulverized the Allied line. As the first rays of the sun illuminated the battlefield, the assault troops boiled out of the German front line and charged forward. On that day the German 7th Army advanced up to 20 km (12.5 miles) on a 40-km (25-mile) front, driving all before it except the 2nd Devons who made a desperate last stand in the Bois des Buttes, holding up an entire division for three hours until they were annihilated.

By 30 May the Germans were in sight of the Marne on a 10-km (1.2-mile) front near Château Thierry and had captured 50,000 prisoners and 800 guns. The attack had been almost too successful and the second phase was repeatedly postponed while the troops were redeployed from this deep salient. Nevertheless, General Oscar von Hutier's men attacked gallantly on 10 June and managed to advance 10 km. In the next three days the battle seesawed as General Henri Foch fed in his reserves and stabilized the front.

The plan remains the same

The German army was tiring. The best and bravest had fallen in the battles between March and June, and yet the Allies had not broken. So the ranks were filled with rear-echelon troops, and also with men released from Russian prison camps and thus not wildly impressed with the prospect of further offensives. Ludendorff's plan remained the same, another attack by the Crown Prince's Army group in the south against the French then the decisive blow against the British in the north. Unfortunately the staffwork was hurried, the preparations obvious to the Allies, and deserters trickled into the French lines with stories of a German attack on the Marne.

In the first two weeks of July General Ferdinand Foch assembled a mighty army in the forest of Villers Cotterets. On Bastille Day a prisoner captured in a raid said the Germans would attack that night and he was particularly keen to retain his gas mask. General Henri Gourard, the fire-eating French general who had lost an arm and had both legs shattered at Gallipoli, ordered his heavy artillery to shell all possible forming up areas an hour before the expected German blow. The Germans came on in their now familiar style in the early hours of 15 July preceded by a ferocious barrage: but the French front line was found to be empty and as they reached the limit of their bombardment, they saw a thick line of uncut wire with the defenders smugly

awaiting them. Some 800 French guns then opened fire, knocking out all 20 German tanks and stopping the offensive in its tracks.

West of Reims the Germans did break through: after a barrage of gas shell the German 7th Army crossed the Marne in boats under cover of a smokescreen. Engineers immediately deployed their pontoons and the reserve artillery galloped forward to cross over. General Henri Petain panicked and tried to halt the westward movement of reserves earmarked for the planned counter-attack on the other side of the salient. General Charles Mangin, the iron-willed commander of the 10th Army, went beserk with rage, describing Petain and his staff as 'a bunch of stinking little grocers'. Foch also remained optimistic and the counter-attack was launched as planned.

As bitter fighting raged around the Marne crossings, Ludendorff congratulated himself on finally drawing in the Allied reserves: on 17 July he began transferring the heavy guns north for his final attack and set out for the Crown Prince's headquarters to finalize arrangements. There was a torrential storm that night, and on the northern shoulder of the Marne salient the Germans were busy trying to stay dry when at 0435 a Brüchmuller-style barrage crashed down on top of them. Shortly afterwards they were attacked by seven corps including Moroccan colonial troops and the US 2nd Division. Some 500 tanks and 2,000 guns supported the infantry, who achieved complete surprise; by mid-morning they had broken through on a 20-km front.

That morning in Mons, Ludendorff was presiding over a conference planning the last big push against the British. Crown Prince Rupprecht and two army commanders were there with chiefs of staff down to corps level. Then the telephones began to ring. By lunchtime Ludendorff knew that his country was staring defeat in the face, and that afternoon he halted the northward progress of his assault divisions and gave them to the Crown Prince to stabilize the Marne front. Thus 18 July was the turning point in the war: 'Hagen' was postponed, never to be revived, and the initiative passed to the Allies.

RE 8 reconnaissance aircraft
By 1918 aircraft were an integral part of army operations, providing timely intelligence of enemy troop movements and direct assistance in the form of ground attack. The RE 8 was one of the most importance machines flown by the Royal Flying Corps, which became the Royal Air Force on 1 April 1918.

Right: **German fighter aircraft, 1918**
The pick of German fighters, 1918. On the left is the Fokker D VII, the best fighter of the war. Next right is an Albatros D V, another first-class aircraft. The greatest ace of the war, Manfred von Richtofen, was killed in April during the offensive on the British front.

Glory days 1918

German troops on the Somme front, April 1918. They had the great satisfaction of driving the British right back over the old Somme battlefield, captured at such heart-breaking cost in 1916. Now it was the turn of the French.

As at Verdun, flamethrower teams spearheaded the attack when the Germans stormed the French trenches on the Chemin des Dames at the end of May. After three days, the Germans were once again within sight of the Marne.

British IX Corps was under French command in May and was the only part of the 6th Army to detect the German preparations. After the front was broken small parties of British and French troops were jumbled together, improvising a defence.

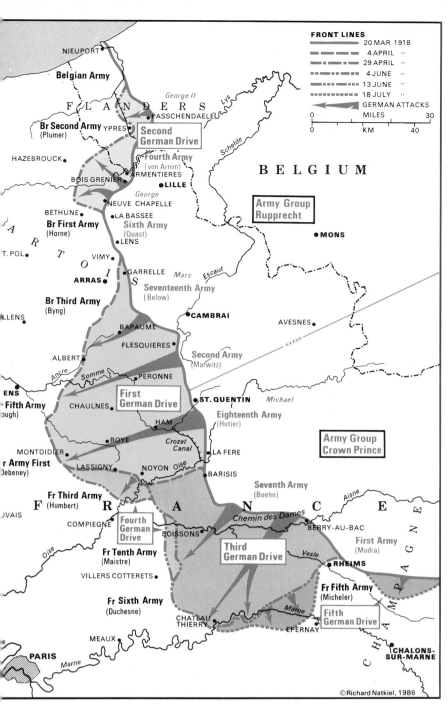

FRONT LINES
- 20 MAR 1918
- 4 APRIL "
- 29 APRIL "
- 4 JUNE "
- 13 JUNE "
- 18 JULY "
- GERMAN ATTACKS

MILES 0 — 30
KM 0 — 40

© Richard Natkiel, 1986

German tank crew on the Marne
The German assault on the Marne included 20 tanks, a mixture of captured British ones and A7Vs such as this. Ponderously slow, even on dry, hard ground, they were all destroyed by French 75-mm field guns on July 15.

German Maxim gun in action
The machine-gunners remained the backbone of the German army in victory and defeat. The MG 08 machine-gun is fitted to the lighter, more portable mounting and the gun crew wear camouflaged cloth covers over their helmets.

The German offensives March–July 1918

Ludendorff's plan was to mount a series of offensives designed to draw in the Allied reserves. When this had been done he would launch 'Hagen': a final blow against Ypres which would break clean through to the Channel ports and win the war. But although the attacks gained ground, they did not smash the Allied armies. By July 1918 it was the German army that was beginning to crack under the strain.

Char d'Assaut St. Chamond

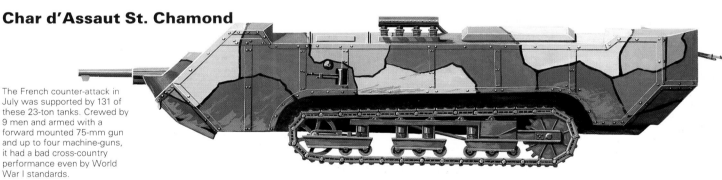

The French counter-attack in July was supported by 131 of these 23-ton tanks. Crewed by 9 men and armed with a forward mounted 75-mm gun and up to four machine-guns, it had a bad cross-country performance even by World War I standards.

A British tank in German hands rumbles forward during training for the next attack. Despite all the pressure, most German divisions went to the rear to practise their new tactics before the great offensives began.

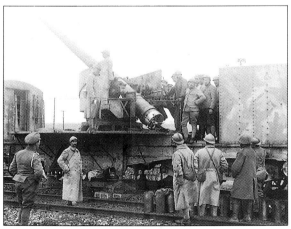

The advancing German armies rapidly out-ran their supplies and were exposed and vulnerable to Foch's counter-attack launched on 18 July. Here a French railway gun pauses at dawn after the French infantry have broken the German line.

A Halberstadt CL ground-attack aircraft is transported on a truck which also tows the fuselage of a French Salmson. The German concentration in the north had not been completed when the French attack broke through on the Marne.

AMIENS: Black day of the German army

The German offensives had not broken the Allied armies. Now the British army prepared to go over to the offensive.

Under the pressure of the German offensive in March, the Allies had at long last created a unified command presided over by the French General Ferdinand Foch. On 25 July 1918 Field Marshal Sir Douglas Haig, General Henri Petain and General John J. Pershing met at Foch's new headquarters near Mélun to review a surprisingly favourable situation: General Erich Ludendorff's fifth great offensive had been utterly defeated by General Charles Mangin's counter-attack, and the Allies now enjoyed numerical superiority.

The Allied plan was for Petain to continue the counter-offensive on the Marne while Haig staged his already prepared attack south and east of Amiens, and Pershing launched his American army at the Saint Mihiel salient. At the conclusion of all three operations, the Allies were to mount a rolling programme of offensives at different points along the line to maintain the pressure on the weakening German armies.

Sir Henry Rawlinson

The task of attacking the Amiens sector fell to General Sir Henry Rawlinson's 4th Army, and the brilliance with which this attack was carried out remained a model for the great set-piece battles of World War II. Haig and Rawlinson planned a gigantic surprise attack using the Canadian and Australian Corps between the River Somme and the Amiens-Roye road. It was to be supported by the entire Tank Corps, 2,000 guns and the full strength of the newly constituted Royal Air Force. The railway line from Amiens to Chaulnes provided a convenient boundary between the Australian and Canadian attacks. One-third of the artillery was to

provide a rolling barrage (a curtain of fire slowly moving ahead of the infantry) and the remainder was to fire on all known German artillery positions. Staffwork was immaculate. The Germans remained in blissful ignorance of the guns and infantry massing opposite their positions; the RAF staged a sharp increase in air activity over the 1st and 5th Army fronts, while wireless activity in the north became similarly heavy. The troops moved in to their forming up areas during the night of 7/8 August until shortly after 0400. The Australian commander, General Monash, remembered: 'In black darkness, 100,000 infantry deployed over 12 miles of front, are standing grimly, silently, expectantly, in readiness to advance . . . Overhead drone the aeroplanes and from the rear, in swelling chorus, the buzzing and clamour of the tanks every moment louder and louder.' The fog which had aided the

German attack in March now gave the Allies the same blessing, and shrouded the whole sector.

Advance Australia

The Australians were already recognized as the finest infantry on any side in the war and on 8 August they again demonstrated why. As the mist cleared at around 1030 the Australian flag could be seen flying from the church tower at Harbonnières, 10 km (6.5 miles) behind the German front line. The Canadians were also volunteers to a man and had demonstrated their fighting abilities at Vimy Ridge in 1917: on 8 August they made equally short work of their opponents and were abreast of Mézières by mid-morning.

From the air, the whole plateau south of the Somme was dotted with troops moving west: infantry, artillery and cavalry pressed on the heels of

Medium Tank Mk. A 'Whippet'

Whippet tanks were lighter and faster than their bigger brethren. Carrying a crew of four and armed with two machine-guns, they were the first serious alternative to cavalry. After the breakthrough on 8 August they created havoc in the German rear areas and the true potential of the tank had at last been realised.

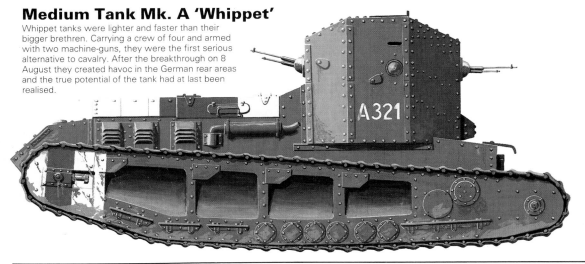

Twelve miles in four days

German troops armed with flamethrowers follow a captured British tank. By July 1918 the Allies had the measure of the new German methods and not even the introduction of mustard gas shells could guarantee a German breakthrough.

Aerial reconnaissance had come of age by 1918. Hard work by the RAF also managed to deprive the enemy of this advantage: the Germans never detected the massive increase in artillery behind the front of Rawlinson's 4th Army.

A Mk V tank heads east at its top speed of 3 mph. The ground south of the Somme over which the British attacked on 8 August was hard, dry and not cut up by shell craters. It was ideal for the tanks and infantry alike. A thick fog also came to the help of 4th Army.

Re-captured British Mk IV tank
As the German army reeled back, their handful of tanks were overrun by Allied infantry. By the summer of 1918 the first purpose-built anti-tank weapons had come into service but the tanks' main enemies were still rough ground and their own temperamental machinery.

German prisoners of war
After World War I German right wingers claimed that the army had not been beaten but 'stabbed in the back'. In fact the German army was smashed completely in the autumn of 1918. Prisoners cheered each other as they marched into British POW camps and red flags appeared behind the German lines.

the retreating Germans, who were thoroughly beaten. Formed bodies of prisoners carried the Allied wounded to the rear and an 18-km (11.2-mile) gap now yawned in the German front line. Whippet tanks raced deep into the German rear and German reserves detraining behind the front were machine-gunned by British aircraft. It was the greatest defeat suffered by the German army since the beginning of the war, and Ludendorff described 8 August as 'the black day of the German army'.

The second day did not quite live up to Rawlinson's hopes but it gained another 5 km (3.1 miles) and another 12,000 prisoners. Resistance began to stiffen between 10 and 12 August as the Germans fell back on to the old Somme battlefield. A derelict area, scarred by old trench lines, heavily cratered and crossed in all directions by tangles of barbed wire, it was covered by two years' growth of wild

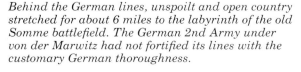

Australians going into the line near Fricourt, October 1918
The Australians were widely recognised as the finest soldiers on either side in 1918. After 31 March the Australian Corps was taken over by General Monash and it spearheaded the offensive on 8 August, making the biggest breakthrough of the day.

vegetation. This was a machine-gunners paradise and by now 10 tired British divisions faced 12 German. Haig broke off the battle and launched the 3rd Army north of the Somme in a new offensive aimed towards Bapaume.

Combined arms attack

Rawlinson's army had advanced 20 km (12.5 miles) in four days, and into the bargain taken 30,000 prisoners, 500 guns and a vast stock of supplies the Germans could ill afford to lose. It was a perfect combined arms operation: infantry, artillery, tanks and aircraft had worked in close harmony. The breakout into open country exposed some weaknesses in a command chain still accustomed to trench warfare, but the Battle of Amiens sounded the death knell of the German army. In the 4th Army prisoner cages, many Germans were delighted that their war was over and cheered the arrival of each fresh batch of prisoners. Although the German front line was still held by resolute machine-gunners and some stubborn divisions, utter chaos reigned in the rear areas. Red flags had begun to appear among large parties of troops who were wandering away from the front. Every army had its breaking point and, at long last, the German army was tottering on the brink.

10th Australian Battalion, Bois de Crepy, 10 August 1918
Having overrun a German artillery battery, the Australians have dug in along an old trench line. On the right is a Vickers gun, barrel by the tripod, ready to advance. Note the Lewis gun and the SMILE rifle fitted to fire rifle grenades.

Behind the German lines, unspoilt and open country stretched for about 6 miles to the labyrinth of the old Somme battlefield. The German 2nd Army under von der Marwitz had not fortified its lines with the customary German thoroughness.

A Sopwith Camel upended on a German support trench: some Germans reported being struck by the undercarriages of low flying British fighters. On 8 August RAF crews were able to watch a whole army on the move as the German front collapsed.

The 4th Army captured 30,000 prisoners in four days, plus 500 guns. The British advance was stopped when it reached the old Somme trench lines but irreparable damage had been inflicted on the German army.

AMERICA AT WAR:
The battle of Meuse-Argonne

On 12 September 1918 the American Expeditionary Force, the largest US army since the Civil War, finally launched its first offensive.

As soon as the leading elements of the American Expeditionary Force arrived in France in 1917, British and French commanders began to demand that the US troops be flung into the line immediately. Fortunately for the American soldiers, General John J. Pershing was as dour and uncompromising a leader as Field Marshal Sir Douglas Haig, with whom he got on splendidly. Even when faced by the awesome combination of David Lloyd George, Georges Clemenceau and Vittorio Orlando, Pershing banged the table and refused to be coerced.

The US Army repeated every mistake made by the British in the raising of the Kitchener armies, but on a greater scale. The peacetime army was a small organization for chasing Indians and Mexicans, and its expansion to European size was a complicated and confusing business. However, by July 1918 Pershing had an army in the front line, ready to attack the Saint Mihiel salient as part of the Allied counter-offensive. He went further and agreed to take over the 145-km (90-mile) front between the Meuse and Argonne and mount a second offensive in late September towards Meziéres.

Pershing had committed his army to mount two offensives within three weeks using the same troops on battlefields 95 km (60 miles) apart, connected by only three bad roads. This would demand immaculate staffwork indeed. The first target was a 520-km² (200-sq mile) bulge between the Moselle and the Meuse with the small town of Saint Mihiel at its apex and the 'Hindenburg Line' along its base. It had been a quiet sector since 1915, a resting place for

divisions burned out in the infernos of Verdun and Ypres, but the Germans had fortified it with customary industriousness. Their concrete bunkers even had piped water and electric light.

On 12 September half a million Americans went into action against the Saint Mihiel salient, catching the Germans in the act of retiring in accordance with General Erich Ludendorff's latest directive. Supported by 100,000 French troops, 3,000 guns and complete air superiority, the American attack captured the whole salient in one day along with 15,000 prisoners and 450 guns. A certain Brigadier General Douglas MacArthur, who led his troops from the front, wanted to push on towards Metz but Pershing stuck to his original scheme on the grounds that the inexperienced army could not so easily alter its plans.

Outstanding staffwork

Some 600,000 American and 22,000 French soldiers now redeployed to the Meuse-Argonne front. There some 4,000 guns had to be assembled in equal secrecy, together with 40,000 tons of shells to enable them to fire off the daily total of 350,000 rounds which a 1918 offensive demanded. That this was managed at all, let alone on time and without the Germans detecting it until too late, was an outstanding achievement.

Meuse-Argonne was one part of the overall Allied offensive in the late Summer of 1918. Six million Allied soldiers were involved in an all-out attempt to defeat the Germans before the dead hand of winter descended on the Western Front. The Americans planned to attack a 39-km (24-mile) front of hill and forest fortified with German thoroughness, and to maintain the surprise US officers visiting the front wore French uniforms so that the Germans still

believed they were facing second-line French divisions.

The bombardment began at 0230 on 26 September, and three hours later the American first wave swarmed over the top. In thick fog, the fighting was confused in the extreme: the centre made little progress against a stubborn German defence, but both flanks broke through to the second enemy line and drove off several desperate counter-attacks. Lieute-

nant Colonel George S. Patton commanded 189 little Renault tanks with characteristic vigour and took Varennes by 0900, four hours ahead of the infantry he was supposed to be supporting. Hit by a shell splinter, he was carried away still giving orders for the next phase of the attack.

When an army begins to disintegrate, the rot begins in the rear areas. This was how the Russian army collapsed in 1917 and where the French mutinies had begun after Nivelle's 1917 offensive. The defeat of the German army followed an identical pattern, so that although the fatal cancer was spreading rapidly, many parts of the front were unaffected even by September 1918. The Americans found the German positions in the Argonne forest were defended with supreme tenacity and military skill. From 27 to 30 September Ludendorff flung in over 20 divisions and the US troops discovered that beating the Imperial German army on ground of its own choosing was no easy business.

Once the element of surprise had gone, the Battle

M1903 Springfield rifle

After being on the receiving end of Mauser rifles during the Spanish-American War, the US Army adopted the Mauser design themselves in 1903. Chambered for the American .30 cal bullet, it was one of the first 'short' rifles designed to be used by both cavalry and infantry.

Towards the Hindenburg Line

American machine-gunners with a French Hotchkiss machine-gun. The AEF's target was a tough one. For four years, virtually undisturbed, the Germans had been fortifying their positions between the Meuse and the Argonne forest.

A light 37-mm gun provides covering fire for US troops fighting in the Argonne forest. Outnumbering the Germans 8:1 and supported by 2,700 guns, Pershing's offensive depended on surprising the defenders before they could rush up reinforcements.

The American staff calculated correctly that the three German divisions holding the front line would be reinforced by another 15 in 3 days. Here a 15-cm gun battery shells the US troops who had managed to break into the second line of the defences.

Halberstadt C V high altitude reconnaissance aircraft
German fliers prepare to take-off on a photo-reconnaissance flight. The C V had a camera fitted in the floor beneath the observer's position. The rear-mounted machine-gun is on a traversable mounting so it can be fired forward, over the pilot if necessary.

Over the top, July 1918
American infantry counter-attack on the Marne supported by French Schneider tanks and preceded by a rolling barrage laid down by French 75-mm and 155-mm guns. Many of the troops carry entrenching tools to dig in on the objective before the inevitable German counter-attack.

Right: German war dog training school
The patrol compose their report which will be carried back to the battalion HQ by the messenger dog. The German infantry wear the coalscuttle helmet with its distinctive lugs on the side. These were for a steel visor which did not prove practical in service.

of Meuse-Argonne followed the pattern of Allied offensives of 1916-17. Communications had broken down, units were scattered and running out of food and ammunition, and the German artillery was back in action. American tactical inexperience had been obvious at the Lys, where the 15th Scottish Division found their dead 'lying in swaths in the cornfields, having obviously been cut down by machine gun fire in thick waves'. The Americans learned the lessons of Loos and the Somme in the wet autumn of 1918, and Pershing's decision to close down the Meuse-Argonne offensive in early October was a sound one. In the north, Haig's great masterpiece, the breaking of the 'Hindenburg Line', was under way and the defeat of Germany only five weeks away.

Renault FT 17 light tank

The 6½-ton, two-man Renault FT introduced what was to become the standard layout of the tank. Its revolving turret carried either a stubby 37-mm gun or a machine-gun. The 'tail' on the hull rear was to improve its trench-crossing ability.

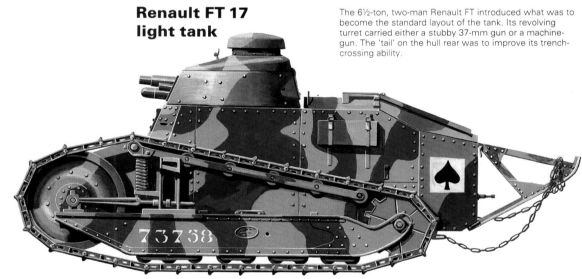

73768

The American attack included 189 of these Renault FT tanks, commanded by Lt. Colonel George S. Patton, who would lead tanks through this region again in 1944. Used en masse the little Renault tanks performed very well.

A French 75-mm gun serves as a mobile anti-aircraft gun for the US Army. Future President Harry S Truman was serving nearby in the 129th Field Artillery Regiment. By the end of September the Americans had advanced about 10 miles.

As the Americans drew nearer to the third and most powerful line of the German defences, 27 enemy divisions stood ready to stop them. The attack had run out of impetus by 30 September but it had been a magnificent effort.

VICTORY IN PALESTINE

Jerusalem was captured by British forces in December 1917. General Allenby now began to plan his final offensive.

After the humiliating failure of the Gallipoli campaign, British action against Turkey was restricted to an advance into Mesopotamia and a stiffening of the garrison in Egypt. The Mesopotamian theatre was soon the scene of a small-scale disaster at Kut, where some 10,000 British and Indian troops were besieged and compelled to surrender in April 1916. Eventually a large British force, mainly of Indian troops, fought its way slowly up the Tigris and Euphrates, but Turkey was to suffer its most fatal blow in Palestine.

The Turks launched several expeditions across the Sinai desert to attack the Suez Canal. These efforts in fact had little chance of success, but were magnified in some quarters to represent a serious threat. General Sir Archibald Murray was tasked with defending Egypt and reported to the War Office that it would be more sensible to advance into Palestine rather than squander resources on fortifying the frontier. He had his way and, through the summer and autumn of 1916, British forces methodically advanced eastwards, building a railway and

extending a pipeline as they did. El Arish fell just before Christmas 1916.

The defence of Egypt had now become the invasion of Palestine without serious prior planning. Unfortunately Murray botched an attack on Gaza in April 1917 and was replaced by the commander of 3rd Army at Arras, General Sir Edmund Allenby. Nicknamed 'The Bull' because of his aggressive appearance and legendary temper, he took over a mixed force of Australian, British and Indian troops and rapidly restored their morale. A series of superbly co-ordinated attacks broke the Turkish defences on the Gaza-Beersheba front and reached the Judean Hills by mid-November. After three weeks of hectic fighting, the Turks retreated and civic leaders emerged from Jerusalem to hand the keys of the Holy City to a British sergeant commanding an advanced post.

Allenby's attempts to push farther north in the spring and summer of 1918 were frustrated when 60,000 men (including most of his best troops) were transferred to France and replaced by raw Indian divisions. However, a Turkish counter-offensive spearheaded by two German battalions was defeated on 14 July at Ghoraniye, Australian cavalry smashing the Turks at Abu Tellul, and the Mysore and Jodhpur lancers charging with magnificent dash to complete the rout at Hijla. The German officer com-

manding the Turks was the victor of Gallipoli, General Otto Liman von Sanders, and he was forced to admit that the Turkish soldier was losing interest in the war.

Allenby's soldiers were supported by a first-class logistic organization which gave them the best possible medical and sanitary conditions, a healthy diet and reasonable rest periods. In such a hot and uncomfortable climate, warfare is very much a logistic business, and the Turkish troops had had to endure years of action with almost no support. They were filthy, verminous, hungry and suffering from cholera, typhoid and dysentery. They were the most stubborn soldiers in the world, but dismal staff work had eroded Turkish fighting power to a dangerously low level.

On 19 September Allenby launched an ambitious offensive designed to decisively defeat the Turkish forces in Palestine. Meticulous concealment measures enabled the attack to achieve complete surprise, and the Turkish front line was immediately ruptured. After the British and Indian infantry had broken through, the Desert Mounted Corps of three cavalry divisions poured through to complete a battle of encirclement. On the Plain of Esdraelon, or Megiddo (the Armageddon of the Apocalypse), the retreating Turkish forces were utterly routed.

Liman von Sanders was nearly captured in his headquarters in Nazareth when he was awakened on the morning of 20 September by the arrival of the 5th Cavalry Division. Clerical staff were left to mount a futile defence with pistols while their commander sped away in his staff car. The Turkish 7th and 8th Armies were streaming north, their retreat hampered by the RAF which launched the first successful aerial interdiction campaign in history. The Turks lost the race to the Jordan crossings and surrendered in droves: in fact the encircling cavalry line was sorely stretched and a determined effort would have broken through, but the Turks had had enough. In one instance 2,800 Turks surrendered to a British lieutenant and 23 men.

Damascus fell to Australian cavalry on 1 October and the 7th Indian Division captured Beirut on the next day. Homs was taken by the 5th Cavalry Division on 16 October and Aleppo was reached on the 25th. The 5th Cavalry division advanced 885 km (550 miles) in 38 days, fighting four major actions in the process and losing only 21 per cent of their horses – a record achievement. Turkish casualties are unknown, but 75,000 of their embittered troops surrendered. Only outside Aleppo did they show a spark of their former brilliance: the rearguard under the command of a certain Mustapha Kemal Pasha (subsequently Kemal Atatürk, founder of modern Turkey) beat off an attack by the 15th Cavalry Division. The Turkish government was toppled early in October and peace overtures commenced: an armistice was finally signed aboard the battleship HMS *Agamemnon* on 30 October. The Ottoman Empire had been destroyed.

Australian Rolls-Royce armoured car
Rolls-Royce armoured cars were based on the Silver Ghost chassis and carried a turret-mounted Vickers machine-gun. This Australian crew have removed the turret roof to reduce the temperature inside.

The road to Armageddon

Indian troops prepare to fire a rifle grenade at the Turkish trenches. Indians formed a high proportion of Allenby's army and in early 1918 the Indian cavalry divisions still in France were transferred to Palestine.

The Turks defied all British efforts to advance north of Jerusalem in the summer of 1918. The rocky hills of Judea lent themselves to a stubborn defence and British raids across the Jordan during the spring had been bloodily repulsed.

The Bedouin guerrilla war, brilliantly co-ordinated by T.E. Lawrence, tied down some 45,000 Turkish troops in defence of the 600-mile Hejaz railway which ran down to the sacred city of Medina.

Australian cavalry trooper, Palestine

Unlike their counterparts in France, the Australian troops in Palestine wore their rakish slouch hats in action. This trooper belongs to the Vickers gun section of his regiment but still wears a bandolier full of .303 ammunition for his Lee-Enfield rifle.

Lewis .303 light machine-gun

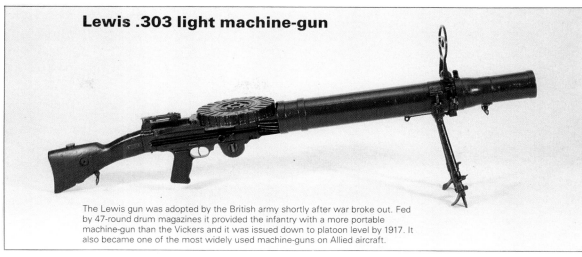

The Lewis gun was adopted by the British army shortly after war broke out. Fed by 47-round drum magazines it provided the infantry with a more portable machine-gun than the Vickers and it was issued down to platoon level by 1917. It also became one of the most widely used machine-guns on Allied aircraft.

Australian Light Horse
Cavalry were of little value on the Western Front by 1916, but in Egypt and Palestine they were still an important weapon. Fighting in conjunction with armoured cars they could outflank the Turkish positions and pursue a beaten enemy to destruction.

The surrender of Jerusalem
Lloyd George's parting remark to Allenby when he left England had been 'Jerusalem by Christmas'. He took the Holy City on 9 December, entering on foot two days later. Here the chief of the municipality and his colleagues stand with the two British sergeants to whom they presented the keys of the city.

SE5a fighter in Palestine, 1918
The RAF mounted the first successful aerial interdiction campaign as the columns of troops and transports fell back along mountain passes.

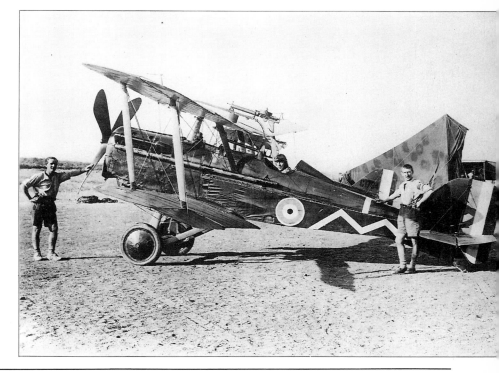

Liman von Sanders replaced Falkenhayn as the German commander in Palestine. His few German battalions were his only truly dependable troops. Here a camel is used to evacuate two German casualties in Judea, summer 1918.

Allenby's attack began on 19 September: the infantry attacked frontally while the cavalry divisions raced around the eastern flank. The Turks fell back in disorder but some were still game: this is part of a headquarters, found to be booby-trapped.

Indian cavalry enter Damascus which was captured by Australian troops on 1 October. The 7th Indian Cavalry Division took Beirut the next day. Allenby's men took 75,000 prisoners for a loss of 5,666 men. Turkey was out of the war.

No Pasaran: The battle of Madrid

July 1936: part of the Spanish army attempts a coup d'etat. The plot fails, but a powerful rebel army is soon advancing on Madrid.

By 1936 every dawn in Madrid found fresh bodies dumped in the gutter: victims of rival death squads. A number of senior army officers plotted a coup d'état, believing that only another period of military rule could restore law and order. Unfortunately what was designed as a traditional *prononciamiento* led to three years of bitter civil war.

The military revolt began on 17 July 1936 and failed immediately. In Madrid the plotters bungled badly and many paid with their lives: loyal army units, the paramilitary civil guard and armed workers' militias soon controlled the capital. The rebels were successful at Valladolid, Burgos, Corunna and Zaragoza. Against all odds they captured Seville, but within the Spanish peninsula the rebels were hopelessly outnumbered. Their only hope was General Francisco Franco's Army of North Africa, cut off from the mainland by the navy, which remained loyal.

Fortunately for the rebels the government concentrated its forces on the defence of the capital and failed to prevent Franco boldly despatching several thousand troops across the Straits of Gibraltar to Algeciras escorted by one elderly gunboat. Reinforced, General Emilio Mola marshalled a small army at Burgos and headed for the capital while Franco headed north for Badajoz.

The rebel troops compensated for their numerical inferiority by superior discipline and fighting power, cutting their way through a rabble of rival militias. A diversion to relieve the beleaguered rebel garrison at Toledo delayed progress, but by October the capital was within reach. However, the republic had powerful friends: tanks and aircraft manned by Soviet personnel arrived to boost the fighting power of the government armies. The militias began to co-operate in the face of the common enemy and the military balance began to swing in the government's favour once again.

The 'fifth column'

Publically Franco and Mola remained confident. Mola spoke of attacking with four columns aided by a secret 'fifth column' of supporters within the capital. The phrase lasted, but the attackers, outnumbered by three to one, failed to break through. On 15 November Moroccan troops managed to storm the University City and despite heavy counter-attacks the Nationalists maintained a bridgehead over the River Manzanares.

The Nationalist units in the University City and

Republican anti-clericalism: disinterring a nun
The entrenched power and wealth of the Spanish church was a prime target of the left-wing parties. While the Nationalist press horrified the world with lurid stories of raped nuns and tortured priests, some of them were sadly true. Digging up graves was a more bizarre gesture of protest.

The Messerschmitt Bf 109 makes its debut
A Bf 109 of the German Condor Legion swoops on republican infantry. Many of the Luftwaffe's finest pilots received their baptism of fire in Spain, and the Nationalists gradually won air superiority. The Bf 109 rapidly established itself as a first-class fighter aircraft and was to remain in service until 1945.

Crushing a revolution

Madrid, June 1936: bodies litter the street after another night of violence. The army believed that only a further period of military rule could restore law and order. Unfortunately the coup led to a three-year civil war.

Women's militia march through Madrid a week after the coup attempt. The main parties and unions all organised their own militias creating a large, but unruly army to defend the capital.

Moroccan troops of the Army of North Africa fight their way north. The Republican leaders made a bad mistake in not trying to stop Franco's troops crossing from Africa. The rebel army made short work of Republican forces in the south.

Casa de Campo were in a dangerous salient and heavy fighting continued past the end of the month as Franco's forces ground their way forward to cut the Corunna road. However, a frontal assault on Madrid was no longer under consideration; instead, the capital was to be encircled and the next major battle was fought to the south around the River Jarama.

Both sides launched offensives on the Jarama front during January and February 1937, the Nationalists now aided by some 45 PzKpfw I and II light tanks and German artillery. On the other hand the Soviets supplied the Republicans with superior T-26 tanks, and in the air their Polikarpov I-16 fighters and Tupolev SB-2 bombers gave the government an equally significant advantage. In bitter winter weather the battle see-sawed for several weeks before petering out in a bloody draw. Franco's forces managed to gain the east bank of the river but failed to cut the Madrid-Valencia road.

In the north the republic scored a major victory over the Italian force sent by Mussolini to assist Franco but failed to follow it up. In May republican forces under General Karol Swierczewski attacked out of Madrid, but the Nationalists had observed the preparations for the offensive and stopped it in its tracks. Tragically, Mola was killed in a plane crash on his way to discuss the situation with General José Varela and the Nationalist forces were deprived of one of their most able commanders.

In July 1937 the Republican forces mounted their most ambitious offensive on the Madrid front, a massive attack from the north planned to cut off Nationalist forces in front of the capital, not unlike the Soviet counter-attack at Stalingrad in 1942. However, internal rivalry and prompt action by the Nationalists prevented the Brunete offensive achieving its main objectives, and Franco mounted a counter-attack towards the end of the month spearheaded by the 4th and 5th Navarrese Divisions. Most of the lost ground was regained, but Franco refused to be tempted into another frontal assault on the capital.

Nationalist victory

Madrid's fate was determined in the north during the summer of 1937 as a Nationalist offensive overran most of Spain's heavy industry. By December the armaments factories were back in operation, now sustaining Franco's war effort, and in the following spring Nationalist troops broke through to the Mediterranean. During the remainder of 1938 the war tipped irrevocably against the Republic.

The Republican troops suffered terribly during the winter of 1938/9. Short of food, warm clothing, weapons and ammunition, they soldiered on but it could not last for ever. Juan Negrin and the communists prolonged Madrid's agony; SIM, their secret police modelled on the Soviet NKVD, dealt ruthlessly with anyone accused of betraying the Republic. It was left to General Sigismondo Casado, commander of the 3rd Army deployed in defence of Madrid, to topple the regime and attempt to negotiate with Franco. On the afternoon of 28 March 1939 Madrid formally surrendered to Nationalist forces.

Polikarpov I-16 fighter

The USSR agreed to help the Spanish government in return for payment in gold. They supplied better tanks than Germany could offer and the I-16 fighter outclassed most Nationalist aircraft. Tricky to fly but highly manoeuvrable, it was armed with twin 20-mm cannon and two machine-guns.

Republican militia captured by the Nationalists
Franco's troops attacking the capital in 1936 were outnumbered by over 3:1 but their superior discipline and skill at arms had enabled them to cut their way through several republican armies on the way to Madrid. In this savage war, prisoners often suffered a grim fate.

German intervention: Heinkel He 111 over Valencia
As it became clear that the UK and France would not risk war over Spain, Hitler provided Franco with a steady supply of weapons, technicians and eventually aircrew. In Spain German aircraft and pilots developed the techniques of close air support that the world would soon know as *Blitzkrieg*.

Fighting in the University City where the nationalists made their deepest advance into the capital in November. Franco called off the attack as it became obvious that his outnumbered forces could not hope to break through.

Junkers Ju 87 Stukas made their first, deadly appearance over Spain in the series of battles in the north which decided the war. Once Franco had overrun Spain's industrial heartland, the republic was doomed.

Nationalist troops ready for the final attack on Madrid, spring 1939. The defenders had endured terrible privation during the winter, living mainly on lentils dubbed 'Dr Negrin's resistance pills' after the name of the communist leader.

THE RAPE OF NANKING: Japan in China

July 1937: The military rulers of Japan determine to carve out a new empire in China which looks invitingly weak.

China has been of overwhelming importance to Japan from earliest times. Much of Japan's culture was copied from her older, more sophisticated neighbour to the west, but emergence in the 1860s from 200 years of isolation led to her rapid industrialization. An awakening imperial and colonial appetite made her leaders cast covetous eyes on the rich pickings offered by the decaying colossus across the China Sea.

The first war with China and the defeat of Russia at the turn of the century meant that Japan became the major East Asian power. Over a period of 30 years Japan won control over Korea, the ex-German treaty ports in China, and finally Manchuria. The rise of Japanese militarism in the 1930s allied to colonial ambition saw Japan cynically manipulate China into war.

The Marco Polo Bridge incident in July 1937 was to lead to the fall of nearby Beijing and marked the start of a new and brutal phase in China's turbulent history. Some 500 miles to the south the great port of Shanghai was the heart of foreign influence and interest in China. Japan was just one of the nations maintaining forces in the city. At first, the Japanese seemed to want to avoid spreading the war to the south, possibly not wishing to antagonize the Western powers.

Chiang Kai-shek had other ideas. With over a million Chinese troops in the Yangtze valley, including 80,000 German-trained soldiers in nationalist units, he felt that the 25,000 Japanese in Shanghai (only 5,000 of whom were fighting men) were vulnerable. In August he moved four divisions of crack troops into Shanghai. The Japanese responded by sending in naval and marine reinforcements.

Japanese invasion

Early Chinese operations were limited to bombarding Japanese shipping, but as a result of abysmal gunnery this was not nearly as effective as the counter-fire of the Japanese naval gunners. Following Chinese bombing of the international settlement, the Japanese decided to play the game for keeps. They issued orders for 300,000 troops, 300 guns and 200 tanks to be ready for action around Shanghai. The Japanese air force bombed Nanking, the Nationalist capital, and established a pattern of bombing other cities.

In Shanghai, positional warfare developed. Japanese reinforcements poured into the city. Chinese forces held off Japanese attacks, but casualties were high. The Chinese hoped that the Western powers would intervene, but in vain.

On 22 August Japan landed the Shanghai Expeditionary Army which drove south towards the

city, beating off Chinese counterattacks along the way. Over the next two months, the Japanese took the towns and villages around Shanghai until the Chinese withdrew to the south west, leaving one battalion, the 'Lone Battalion', in the city.

On 5 November the retiring Chinese were outflanked by the landing of the Japanese 10th Army in Hangzhou Bay to the south. As the Japanese drove north to link with the forces in Shanghai, the Chinese retreat threatened to become a rout.

By 9 November the Chinese were trying to set up a defensive line 80 miles to the east, but they were too late. Pouring more and more troops into the region, the Japanese began a drive up the Yangtze, ferrying their forces in hundreds of flat-bottomed boats. On 10 November the Japanese took Song

Jiang behind the Chinese right flank.

Back in Shanghai the battle raged on, but Japanese numbers began to tell. Three months of fighting had razed several square miles of the city before the final mopping up of pockets of resistance was ended.

The only effective fighters in the huge Chinese army were Chiang's 80,000 German-trained troops. But the battle for Shanghai cost the Chinese army 60 per cent of its best troops, and a higher proportion of its officers. The coming Japanese drive on Nanking was to cost even more.

With 250,000 troops in and around Shanghai the Japanese could launch an attack on the capital quickly. The route between Shanghai and Nanking was bombed and strafed mercilessly, and it was

The modern samurai in action

Many of the Great Powers maintained forces in China but in 1937 the Japanese planned to conquer a large part of the divided Chinese nation. The cruiser Yubari *is seen here at Shanghai where the Chinese made their first bid to oust the invaders.*

After the Chinese counter-attack at Shanghai reinforcements were rushed in by the Japanese navy despite ineffectual Chinese attempts to drive the warships away. Here an armoured column of Japanese marines heads inland.

The fighting at Shanghai lasted from late August to early November when the beaten Chinese forces fell back towards the Nationalist capital, Nanking. The Japanese swiftly overran the remaining positions and advanced on Nanking on 1 December.

Left: A Nationalist Chinese soldier
The Nationalists' best troops had been trained by a German military mission and German equipment was in widespread use although much of it dated from World War I. Unfortunately, the issue of coal-scuttle helmets and Mauser automatic pistols did not turn men into German soldiers.

Right: On the road to Nanking
Japanese soldiers perform their ablutions with the aid of a curious bucket bath. Although the Japanese won a crushing victory in 1937, the invasion committed Japan to a protracted war which tied down nearly a million troops during World War II. It was to prove a fatal diversion of effort.

Below: Code of the Warrior
Samurai swords were more than a proud symbol, they were put to use by the Japanese army until 1945. A medieval warrior caste armed with modern weapons, the Japanese officer corps dominated Japan's social, cultural and political life. Its reckless military adventurism was to lead Japan into the ultimately disastrous war with the USA.

Type 95 Light Tank

The Japanese army was equipped with a range of light tanks similar to those in service with European armies. Prototypes of the Type 95 were tested under combat conditions in China before it entered full scale production. It had a crew of four and was armed with a 37-mm gun and two machine-guns. The Chinese had few anti-tank weapons and only a handful of operational tanks.

obvious to the Chinese commanders that when the Japanese moved, Nanking would fall. Nevertheless, Chiang Kai-shek insisted that the capital, and the tomb of Sun Yat-sen, be defended. General Tang Sheng-zhi, a man of more optimism than ability, was put in command.

On 1 December the Shanghai Expeditionary Army began the march on Nanking. Within five days the left wing was within sight of the capital, whose population had been swollen by more than 250,000 Shanghai refugees. On 9 December an artillery bombardment began. By 13 December Tang's army had been routed and the Japanese were entering the city. And the Rape commenced.

Even in a decade whose leading lights were Hitler and Stalin, the Rape of Nanking stands out as a horror unmatched in modern warfare. The Japanese troops were out of control. Murder, looting and rape were the orders of the day. People were buried alive, or roasted over open fires, or dipped in acid. Bodies in their thousands were thrown into the Yangtze.

The total death toll in Shanghai is unknown but as many as 300,000 civilians may have been slaughtered in less than two months. At least 20,000 were killed on the first day.

By the end of 1937, Japan was thus master of both the old and new capitals of China, Beijing and Nanking. But the war was far from over. Resistance to the invaders was to continue for a further eight years of blood and sacrifice.

The Japanese army took just five days to reach Nanking and its heavy artillery was in position to begin the bombardment by 9 December. The Nationalist defenders were in no condition to resist the ferocious Japanese assault.

Japanese guns bombard the South Gate of Nanking while infantry wait to attack during bitter street fighting on 12 December. The Japanese were far more organized and had better weapons and equipment than their Chinese opponents.

Breaking through the defences on 13 December the Japanese army embarked on an orgy of atrocity and destruction. The defenceless population was slaughtered wholesale, a grim foretaste of the moral worth of the Japanese armed forces.

Adolf Hitler at a pre-war Nazi Party rally. The Versailles Treaty that ended the Great War also sowed the seeds of future conflict. Few Germans could accept the loss of territory to Poland, and the legend grew that the Army had been 'stabbed in the back'. Hitler was by no means the first German leader to champion this myth, but his political skill eventually brought him absolute power. After just six years in power he was ready to challenge the verdict of 1918.

THE BLITZKRIEG BEGINS: Poland overrun

September 1939: Hitler gambles he can attack Poland without triggering another European conflict.

On 31 August 1939 Hitler ordered the invasion of Poland. The following day the UK and France demanded the instant withdrawal of all German forces and, in the face of the contemptuous silence with which this was greeted in Berlin, consulted on how best to implement their promises to Poland. That they must be implemented was unanimously agreed: but how, when and where were matters for lengthy discussion, and indeed remain the subject of controversy.

An ultimatum was sent – and ignored. At 11 am on 3 September 1939, Chamberlain broadcast the news that the UK was now at war with Germany. The world would realize, he felt sure, what a bitter disappointment it was to him.

Luftwaffe in action

At 0445 on 1 September, bombers and fighters of the Luftwaffe crossed the Polish frontier and began their systematic destruction of Polish airfields and aircraft, of road and rail centres, of concentrations of troop reserves, and of anything which intelligence or observation had indicated as likely to house command headquarters of any status. The first Blitzkrieg had begun.

Poland was an ideal theatre for such warfare. In addition to being fairly flat (and at this time dry and hard-surfaced), her frontiers were much too long for them to be well defended. She was, moreover, flanked by her enemy on both sides – East Prussia to the north and the newly occupied Czechoslovakia to the south – and the most valuable areas of the country lay between those flanks. Poland, in fact, protruded like a tongue into hostile territory – and her armies in September 1939 were deployed in that tongue, instead of behind the river lines of the Vistula and San where their defences would have been stronger. But the fatal weakness in Poland's defences lay in her lack of armour, for the bulk of the army consisted of 30 divisions of infantry supported by 11 brigades of horsed cavalry and two motorized brigades. Against them were to be launched six German armoured divisions and eight motorized divisions, together with 27 infantry divisions whose main role would be to engage the attentions of the Polish infantry while the German mobile forces raced around the flanks to strike at the centres of control and supply.

One hour after the Luftwaffe had struck, Army Group South under General Gerd von Rundstedt smashed its way forward: the 8th Army on the left wing driving for Lodz, the 14th Army on the right aimed for Krakow and the line of the River Vistula, and the bulk of the armour of the 10th Army under General Walther von Reichenau in the centre piercing the gap between the Polish Lodz and Krakow

Armies, linking with 8th Army mobile units and racing on for Warsaw.

By 4 September, 10th Army spearheads were 80 km (50 miles) into Poland, curving up towards the capital and isolating the Lodz Army from its supplies, while to the south 14th Army tanks had reached the River San on each side of Przemysl.

Meanwhile Army Group North under General Fedor von Bock was driving down from Pomerania and East Prussia: the 4th Army along the line of the Vistula towards Warsaw, and the 3rd Army along the line of the Bug towards Brest-Litovsk, Lwow and eventual junction with the 14th Army coming up from the Carpathians.

Thus two huge encirclements would take place, the outer intended to block any escapees from the inner – and at the end of the first week only the immediate confusion of battle masked the extraordinary success of the German attack. The inner pincers had certainly met successfully, but the chaos inside the trap was such that no-one could be sure what was happening. Polish columns marched and counter-marched in frantic efforts to make contact either with the enemy or with their own support, and in doing so raised such clouds of dust that aerial observation could report nothing but general movement by unidentified forces of unknown strength, engaged in unrecognizable activity in pursuit of incomprehensible aims.

Fighting at Bzura

As a result there was some doubt at German headquarters whether or not the bulk of the Polish forces had been trapped, therefore 10th Army armour was wheeled north to form another block along the Bzura, west of Warsaw. Here was fought the most bitter battle of the campaign, but it could only end in defeat for the Poles. Despite their desperate gallantry, they were fighting in reverse against a strong, well-entrenched enemy who had only to hold on to win, and after the first day they were harried from behind by troops of the 8th Army from the southern group and of the 4th Army from the north. It is hardly surprising that only a very small number managed to break through the German armoured screen to join the garrison at Warsaw – where they very soon found themselves again cut off from escape to the east by the outer encirclement.

From this double encirclement only a small fraction of the Polish army could hope to escape, and on 17 September even this hope was dashed. The contents of the secret clauses of the Russo-German Pact signed the previous month were cruelly revealed when the Red Army moved in from the east to collect its share of the spoils; Poland as a nation ceased to exist and a new international frontier ran from East Prussia past Bialystok, Brest-Litovsk and Lwow as far as the Carpathians.

SS armoured car in Danzig
The Germans organized an SS unit in the free city of Danzig during August 1939 and at the outbreak of hostilities it joined the Danzig police in an assault on the Polish-held post office and the Westerplatte fortress.

PZL P23 Karas
Poland fielded about 100 of these light bombers in 1939 but they had little impact. The Polish air force was unable to mount a coherent air defence after 6 September. 327 Polish aircraft were destroyed, many on the ground, and 98 flew to neutral Rumania as the defeat of Poland became inevitable.

Right: The fifth partition of Poland
The German plan was to defeat the Polish army in a classic battle of encirclement. The Poles fought stubbornly, but the professionalism and numerical superiority of the German army made the result a foregone conclusion.

Thirty-six days

Polish cavalry mobilised for war, 30 August 1939. Poland's 11 cavalry brigades were intended to fight as they had done in the 1920s but they were badly handled. Insistence on carrying lances and sabres was a romantic but futile gesture.

German armour presses east, 3 September. The rapid advance of the German armoured divisions quickly penetrated the Polish defences and prevented a stable front ever being established.

Refugees flee before the advancing Germans, 7 September. In scenes which were to be repeated all over Europe during the next two years, the Polish roads were choked with civilians hurrying away from the fighting.

Polish infantryman 1939
The Polish army was poorly equipped and its troops poorly led. Despite weak strategic direction and a reckless enthusiasm for offensive tactics, the Polish soldier resisted for 36 days. 66,000 Polish troops were killed in action and 130,000 wounded.

Above: The unholy alliance. In 1939 and not for the first time, Germany and Russia shook hands over the corpse of Poland. The Red Army invaded on 17 September but Stalin's opportunism bore bitter fruit. The Red Army left its fortified border zone and in 1941 would face the Germans in the open.

Panzer I armoured command vehicle. Radzymin, 27 September
In the black uniform of German tank crew, a young commander leads a column of German armour along the road to Warsaw. The white cross was used as a recognition sign on German vehicles during the Polish campaign.

GERMAN ATTACKS 15/27 SEPTEMBER
POLISH BZURA POCKET
RUSSIAN ATTACKS 17/27 SEPTEMBER

MILES 200
KILOMETERS 300

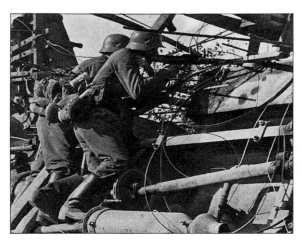

A German machine-gun team in action on the outskirts of Warsaw. The government fled to Rumania but the capital held out until 27 September despite heavy German aerial and artillery bombardment.

A German soldier hurls a stick grenade at a Polish position in Warsaw. Many Germans who fought in both campaigns said the fighting in Poland was much tougher than during the invasion of western Europe the following summer.

The end: 400,000 Polish soldiers surrendered, many to endure appalling conditions in German PoW camps. Meanwhile in the east in Katyn forest, the Red Army murdered vast numbers of captured Polish officers.

INCREDIBLE VICTORY: Battle of the River Plate

Hitler's 'pocket battleships' were expressly designed to be fast enough to outrun any vessel their 28-cm guns could not sink.

Although history affords no example of war against commerce in itself defeating a major maritime power, the Kaiser's fleet had come close enough to success against the UK to encourage Hitler to try again. Among ships built expressly for the purpose were the three 'Deutschland' class 'pocket battleships' (more correctly 'armoured ships') which were designed with long range and economical diesel machinery to give a speed greater than that of any more powerful ship, while armament and protection were on a scale to be more powerful than any faster ship.

Toward the end of August 1939, before the actual outbreak of hostilities, two of these ships, KMS *Deutschland* and KMS *Admiral Graf Spee*, together with their dedicated supply ships, left for their war stations in the North and South Atlantic respectively. Beginning with the 5,050 grt Booth liner *Clement* near Pernambuco on 30 September, the *Graf Spee* destroyed several independently-routed merchantmen during wide-ranging depredations over the next few months. No fewer than eight separate Anglo-French hunting groups were formed to catch her.

Raider warning

On 2/3 December 1939 two British ships, *Doric Star* and *Tairoa*, were sunk in mid-ocean. Each transmitted a raider warning and position which, when plotted, indicated that the German ship's course was toward the rich traffic in the Rio de Janeiro – River Plate area. This region was in the ambit of Commodore Henry Harwood, whose South American Cruiser Division was known as Force 'G'. Having picked up the merchantmen's distress signals, Harwood was convinced that Captain Hans Langsdorff, in the *Graf Spee*, was making for the Plate estuary and at a speed that indicated arrival on or about 13 December. He accordingly concentrated his three available cruisers, the 203-mm (8-in) HMS *Exeter* (flag) and the 152-mm (6-in) sisters HMS *Ajax* and HMS *Achilles* (the latter New Zealand-crewed) some 240 km (150 miles) off the Uruguayan coast on 12 December and thoroughly briefed his captains regarding his intentions.

Sure enough, at 0608 on 13 December *Ajax* sighted the enemy, unexpectedly to the north-westward. Langsdorff was, in fact, loitering in expectation of intercepting a small convoy whose presence he suspected through papers taken from a further British ship, the *Streonshalh*, sunk on 7 December without any transmission. Backlit by the early

dawn, Harwood's ships had been sighted by *Graf Spee* at 0530 and, taken to be the convoy, were already being approached.

Harwood was presented with a formidable adversary. Against him Langsdorff could deploy six 280-mm (11-in) guns in two triple turrets and eight 150-mm (5.9-in) weapons.

Within 8- and 6-inch gun range, the German ship's 80-mm (3.15-in) vertical armour would prevent vital damage. Only in speed did the British have the advantage and this was used to good effect, the three cruisers working in two divisions. *Exeter* approached from the south while the two faster light cruisers worked around to the east; each division could thus spot the fall of shot for the other and, it was hoped, force *Graf Spee* to split the fire from her main battery.

Langsdorff opened fire at 0617 at about 17350 m (19,000 yards) and, after some initial uncertainty, concentrated on the main threat, *Exeter*. He enjoyed a further advantage over the British in having one of only two ships in the German fleet fitted with a radar that could be used for gunnery purposes. Within minutes *Graf Spee* had found the range, three 280-mm shells smashing *Exeter*'s bridge and putting her forward turrets out of action. Badly on fire and with an increasing list to starboard, she struggled gamely on, steering from local control and firing only from her after turret. At 0640 her condition was so dire that she fired a salvo of torpedoes to cover a manoeuvre designed to open the range.

Despite his obvious success Langsdorff, an ex-destroyer man, seemed very concerned at the torpedo threat posed by the two light cruisers. Their

HMS Exeter after her refit
Exeter was badly damaged by *Graf Spee* and returned to England to refit after temporary repairs were carried out in the Falkland Islands. She was subsequently deployed to the Far East and sunk by Japanese cruisers in the Java Sea on 1 March 1942.

Dutschland fires her aft main armament
Deutschland's 28-cm guns in action during her successful commerce-raiding cruise in the North Atlantic. The elusive German raider sank the British armed merchantman *Jervis Bay* before returning to Germany.

HMS Ajax fires a salvo from her aft 6-in guns
Graf Spee's 3-in armour belt and heavily protected turrets were proof against the 6-in guns of *Ajax* and *Achilles* except at close range. By contrast, neither of the British light cruisers could have withstood a few hits from *Graf Spee's* main armament.

Voyage of no return

The Royal New Zealand Navy's 'Leander' class cruiser Achilles *joined the Royal Navy's South Atlantic Squadron for the operations against the German raiders. The* Graf Spee *was off the Brazilian coast when the war began.*

Graf Spee *was intercepted on 13 December. Here* Achilles *trains the guns of 'X' and 'Y' turrets on the* Graf Spee. *The 6-in guns are at maximum elevation but still not in range, although the* Graf Spee *could quickly score hits at 19,000 yards.*

Graf Spee *and* Deutschland *steam down the English Channel in 1939 before the outbreak of war. By the time the UK declared war the German raiders were on station in the Atlantic accompanied by their logistic support ships.*

'Deutschland' class 'pocket battleship'

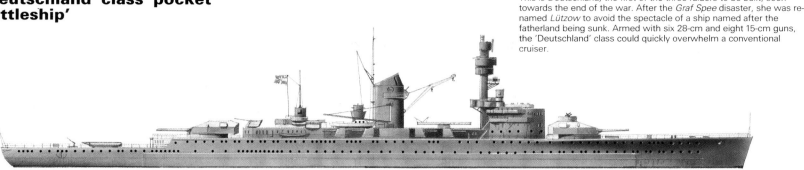

This is *Deutschland*, the first of the three raiders to be built, seen towards the end of the war. After the *Graf Spee* disaster, she was renamed *Lützow* to avoid the spectacle of a ship named after the fatherland being sunk. Armed with six 28-cm and eight 15-cm guns, the 'Deutschland' class could quickly overwhelm a conventional cruiser.

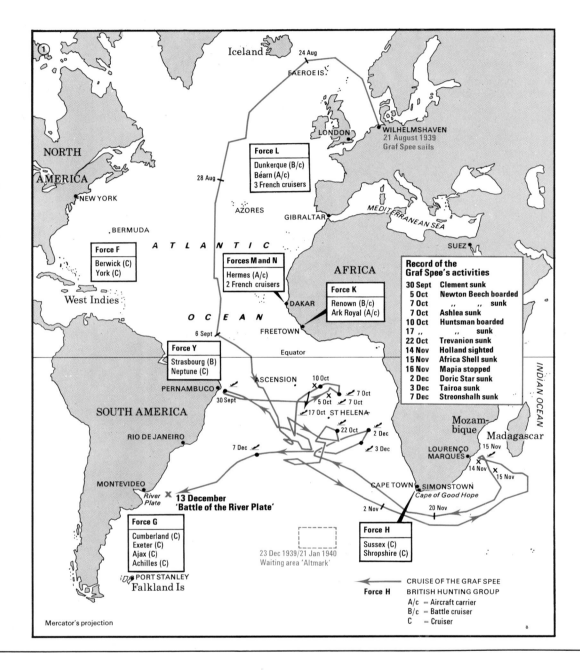

Record of the Graf Spee's activities

30 Sept	Clement sunk
5 Oct	Newton Beech boarded
7 Oct	,, ,, sunk
7 Oct	Ashlea sunk
10 Oct	Huntsman boarded
17 ,,	,, sunk
22 Oct	Trevanion sunk
14 Nov	Holland sighted
15 Nov	Africa Shell sunk
16 Nov	Mapia stopped
2 Dec	Doric Star sunk
3 Dec	Tairoa sunk
7 Dec	Streonshalh sunk

CRUISE OF THE GRAF SPEE
Force H → BRITISH HUNTING GROUP
A/c = Aircraft carrier
B/c = Battle cruiser
C = Cruiser

Mercator's projection

feints resulted in his changing course by steps from the original south-east, through east and north eventually to west, i.e. back towards the Uruguayan coast. While *Exeter* had hit the German only twice, the light cruisers had scored a possible 13 times and, while their 152-mm shells caused little significant damage, the psychological effect on Langsdorff was considerable.

At 0716 *Graf Spee* had made a sudden turn as if to finish off the still present *Exeter*, but had been immediately closed by the others which deterred her at the cost to *Ajax* of three hits, which deprived her of the use of two turrets. With *Exeter* obliged to steer southward to the dubious shelter of the Falklands, the two light cruisers were dodging main and secondary battery fire at ranges down to 7300 m (8,000 yards) and, as the German patently could not be stopped, lost bearing and took up a shadowing role with the idea of a further attack after dark. *Ajax* was now down to three guns and only 20 per cent ammunition.

Surprisingly, Langsdorff was obviously determined to make for Montevideo instead of the more obvious sanctuary of the open ocean, and fired only when the British approached too closely. Early on the morning of 14 December he duly entered neutral waters with a still fully battleworthy ship and 36 dead (the British had suffered 72).

International law obliged the ship to leave within 24 hours but the Germans asked for more, to effect necessary repairs. This accorded with British aims to delay her even more to allow the concentration of reinforcements. The diplomatic battle was matched by careful use of misinformation that appeared finally to convince Langsdorff that the aircraft-carrier HMS *Ark Royal* and a battle-cruiser awaited him.

On the morning of 17 December *Graf Spee* moved out into international waters in the estuary, her crew left and she was blown up, the resulting column of smoke clearly visible to the British ships outside. These comprised just the *Ajax*, *Achilles* and the newly-arrived *Cumberland* (able to steam on only two shafts).

On 20 December the disillusioned Langsdorff shot himself. Napoleon had once observed that morale was to *matériel* as three was to one. Never was it more true.

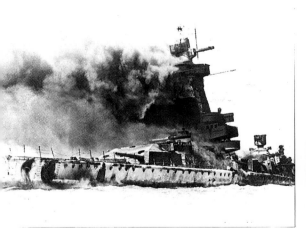

Graf Spee *broke off the action and retreated to Montevideo. Bluffed into believing that a battle-cruiser and an aircraft carrier awaited him, Captain Hans Langsdorff sailed down the estuary and scuttled his ship.*

Ajax *and* Cumberland *after the news of* Graf Spee's *blowing up has been received. All ships cleared lower decks and the crew of* Ajax *can be seen mustered at every vantage point to watch the end of the* Graf Spee.

Graf Spee *settled in the water, burned out. Langsdorff could not live with the humiliation of his action and shot himself on 20 December.*

BATTLE FOR FINLAND: The Winter War

In 1939 the USSR expands its border at the expense of several neighbouring countries. But Finland refuses to be coerced.

Poland was not the only country that figured in the secret clauses of the 1939 Russo-German Pact. They also mentioned the Baltic republics of Estonia, Latvia and Lithuania, together with Finland, placing them all 'within the sphere of interest of the USSR' – and Joseph Stalin, having watched Hitler's army conquer one small nation so spectacularly, seems to have felt that it was time for the Red Army to bring him similar gains.

Political pressure – and geographic realities – were enough to persuade the three Baltic republics to sign treaties of mutual assistance which allowed the USSR to establish garrisons and bases within their borders; but Finland felt herself protected in her most vulnerable area by the Gulf of Finland and Lake Ladoga, and by the wilderness of forest, swamp, lakes and sheer arctic distances which made up her eastern frontier, stretching from Lake Ladoga up to the Arctic Ocean. The Finns also believed that the spirit and training of her armed forces would be enough to hold the first onslaught, and that the sight of their own David fighting off the Soviet Goliath would evoke first sympathy and then active aid from the rest of the world.

Overwhelming odds

And when, on 28 November, after two months of verbal bullying by Molotov and defiance by the Finnish leaders Paassikivi and Tanner, the USSR broke off negotiations and attacked the Finnish defences two days later, it looked at first as though the Finns had been right. Certainly, all Western Europe and the USA applauded the Finnish stand – and Finnish military successes at first exceeded all expectations. Despite the size of the Finnish army (at its peak it could never produce and support more than 16 divisions), despite its acute shortage of artillery and heavy ammunition, despite its shortage of transport, signals equipment and total lack of armour, it held the Soviet attack which came up through the Karelian Isthmus, along the whole of the Mannerheim Line (the main Finnish defences) from the Gulf of Finland to the River Vuoksi, and between there and Lake Ladoga they held the Soviets in their forward positions *in front* of the line. The Finnish II and III Corps, in fact, beat back the Soviet 7th and 13th Armies, inflicting astonishing losses on the Red Army infantry by the accuracy of their rifle and machine-gun fire, and on the Soviet tanks with petrol bombs. By 22 December, after six days of pointless battering against a seemingly impregnable line, the Soviets broke off the action and withdrew, obviously to re-group – and to re-think.

Finland defiant

Matters had not gone so well for the Finns north of Lake Ladoga. The six divisions of the Soviet 8th

Motti tactics: Finnish troops examine Soviet dead
The long columns of Soviet troops pressing into central Finland were cut to pieces in December. Chopped into pockets ('mottis') some 30,000 Soviets were killed or captured around Suomussalmi, many frozen to death after their supplies ran out. The Soviet 44th and 163rd Divisions were annihilated.

Russian assaults on Finland
The Winter War was fought in a sparsely inhabited land of forest and swamp with a savage winter climate. From south of Oulu the countryside was heavily wooded and bad going for mechanized units. Following the German invasion of Russia in 1941, Finland swiftly recaptured the territories it lost in 1940, only to lose them and other areas after World War II.

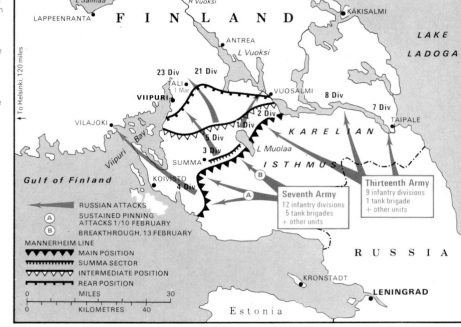

Slaughter in the snow

The Soviet attack began on 30 November 1939. Finnish forces were outnumbered 3:1 and desperately short of modern military equipment. This officer is in part of the 'Mannerheim Line', the vital defensive belt across the Karelian isthmus.

The Red Army came unstuck immediately. Apart from in the far north, its troops suffered heavy losses for negligible gains. Armour, like this T-26 tank, was picked off by the handful of Finnish anti-tank guns and the appalling weather added to the chaos.

Bewildered Soviet prisoners left behind after the Soviets retreated from central Finland at the end of December. The Finns captured vast quantities of sorely needed military equipment from the Soviets in the battles around Suomussalmi.

Finnish machine-gunners in action
The Soviet attacks in December 1939 were so poorly managed that Finnish machine-gunners were presented with thick waves of Soviet infantry with no effective support from tanks or artillery. The ensuing bloodbath stopped the Red Army in its tracks.

Reindeer and Finnish ski troops, Lapland, January 1940
The Soviet 14th Army based at Murmansk launched a vigorous offensive aimed at Petsamo to forestall a possible Anglo/French landing. It was the one area where the Finns were unable to stop the Soviet advance and they fell back towards the Norwegian border.

Suomi M1931 9-mm sub-machine gun

Finnish troops were desperately short of equipment and their difficulties were exacerbated by the sheer variety of different weapons provided by friendly countries. The Suomi was Finnish-made and one of the best SMGs available. It was tough, accurate, reliable, and always in short supply.

Army crossed the frontier and advanced implacably to the line of Finnish defences between Kitelä and Ilomantsi. But in doing so they had given some hostages to fortune: incredibly, the Soviets had no ski troops, whereas every Finnish soldier was well trained on skis and many were expert in their military exploitations. Soviet divisions thus found themselves cut off from communication and supplies; small formations were decimated, some units annihilated.

Much farther north at Suomussalmi the Soviet 163rd Division was surrounded, subjected to concentrated small-arms and short-range artillery fire until 29 December, when it broke completely, the survivors fleeing across the frozen wilderness leaving 11 tanks, 25 guns and 150 lorries to the elated victors.

But of course, it could not go on. First of all, although the UK, France, the USA and Sweden all professed a desire to help, they produced very little of it – the first two because they needed for their own use every man and every weapon they could produce, the others because of their carefully cultivated neutrality; and secondly, when plans were laid to send British and French reinforcements in, Sweden refused to allow them passage.

By early January, Stalin had decided to bring it all to an end. Command of the campaign was given to

General Semyon Timoshenko, siege artillery was brought up, and on 15 January 1940 the systematic destruction of the Mannerheim Line commenced. As the Finns had no long-range artillery they could mount no counter-battery fire; Finnish troops spent the days in the trenches connecting the strongpoints, their nights desperately trying to reconstruct the smashed concrete boxes, the obliterated gunposts: and soon on every night they had also to beat off Soviet tanks, supported by infantry brought up on towed sledges. Sheer exhaustion spelt the end of the Mannerheim Line – and in due course of every other defence line the Finns could man.

The road to Helsinki

By the beginning of March the Soviets had driven them back to Viipuri, and from there the Finnish line curved back almost to Tali and on to Vuosalmi, then to the water-line at Taipale on Lake Ladoga. On 3 March Timoshenko sent a battalion and a brigade across the ice to Vilajoki. So the Finnish positions were turned – and the road to Helsinki open.

On 13 March, bowing to the inevitable, Prime Minister Ryti signed the Treaty of Moscow, which returned the Russo-Finnish border more or less to where Peter the Great had drawn it in 1721; where, in fact, it remains today.

Private, Red Army Rifle Division,

This Soviet soldier wears the standard army greatcoat and high boots which were often replaced by American-manufactured ankle boots. The curious cap is the *budionovka* which proved impractical in Finland, fur caps being much warmer. The red colour patches indicate arm of service.

Stung by this humiliating defeat, Stalin fed in overwhelming numbers of troops against the Mannerheim Line. The spring thaw was late, and the Soviets were able to outflank some of the defences by attacking over the frozen sea.

Helsinki burns after a Soviet air raid. The last weeks of the war became very bitter as the furious Red Army sought revenge for its initial defeats. The Finns lost 62 aircraft in action but destroyed 208 enemy aircraft.

On 13 March, Finland signed a peace treaty surrendering part of her territory to the USSR. Here a column of Finnish lorries evacuate some of the population of Viipuri. The Finns sustained 24,000 casualties and the Soviets over 200,000.

BREAKTHROUGH AT SEDAN

10 May 1940: The long awaited German offensive in the West begins. The French border defences are outflanked.

Shortly after 0230 on the morning of 10 May 1940, 64 men of the German army crossed the Dutch frontier; this was the pinpoint of invasion. Three hours later glider-borne troops dropped over the Belgian border to capture and demolish the huge fortifications at Eben-Emael; five minutes later the 30 divisions of Army Group 'B' under General Fedor von Bock flooded forward across the frontiers from Maastricht up to the coast at the Ems estuary, while to the south General Gerd von Rundstedt's

Army Group 'A' of 44 divisions, including the main striking force of seven Panzer divisions under General Ewald von Kleist, struck forward into the Ardennes – the wooded country which French military commanders had been proclaiming impassable for tanks since 1919.

Allied advance

And with an almost suicidal alacrity which brought tears of joy to Hitler's eyes, the Allied armies in the north – five divisions of the British Expeditionary Force, eight divisions of the French 1st Army on their right and seven divisions of the French 7th Army up on the coast around Dunkirk – left the defensive positions they had spent the bitterly cold winter so arduously preparing, and moved forward to join the Belgian army in accordance with the Dyle Plan, which envisaged a defensive line running along the Dyle and Meuse rivers. There were obviously some difficulties to be overcome on the way, for the Luftwaffe was busy overhead all the time, and this was the occasion for the baptism of Allied troops by dive-bombing – it took time for them to become accustomed to the nerve-shaking

Surrender of a Char B1 heavy tank
A few sorties by these monstrous tanks caused the Germans momentary alarm since they were impervious to the standard 3.7-cm anti-tank gun. Unfortunately French logistic arrangements beggared description and many were captured as they ran out of fuel.

Knocked out Renault FTs
The French army possessed 3,000 tanks in 1940, some of them technically superior to German armour. However, these two-man World War I tanks stood little chance in 1940: two stand silent and one has exploded after a penetrative hit from armour-piercing shell.

Through the Ardennes
The German plan was an audacious gamble which had captured Hitler's imagination but alarmed several of his senior commanders. Success depended on the German armour debouching from the Ardennes forest before the French could deploy a blocking force. In the event, the German spearheads reached the Meuse in two days: Like the Second Empire before it, the Third Republic perished to the sound of gunfire at Sedan.

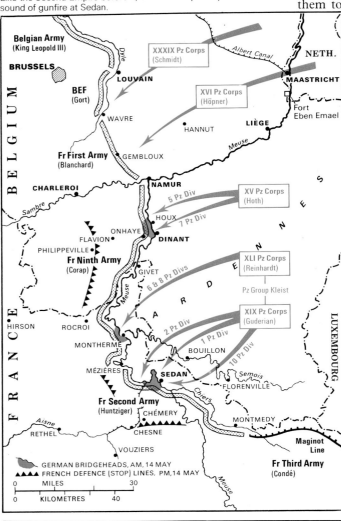

Hotchkiss H-39 two-man light tank

Armed with a 37-mm gun which could penetrate the armour of only the lighter German tanks, the H-39 was hopelessly outclassed in 1940. The German army captured hundreds of them and pressed them into service later in the war on anti-partisan operations in the USSR and Balkans.

Six days to disaster

French troops in Paris, October 1939. Having been reduced virtually to a militia during the 1930s, the French army was mentally and physically incapable of attacking Germany while Hitler was busy in Poland.

German troops pressing through the Ardennes forest, outflanking the Maginot Line. Encountering only light resistance, they reached the Meuse in two days and broke the French front wide open.

A Renault R-35 lies burning as the Blitzkrieg continues: on 16 May the Allied armies north of the Maginot Line officially began a three-day withdrawal. In fact the retreat would only end with surrender of France.

For you the war is over: French POWs
The breathtaking pace of the German advance quickly demoralised the French army. While the French high command manoeuvred pins on their maps, the bewildered soldiery began to surrender. There were several gallant stands but there was no strategic co-operation.

howl which accompanied it. Moreover, roads were soon choked by refugees fleeing ahead of von Bock's advancing infantry.

Nevertheless, by the evening of 14 May, the Allied line was formed. From the mouth of the Scheldt to just north of Antwerp stood three divisions of the French 7th Army; the 80 km (50 miles) south-east to Louvain were held by 13 divisions of the Belgian army; between Louvain and Wavre the front was held by the BEF and from Wavre to Namur by six divisions of the French 1st Army. Some of the battalion and brigade commanders were dismayed by the fragmentary nature of the defences they now occupied – especially compared with those they had just left – while the divisional and higher commanders were alarmed by news of events farther to the south. But as yet none of them was aware of the fact that von Bock's slowly advancing army group was in fact 'the matador's cloak', tempting the mass of the Allied armies forward into the trap which would release von Kleist's Panzer group for the killing thrust.

Race to the Meuse

This was not merely the plan; it soon became the reality. Crashing through the 'impassable' Ardennes as though on a peacetime exercise and brushing aside the French light cavalry unit which had been sent out to 'delay' them, the three divisions of General Heinz Guderian's XIX Panzer Corps were across the French frontier and had reached the Meuse on each side of Sedan by the afternoon of 12 May; by evening German armour controlled the right bank of the river up as far as Dinant. They were across the river within 24 hours (French High Command estimates, once they had got over the shock of the German arrival on the Meuse, were that the crossing would take at least four days to organize and two to carry out). By the morning of 14 May Guderian had two bridgeheads consolidating, while up at Dinant the 7th Panzer Division of General Hermann Hoth's XV Panzer Corps (commanded by Generalmajor Erwin Rommel) had formed yet another bridgehead in the face of desperate but sporadic French resistance.

Screaming Stukas

Early on 15 May the flood burst into France. From each of the bridgeheads the Panzers roared out, preceded on every advance by a cloud of screaming Stukas, covered against attack from British or French fighters by marauding Messerschmitts. Refugees choked the roads, harried by Luftwaffe fighters, bullied by frightened and demoralized soldiers or gendarmes of their own side, or forced into the ditches by strange, ominous, foreign vehicles manned by blond young giants who waved triumphantly at them, rarely deliberately harming them but leaving an impression of invincibility. That evening, German Panzers were reported only

In the wake of the Panzer divisions
The armoured formations which achieved such startling success in 1940 represented a small proportion of the German army. The bulk of the infantry divisions were equipped much like their fathers in 1918 but they faced a very different opposition. The British and French armies were not the competent, victorious forces of 20 years before, but had deteriorated to a very low professional standard.

12 miles from Laon, and when Edouard Daladier, then France's Minister of National Defence, ordered a counter-attack, the French commander-in-chief, General Maurice Gamelin, replied that he had no reserves because the bulk of French strength was locked up in the outflanked Maginot Line. At the same time Gamelin announced that he could no longer take responsibility for the defence of Paris, and he issued orders for a general retreat of all French forces in Belgium. A copy of these orders came, solely by good fortune, to the notice of the British commander-in-chief, Field Marshal Lord Gort, enabling him to ensure that the BEF divisions on the Dyle were not left there on their own.

After the first few days of the German invasion, refugees poured westwards, hampering road movement and adding to the confusion. The Luftwaffe seemed to be everywhere and the incessant dive-bombing further reduced Allied morale.

Sedan in June 1940 after the tide of battle had passed. The French army had relied too long on débrouillage (muddling through). It availed them nothing against the cold-eyed professionalism of the German army.

In six days the German army had shattered the Allied defences in the west. A fortnight after the offensive began the BEF was in full retreat to the Channel ports and the French were staring defeat in the face.

THE FALL OF FRANCE: Escape from Dunkirk

Nightfall, 26 May 1940: Calais is stormed by the Germans and the BEF, the French 1st Army and the Belgian forces are hemmed in with their backs to the sea.

When the Germans broke through the Allied line in France during May 1940, there were still considerable French forces to the south of the breakthrough, and even larger forces – including the British Expeditionary Force – to the north. Between them, could they not first manoeuvre to channel and then contain the German breakthrough, then counter-attack from both north and south and so cut the enemy spearheads off from their main sources of supply and support?

In the depths of their despondency, the French leaders were reluctant to admit the practicability of such a scheme, pleading lack of air strength unless Churchill were to abandon all thought of retaining RAF fighter squadrons for the defence of Britain and send them all to France instead. Even then it seemed most likely that the German forces would be either on the Channel coast or in Paris – or both – in a matter of days, in which case the British and French armies to the north most probably faced early dispersion and disintegration and, unless a general armistice saved them, possibly physical destruction.

Muddle through

Churchill was home by the morning of 17 May, but before he left he managed to instil something of his own dogged courage into the French leadership, so that they at least agreed to order some form of counter-attack on the German spearheads as he had suggested. But at the pace of Allied military planning it was four days before it could be attempted, and even then it was bungled.

By the evening of 20 May General Heinz Guderian's tank spearheads had reached Abbeville at the mouth of the Somme, and at this point their line was

Dunkirk after the evacuation
An abandoned Renault R-35 light tank lies among burned out vehicles. As the German 18th Army fought its way into the town the Luftwaffe provided round-the-clock air strikes against which there was little defence.

Wreckage of a Spitfire shot down over Dunkirk
With the skies dominated by the Luftwaffe, many soldiers wondered loudly where the RAF was. In truth the RAF flew sortie after sortie from its bases in Kent to cover the evacuation. Between 27 and 30 May the RAF shot down 179 German aircraft for the loss of 29.

as attenuated as it ever would be. On 21 May four British infantry brigades and the 1st Army Tank Brigade were launched southwards from Arras, in theory supported by two French infantry divisions on one flank and one light mechanized division on the other, while equally strong French forces were assumed to be attacking up from the south to meet them.

Evacuation planned

In the event, only the British forces and the French light mechanized division moved at all, and they quickly found themselves blocked by General-major Erwin Rommel's 7th Panzer Division, which after a brisk battle (it at least managed to worry Rommel seriously) drove them back to their original positions and threatened them with encirclement. By the evening of 23 May Field Marshal Lord Gort was withdrawing the British brigades farther north, and two days later it became evident to him that only a rapid retreat to the coast and evacuation to England would save even a quarter of his command.

On his own responsibility he issued the necessary orders; the British III Corps withdrew to the beaches on each side of Dunkirk, the I Corps fell back to hold the western flank with one French division on their right and the British II Corps on their left, while the Belgian army held the eastern end of the perimeter. However, on 28 May King Leopold of the Belgians signed an armistice with the Ger-

mans, the Belgian army ceased to exist and a large gap yawned on the left of the British positions – filled during that night by a manoeuvre of extraordinary difficulty carried out with admirable efficiency by the 3rd Infantry Division under command of Major-General B. L. Montgomery. It is not too much to say that this operation saved the British Expeditionary Force.

Battle on the beach

Now Operation 'Dynamo' began – the attempt to evacuate the British army and as many French soldiers as possible from the trap into which they had been lured. Over a thousand boats took part in this evacuation, varying in size from a Royal Navy anti-aircraft cruiser down to yachts which were sailed across the Channel by their owners from a hundred tiny slips along the south coast or along the reaches of the Thames. At least 50 of these craft were sunk; many of the yacht owners were killed or wounded; but an astonishingly large number of soldiers were saved to fight again, and to form the basis of new armies.

The highest hopes before the evacuation began were that perhaps 50,000 men might escape capture or worse; in the event 338,226 reached the shores of Britain during those miraculous nine days, of which, on Churchill's insistence, over 100,000 were French. He had returned to Paris on 31 May, and there agreed that British troops would share in holding the rearguard with French formations, and that French troops in the bridgehead would be evacuated in the same proportion as the British. As it happened, French formations were fighting furiously to the south of the bridgehead (thus holding back powerful German forces which would otherwise have been free to attack Dunkirk), and these never reached the sea. Many of those that did arrive towards the end of the operation refused the chance to escape, and the last ships to sail were thus almost empty. As quite a large number of French troops who did get away quickly decided that they did not care for life in Britain and chose to return to France (where most of them soon found themselves in German prison-camps), Churchill's well-meant gesture was to a great extent wasted.

'We shall defend our island'

But, to the British people, the escape of the bulk of the BEF at Dunkirk was a miracle. To such an extent did their spirit rise, indeed, that Churchill found it necessary to sound a cautionary note. 'We must be very careful not to assign to this deliverance the attributes of a victory,' he said in his report to Parliament; 'wars are not won by evacuations.' He then went on to finish his speech with what was to become one of the most famous passages of rhetoric in British history:

"Even though large tracts of Europe and many old and famous States have fallen or may fall into the grip of the Gestapo and all the odious apparatus of Nazi rule, we shall not flag or fail. We shall go on to the end. We shall fight in France, we shall fight on

The defeat of the BEF

British troops arrive in France, autumn 1939. They had 9 months in which to prepare for a full-scale conflict in Europe. The German army had been making itself ready for six years.

The winter of 1939-40 was spent digging in along the Belgian frontier. Political leadership remained unspeakable: 'I don't think the Germans have any intention of attacking us,' said Chamberlain to Major-General Montgomery in December.

The Germans overran the Low Countries in the blink of an eye, then smashed the French front apart in two days. Meanwhile the BEF entered Belgium to find its right flank suddenly menaced by the enemy advance.

the sea and oceans, we shall fight with growing confidence and growing strength in the air; we shall defend our island, whatever the cost may be. We shall fight on the beaches, we shall fight on the landing-grounds, we shall fight in the fields and in the streets, we shall fight in the hills; we shall never surrender; and even if, which I do not for a moment believe, this island or a large part of it were subjugated and starving, then our Empire beyond the seas, armed and guarded by the British Fleet, would carry on the struggle, until, in God's good time, the New World, with all its power and might, steps forth to the rescue and liberation of the Old."

The long wait on the dunes
The crowded beach at Dunkirk where 224,717 British troops were brought off by the Royal Navy and hundreds of volunteer civilian craft. Over 100,000 French soldiers were also evacuated but many chose to return home after the surrender.

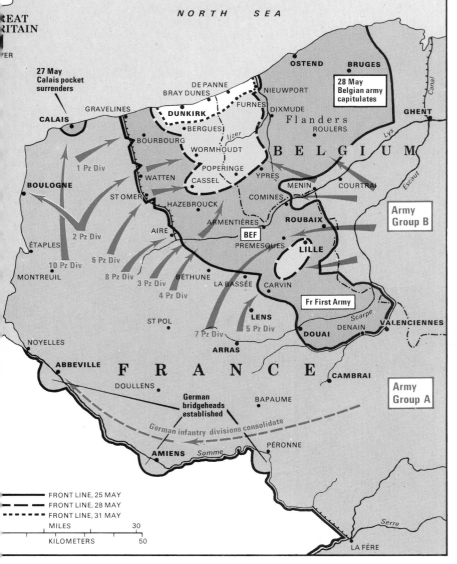

Front lines / map legend:
- FRONT LINE, 25 MAY
- FRONT LINE, 28 MAY
- FRONT LINE, 31 MAY

MILES 30
KILOMETERS 50

Fleeing from Europe
The BEF of 1939-40 was a far cry from the magnificent army of 1914. Utterly unprepared to wage war in Europe it was ignominiously defeated by the very opponent it had beaten in 1918. Fortunately Lord Gort, the C-in-C, ignored the ill-considered orders emanating from London and fell back to Dunkirk. He saved the BEF to form the nucleus of a new British army.

7th Panzer Division, 1st June 1940
Photographed by their commander, Erwin Rommel, from his Fieseler Storch command aircraft, 7th Panzer Division heads for Rouen. After Dunkirk there were still 140,000 British troops left in France. Rommel's men took the surrender of the 51st Highland Division at St Valéry.

Vickers Light Tank
This 5-ton, 3-man light tank armed with a machine-gun was designed for reconnaissance but proved unable to match comparable German AFVs. British armour was committed piecemeal in 1940 without proper support and was predictably defeated.

A knocked-out Vickers tank marks another stand. The BEF found itself conducting a dispiriting withdrawal. Churchill in London and the French commanders in Paris, equally ignorant of the true situation, ordered counter-attacks towards Cambrai.

By 25 May the BEF was in dire peril: the Germans were advancing rapidly along the coast, threatening to overrun the ports. Lord Gort fell back to Dunkirk, saving the BEF from certain destruction. Here a Bf 110 prowls above the doomed port.

June 1940: the German army was now the master of Europe. Only the English Channel stood between the UK and surrender, for there could be little doubt what would follow if the German army could land in strength on the coast of England.

THE BATTLE OF BRITAIN: Victory of The Few

22 July 1940: the German army prepares for the invasion of Britain. First the Luftwaffe must win aerial supremacy then the army can land and the war will be over.

Following the invasion of Norway and the fall of France and the Low Countries in May and June 1940, and as the RAF set about dressing its wounds, the Luftwaffe moved up to bases lining the coasts facing the British Isles. For the all-out air attack, intended to eliminate RAF Fighter Command in preparation for Operation Sea Lion, an invasion of the islands, the Luftwaffe disposed its forces in three air fleets. Luftflotte III was based in north-west France, Luftflotte II in north-east France and the Low Countries, and Luftflotte V in Norway and Denmark.

By early July the German air forces facing the UK fielded about 2,800 aircraft, comprising 1,300 Heinkel He 111, Junkers Ju 88 and Dornier Do 17 bombers, 280 Junkers Ju 87 dive-bombers, 790 Messerschmitt Bf 109 single-seat fighters, 260 Messerschmitt Bf 110 and Junkers Ju 88C heavy fighters and 170 reconnaissance aircraft of various types; of these totals roughly half were immediately combat-ready.

At the head of Fighter Command, Air Chief Marshal Sir Hugh Dowding divided his air defences into three Groups, No. 11 in the south under Air Vice-Marshal Keith Park, No. 12 in the Midlands under Air Vice-Marshal Trafford Leigh-Mallory and No. 13 in the north under Air Vice-Marshal Richard Saul; a fourth Group, No. 10 under Air Vice-Marshal Quintin Brand, would shortly be added to cover the south-west.

Dowding disposed a total of 640 fighters at the beginning of July 1940, including 347 Hawker Hurricanes, 199 Supermarine Spitfires, 69 Bristol Blenheim night-fighters and 25 Boulton Paul Defiants; slightly over half his strength was deployed in the south, the key airfields of Biggin Hill, Kenley, Croydon, Hornchurch, Manston and Tangmere constituting a defensive ring round London and the Thames estuary. To provide early warning and a degree of fighter control, the south and east coasts were covered by a network of radar stations which could detect approaching raids at a distance of about 160 km (100 miles).

The German attacks of July, aimed principally at shipping and coastal targets in the south, proved something of a strain on the British pilots who were obliged to fly standing patrols over the convoys until the German tactics were recognized for what they were, and orders given not to engage enemy fighters unnecessarily. British losses in the July combats amounted to 77 fighters, of whose pilots roughly half survived. A particularly savage combat on 19 July had shown the two-seat Defiant to be unsuitable for day fighting, and it was temporarily withdrawn out of harm's way.

The onset of the main assault on 8 August was competently countered by Park's squadrons, whose pilots quickly spotted the weaknesses of the Junkers Ju 87 and Messerschmitt Bf 110, and set about effective tactics to deal with them. The appearance of large formations of Messerschmitt Bf 109s, which were superior in most respects to the Hurricane, caused the British controllers, where possible, to order their Spitfires against the enemy fighters, while the Hurricanes fought the slower, lower-flying bombers.

Northern raids

By now raids were penetrating farther inland, and on 15 August the aircraft of Luftflotte V attempted to attack targets in northern England, but suffered so badly that such raids were not repeated during the Battle.

A reappraisal of the tactics being employed by the Luftwaffe led to a marked shift during the next phase of the attack which began at the end of August. Following complaints by the Bf 109 pilots that they were badly handicapped when employed in the bomber-escort role, the *Jagdgeschwader* were allowed to resume 'free chase' tactics over southern England, frequently catching the RAF fighters either during take-off or landing, or as they returned short of fuel and ammunition after combat.

This was unquestionably the most successful phase from the Luftwaffe's viewpoint and would

---

RAF Fighters, Summer 1940

Hawker Hurricane Mk I, 85 Squadron, Royal Air Force
85 Squadron was commanded by Squadron Leader Peter Townsend who shot down six enemy aircraft during the battle. Highly manoeuvrable, if slower than its opponents, the Hurricane was a tough aircraft, designed by the redoubtable Sydney Camm. Its eight 0.303-in machine-guns packed a considerable punch and Hurricanes shot down more enemy aircraft than all the other defences put together.

Supermarine Spitfire Mk IIA, 41 Squadron, Royal Air Force
This Spitfire was flown by Squadron Leader D. O. Finlay when 41 Squadron was based at Hornchurch in December 1940. Air Chief Marshal Dowding had resisted demands to send his Spitfires into the battle for France, thus husbanding his most modern fighters for the battle to come. Also armed with eight 0.303-in machine-guns, the Spitfire was well matched with the Bf 109. Victory usually went to the better pilot.

From 'Sea Lion' to the Blitz

Ju 87 Stuka dive-bombers played a major role in the initial attacks on coastal shipping and were a deadly threat to the radar stations. However, they proved hopelessly vulnerable to RAF fighter aircraft and suffered heavy losses.

RAF Hurricanes scramble: thanks to the radar stations, Fighter Command was able to co-ordinate its defences far better than the Germans had anticipated. The RAF also had the advantage of fighting above its own ground.

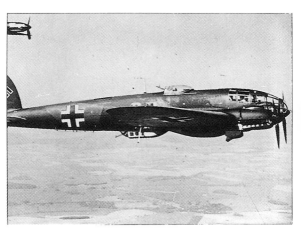

On 11 August the Luftwaffe began to bomb Fighter Command's airfields and radar stations. Four days later the Luftwaffe was in action from Hampshire to Northumberland as German aircraft based in Scandinavia joined in a co-ordinated assault.

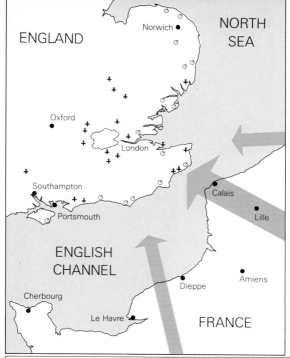

ENGLAND

NORTH SEA

Norwich

Oxford

London

Southampton

Portsmouth

ENGLISH CHANNEL

Cherbourg

Dieppe

Le Havre

FRANCE

Calais

Lille

Amiens

Luftwaffe attacks on southern England, August 1940
The Battle of Britain began at the start of August 1940 with a series of German air strikes on coastal shipping and Channel ports. On 11 August the Luftwaffe started to raid inland, concentrating on front-line airfields and the vital radar stations. The tempo increased until by mid-August the Luftwaffe was mounting up to 1,800 sorties a day. The UK's security depended on a dwindling number of irreplaceable young pilots.

Right: Stripping a crashlanded Ju-88
The RAF had a considerable advantage fighting over its own territory: British pilots who bailed out could quickly return to action while German aircrew were captured. German aircraft which crash landed could be studied for their intelligence value. However, the remorseless onslaught against the RAF's frontline airfields was beginning to succeed by late August. Meanwhile, elements of the German army practised embarkation drills with varying degrees of enthusiasm.

Luftwaffe Aircraft over England

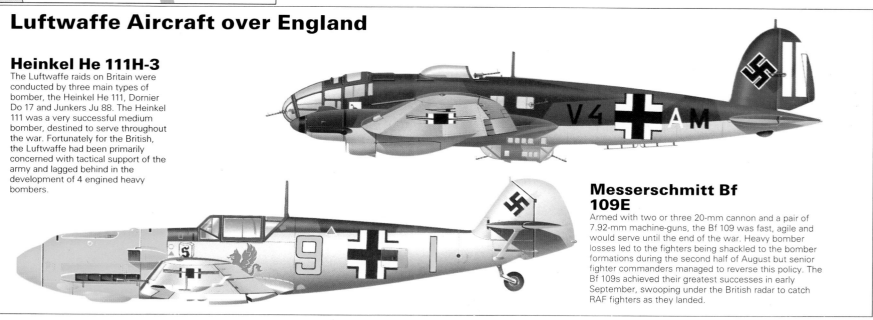

Heinkel He 111H-3
The Luftwaffe raids on Britain were conducted by three main types of bomber, the Heinkel He 111, Dornier Do 17 and Junkers Ju 88. The Heinkel 111 was a very successful medium bomber, destined to serve throughout the war. Fortunately for the British, the Luftwaffe had been primarily concerned with tactical support of the army and lagged behind in the development of 4 engined heavy bombers.

Messerschmitt Bf 109E
Armed with two or three 20-mm cannon and a pair of 7.92-mm machine-guns, the Bf 109 was fast, agile and would serve until the end of the war. Heavy bomber losses led to the fighters being shackled to the bomber formations during the second half of August but senior fighter commanders managed to reverse this policy. The Bf 109s achieved their greatest successes in early September, swooping under the British radar to catch RAF fighters as they landed.

have quickly brought the defences to their knees had the Germans persisted. However, exasperated at continuing losses, Goering ordered the attack to switch from the RAF to the British civilian population with a sudden massive attack on East London in the late afternoon of 7 September.

This marked the turning point of the whole battle, and the easing of pressure on the fighters allowed them a much-needed respite. In the course of further heavy daylight attacks on London, particularly on 15 September and on south east England at the end of the month, the Germans took a heavy beating; the British fighter pilots no longer had to fight over their airfields and could concentrate on the great armadas making their way ponderously towards some unfortunate town or city.

It was at this time that the differing tactics favoured by Park and Leigh-Mallory came into

sharp focus, the former advocating use of single squadrons (because of the short time available in the south to assemble larger forces) and the latter favouring the committing of whole fighter wings to battle. Both men were probably justified in their own combat environments and it must be said that, given adequate warning, Park himself tried to employ two or three squadrons simultaneously. There were, however, occasions when Leigh-Mallory's wing tactic failed to operate efficiently as a result of the time taken to assemble.

The daylight Battle of Britain cost the Luftwaffe a total of 2,020 aircraft destroyed, and more than 5,200 aircrew killed or missing; as with the RAF's losses in France, a high proportion of these men were the most experienced in the German air force, and had been responsible for evolving and proving the battle tactics employed. Nevertheless, whereas

the British could regard the final outcome of the Battle of Britain as a resounding victory, it was by no means the end of the air assault, which now continued (with very different results) under cover of darkness.

The cost of victory in the daylight Battle of Britain was heavy. Considerable damage was suffered at many of the key airfields, of which some were temporarily abandoned for operational purposes. The cost in aircrew lives was heavy, more than 500 men being posted killed or missing, yet on the last day of the Battle (31 October) Fighter Command possessed eight more squadrons in the front line than on the first day, and replacement pilots were arriving from the training schools twice as fast as in July to continue a tradition that would for ever be remembered by a grateful nation: survival had been achieved through the prowess in combat of just 3,030 airmen.

The bombers were supposed to be escorted by the twin-engined Messerschmitt Bf 110, but this proved unable to deal with single-engined RAF fighters. The roving groups of Bf 109s were then forced to fly close escort, which severely restricted them.

A Dornier Do 17 after a crash landing in Britain. The Luftwaffe lost over 2,000 aircraft and 5,000 aircrew in its bid for aerial supremacy. Ironically, the Germans were within an ace of victory when they switched to bombing London.

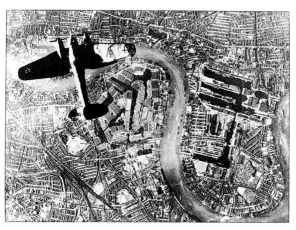

A Heinkel He 111 over the east end of London. At the end of August when the RAF's fighter bases were practically untenable, the Luftwaffe was ordered to attack London instead. The RAF recovered and 'Sea Lion' was postponed for ever on 11 September.

OPERATION JUDGEMENT: The Taranto Raid

While the Japanese navy was planning its attack on Pearl Harbor, the Royal Navy was planning a very similar operation.

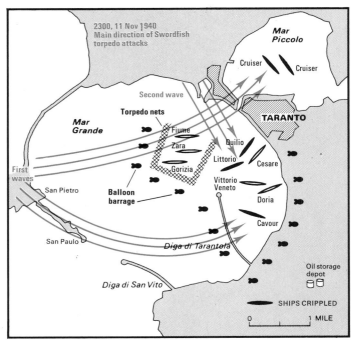

On the night of 11/12 November 1940 21 Fairey Swordfish torpedo-bomber biplanes of the Fleet Air Arm struck at the Italian fleet in Taranto harbour and, in the first major and successful strike by naval aircraft, effectively redressed in British favour the balance of sea power in the Mediterranean.

Italy's entry into the war in June 1940 and the subsequent elimination of the French fleet had given the Axis superiority at sea in the Mediterranean, a situation that seriously threatened British convoys sailing to the UK with vital food, forces and munitions from the dominions east of Suez. Moreover, following Italy's attack on Greece in October that year, undisputed use of the Aegean and Adriatic by the Axis powers posed considerable difficulties in the support of any British foothold in the Balkans that might be considered.

Key to any operations in the central Mediterranean by the Royal Navy lay in the continued use of Malta, both as a naval and air base, and it was with a fine sense of history that it had been intended to bring the Italian fleet to battle on 21 October (Trafalgar Day) with a British fleet of four battleships and battle-cruisers, two carriers (HMS *Eagle* and *Illustrious*), 10 cruisers and four destroyer flotillas. Despite the sailing of two convoys through the Mediterranean, the Italian fleet (comprising five battleships, 14 cruisers and 27 destroyers) declined to leave its base at Taranto; moreover, following a number of near misses from Italian bombers, the carrier *Eagle* was suffering mechanical troubles, necessitating the transfer of her Swordfish aircraft to the *Illustrious*.

Wave top recce

The action was accordingly postponed, and as a preliminary step a reconnaissance of Taranto was ordered on 10 November. A Martin Maryland of No. 431 Flight, RAF, flown by Pilot Officer Adrian Warburton, was despatched from Malta that day and, following an epic wave-top tour of the enemy port carried out in the face of intense flak, full details of the Italian fleet's dispositions were brought back and reported to Rear Admiral Lumley Lyster, the flag officer aboard *Illustrious*. The same evening the crew of an RAF flying-boat reported that a sixth Italian battleship had also entered Taranto.

Encouraged by the survival of the Maryland, Lyster decided to launch a strike against the Italian ships where they lay, and on the evening of 11 November two waves of Swordfish flew off *Illus-*

trious at a position 275 km (170 miles) south-east of Taranto. The first formation, led by Lieutenant Commander Kenneth Williamson, comprised 12 aircraft (six with torpedoes, four with bombs and two with bombs and flares); the second wave of nine aircraft (five with torpedoes, two with bombs and two with bombs and flares) followed 40 minutes later, led by Lieutenant Commander John Hale.

Despite the obvious significance of the Maryland's appearance over the naval base on the previous day, the Italians were evidently caught completely unaware when Williamson's aircraft swept into Taranto harbour; added to this was the fact that the balloon barrage, which had been expected to cause some embarrassment during the attack, had been almost wholly destroyed by storms the day before. Moreover the Italians had decided against

the use of anti-torpedo nets on the pretext that they restricted the movement of their ships.

Two flares quickly disclosed the position of the new battleship *Littorio* (35,000 tons), and with three torpedoes she was promptly sunk at her moorings. Two older battleships, *Conte di Cavour* and *Caio Duilio* (both of 23,600 tons) were also hit, the former never to sail again and the latter, beached to prevent her sinking, severely crippled. In the inner harbour a heavy cruiser and a destroyer were also hit.

In due course the gun defences came into action and two Swordfish were shot down, including that flown by Williamson himself, although he and his crewman survived to be taken prisoner. Another Swordfish failed to release its torpedo.

At a single blow, half Italy's battlefleet had been put out of action, a blow from which the Italians

Four out of six

July 1940: battleships Conte di Cavour *and* Cesare *in Heraklion harbour, Crete. Only timid leadership was preventing the Italian navy from dominating the Mediterranean.*

Cunningham's plans were made possible by the arrival of HMS Illustrious *in September. Probably the toughest aircraft-carriers of their time, the 'Illustrious' class carried 45 aircraft.*

The Swordfish attacked in two waves, the first taking off from Illustrious *at 20.40, and the second at 21.30 from a position some 180 miles south east of Taranto. They achieved complete surprise.*

Fairey Swordfish, 813 Squadron, Fleet Air Arm

The Fairey Swordfish carried a two or three-man crew and was armed with a single 18-in torpedo or 8×60lb rockets. It was slow, being capable of only 138 mph at sea level, but at Taranto this was not a disadvantage.

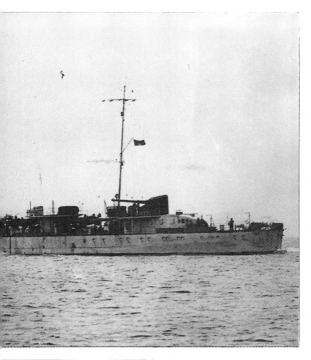

'Zara' class heavy cruiser
Three of the 'Zara' class cruisers were lying in the centre of the Mar Grande when the Swordfish made their attack. In addition to their main armament each carried 16 dual-purpose 100-mm guns: a powerful anti-aircraft battery in itself.

'Soldati' class destroyer
The Italian navy included large numbers of well-armed destroyers. Like most classes of Italian warship they were built for speed and the lightness of these destroyers' design betrayed them after the battle of Sirte when two foundered in heavy seas.

Vittorio Veneto
Vittorio was not hit during the Taranto raid but her sister ship *Littorio* suffered three torpedo hits leaving her under repair until April 1941. Capable of 30 kts and armed with high velocity 381-mm guns, these magnificent battleships seriously threatened the British position in the Mediterranean.

never fully recovered. On numerous occasions during the following three years their fleet declined battle with the Royal Navy, having been deprived of capital ship superiority. In the naval Battle of Cape Matapan on 28 March 1941, when a powerful force of Italian battleships might otherwise have severely crippled Admiral Sir Andrew Cunningham's Mediterranean Fleet, the two enemy capital ships (albeit one of them damaged) sought safety by flight, leaving three cruisers and two destroyers to be sunk by the Royal Navy. In the subsequent evacuation of Greece and Crete by British forces, losses among ships of the Royal Navy were grievous, being in the main inflicted from the air. Had the bulk of the Italian battlefleet been intact at that time losses would have been immeasurably worse.

HMS *Eagle* in the Mediterranean
HMS *Eagle*, seen here after Taranto, was unable to take part in the raid as planned. She had sustained considerable damage from numerous near-misses during enemy air attacks off Calabria. Some of her Swordfish and their crews were transferred to *Illustrious* for the attack.

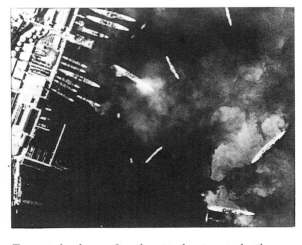

Taranto harbour after the attack: at a stroke the Italian fleet had been reduced from six battleships to two. The Royal Navy could now look forward to a fleet action with considerable confidence.

Littorio lies forlornly on the harbour bottom only six months after she had been completed. Struck by two torpedoes on the starboard side forward and one on the port side aft, she took six months to repair.

One of the two Swordfish shot down is recovered from the sea by the Italians. Two airmen were killed and two captured, but the Italian battlefleet was crippled.

O'CONNOR'S VICTORY: Operation Compass

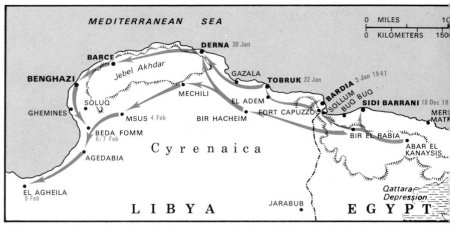

August 1940: The Western Desert Force plans to raid the Italian armies menacing Egypt.

The Italian invasion of Egypt in September 1940 ground to a halt at Sidi Barrani, 96 km (60 miles) short of Mersa Matruh, having apparently run out of petrol, water and perhaps energy. The leading Italian formations then spent the next two months building a number of fortified camps running in a quadrant out into the desert from Maktila on the coast to Sofafi at the top of the Escarpment, and stocking them with food, wines, excellent soft furnishings for the officers' and senior NCOs' quarters, some well-sited artillery and some ammunition.

On 9 December General Richard O'Connor launched Operation Compass, a 'five-day raid' by both divisions of the Western Desert Force, intended to attack and perhaps destroy two or more of the fortified camps, menace the others on the Escarpment, shell Italian barracks and garrisons in Sidi Barrani and Maktila, and, if all went well, advance as far as the frontier wire and destroy any other enemy installations there. They were then to collect as many prisoners as possible before withdrawing either along the coast to Mersa Matruh or down into the desert.

It caught the Italians totally by surprise, the majority of the garrisons in the course of preparing breakfast. The shock of the attack was total. Ponderous and irresistible, the line of Matildas appeared over the crest half a mile from the main entrances to the camps, brushed aside any vestige of defence put up against them, burst through the gateways and fanned out across the camp areas like avenging furies. They were impervious to any fire, even from the Italian artillery, and only minefields could have stopped them – and they were all on the far sides of the camps.

Nibeiwa was in British hands by noon, the Tummar camp to the north by evening and the camp nearest to the coast surrendered the following morning without firing a shot. Meanwhile Sidi Barrani had been occupied, the forward patrols of the 7th Armoured Division were probing westwards to the wire, and by the evening of 10 December one of the greatest problems facing Western Desert Force was dealing with some 20,000 prisoners. Operation Compass was succeeding beyond the wildest dreams and if exploited could go much farther than the limits of the 'five-day raid'.

Bardia was surrounded by the Australians by 17 December and assaulted by them on 3 January; by the evening of 6 January the last Italian defences had collapsed, thousands more prisoners were trudging eastwards, and one British armoured brigade – the

The race into Libya
O'Connor's staggering victory was made possible by the herculean efforts of his troops. In the long race across Cyrenaica the wear and tear on men and machines was severe and by the end of the operation only 20 per cent of British vehicles were still operational.

On the road between Sollum and Sidi Barrani, January 1941
The Italians christened this stretch of desert highway 'The road to victory'. That it certainly became, but not in the way they had hoped! Here a Fiat CR 42 fighter lies wrecked on a captured airstrip. The Italian markings have been stripped off by souvenir hunters.

500 miles in two months

The Italian invasion of Egypt penetrated only 50 miles (calculated to satisfy Mussolini). The Italian forces then dug in and awaited events. They did not anticipate a vigorous counter-attack, and O'Connor disguised his preparations as a training exercise.

7th Armoured Division swept around Sidi Barrani to cut it off from the west while 4th Indian Division attacked from the south on 9 December. The Italians who had expected any British attack to come directly from Egypt were surprised and routed.

Australians examine an L6/40 light tank knocked out during the fighting. In the first two days, O'Connor had taken 20,000 prisoners and smashed the Italian forces in Egypt. But he was not content to stop. The vital port of Tobruk seemed within reach.

Victor of Sidi Barrani: Matilda tank

Capable of no more than 8 mph and cursed with the ineffective 2-pdr gun for main armament, the ponderous Matildas were all but invulnerable to light anti-tank guns. The Matilda regiment sent out from England spearheaded the attack on the Italian camps around Sidi Barrani.

Milizia Volontaria Per La Sicurezza Nationale
The MVSN, popularly called 'Black Shirts', were Mussolini's Fascist militia. 340,000 strong on the outbreak of war they fought under the command of the Italian army but retained their distinctive shirts, collar patches and black fezes with tassels.

Colonel, Italian army, 1940

Italian regular troops wore a grey/green uniform but the army in North Africa generally wore the colonial khaki uniform. This officer wears the lighter *cordellino* twill uniform and carries a Beretta pistol. For field service dress the cap badge was supposed to be embroidered in black.

flag which he had just taken down.

The following morning new orders reached the men of Western Desert Force: they were now to mount a raid on Benghazi, so their advance must continue westwards, the Australians moving on Derna, 7th Armoured Division concentrating at Mechili, on the Trig el Abd, south of the Jebel Akhdar bulge. They were there by 2 February.

Excitement kept them all going. They were driving vehicles in dire need of service and maintenance, over appalling country about which almost nothing was known except that it led in the right direction. They had aboard the vehicles two days' supply of food and water, just enough petrol to get them to the target area – and as much ammunition as they could find room for; God only knew what would happen when it ran out.

But the leading armoured cars were chasing an astonished garrison out of the fort at Msus by the afternoon of 4 February, the first cruiser tanks arrived there the following morning, and by that afternoon guns and infantry of the Support Group had raced down to Antelat and then across the coast road at Beda Fomm. By 1600 a battalion of the Rifle Brigade was established across the road with gun positions in support to their rear and armoured cars patrolling the stretch of beach on their left. Altogether, the force consisted of about 600 men.

Italian counter-attack

When the morning came one small attack was launched against the British lines, by 13 M13 tanks which had been brought up to the head of the column during the night; but it was met by a storm of fire – which in fact emptied the artillery magazines and left many riflemen with the prospect of using their bayonets as a last resort. When the smoke of battle cleared, the astonished watchers saw 13 smoking and stationary Italian tanks, some with their tracks blown off, some with their crews shot by fire through turrets or hatches, one stopped only yards from the tent from which the action had all been directed.

In ten weeks, General O'Connor's force had advanced 800 km (500 miles) and destroyed the Italian 10th Army, taking 130,000 prisoners including seven generals – at a cost to themselves of 550 killed or missing, and 1,373 wounded. It was a remarkable feat by any standards and now, despite the condition of the bulk of their equipment, all the men of the force from O'Connor down to the youngest private were sure they could drag themselves farther, on and into Tripoli, thus driving the Italians completely out of North Africa – possibly even out of the war altogether!

With this in mind, O'Connor's chief staff officer travelled post-haste back to Cairo. He arrived early on the morning of 12 February and at 1000 was ushered into General Wavell's office.

All the maps of the desert which had previously covered the long wall were gone; in their place was a huge map of Greece.

'You see, Eric,' said Wavell, gesturing towards it. 'I am planning my spring campaign!'

Developments in the Balkans had conspired to rob O'Connor and his men of their greatest victory.

7th – had reached El Adem on their drive to seal off Tobruk. Their engines needed overhaul, their tank tracks had already grossly exceeded their statutory mileage, the drivers' eyes were red-rimmed and everyone was hungrier and thirstier than they had believed possible – but they were winning and this made up for everything.

The Australian 19th Brigade and the riflemen of the 7th Support Group arrived on the Tobruk perimeter on 12 January, the other two Australian brigades following on the 17th. On 21 January, covered by the guns of the Support Group and the small-calibre fire of the tanks, the Australian infantry mounted the first attack on Tobruk. It was all over in 36 hours: few of the Italian posts were held with any degree of determination, and the naval garrison around the port gave up without a shot fired, an Australian trooper hoisting his slouch hat to the top of the main flagpole in place of the Fascist

Tobruk was a major strategic prize and was first attacked by the Australians on 21 January. In 36 hours of fighting, the port fell and 27,000 more Italians surrendered to swell the numbers in the British cages to 100,000.

More prisoners were brought in but O'Connor knew if he could cut inland from Mechili to Beda Fomm he could block the retreat of the Italian forces hurrying west along the coast road. The first British forces reached Beda Fomm on 5 February.

The final phase: 6-7 February 1941. Italian troops caught east of Beda Fomm fight desperately to break through. The 10th Army surrendered shortly after dawn. 30,000 British troops had taken 130,000 prisoners.

THE BATTLE OF CAPE MATAPAN

March 1941: Prodded into action by the Germans, Italy dispatches a strong naval force to Greek waters to counter the British.

In March 1941, with Germany plainly about to invade Greece (in support of her ally Italy), the British shipped over substantial army strength from North Africa. After German insistence that the Italian fleet stop this flow, the battleship *Vittorio Veneto* and four destroyers left Naples on the evening of 26 March, linking the following morning with the 3rd Division of three 203-mm (8-in) cruisers and three destroyers out of Messina. Within hours they were joined further by the 1st Division, comprising the 203-mm cruisers *Fiume*, *Pola* and *Zara* with four destroyers from Taranto, and the 8th Division of two 152-mm (6-in) cruisers and two destroyers from Brindisi. The objective was for the latter two divisions to sweep along the north coast of Crete and the remainder along the south, but much-increased Axis aerial reconnaissance, together with decrypts of intercepts, had alerted the British to the general intention.

Admiral Sir Andrew Cunningham, commander-in-chief Mediterranean, discreetly removed all convoys from the danger area and, following a first sighting of the 3rd Division by a British aircraft shortly after noon on 27 March, some 130 km (80 miles) east of Sicily and steering eastward, he directed a light force to be at a point off Gavdo Island, southern Crete at dawn on 28 March. This force comprised four 152-mm cruisers and four destroyers under Vice-Admiral Sir Hugh Pridham-Wippell, diverted from the Aegean. Cunningham sailed the main battlefleet of the battleships HMS *Warspite*, HMS *Valiant* and HMS *Barham*, the new carrier HMS *Formidable* and nine destroyers immediately after dark, at 1900 on 27 March. Unfortunately *Warspite* had condenser problems which limited speed to 22 kts.

Italian caution

Once it knew its force had been sighted, the Italian high command vacillated and then cancelled the sweep to the north of Crete, ordering the full force to reconcentrate to the south of the island. At dawn on 28 March, the *Vittorio Veneto* group had the 3rd Division some 16 km (10 miles) ahead and the remainder about 24 km (15 miles) astern when their reconnaissance aircraft sighted Pridham-Wippell. Being ahead, the powerful 3rd Division was ordered at 0635 to intercept. At this point Cunningham, unknown to the Italians, was some 145 km (90 miles) farther to the south-east, which was the reason why it was 0740 before a *Formidable* aircraft made contact.

Pridham-Wippell, whose 152-mm gunned ships were in any case outclassed, used his superior speed to keep the range open and lure the Italians back onto his commander-in-chief, but at 0850 the Italian Admiral Angelo Iachino ordered his cruisers to

In the nightmare of the dark

Zara sailed with sister-ships Fiume *and* Pola, *two light cruisers and four destroyers. Another cruiser force* (Trente, Trieste *and* Bolzano) *also sailed ahead of* Vittorio Veneto. *By dawn on 27 March, three Italian squadrons were south of Crete.*

As Iachino feared, reconnaissance aircraft promised by the Germans never appeared but one of Vittorio's *spotter planes located Pridham-Wippell's cruisers at 0643. Cunningham's battle squadron, including* Barham (above) *was 55 miles away and closing.*

HMS Formidable's *second air strike put a torpedo into* Vittorio *at about 15.15. It slowed her, but not enough for Cunningham to catch her before dusk. Eight more torpedo bombers plus two from Maleme attacked again at sunset.*

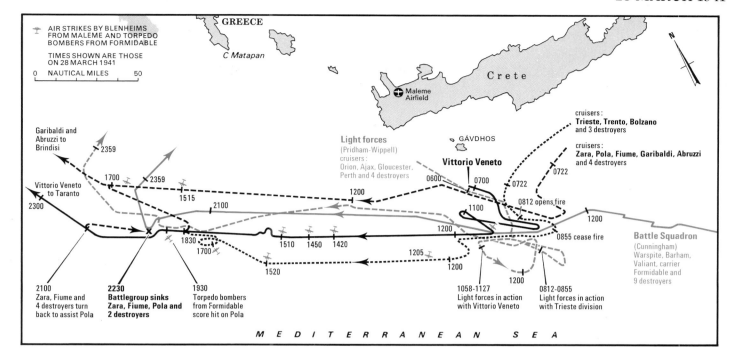

GREECE

C Matapan

Crete

Maleme Airfield

A broadside from *Vittorio Veneto*
The earlier accurate shooting of the Italian navy was conspicuous by its absence at Matapan. *Vittorio* fired 94 rounds of 381-mm shell at Pridham-Wippell, straddling the British cruisers several times but failing to score any hits.

Garibaldi and Abruzzi to Brindisi

2359

1700

2359

Vittorio Veneto to Taranto

2300

1515

2100

1200

Light forces (Pridham-Wippell) cruisers: Orion, Ajax, Gloucester, Perth and 4 destroyers

GÁVDHOS

Vittorio Veneto

0600

0700

0722

cruisers: **Trieste, Trento, Bolzano** and 3 destroyers

cruisers: **Zara, Pola, Fiume, Garibaldi, Abruzzi** and 4 destroyers

0722

0812 opens fire

1100

1200

1200

1200

0855 cease fire

1830

1700

1510 1450 1420

1205

1520

1200

Battle Squadron (Cunningham) Warspite, Barham, Valiant, carrier Formidable and 9 destroyers

The Italian sortie 26-28 March 1941
Admiral Cunningham learned of the Italian sortie the night before and immediately ordered the troop convoys clear of the area. Vice-Admiral Pridham-Wippell led 4 cruisers and 4 destroyers to rendezvous with Cunningham's battleships and bring the Italians to battle.

2100
Zara, Fiume and 4 destroyers turn back to assist Pola

2230
Battlegroup sinks Zara, Fiume, Pola and 2 destroyers

1930
Torpedo bombers from Formidable score hit on Pola

1058-1127
Light forces in action with Vittorio Veneto

0812-0855
Light forces in action with Trieste division

M E D I T E R R A N E A N   S E A

---

break off the chase and the entire force reversed its course, to abandon the whole operation.

The British, however, followed suit, dogging the larger Italians just outside gun range until Iachino, exasperated, sent back *Vittorio Veneto* to deal with them. Suddenly Pridham-Wippell was fleeing at high speed from a battleship firing unpleasantly accurate 381-mm (15-in) salvoes and the returning 3rd Division. By 1050 the British were having to make smoke and zigzag, while being unable to reply at the range, but they escaped at 1115 when six of *Formidable*'s Swordfish carried out a torpedo attack. They failed to register a hit but at 1130 persuaded the Italian admiral again to turn for home.

The retreating enemy looked like outpacing Cunningham's venerable fleet but, following several further unsuccessful air strikes, they were greatly delayed by an eventual torpedo hit on *Vittorio Veneto*'s port quarter. It was already 1510 and they needed to be slowed further before dark. By forming up into a tight, five-column formation, Iachino saved his flagship from further damage but the heavy cruiser *Pola* was hit at dusk, stopped completely and was left behind.

Pridham-Wippell's light forces were pressing ahead to gain contact with the reluctant Italians, their commander pondering on what he would do when this actually came about, when Iachino at 1945 was warned of a British presence some 120 km (75 miles) astern of him. This was actually Cunningham but, still not suspecting the latter's presence, the Italian admiral at 2018 ordered back the *Pola*'s division mates, *Fiume* and *Zara*, to defend her against what were anticipated to be British light cruisers.

Radar report

It was a very dark night, overcast and quiet. At 2015 the only radar-equipped ship in Pridham-Wippell's group, HMS *Ajax*, detected a large stationary ship. While the light forces reported it and kept moving, Cunningham, influenced by earlier optimistic reports from *Formidable*'s pilots, believed the ship to be *Vittorio Veneto* and closed in. *Valiant*'s radar acquired the mysterious target at 2203 and, 20 minutes later, all three battleships were swinging to open their arcs before opening fire when, suddenly, two further darkened ships were sighted. They were *Fiume* and *Zara* – oblivious of the British presence,

and were illuminated by the cold finger of the searchlight of the destroyer HMS *Greyhound* at the instant that the first 381-mm salvoes crashed out. At 3500 m (3,800 yards) whole groups of six and eight of the great projectiles entered the hulls of the hapless ships, whose main armament was still trained fore and aft and whose crews had been rigging for towing.

They were reduced to wreckage within five minutes and fire was checked as the battleline evaded an Italian destroyer torpedo counter-attack. This was parried by the British screen with two enemy ships, *Alfieri* and *Carducci*, sunk.

During this brief carnage *Pola*, devoid of all power, lay in the darkness as a helpless witness. Recognizing destruction as inevitable her crew attempted to scuttle her. She eventually had her remaining crew removed at 0300 by HMS *Jervis*, who then finished the job with two torpedoes.

While Iachino's remaining force reached home safely, it had been a satisfactory night's work for the British who, following the lesson of Jutland 25 years before, had trained for night-fighting where the Italians had not contemplated it.

British flagship HMS *Warspite*

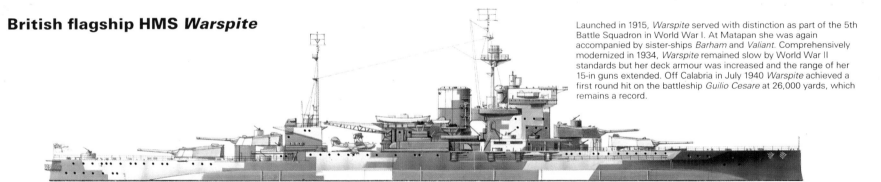

Launched in 1915, *Warspite* served with distinction as part of the 5th Battle Squadron in World War I. At Matapan she was again accompanied by sister-ships *Barham* and *Valiant*. Comprehensively modernized in 1934, *Warspite* remained slow by World War II standards but her deck armour was increased and the range of her 15-in guns extended. Off Calabria in July 1940 *Warspite* achieved a first round hit on the battleship *Guilio Cesare* at 26,000 yards, which remains a record.

Italian AA fire prevented the last air strike hitting Vittorio, *but one plane attacked the cruiser* Pola *instead. The torpedo struck amidships and left her dead in the water. Iachino left her to her fate and made best speed for home.*

Iachino then changed his mind and sent Fiume *(above),* Zara *and four destroyers to* Pola*'s rescue. He knew British cruisers might make a night attack but had no idea the British battle squadron was so near.*

Pola *was located by radar and the others were spotted visually at 2½ miles. The peaceful night turned into a nightmare of destruction as* Fiume *and* Zara *were torn apart immediately, while* Pola *was sunk by destroyers.*

DEATH FROM ABOVE:
The Airborne Invasion of Crete

April 1941: The German army advances remorselessly through Greece. Attention turns to the island of Crete.

The fall of Crete, 20-31 May 1941
The three airfields at Maleme, Retimo and Heraklion were the key to Crete. The Germans gambled that by using all available paratroops together against all three airfields they would capture one of them. Then ground troops could be flown in by transport aircraft.

Night, 31 May, Final Commonwealth forces evacuated from Crete

German airborne and paratroop landings, 20 May

By the end of April 1941 the last of the Allied survivors of the disastrous Greek campaign had arrived in Crete, and as it was obvious to many that the island would certainly be the next target of Hitler's aggression, the wounded, unfit and non-combatant were evacuated to Egypt. Major General Bernard Freyberg, VC then assessed the forces at his command and set about deploying them for the defence of the island.

Two brigades of his own New Zealanders (the 4th and 5th) he posted around the vital Maleme airfields and supported them with three Greek battalions; in the Suda Bay area he left some 2,000 men of the Mobile Naval Defence Organisation and added one British, one Australian and one Greek battalion; to the Retimo section he sent three Australian infantry battalions and their machine-gun support, plus two more Greek battalions; and to Heraklion he sent the two remaining battalions of the British 14th Brigade, one Australian battalion, a medium artillery regiment with rifles but no guns, and two more Greek battalions. By May 7 they were all in position, numbering some 15,000 British, 7,750 New Zealanders, 6,500 Australians and 10,200 armed Greeks. By the end of the month another British infantry battalion, 22 elderly tanks and 49 pieces of artillery had joined the garrison from Egypt.

They all trained, dug defences – and waited.

At dawn on the morning of 20 May they heard a new note in the intensity of the early morning Luftwaffe 'hate', like that of an approaching swarm of bees. As it rose in a crescendo, the New Zealanders at Maleme saw a huge fleet of transport aircraft coming towards them across the sea, and as these arrived overhead the sky blossomed with a thousand parachutes – and the Battle for Crete began.

Assault on Maleme

Operation 'Merkur' called for airborne landings, in two waves, at four places along the north coast of Crete. Gliderborne soldiers and paratroops would assault and capture Maleme airfield and hold it until 5th Mountain Division units could be flown in; the 3rd Paratroop Regiment would drop around Galatas and Canea and then, reinforced by the men from Maleme, drive east and take control of the Suda Bay area. The second wave would consist of two more

paratroop regiments with their artillery who would drop at Retimo and Heraklion during the afternoon. In the meantime seaborne support would arrive off Maleme during the evening, more the following morning off Heraklion, and once Suda Bay was in German hands as many Panzers as possible would be landed. Altogether 22,750 elite German troops were to be put ashore, carried and protected by over 1,200 aircraft.

Yet by the end of the first day it seemed to their commander, Generalleutenant Kurt Student, that this powerful force was about to suffer the first German defeat since 1918. They were being beaten by the remarkable shooting of the New Zealanders and Australians, many of them farmers who had shot for the pot since childhood. Several of the paratroop units were wiped out before they hit the ground, only those fortunate enough to be dropped away from Freyberg's concentrations escaping.

One such unit was from the Assault Regiment,

The Victors: German paratroopers on Crete
The 7th Air Division sustained nearly 50 per cent casualties during the attack on Crete, mostly during the first day. Although the German parachute arm was to be expanded later in the war, it was never to attempt another opposed landing of this kind.

Mopping up operations: house-to-house searches
Some 12,000 British troops were left behind after the evacuation and the Germans searched the island thoroughly. Like the Turks before them, the Germans soon discovered that suppressing Cretan resistance was exceedingly difficult.

Hitler's Pyrrhic Victory

Under Wavell's command six successive British commanders did nothing to fortify Crete. General Freyberg thus had to improvise defences at the last moment. On 20 May the Junkers Ju 52s were preceded by 660 fighters and bombers.

Members of a heavy weapons platoon form up after landing. The Germans planned to land on unoccupied positions but many formations found themselves floating down directly on to New Zealand, Australian, British or Greek troops.

For the first time, the Germans found themselves pinned down by a British force which counterattacked effectively. On the afternoon of 20 May it appeared to many German officers that they had bitten off rather more than they could chew.

78

dropped by mistake so far west of Maleme that it could take no part in the immediate battle. But the men coalesced and marched west towards Tavronitis Bridge, arriving in time to help beat off a New Zealand counterattack – and worry the New Zealand commander. Lieutenant Colonel Andrew, VC, DSO, commanding 22nd New Zealand Battalion around Point 107, realized that the nearby German force was powerful and now concentrated. As his radio sets had broken down he was out of touch with two of his companies, had grave doubts about the other and could get only weak and sporadic communications from his HQ. Feeling that dawn might bring such an attack as might overwhelm his decimated battalion, Andrew withdrew to his reserve position in order to have his flanks covered by his neighbours. In doing so he uncovered Point 107 and with it a corner of Maleme airfield.

It is not too much to say that this move lost the Allies the Battle of Crete. By noon Student had realised that Maleme airfield was now his for the taking, and he sent in all his remaining paratroops, plus more mountain division units, in Junkers Ju 52s which flew unhesitatingly through devastating fire to crash-land on the slowly expanding space held by the paratroops, until they had packed overwhelming force into it. They then proceeded to follow Student's orders to 'roll up Crete from the west'.

There were still five days of bitter action to be fought before it became evident to Freyberg that his own force was being inexorably whittled away while Student's was being regularly supplied and reinforced. On 26 May Freyberg ordered a withdrawal by all his forces across the mountains to the south coast, and asked General Sir Archibald Wavell to organize an evacuation from beaches around the village of Sfakia. A commando battalion had been landed, and this formed a beach-head around the village. Into this over the next few days the exhausted remains of Freyberg's command made their painful way.

British evacuation

The Royal Navy lifted men off the beaches from 27 to 31 May, but then the perimeter was breached and the German forces closed in. Some 13,500 Allied servicemen were taken prisoner and nearly 2,000 had been killed; the Royal Navy lost three cruisers and six destroyers sunk.

But for the Germans it had been a Pyrrhic victory. Of the 8,500 airborne soldiers, 3,764 had been killed, mostly on the first day, and the price in aircraft startled Hitler to such an extent that he declared that he would never again authorize such an operation. Crete was an Allied defeat – but it was also 'the grave of the German paratroops'.

HMS York abandoned at Suda Bay
The Luftwaffe had achieved complete supremacy in the air and inflicted severe losses on the Royal Navy. The short nights made it impossible for seaborne supplies to sustain the defenders so once Maleme airfield had fallen, Crete was doomed.

Junkers Ju 52/3m g4e based at Corinth, May 1941

German paratroopers arrived over Crete in Ju 52s, each carrying 12 soldiers and their equipment. The aircraft flew in tight vics of three at 150 mph, 60 yards apart, at about 400 ft. Speed was reduced to about 100 mph for the men to jump. After they were out, four containers full of arms, ammunition and stores were also dropped.

Thanks to an unfortunate withdrawal by one battalion, Maleme fell into German hands on 21 May. Student promptly landed 600 paratroops and by the end of the day the first transports were ferrying over the 5th Mountain Division.

The weak British air defences shot down eight of the first wave of Ju 52s and a few more were brought down later. The RAF had long abandoned the island, having insufficient aircraft seriously to challenge the Luftwaffe.

Suda Bay, the former British naval base on the north coast, shortly before the garrison retreated south over the mountains to Sfakia. After Norway, Dunkirk and Greece, some British troops openly referred to the army as 'the evacuees'.

THE HUNT FOR THE BISMARCK

May 1941: The battleship *Bismarck*, pride of Hitler's navy, steams into the North Atlantic to attack the UK's vital convoys.

On 18 May 1941 in company with the new heavy cruiser KMS *Prinz Eugen*, the 41,700-ton battleship KMS *Bismarck* sailed from Gotenhafen (Gydnia) on Operation 'Rheinübung'. It was to be a raid on Atlantic commerce and was well supported by pre-positioned auxiliaries. It was to occupy the final 10 days of her short career.

As 11 convoys were at sea or preparing to sail, the British Admiralty was gravely perturbed when, on 21 May, the Germans were reported passing through the Skagerrak. Photo-reconnaissance then confirmed their presence, topping up with oil fuel at Bergen.

Rapid dispositions were made. To reinforce the heavy cruisers HMS *Norfolk* and *Suffolk*, already patrolling the ice-encumbered waters of the Denmark Strait (between Iceland and Greenland), the battle-cruiser HMS *Hood* sailed from Scapa in company with the battleship HMS *Prince of Wales* and six destroyers. Two light cruisers were patrolling the Iceland-Faeroes gap and when, late on 21 May a further flight over Bergen showed both Germans to have left, Admiral Sir John Tovey, commanding the Home Fleet, sailed from Scapa towards the area with the main body of the Home Fleet, which included two capital ships and a carrier.

Into the fogbanks

Weather conditions did not favour aerial reconnaissance and the next sighting of *Bismarck* was by *Suffolk*, entering the narrow gap between the ice-edge and the minefield at the northern end of the strait. Only 11.25 km (7 miles) distant, the British cruiser took rapid cover in a nearby fogbank, informing both her consort and the commander-in-chief. Though coming under fire from time to time, the two cruisers hung on to the enemy throughout the night of 23 May, greatly assisted by their primitive radars. Their performance was copybook, delivering the Germans to the *Hood* group, which established visual contact at 0535 on 24 May.

Vice-Admiral Launcelot Holland wore his flag in an imposing but unmodernized ship whose lack of sufficient horizontal protection rendered it imperative that she engaged a powerful opponent at short range, where flat trajectories would present her thicker vertical armour to major-calibre projectiles. Unfortunately, a necessary change of course during the night had caused Holland to lose bearing and battle was joined at 22850 m (25,000 yards), with Vizeadmiral Günther Lütjens in *Bismarck* slightly forward of the beam. In order to close the range, the British ships steered a course that rendered them unable to bring their full armament to bear, an unfavourable situation compounded by the brand-new *Prince of Wales*'s forward turrets suffering continuous failures and *Hood* herself probably firing at the *Prinz Eugen*, which had a profile very similar to that of *Bismarck*. The latter also had the advantage of a superior gunnery radar, opening an accurate fire at 0553.

At this range, her salvoes were plunging at a steep angle and the third one found *Hood* after just seven minutes. She blew up in a massive explosion that only three men survived.

Now alone (her destroyers had earlier been detached) *Prince of Wales* fought on, down to ranges of 16450 m (18,000 yards). Despite gunnery problems, she hit the *Bismarck* with two 356-mm (14-in) shells before being obliged to break off the action with increasing damage. Lütjens was sufficiently perturbed to signal his intention to abandon his mission and return to a French port.

Fortunately for the British, *Norfolk* and *Suffolk* remained in contact and, as Tovey strove to close the 480 km (300 miles) that still separated his HMS *King George V* and HMS *Victorious* from Lütjens, the Admiralty hurriedly arranged reinforcements. From Gibraltar was sailed Force H, with the carrier HMS *Ark Royal*, while battleships, including the 406-mm (16-in) HMS *Rodney*, were released from their convoys.

KMS Prinz Eugen

Prinz Eugen was a 'Hipper' class heavy cruiser displacing nearly 20,000 tons at full load and armed with 8 x 20.3-cm guns. After escaping to Brest she joined *Scharnhorst* and *Gneisenau* on their celebrated dash up the Channel and back to Germany.

Five days to disaster

Bismarck and Prinz Eugen *put to sea on 18 May. Intelligence reports from British sources in Sweden plus aerial reconnaissance flights enabled the Royal Navy to detect the German operation on the evening of 22 May.*

Bismarck *firing on* Hood: *at 0600 on 24 May the German battleship's fifth salvo straddled* Hood *and she disintegrated in a collossal explosion.* Prince of Wales *fought on gamely but began to take serious punishment before breaking off the action.*

King George V *and the aircraft carrier* Victorious *were still 300 miles away but were close enough by the night of 24 May for an air strike to be mounted. Nine aircraft attacked shortly before midnight but a single hit had little effect.*

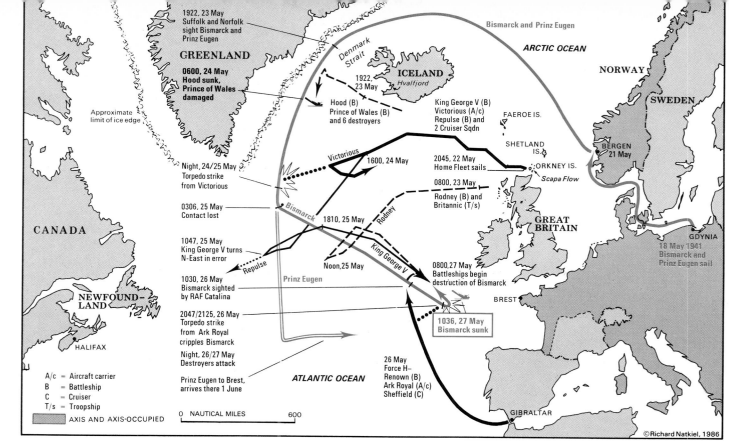

Left: In home waters
The broad beam of *Bismarck* is instantly apparent. She was a powerful vessel but her design suffered from Germany's long break from naval construction between the wars. Nevertheless her speed and 8×38.1-cm guns made her a serious menace to Britain's Atlantic artery.

The cruise of the Bismarck
The *Bismarck's* raid was designed to disrupt the Atlantic convoys. The plan was sound enough but should have been abandoned after HMS *Prince of Wales* holed *Bismarck's* fuel tanks.

HMS *King George V*
Launched, like *Bismarck*, in February 1939, *King George V* was smaller and lighter than the German battleship. Her sister-ship *Prince of Wales* inflicted enough damage to ruin *Bismarck's* commerce-raiding sortie and on 27 May, *King George V* and HMS *Rodney* avenged the loss of the *Hood*.

During the night of 24/25 May *Victorious* closed sufficiently to launch a small force of nine radar-equipped torpedo aircraft. The single hit that they achieved did not slow the battleship, while the latter made a successful feint to cover the detachment of *Prinz Eugen*. These irregular manoeuvres succeeded also in causing the tracking cruisers to finally lose touch, with the result that at 0306 on 25 May all contact with *Bismarck* was lost, with Tovey only 160 km (100 miles) short.

Only after 30 hours of anxious search was Lütjens relocated by a Consolidated Catalina of No. 209 Squadron. *Bismarck* was making for Brest, now only 1125 km (700 miles) away, and Tovey, still 160 km distant to the north, needed to slow her in order to be able to force an action. By great good fortune Force H was well placed, and an aircraft from *Ark Royal* established contact before noon on 26 May, the cruiser HMS *Sheffield* being sent ahead to consolidate the sighting. In marginal flying conditions, however, *Ark Royal's* first strike of 14 torpedo aircraft found and attacked the *Sheffield* in error. She survived nevertheless and acted as a waypoint for a second strike at about 2000.

In the conditions a co-ordinated attack was out of the question, individual aircraft dropping their torpedoes on opportunity between 2047 and 2125. Two further hits were scored, one severely damaging the fugitive's steering gear.

As darkness fell *Sheffield* vectored-in five destroyers (under Captain Sir Philip Vian in HMS *Cossack*), including the Polish *Piorun*. These probed and tormented their great adversary throughout the night as she steered a meandering course toward sanctuary. Almost miraculously the destroyers sustained little but splinter damage, while scoring two, or possibly three, more torpedo hits.

With the hopeless dawn of 27 May, *Bismarck's* weary gunners could still see a destroyer in each quadrant as nemesis loomed in the shape of Tovey's *King George V*, in company with *Rodney*. Manoeuvring independently, these opened fire at 0848 in gale conditions. By 1015 *Bismarck* was a silent, blazing ruin and was finished off by torpedo from the cruiser HMS *Dorsetshire*. It is a moot point whether gunfire alone could have effected her destruction.

HMS Norfolk

Norfolk and *Suffolk* were both 'County' class cruisers: good sea boats displacing up to 14,000 tons and armed with 8 × 8-in guns. Their primitive radar sets were of limited value and they first spotted *Bismarck* visually. Dodging in and out of fog banks they came under fire but escaped damage.

Prinz Eugen returns to Brest. Short of fuel, she was ordered to make her own way home. Meanwhile Lütjens, wrongly believing the British were still tracking him by radar, signalled to Germany and betrayed his position.

Bismarck seen from Prinz Eugen just before the cruiser parted company. She is a little low in the water after the underwater damage from Prince of Wales which penetrated her fuel tanks, reducing her speed by 2 knots.

Monstrous shell splashes rise from the sea aft of the doomed battleship. Her steering crippled by a torpedo from one of Ark Royal's Swordfish, she was smashed to pieces by Rodney and King George V. Of her crew of 2,192 only 115 were saved.

PANZERGRUPPE GUDERIAN: The Drive on Smolensk

The plan is audacious: in just 8 weeks the German army will blitzkrieg its way through the Red Army to dictate peace in Moscow.

'When Barbarossa is launched,' declared Hitler, 'the whole world will hold its breath!', and indeed the forces massed along the Soviet frontier from the Arctic Circle to the Black Sea during that early summer of 1941 represented the greatest concentration of military force the world had seen to that date.

Three German army groups had under command 80 infantry divisions, 18 Panzer divisions and 12 motorized divisions, while behind them waited another 21 infantry, two Panzer and one motorized divisions in reserve: some two million men, 3,200 tanks and 10,000 guns. Already in position by mid-June to supply them were enough stores dumps, fuel and ammunition reserves to feed them over a 565- to 645-km (350- to 400-mile) advance, and 500,000 lorries waited in massed parks from East Prussia to Rumania to rush it forward on demand. To the modern mind the only questionable (indeed alarming) figure to emerge from the tables of statistics among the planning memoranda for Operation 'Barbarossa' is that for 'stabling': 300,000 horses were to play an apparently essential part in this monumental military exercise.

The disposition of the army groups (and the directions of their advances) were dictated to a large extent by one inescapable geographical factor, namely the Pripet Marshes, a virtually uncrossable swamp nearly 160 km (100 miles) from north to south and 480 km (300 miles) from east to west, dividing Belorussia from the Ukraine. Because of this, there could be little contact during the first stage of the operation between Army Group South launched from Lublin towards Kiev and the lower reaches of the River Dniepr, and the two groups to the north. These were Army Group Centre aimed first at Smolensk and then (at least in the minds of the military leaders) at Moscow, and Army Group North launched out of East Prussia first towards Lake Peipus and then Leningrad.

Victory in eight weeks

It was in the northern sector that the greater weight of the attack lay: 50 infantry, 13 Panzer and nine motorized divisions between the groups and, of the two, Army Group Centre was the stronger. Under the command of the icily aristocratic Generalfeldmarschall Fedor von Bock were two infantry armies, the 9th and the 4th, and two Panzer formations, III Panzergruppe under General Hermann Hoth and II Panzergruppe under General Heinz Guderian. These were the armies whose commanders intended to reduce Napoleon's feat of arms of 129 years earlier to historical obscurity, for they planned to reach Moscow in less than eight weeks and to annihilate the Soviet army in the process.

In this hope they were encouraged by Hitler, who had assured them 'We have only to kick in the front door and the whole rotten Russian edifice will come tumbling down!'

Guderian's first task was to throw his Panzergruppe across the River Bug on each side of the fortress of Brest-Litovsk, capture the fortress and then drive precipitously forward with his armoured spearheads towards the city of Minsk, curving up to it from the south to meet Hoth's spearheads coming down from the north. Thus would the Soviet forces immediately behind their attack fronts be isolated in a huge cauldron in which, once their supplies had run out, they would have little alternative but to surrender.

This was all achieved in five days of breathtaking exhilaration which seemed to confirm Hitler's pronouncements and the optimism of the Wehrmacht leaders. On the afternoon of 27 June the leading tanks of the 17th Panzer Division drove into Minsk to meet the spearheads of Hoth's III Panzergruppe, which had covered 320 km (200 miles) in five days and accomplished the first stage of their mission.

But behind them they had left pockets of Soviet troops who, unlike those enemy forces similarly encircled the year before in France, showed little inclination to lay down their arms and surrender. There were four of these pockets: the fortress at Brest-Litovsk, six divisions around Bialystok, six more at Volkovysk, and another 15 between Novo-

Gefreiter, German army, summer 1941

Armed with an MP38/40 sub-machine gun, this NCO wears the basic German army uniform of 1941. He has part of a rubber inner tube around his helmet to add local camouflage. Since victory was anticipated before the autumn, no winter clothing was prepared.

House-to-house fighting in Zhitomir
A 10.5-cm gun fires on isolated Soviet troops fighting on 80 miles west of Kiev. As Guderian and Hoth's Panzer divisions raced north of the Pripet Marshes, vast numbers of Red Army soldiers were left in the Ukraine exposed to encirclement.

In the footsteps of Napoleon

The Soviet air force was caught on the ground by the Luftwaffe, many of its aircraft packed closely together on temporary airfields while the permanent runways were modernised.

After just five days, the leading troops of II Panzergruppe were entering the city of Minsk, 200 miles inside the USSR. Countless Soviet units were isolated in Belorussia and some started to try to fight their way east.

The ill co-ordinated Soviet units were repeatedly defeated as the German Panzer divisions pressed eastwards. The pace unnerved some senior officers but Guderian disobeyed orders and resumed the advance on 1 July.

grudok and Minsk itself. The task of first containing and then destroying and capturing them was assigned, in Hoth's and Guderian's minds, to the German infantry of the 4th and 9th Armies trudging stolidly behind the Panzer divisions.

Not surprisingly, arguments arose. Guderian and Hoth were convinced that they must immediately race further ahead, first to Smolensk and then to Moscow, confident that speed would prove the decisive factor in this campaign. And with a burst of that insubordination which was later to mark the whole of the Russian invasion, on 1 July Guderian and Hoth released Panzer units towards the next obstacle, the River Beresina, and were threatened with court martial for so doing by their immediate superior, General Günther von Kluge.

On the same day, Guderian's Panzers met for the first time a Soviet T-34 tank, which blocked their advance for three hours, knocked out five PzKpfw III tanks and was only removed by an attack from the rear with an 88-mm (3.46-in) gun. Fortunately no more T-34s were encountered in the area and then, on 3 July, the order came for the next stage of the advance. So from his illicit bridgehead over the Beresina, Guderian launched the 18th Panzer Division towards the River Dniepr, which was reached on 5 July.

The next three weeks were occupied with the hardest fighting II Panzergruppe had yet experienced, for although advanced units of the 29th Motorized Division reached Smolensk on 16 July, fierce fighting still raged behind them and there was as yet no sign of Hoth's III Panzergruppe spearheads. For 10 days II Panzergruppe had three separate objectives to pursue: to bar the Soviet forces it had bypassed since crossing the Dniepr from escape south or east, to seek contact with III Panzergruppe fighting its way down from the north-west, and to widen its hold on the land east of Smolensk (towards Roslavl and the River Desna at Elnya) into a solid bridgehead for the final thrust towards the Germans' great goal, Moscow.

But on 29 July Hitler's adjutant, Colonel Schmundt, arrived at Guderian's headquarters, bringing with him Hitler's felicitations and the Oak Leaves to the Knight's Cross (Guderian was only the fifth man in the army to receive them) and also the first hint of changes of plan and emphasis.

Moscow was perhaps not so important after all. The rolling wheatlands of the Ukraine would provide the granary from which the ever-growing Axis armies could be fed and, moreover, down in that direction lay the Baku oilfields.

Moscow could wait. Guderian for the moment must go no further east.

Ju 87 Stukas over the USSR, July 1941
Just as in Poland and France, the Stuka dive-bombers proved extremely effective in the USSR. The Soviet fighters were all but driven from the sky by the Luftwaffe, allowing the bombers to wreak havoc on the Red Army which had no answer to well co-ordinated tank and airpower.

Captured partisans executed in Minsk
The war in the East was characterized by ruthless barbarity from the start, practiced by both sides. Prisoners of war were simply a source of slave labour and civilians remotely suspected of guerrilla activities were summarily slaughtered.

Sorting refugees from Soviet troops cut off behind the German lines: the German infantry were hard pushed to overrun the many pockets of resistance left in the wake of the Panzer divisions.

Vitebsk: 100 miles short of Smolensk. The breakneck advance of II Panzergruppe was only halted by Hitler's indecision over strategic priorities. Guderian's armoured forces were ordered to stop and assist in a new drive to the south.

Hitler decided not to attack Moscow but to plunge into the rolling wheatfields of the Ukraine. Ahead lay the Soviet oil reserves at Baku. The Ukrainians were delighted to be freed from communist rule and many at first welcomed the German army.

OPERATION CRUSADER

November 1941: Spearheaded by 700 tanks, British forces advance to relieve Tobruk and drive the Axis forces back into Libya.

Within two months of his arrival in North Africa, Lieutenant-General Erwin Rommel had reversed the military balance in the desert war. The British forces were driven back, Lieutenant-Generals Philip Neame and Richard O'Connor were captured and the Axis forces surrounded Tobruk. A British counterattack in May made little headway and Operation 'Battleaxe' in June was nothing short of disastrous. The UK's home defence forces were stripped of equipment to sustain another desert offensive but the attack broke down with the loss of 91 tanks. The standard of training of British officers and troops, and the durability of their equipment were cruelly exposed as well below those of the German army.

Four months later, the British returned to the offensive with Operation 'Crusader'. General Sir Archibald Wavell had been replaced by General Sir Claude Auchinleck in July and his desire to reorganize and train the men under his command was sharply at odds with the cabinet's demand for rapid results. By November the army in the Western Desert, now christened the 8th Army, consisted of XIII and XXX Corps. They included three infantry divisions and a Guards brigade, plus a tank division of three brigades and an independent infantry support tank brigade. The force included some 500 cruiser tanks and 200 Matilda and Valentine infantry support tanks.

Panzergruppe Afrika

The Germans had reorganized too: in August all German and Italian formations in the forward area were designated Panzergruppe Afrika under Rommel's command. This comprised the two Panzer divisions of the Deutsches Afrika Korps (15th and 21st, commanded by General Cruewell) plus five Italian infantry divisions. The DAK was soon reinforced by a fresh German division later designated the 90th Light Division. The Axis forces were heavily outnumbered in armour with 240 German tanks, including 70 Panzer II light tanks, while the Italian Ariete Division fielded some 140 vehicles.

The offensive opened on 18 November with the British 7th Armoured Division advancing some 40 miles expecting to trigger a German counterattack and meet it on ground of its choosing. But Rommel, his eyes fixed on Tobruk, ignored it. A second advance took place on the next day, opening a gap between XIII and XXX Corps. The movements which followed were bewildering in the extreme as fast-moving mobile forces manoeuvred in the open desert.

7th Armoured Division's two brigades enjoyed widely differing fortunes on 13 November: 22nd Armoured Brigade ran into the Italian Ariete Division and was badly mauled, while 7th Armoured Brigade captured the airstrip at Sidi Rezegh. 21st Panzer Division detached its 120-strong tank regiment and four 88-mm (3.56-in) guns and fought the British 4th Armoured Brigade to a standstill. On 20 November 15th Panzer Division met the 22nd Armoured Brigade and forced it back. The size of the British offensive was now obvious to Rommel and he withdrew the DAK to the Sidi Rezegh ridge on 21 November.

Towards Tobruk

The British forces on the ridge were attacking towards Tobruk. 7th Armoured Brigade's attempt to breakthrough was stopped with heavy losses to the anti-tank guns of the 90th Light Division. As 7th Armoured attacked towards the port it was taken in the rear by the DAK, advancing from the east. Behind them came 22nd and 4th Armoured Brigades who thought they were following up a beaten enemy! By dusk on 21 November, the eastern edge of Sidi Rezegh ridge was in German hands and everyone was confused as to the true situation.

15th and 21st Panzer Divisions struck at Sidi Rezegh, recapturing the airfield there on 22 November. The next day they broke through the British front, joined with the Ariete Division and annihilated 5th South African Brigade. Still outnumbered, but by now utterly confident in the superior fighting power of his men, Rommel headed for Egypt. 21st Panzer Division led the way with Rommel at its head. The German forces swept through British supply dumps, logistic columns and regrouping British armour; nothing seemed to stand in his way.

The 'dash to the wire'

Although the German counterattack had inflicted serious damage on the British forces and completely dislocated the British offensive, Rommel left very substantial units in his rear. His 'dash to the wire' had been premature. In his absence the New Zealand Division of XIII Corps advanced along the Trigh Capuzzo, reaching El Duda on 26 November. The following day it punched through the forces surrounding Tobruk and linked up with the garrison.

Rommel quickly realized his error and turned his armoured columns around to counterattck the New

Waltzing Matilda
Pennons fluttering in the desert breeze, British Matilda tanks prepare to resume their stately progress across the desert. British tanks suffered most of their losses from enemy anti-tank guns, 22nd Armoured Brigade coming badly unstuck charging dug-in guns of the Italian Ariete division at Bir El Gubi.

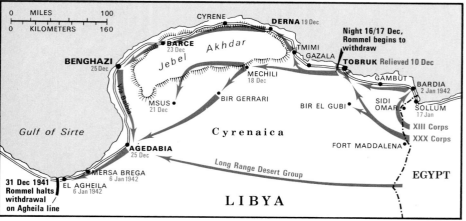

The relief of Tobruk
The British offensive generated a colossal melee in the desert where enemy columns could come from any direction and central control of the battle broke down. Despite his initial optimism, Rommel was finally compelled to withdraw and eventually fell back to his starting point of 12 months earlier. He redeemed his reputation with a masterly attack from El Agheila which marred the success of Operation Crusader.

El Agheila and back

Tobruk was important because it was a major port: if Rommel could capture it his forces would have a supply source close to the Egyptian frontier. Here, Australian gunners fire on the besieging Axis forces with captured Italian artillery.

The British offensive opened on 18 November with the 8th Army enjoying a substantial numerical advantage in armour. Rommel disregarded the attack for the first few days, determined to capture Tobruk while detached forces held up the British.

Italian anti-tank gunners engage British forces sortieing from Tobruk to assist the British relieving force. To the east of Tobruk numerous mechanized columns manoeuvered in the open desert in a very confusing fluid battle.

Zealanders. From 28 November to 1 December, the New Zealand Division received the undivided attention of the Afrika Korps but fought off attack after attack. German casualties now exceeded 4,000 and supplies of fuel and ammunition were running very low. All Axis supplies had to run the gauntlet of Royal Navy and RAF attack in the Mediterranean and the 140 tanks already lost would be difficult to replace. With deep reluctance, Rommel ordered his forces to withdraw to Gazala.

Desert Fox at bay

The German retreat did not stop there but eventually continued to El Agheila, the startline for Rommel's original desert offensive 12 months earlier. The British forces then proceeded to re-enact the disaster of the previous year. Once more, an armoured formation completely fresh to the desert was deployed at the front on the assumption that Rommel could not possibly attack again for several months. On 22 January 1942, Rommel confounded British calculations and attacked. The British 2nd Armoured Brigade was routed at Msus on 25 January and the 8th Army retreated to Gazala, losing in the process 72 tanks, 40 guns and what confidence it still had in its leaders.

Curtiss Tomahawk Mk IIB

Operation Crusader involved 1,000 British and Commonwealth aircraft which were heavily outnumbered by the Axis forces. This Tomahawk wears the ferocious colourscheme of No. 112 Squadron, RAF, which was based at Sisi Haneish as part of No. 258 Wing during the offensive.

Again, the taste of victory
Soldiers of the Afrika Korps head towards Egypt in a captured British lorry with a large swastika flag on the bonnet as an aerial recognition marker. Provided spares could be obtained, British lorries were sometimes preferred by German troops as their Opel Blitz's double rear tyres tended to clog with sand and bog the vehicle down.

Below: The Luftwaffe at play
Men of I/JG 27 soak up rays and play cards by a Messerschmitt Bf 109E. The Luftwaffe provided 600 of the 1800 Axis aircraft which fought in Operation Crusader. Both sides were fully aware that losing the air battle would mean defeat since ground forces were entirely dependent on endless columns of motor transport.

The Desert Fox during 'Crusader'
Rommel studies a map laid on the mudguard of a half-track, 26 November 1941. Determined to retain the initiative he personally led 21st Panzer Division towards the Egyptian frontier: a decision which proved to be a dramatic miscalculation.

Believing he had defeated most of the British armoured formations, Rommel led the DAK towards the Egyptian frontier. But as he overran several rear echelon units, intact British forces behind him broke through to Tobruk. Rommel raced back into Libya.

In the last days of November, the Axis forces counter-attacked ferociously at Tobruk but failed to isolate the port once more. The DAK had incurred heavy losses and its logistic position was impossible. With deep reluctance, Rommel retreated westwards.

In January 1942 Rommel suddenly sprang back into action, attacking the newly arrived 2nd Armoured Brigade. Hopelessly wrong-footed, the British suffered a defeat which cast a dark shadow over the achievements of November and December.

STALIN'S WINTER OFFENSIVE

Never having visited the front himself, Stalin decides on a wholesale offensive from Finland to the Black Sea.

By mid-December some of the effects of the gigantic Soviet mobilization system were being seen. The Red Army now had more than four million men under arms, though there were not always weapons for them and a large proportion of the soldiers were totally untrained: no matter – they could be fed into battle, pick up arms where they found them and, to use one of Churchill's expressions, 'always take one with them'. And they had one advantage over the German enemy: they were warmly clad, for every Soviet citizen knows about the Russian winter which was coming as such a shock to the invaders.

The Orel sector, March 1942
German soldiers help civilians out of a bunker during the last phase of Stalin's ill-conceived offensive. They did not know it, but Stalin's rigid insistence on attacking was doing to the Red Army what Hitler's 'no retreat' orders had done to the German army.

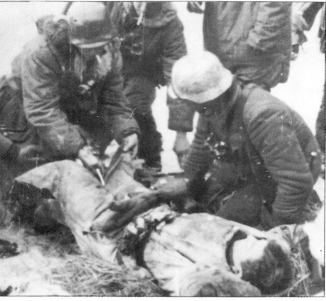

SS aid post, winter 1941
Confident of victory before winter, the German army had pitifully little warm clothing. Boots stuffed with straw and newspaper, and suffering from snow blindness and frostbite, the German troops suffered badly.

On 5 December, on Stalin's instructions, the Red Army went over to the offensive on both the Kalinin and West Fronts in order to push the German Army Group Centre back from Moscow. On the following day they were joined on their left flank by the armies of South-West Front – 15 armies altogether, plus one cavalry corps, and if the Soviet army of those days barely exceeded a German corps in manpower, this first counter-offensive was nonetheless conceived on a grand scale. And because it was attacking forces at the end of lengthy communications and supply lines, forces who were also tired from their recent efforts – and suddenly ragged and freezing – the counter-attacks succeeded despite the lack of heavy weapons or armour to support them.

Gradually German armies were levered away from

T-34/76 tank, winter 1941

The Soviets had husbanded the bulk of their T-34s in readiness for the winter counter-offensive. They had their greatest impact in the counter-attack launched from Moscow which drove the Germans back from the capital. Fast, well armed and well-armoured, the T-34 had only one serious weakness, its lack of a radio.

Stalin's Grand Strategy

Ill-equipped for the weather conditions, the German forces near Moscow were driven back in disarray in December 1941. Zhukov and others recognised that this success should be exploited by more Soviet attacks against Army Group Centre.

T-34s in Moscow, during the last days of 1941. Without consulting his front-line generals, Stalin decided to launch an offensive on all fronts instead of reinforcing the success near the capital.

The Soviet offensives gained ground in many areas because the Germans were simply in no condition to hold the entire front. However, the thinly spread Soviet effort achieved no fatally damaging penetration of the German front.

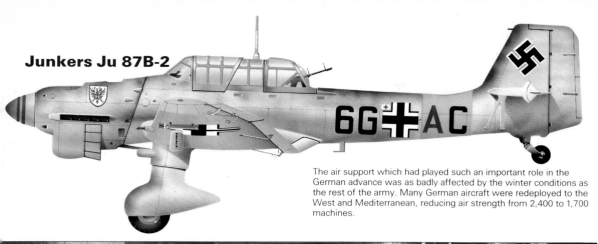

Junkers Ju 87B-2

The air support which had played such an important role in the German advance was as badly affected by the winter conditions as the rest of the army. Many German aircraft were redeployed to the West and Mediterranean, reducing air strength from 2,400 to 1,700 machines.

General Georgi Zhukov had few questions to ask, but a number of statements to make. At both the northern and southern ends of the proposed offensive line, he claimed, German forces had had time to build and occupy strong defences; in the centre, however, the present pressure on Army Group Centre had not only pushed the Germans back, it had also thrown them into considerable organizational chaos. Here, undoubtedly, lay chances for great Red Army gains should it be possible to supply them with sufficient reinforcement and re-equipment – but it was certainly not possible to reinforce and resupply the entire length of the front; therefore the proposed actions on the wings should be abandoned, and everything concentrated in the centre.

His words fell on deaf ears; Stalin held to his plans. As the meeting broke up Shaposhnikov said to Zhukov, 'You were wasting your time arguing; the Supremo had already decided. The directives have already been sent to the Fronts.'

'Then why did he ask our opinion?' asked Zhukov.

'I don't know, my dear chap, I don't know,' replied Shaposhnikov, sighing heavily.

Zhukov was, of course, right. Stalin by dictatorial decree might be able to produce another three or four armies from the apparently limitless population of the USSR, but that decree would not produce weapons of quality or weight with which to arm them. Nor within days would it provide the training those armies needed to use the weapons with expertise – certainly not the expertise of the German soldiers against whom they would be pitted. Nevertheless, attacking across 1600 km (1,000 miles) of front, they did push the Germans back between 80 and 320 km (50 and 200 miles), partially cleared the Kalinin, Moscow, Orel and Kursk regions, and below Kharkov drove in a deep salient (known later as the Izyum Bulge) between Balakeya and Slavyansk which penetrated nearly 130 km (80 miles) to reach the banks of the Orel River in the north and Lozovaya in the south.

Grinding to a halt

But these gains were made almost as much by the willingness of the German forces to go back – despite the draconian penalties for doing so threatened by Hitler – as by Soviet pressure, and as soon as conditions favoured a stubborn German defence, then Soviet lack of experience and supply shortages compelled a halt to the advance. At times, according to Zhukov, their main purpose in attending STAVKA meetings was literally to wheedle out of Stalin 10 or 16 more anti-tank rifles, a hundred light machine-guns or, even more vital, mortar and artillery shells. At times guns were limited to one or two shells a day – and that when the Red Army was supposed to be conducting a vigorous counter-offensive along a 1600 kilometer front!

A few more small but terribly expensive gains were made, but by March even Stalin had to admit that the winter offensive was over. Until Soviet industry could produce armaments in vast quantities the best that could be expected of the Red Army was that it might hang grimly on and, in doing so, gather experience at all levels.

Repairing a BT tank
Isolated in his Kremlin bunker, surrounded by sycophantic officers, Stalin had no understanding of the difficulties faced by front-line Soviet soldiers. Despite courageous efforts the Red Army lacked the equipment and training to mount a full-scale attack all along the line.

the outskirts of Moscow, the pincers on each side bent back. And if the distances the Red Army advanced during those days were miniscule compared with those of the German army in the summer, this did not affect the fact that the Red Army was going forwards, the Wehrmacht backwards – with inevitable effects upon their morale, and upon Stalin's. On 17 December he issued orders to armies of the Leningrad Front and to the Volkhov and North-West Fronts beside them. They were to drive south-west against German Army Group North, both to check the encirclement of Peter the Great's city and to prevent a link-up between German and Finnish forces. Stalin also planned to drive a wedge between Army Groups North and Centre with a drive by the 4th Shock Army, aimed – with rather extravagant optimism – at Smolensk.

Far to the south Stalin's directives also launched 20,000 men in 14 transports and a Force 8 gale across nearly 160 km (100 miles) of the Black Sea, from Novorossiisk to the Kerch Peninsula, where they landed to pose what General Erich von Manstein admitted was a serious threat to his 11th Army besieging Sevastopol. Then on 5 January, at a suddenly convened meeting of STAVKA (Soviet high command), Stalin announced an all-out offensive along the entire front from the Baltic to the Black Sea.

It was certainly a grandiose plan. The main blow was to be delivered in front of Moscow by the armies of the Western, Kalinin and Bryansk Fronts with the left wing of North-Western Front, all against Army Group Centre. Army Group North was to be defeated by the Leningrad Front, the right wing of the North-Western Front and the Baltic Fleet; Army Group South was to be flung out of the Donbass by the South-Western and Southern Fronts, while the Crimea was to be liberated by the Caucasus Front and the Black Sea Fleet. All offensives were to start immediately; were there any questions?

Hitler, as oblivious to front-line reality as Stalin, ordered no retreat but these German soldiers have had enough and surrender to Soviet troops on the Moscow front. Elsewhere the Soviet offensive gained up to 200 miles.

Evidence of German atrocities came to light as the Soviets advanced. This, in turn, led to increasingly barbaric treatment of captured Germans, and the war in the East became steadily more brutal.

German counter-attacks stabilised the front in a few sectors but it was the arrival of the spring thaw in March which stopped most operations by immersing the front in mud. By attacking on so wide a front, Stalin had missed a valuable opportunity.

DAY OF INFAMY: Pearl Harbor

Sunday 7 December 1941: The US Pacific Fleet lies peacefully at anchor unaware that 183 hostile Japanese aircraft are approaching.

Rich in ambition but poor in natural resources, Japan had long planned the creation of a so-called Greater East Asia Co-Prosperity Sphere, and the straits of the European colonial powers by 1941 stimulated her to occupy part of French Indo-China in July 1941. In response the USA, the UK and the Netherlands Indies staged a potentially crippling embargo on oil exports to Japan which, from this point, saw war as inevitable. It was to take the form of a rapid conquest to the defined limits of the Sphere, followed by bargaining with the Western powers from a position of strength and before their superior industrial capacity could be brought to bear, obliging them to accept the status quo as a condition for peace.

The Far Eastern forces of the warring European powers had been drastically thinned, but the US Navy's Pacific Fleet, based on Hawaii, was a major threat and would react strongly to any violation of American territory. It needed to be eliminated – a requirement simplified by its being concentrated within Pearl Harbor. British strikes against Oran, and more particularly Taranto, had confirmed the results of exercises already conducted by the Japanese of the feasibility of causing great damage with little loss. Japan had set a precedent in 1904 for attacking without the formalities of declaring war. All the ingredients were there for a pre-emptive attack on Pearl Harbor.

The commander-in-chief of the Combined Fleet, Admiral Isoroku Yamamoto, entrusted the attack to Vice-Admiral Chuichi Nagumo, with the six largest of Japan's 10 carriers. Between them they could stow about 450 aircraft, equally divided between torpedo bombers, dive-bombers and fighters. Reconnaissance was largely the province of the especially developed long-range Aichi E13A ('Jake') floatplanes, carried by the escorting battleships and cruisers, particularly the *Tone* and *Chikuma*, modified to carry six each. By this means the strike capacity of the carriers was considerably enhanced.

Special shallow-running 450-mm (17.7-in) torpedoes and 800-kg (1,764-lb) armour-piercing bombs modified from 356-mm (14-in) shells were developed and exhaustively tested. No less than 27 submarines, some carrying midgets, were sailed to the area of Hawaii during November 1941, though they were destined to play little part in the action. Nagumo's force, having assembled in the Kuriles in great secrecy, sailed on 26 November. At easy speed, with refuelling tankers in company, the force took a circuitous route through the desolate and deserted northern Pacific. Concealed by continuous thick weather it arrived totally undetected at its launch point, 440 km (275 miles) due north of Hawaii early on Sunday, 7 December.

At first light floatplanes had confirmed the composition of the American fleet at Pearl and that no ships were at sea in the flightpath, but that the most-desired targets, the American carriers, were absent. (Of the three carriers in the Pacific, USS *Enterprise* and *Lexington* were at sea delivering Marine Corps aircraft to Wake and Midway, while USS *Saratoga* was at San Diego).

Into the dawn

So poor was the weather that Nagumo began launching early, at 0530, the 51 dive-bombers, 49 high-level bombers, 40 torpedo aircraft and 43 fighters being formed up by 0615. This prompt start inadvertently saw the raid being delivered ahead of the declaration of war, instead of a nominal 30 minutes afterward, as had been planned.

Clear weather was found over the islands and, in the exhilaration of the moment and despite all planning, all types of aircraft attacked simultaneously.

At 0755 all six US airfields were dive-bombed, then strafed to complete the job and prevent any fighters taking off. Simultaneously, achieving complete surprise, the remaining 140 aircraft fell on the fleet, virtually without opposition. Seven battleships were moored off Ford Island in what was termed 'Battleship Row', an eighth (*Pennsylvania*) being in dock in the Navy Yard. These were the Aunt Sallies and, within minutes, the *West Virginia* had absorbed seven torpedoes. She was still settling in the shallow water when, at 0810, the next in line (*Arizona*) was shattered by a devastating explosion

Aichi D3A 'Val' dive bomber

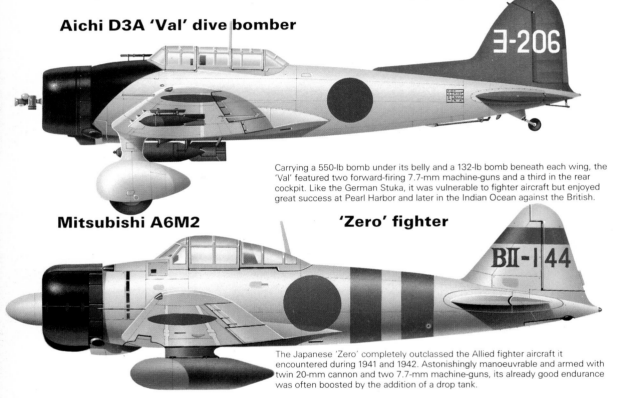

Carrying a 550-lb bomb under its belly and a 132-lb bomb beneath each wing, the 'Val' featured two forward-firing 7.7-mm machine-guns and a third in the rear cockpit. Like the German Stuka, it was vulnerable to fighter aircraft but enjoyed great success at Pearl Harbor and later in the Indian Ocean against the British.

Mitsubishi A6M2   'Zero' fighter

The Japanese 'Zero' completely outclassed the Allied fighter aircraft it encountered during 1941 and 1942. Astonishingly manoeuvrable and armed with twin 20-mm cannon and two 7.7-mm machine-guns, its already good endurance was often boosted by the addition of a drop tank.

Soryu, 2nd Carrier Division 1941

Displacing only 19,800 tons, *Soryu* carried 63 aircraft: 21 Mitsubishi AGM 'Zero' fighters, 21 Aichi D3A 'Val' dive-bombers and 21 Nakajima B5N 'Kate' torpedo-bombers. She later participated in attacks on Ceylon, Darwin and the Dutch East Indies before being sunk at Midway.

Throwing down the gauntlet

Fortunately for the US Navy, none of its three aircraft-carriers in the Pacific were at Pearl when the Japanese struck. Lexington, seen here, was delivering Marine Corps aircraft to Wake Island.

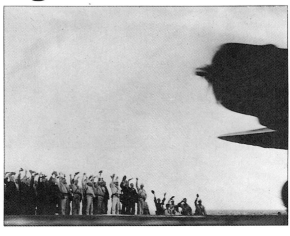

The first wave of 183 aircraft took off at 05.30, found clear weather over the target and attacked just before 08.00. The fleet was looking forward to another peaceful Sunday morning and the Japanese met little opposition.

A Japanese photograph taken early in the attack shows the battleships moored along battleship row, unable to offer a coherent defence. Only Nevada managed to get up steam before the arrival of the second wave.

USS Nevada lies burning
A modernized World War I dreadnought, the *Nevada* had improved underwater protection but this did her little good at Pearl Harbor. Completed in 1916, she introduced the revolutionary concept of 'all or nothing' armour protection. *Nevada* was eventually re-floated but her sister-ship *Oklahoma* was sunk.

as the eighth AP bomb to hit her penetrated to a magazine. USS *Oklahoma* took five torpedoes and was already on her way to capsizing while the two that had struck the *California* were also to put her eventually on the bottom. *Nevada*, hit by one torpedo, got under way but beached herself when bombed by the second wave. Only *Maryland* and *Tennessee* escaped with moderate damage. Some damage was caused to ships in the Navy Yard: two destroyers were sunk in dock and a third, the *Shaw*, exploded spectacularly.

The second wave of 167 Japanese aircraft arrived at about 0900 and added to the general level of damage while meeting a higher level of resistance. Nagumo did not mount a third strike. Uncertain of the whereabouts of the American carriers, nervous of the number of bombers known to be stationed on the island and informed by the returning second wave that most of the target area was, in any case, obliterated by dense palls of smoke, he pulled away to the north and was never sighted by the Americans.

For the loss of 29 aircraft he had secured a significant, but not decisive, victory. In addition to the damage to the fleet, nearly 200 US aircraft had been destroyed, mostly on the ground. A foolish oversight in planning had left undamagd the extensive tank farms, the dockyard installations and the submarine base. Pearl Harbor was still functioning and the carriers were still intact. Of equal importance, the Americans were fired with a dreadful resolve to avenge the 2,403 lives that had been lost.

Pearl Naval Station ablaze
All six airfields on Oahu were attacked, most American fighter planes being destroyed on the ground. Fortunately the majority of dockyard installations remained intact and the damage, although spectacular, had not crippled the Pacific Fleet.

The second wave of Japanese planes struck at 09.00 and Nevada was hit repeatedly and beached. Nagumo decided against a third strike after the glowing damage reports received from his aircrew, and the Japanese fleet steamed away.

USS West Virginia *and* Tennessee: *the latter had in fact, escaped serious damage but* West Virginia *was resting on the bottom after seven torpedo hits. For the loss of less than 30 aircraft, the US battleship force had been crippled.*

Pennsylvania *was in the dockyard during the attack and not badly hit. The Japanese attack committed them to a war against the most powerful industrial nation in the world. It was a military victory but a political disaster.*

DEATH ON THE NEVA: The Siege of Leningrad

Anti-aircraft guns in action
German and Finnish aircraft bombed Leningrad repeatedly but failed to permanently destroy the arms and tank factories within the city. Once supplies could be brought across Lake Ladoga in the winter, the defences took on a new lease of life.

1 September 1941: The German Army Group North begins to bombard the sprawling city of Leningrad.

Leningrad was one of the primary objectives of the opening phase of Operation 'Barbarossa' in June 1941. The German invasion of the USSR was planned to take place along three main axes, the most northerly of which was the responsibility of Army Group North under the command of Generalfeldmarschall Wilhelm Ritter von Leeb and, paradoxically, such was the success of the opening phase of the campaign that was to cost Germany the war, that in five days Army Group North had covered half the distance to Leningrad.

But at that point a series of massive battles on the central front started to divert the impetus away from the north. The reduced Army Group North forces

Aboard a Sturmgeschutz
A German assault gun fitted for winter warfare with additional wide tracks. Try as they might, the Germans could not stop the trickle of supplies reaching the city during 1942 and attacks on the perimeter became increasingly costly.

The Leningrad lifeline
By clinging tenaciously to the southern shores of Lake Ladoga, the Soviets managed to keep a supply line open to Leningrad. In winter the lake froze solid enough for trucks and even a light railway to pass over. Under air and artillery bombardment, the winter road over the lake was a dangerous route indeed.

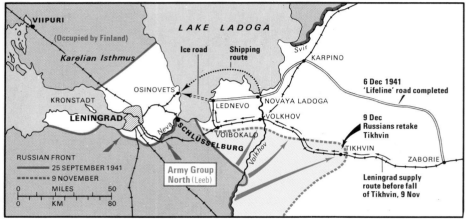

still moved towards the 'Cradle of the Revolution' but at a reduced speed, so that it was not until September that the approaches to the city were in sight. By that time the defenders had sensed their danger and the populace was put to work to construct defences and anti-tank ditches on the approaches. The Germans themselves assisted this defence by constantly diverting their efforts southwards away from their objective as the approaches to Moscow beckoned, but eventually a definite operational plan to take the city was made. The Finns, the reluctant allies of Germany, were coerced into joining the campaign but did little more than cross the Svir river and establish themselves around Lake Ladoga.

By the time the Germans were ready over one million civilians inside Leningrad had rendered their perimeter into a state fit to defend. When the full German attack took place it almost immediately became bogged down in a myriad of defensive posi-

7.62 mm PPS-43 sub-machine gun

In 1942 a Leningrad engineer, A. I. Sudarev, produced a simple sub-machine gun mainly from sheet metal stampings. Designated PPS 42, it became one of the main weapons of the people and garrison. After the siege was over, it was improved and placed in mass production as the PPS-43 to become a standard Red Army weapon for the rest of the war.

The Rise and Fall of Army Group North

German troops of Army Group 'North' advance through Lithuania in the summer of 1941. Hitler's inability to decide whether to go for Leningrad, Moscow or the Ukraine in 1941 eventually denied him all three.

The German grip on Leningrad was weakened in December 1941 as the Red Army counter-attacked from Moscow, shattering the freezing German defenders. Nevertheless, the lack of food and fuel within the city led to catastrophe.

German shelling along the Nevski Prospect. Dead bodies in the streets were so common in the winter of 1941-42 that they no longer excited comment. Over half a million people died in Leningrad, mostly of cold, malnutrition and disease.

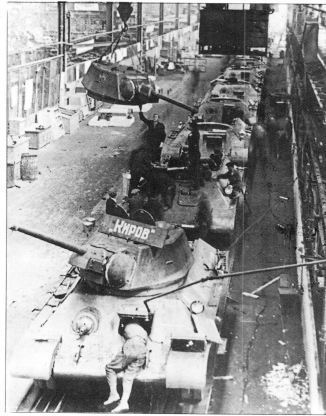

Inside a Leningrad tank factory, 1943
Towards the end of the siege, Leningrad had once again become a major source of Soviet armaments. In 1942, tanks completed here drove out of the gates and straight into action.

Sailor of the Baltic Fleet 1943

Many men of the Baltic Fleet served as soldiers during the siege of Leningrad and the ships' guns were employed in the defence of the city. Wearing the distinctive striped T-shirt under his quilted combat jacket, this sailor carries a PPSh-41 sub-machine gun.

tions, anti-tank obstacles and ditches. The Luftwaffe carried out constant bombing raids, but the German forces were held. Throughout the attack the German local commander, Generaloberst Hermann Hoth, was restricted by the fact that the bulk of his offensive forces were required to take part in operations to the south, against Moscow, but he used these forces at the very time they were requested to move south. Thus Leningrad made its first major contribution by absorbing forces that might have made all the difference in the battle for Moscow.

The long blockade

The attack on the Leningrad perimeter died out by the middle of September and there began the siege that was to last until the late spring of 1943. It was a rather loose form of siege as the German forces involved could never fully control the whole city boundary and Lake Ladoga could usually be kept open. The Finns did little to assist the Germans, but a city the size of Leningrad requires a great deal of food and other supplies just to exist and these supplies were never forthcoming through the German lines. The civilian population of Leningrad suffered dreadfully. Throughout the winters of 1941/2 and 1942/3 thousands died of cold and hunger to the extent that bodies lay in the streets for days because no one had the strength or time to bury them.

Supply shortage

The front-line soldiers received the bulk of what food and supplies were available, but there was little enough of that and food could only be obtained by small-scale forays through the loosely-held German lines. Weapons and ammunition supply were a constant headache for the Soviet commanders, who had

been allowed to form their own independent Soviet to conduct their own defence, and they used the slender supply lines that came across the Lake Ladoga ice during the winters only for the movement of ammunition and other such material.

Leningrad could supply some of its own defence materials, for it had long been one of the major industrial centres of the USSR. The KV tank factory inside the perimeter continued to build tanks throughout the siege. As they were completed they ran off the lines straight into battle, while machine tools from other factories were used to produce small arms and spares, among them the remarkable 7.62-mm PPS-42 which was made more with consideration to what machine tools were available rather than any design refinements.

German retreat

Despite constant artillery bombardment by the Germans and constant small-scale raids, Leningrad held on. By early 1943 the worst was over: the Germans had lost the vital strategic initiative and they fell back to the west leaving the approaches to Leningrad open. Battles still took place along the coastlines to the west of the city, but it had held and the worst siege of the war was over. Leningrad had won through, although at fearful cost.

Army Group North abandoned its efforts to capture the city by storm in the autumn of 1941. Although the Leningrad front produced a steady stream of casualties until 1943 there was no longer any prospect of an all-out assault.

January 1943: the Volkhov and Leningrad Fronts join up to relieve the city. Meanwhile, at the other end of the USSR, the pitiful remnants of the German 6th Army were hemmed into one corner of the ruined city of Stalingrad.

November 1945: German prisoners are paraded through Leningrad to the delight of the survivors of the siege. Many of these POWs will remain in the USSR for years in revenge for the German treatment of captured Soviet soldiers.

CORAL SEA: Carriers in action

Japan threatens New Guinea. A new kind of sea battle is in prospect, where the triumphant Imperial navy suffers a set back.

Douglas SBD Dauntless dive-bomber

Capable of 245 mph and with a range of 1,100 miles, the SBD was the most effective American strike aircraft at Coral Sea and Midway. Swooping from 18,000 ft they attacked *Shokaku* and *Zuikaku*, dropping single 1,600-lb bombs which were able to pierce clean through Japanese deck armour.

To further their intentions of cutting lines of communication between the USA and Australia, Japan in April 1942 mounted Operation 'MO'. Its aims were to capture the southern New Guinea town of Port Moresby by seaborne landing and to establish a seaplane reconnaissance base on Tulagi, farther to the east in the Solomons. Where a small force would suffice to take the undefended Tulagi, the dozen transports of the Port Moresby group were covered by an escort that included the new light carrier *Shoho*. As the move was fully expected to attract elements of the American fleet, Vice-Admiral Takeo Takagi was to double the Solomons chain with the two big carriers *Shokaku* and *Zuikaku* and take them from the rear.

Codebreaker success

Even at this early stage of the war, however, the Americans could decode sufficient enemy intercepts to gauge Admiral Isoroku Yamamoto's intentions and CINCPAC (Admiral Chester Nimitz) despatched Rear Admiral Frank Fletcher's TF17 to the area. Built on the carriers USS *Lexington* and *Yorktown*, this force was already in the Coral Sea on 3 May when news came of the landing on Tulagi. *Yorktown* diverted to conduct three separate air strikes during 4 May, which caused little damage but advertised Fletcher's presence to Takagi. The latter could not get into strike range until 5 May, however, by which time *Yorktown* had rejoined her partner farther to the south.

While neither carrier force could locate the other during the 5/6 May, the Port Moresby group, which had departed Rabaul on 4 May, was located, reported and attacked by Allied land-based aircraft. Reacting on cue, Fletcher moved across the Coral Sea to attack it further.

Carrier battle begins

Early on 7 May both carrier forces staged air searches. Takagi located the American oiler *Neosho* and her single destroyer escort. Reporting the tanker as a carrier, the pilot brought down a full-scale air attack from the Japanese carriers which, while it caused the eventual loss of the two ships, almost certainly saved Fletcher from discovery at a critical juncture. As it happened, the Americans had located elements of the Port Moresby group and as these, too, were wrongly reported as including two carriers, Fletcher launched two-thirds of his air strength at what he believed to be Takagi.

Knowing themselves to have been located the Japanese temporarily reversed the course of the transports. As a result the full force of the American attack fell upon the luckless *Shoho*, which could muster only 21 aircraft in total. Engaged herself in launching aircraft, she could offer little resistance:

the combined gunfire of the group kept the *Lexington*'s aircraft at a distance but the *Yorktown*'s, following immediately behind at 1025, bore through the flak and overwhelmed her.

Within the space of 10 minutes she was hit by 13 454-kg (1,000-lb) bombs, possibly seven torpedoes and a crashing Douglas SBD, and sank, shattered. Only three aircraft were lost in this first example of carrier-against-carrier warfare, but Fletcher had been fortunate in remaining undiscovered while his main strength was thus diverted. Recovering his victorious aircraft, he retired under the cover of heavy frontal cloud. Surprised by *Shoho*'s loss, the Japanese deferred the progress of their transports still further.

Dawn on 8 May saw the two carrier groups only 320 km (200 miles) apart. By 0720 each had located the other and each launched an air strike at a maximum strength. By this time it was Takagi concealed beneath murky weather but he was found by *Yorktown*'s aircraft at about 1030. The still inexperienced Douglas TBD crews wasted their torpedoes through dropping at too great a range and at the wrong bearing to take account of the speed of the Japanese. The dive-bombers succeeded in hitting *Shokaku* twice, one hit forward damaging the flightdeck to the extent that she could not launch further aircraft. Most of *Lexington*'s aircraft failed even to find the

Japanese but one that did arrive put a further bomb into the carrier at about 1140.

In the meantime, the mixed 69-plane Japanese strike had been detected in time by Fletcher's radar but arrived as the defensive fighter screen was being changed. A bomb went deep into the *Yorktown* at 1120 but, though severely damaging her, failed to put her out of action. Simultaneously, *Lexington* was attacked by a small group of torpedo bombers which, coming from either bow, succeeded in hitting her twice. A synchronized dive-bombing attack also scored two hits. Her elevators were jammed in the raised position, though initially the flightdeck could still be used. Unfortunately, her Avgas system had been badly shaken, releasing highly explosive vapour. At about noon came the first of a series of gas explosions that were to wrack the great ship, causing fires that became progressively uncontrollable. All possible aircraft were flown to *Yorktown* and the ship abandoned at 1700, later to be sunk by torpedo.

The effect of the Coral Sea action was to oblige the Japanese to abandon their seaborne invasion of Port Moresby. Any further attempts were out of the question because of the imminent fleet operation against Midway. The presence of Takagi's two big carriers at the latter action might have proved decisive, but the 'MO' operation caused their absence.

Nakajima B5N torpedo bomber

Codenamed 'Kate' by the Allies, this three-man aircraft was the best torpedo-bomber in the world in 1942. Capable of 235 mph and with a range of 1,237 miles, its only weakness was the defensive armament – a single 7.7-mm machine-gun in the rear cockpit.

"Scratch one flat-top!"

Yorktown launched her dive-bombers at the Japanese landings on 4 May but inflicted little damage. She rejoined Lexington. *On 7 May the Japanese mistook an oil tanker for a carrier and attacked her instead of Fletcher's carriers.*

US reconnaissance aircraft located an enemy carrier force and Fletcher launched a full strike. The squadron turned out to be the Japanese group heading for Port Moresby. Here the small Japanese carrier Shoho *takes her fatal torpedo hit.*

Shortly after dawn on 8 May US and Japanese carrier fleets had located each other. Both launched full air strikes at a range of 200 miles. Yorktown's Devastator torpedo-bombers were the first to engage, attacking Shokaku at 10.30.

The one that got away:
Shokaku
A Dauntless flown by Lt
Powers of *Yorktown* scored a
direct hit on *Shokaku* at the
cost of both crew members'
lives. The carrier survived, but
she lost most of her air group
at Coral Sea and was thus
unable to take part in the
Midway operation.

The collapse of Operation
'MO'
The Japanese amphibious
assault on Port Moresby was
abandoned after the sinking of
Shoho removed its fighter
cover. In the subsequent
exchange of air strikes the
Japanese lost 86 aircraft
which prevented *Shokaku* or
Zuikaku fighting at Midway
where they could have made
all the difference.

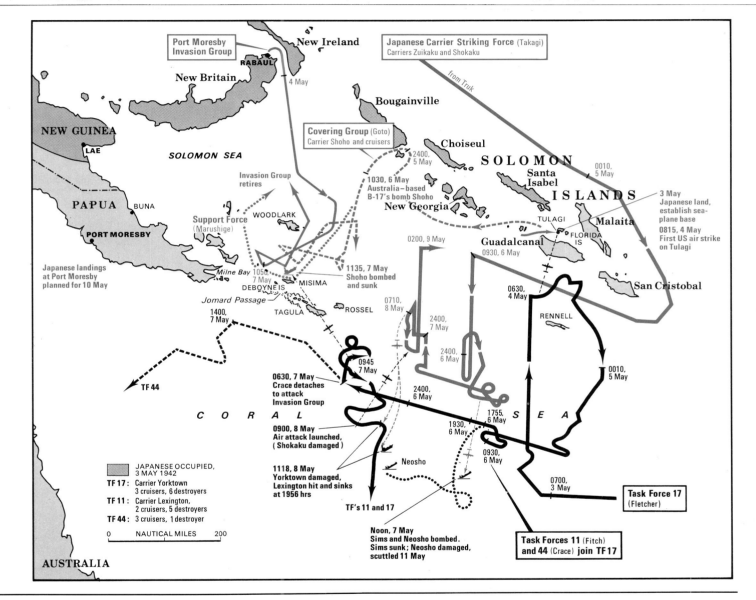

Port Moresby Invasion Group

New Ireland

Japanese Carrier Striking Force (Takagi)
Carriers Zuikaku and Shokaku

RABAUL

New Britain

4 May

from Truk

Bougainville

NEW GUINEA

LAE

SOLOMON SEA

Covering Group (Goto)
Carrier Shoho and cruisers

2400,
5 May

Choiseul

SOLOMON

Santa
Isabel

0010,
5 May

PAPUA

BUNA

Invasion Group
retires

New Georgia

ISLANDS

3 May
Japanese land,
establish sea-
plane base

Support Force
(Marushige)

WOODLARK

1030, 6 May
Australia–based
B-17's bomb Shoho

TULAGI

0815, 4 May
First US air strike
on Tulagi

PORT MORESBY

0200, 9 May

FLORIDA
IS

MALAITA

Japanese landings
at Port Moresby
planned for 10 May

Milne Bay 1050,
7 May
MISIMA

1135, 7 May
Shoho bombed
and sunk

0930, 6 May

Guadalcanal

0630,
4 May

San Cristobal

DEBOYNE IS

Jomard Passage

TAGULA

ROSSEL

0710,
8 May

RENNELL

1400,
7 May

2400,
7 May

0010,
5 May

TF 44

2400,
6 May

C O R A L

0945
7 May

0630, 7 May
Crace detaches
to attack
Invasion Group

2400,
6 May

1755,
6 May

S E A

0900, 8 May
Air attack launched,
(Shokaku damaged)

1930,
6 May

0930,
6 May

1118, 8 May
Yorktown damaged,
Lexington hit and sinks
at 1956 hrs

Neosho

0700,
3 May

Task Force 17
(Fletcher)

JAPANESE OCCUPIED,
3 MAY 1942

TF 17: Carrier Yorktown
3 cruisers, 6 destroyers

TF 11: Carrier Lexington,
2 cruisers, 5 destroyers

TF 44: 3 cruisers, 1 destroyer

TF's 11 and 17

AUSTRALIA

0   NAUTICAL MILES   200

Noon, 7 May
Sims and Neosho bombed.
Sims sunk; Neosho damaged,
scuttled 11 May

**Task Forces 11 (Fitch)
and 44 (Crace) join TF 17**

Shokaku or her sister-ship Zuikaku *manoeuvres
frantically as the American aircraft attack. The
carriers combed the tracks of the TBD's torpedoes
but* Shokaku *took a 1,000-lb bomb on her flight
deck, putting her out of action.*

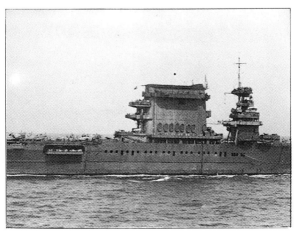

The Japanese air strike put two torpedoes into
Lexington *and scored bomb hits on both US
carriers. However, both vessels survived and
recovered their own planes. This is the last known
picture of* Lexington *in operational condition.*

Coral Sea *appeared to be a resounding American
victory until* Lexington *suffered a series of
explosions which tore her apart. However, although
the loss of* Lexington *was a bitter blow, Japan's
advance on Australia was stopped.*

BATTLE ON THE KOKODA TRAIL: New Guinea 1942-3

Coral Sea ended Japanese plans for an amphibious invasion of Port Moresby. Now it was the turn of the Japanese army.

While the main drive of the great Japanese offensive during the months following Pearl Harbor had been to the south-west of the home islands, on each side of a central axis aimed at Singapore, the Japanese commanders also appreciated that in the end they would have to defend themselves from American forces from the east. They had therefore consolidated control of the island chains to the south – the Marianas, the Carolines and especially the island and harbour of Truk – and as early as 23 January 1942 they had put a small force ashore at Kavieng in New Ireland, then one at Rabaul on New Britain, where their force of 5,000 quickly overcame the 1,400 Australian troops garrisoned there.

In early March Japanese troops landed unopposed at Lae and Salamaua in Huon Bay on the north coast of New Guinea, and busied themselves for several weeks building up stores and workshops for a possible further advance to the south. Because they were subjected to so little interference – even while they built a fair-sized airfield of obvious tactical importance – and as they soon heard that a large fleet was sailing from the Carolines to capture Port Moresby, they remained fairly confident that their progress to the south would be comparatively easy, their greatest problems being presented by the admittedly difficult terrain.

The defeat of the invasion force at the Battle of the Coral Sea put an end to such comfortable assumptions, however, though not to headquarters plans for the capture of Port Moresby: as the Japanese navy had failed to reach the place, then the Japanese army would do so. But the necessary reorganization took time, and meanwhile the Australian presence in the area increased.

Already Australian commandos – independent companies – had been harassing the Japanese perimeters, and in April they were joined by another company. Shortly afterwards two Australian brigades arrived at Port Moresby, another was sent to Milne Bay on the eastern tip of the peninsula and two battalions were ordered to push up and over the Owen Stanley Range along the Kokoda Trail to try to reach Buna on the north coast. There they were to construct an airfield from which the Japanese positions along the coast could be attacked.

Landings at Buna

Not surprisingly, the Japanese reacted swiftly and in some strength. On 21 July 2,000 men went ashore at Buna (the Australian battalions were still on their way); by the end of the month 13,500 men of Lieutenant-General Harukichi Hyakutake's 17th Army had followed them, driven south along the trail sweeping up the independent companies as they went, almost effortlessly driving back the two battalions as well, and by 27 July had arrived at Kokoda. By mid-August they were driving even farther south, though by now Lieutenant General F. F. Rowell, commanding the Australians, had pushed more men up to meet them, while Australian and American fighter aircraft were very effectively shooting up the narrow and overflowing Japanese communications. Once again, that iron law was coming into operation: the Japanese were nearly 160 km (100 miles) of appalling going from their bases, the Australians were only 50 km (32 miles) from theirs.

Moreover, the Australians had their homeland with many more divisions, many more aircraft and, compared with the Japanese, a positively inexhaustible storehouse, just behind them.

The Japanese advance was stopped by 25 August, but on the following day the second prong of the Japanese attack formed with a landing of nearly

Japanese private first class

Armed with a Type 100 8-mm sub-machine gun, this Japanese soldier wears the standard uniform of the Japanese armies fighting in the Pacific. Instead of boots he wears canvas *tabi* and he has a steel helmet on top of his field cap with neck flaps.

Across the Owen Stanley Mountains

In the first months of 1942, Japanese troops were landed in New Guinea and New Britain to begin the conquest of the south west Pacific. The eastern coast of New Guinea and Papua was occupied and the army prepared to advance on Port Moresby.

To stop the Japanese, the Australians had to defend the Owen Stanley mountain range: 13,000-ft peaks covered in dense rainforest. It was probably the most demanding battlefield of World War II.

By 27 July, the Japanese 17th Army had fought its way up into the mountains and reached Kokoda. In the next three weeks the Japanese continued to push the Australians back in a series of savagely fought rearguard actions.

Mitsubishi A6M2, 6th Kokutai, 1942

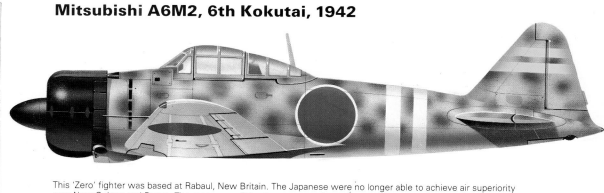

This 'Zero' fighter was based at Rabaul, New Britain. The Japanese were no longer able to achieve air superiority over New Guinea and Papua. The resources of the Japanese empire were not able to sustain operations over such an ocean-wide theatre of operations.

'When the mist was on the rice fields'
Advancing through a paddy field, Australian troops wear a mixture of issue kit but one has acquired an American helmet and the Thompson gun to go with it. The Australians sustained nearly 6,000 casualties in action but many more were incapacitated by tropical diseases.

Towards Port Moresby
As the Japanese advanced higher into the mountains and away from their beach-head at Buna, their difficulties were acute, with every round and every ration having to come over a hundred miles of mountainous jungle.

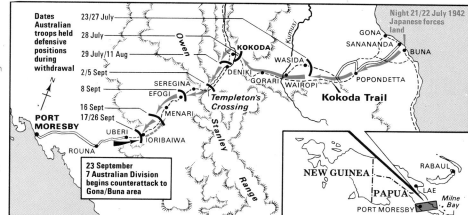

2,000 men at Milne Bay. But their intelligence was at fault for they had expected to find only two or three companies of Australian infantry there, as guard to the small airfield. Instead they found nearly two brigades (the first had been reinforced), two fighter squadrons and batteries of well sited artillery, and although after five days of fierce fighting the Japanese – who had landed a few tanks – did reach the edge of the airfield they were gradually driven back, their casualties mounting implacably and on 6 September the survivors were evacuated. Japanese soldiers had at last been forced to retreat!

It was beginning to happen, too, on the Kokoda Trail. Both the 6th and 7th Australian Divisions were now concentrated in Papua, and on 23 September General Sir Thomas Blamey arrived to take command. Slowly but relentlessly, the Australians began to force the Japanese back up the 'golden stairs' from Uberi, the 'stairs' formed by steps some 25 to 45 cm (10 to 18 inches) in height, the front edge of the step consisting of a small log held by stakes, with behind it little but mud and water; and they rose 365 m (1,200 ft) in the first 5 km (3.2 miles)!

For the Australians the physical exhaustion of just climbing the 'stairs' was almost unsupportable, and were it not for the 'fuzzy-wuzzy angels' – Melanesian porters who carried everything (and almost everyone) with a loyalty and enthusiasm which astounded all who saw it – the job would have taken ten times longer. As it was, by early October

the leading Australian brigade had reached Templeton's Crossing at the ridge of the Owen Stanley Range, and by 17 October had forced the Japanese away from three positions they had formed there – though hunger must have played its part in the Japanese defeat, for evidence of cannibalism was found, and most of the bodies of the dead Japanese soldiers were thin and discoloured with starvation and disease. Allied control of the air was beating them just as much as the assault on the ground.

The Australians retook Kokoda on 2 November and reopened the airfield there from which they could be well supported all the way to Buna. An attempt by the Japanese to stand on the Kumusi river was thwarted by flank attacks by fresh Australian and American troops, and their final stand at Buna came to an end on 21 January 1943, when more Australian and American troops were brought up along the trail and even more were landed along the north coast, isolating the Japanese garrisons at Lae and Salamaua.

The New Guinea campaign cost the Japanese over 12,000 men, the Australian battle casualties amounted to 5,700 and the American figure was 2,800 – but at least three times as many had succumbed to tropical hazards from malaria to sheer heat exhaustion.

But they had proved that they could fight and beat the Japanese, even in such appalling conditions – so long as they had air supremacy.

Fuzzy-Wuzzy Angels: the Allied forces relied heavily on local porters to carry everything from ammunition to wounded. They alone seemed able to cope with the tortuous steps of the Kokoda Trail.

The long withdrawal ended in September. On the 23rd, the Australians counter-attacked, driving the Japanese from Uberi. All Japanese supplies had to come from the other side of the mountains while the Australians were within 30 miles of their base.

Australians go ashore on the Huon peninsula during September. As the Japanese were steadily pushed back up the Owen Stanleys, Allied troops landed on the south eastern coast of Papua and the Japanese drive on Australia was now defeated.

The Battle of Sevastopol: Conquest of the Crimea

Soviet forces in the eastern Crimea are overwhelmed in May 1942. Only the fortress of Sevastopol still holds out against the invaders.

The Soviet attempt to relieve Sevastopol by landing a force of 20,000 men on the Kerch Peninsula during December 1941 had resulted in the formation of bridgeheads around the town of Kerch and the port Feodosia. There had followed a build-up of strength until by April five Red Army brigades had been formed, consisting of nearly a quarter of a million men, together with some supporting artillery and 200 tanks. This was a considerable force, but it had been fed in piecemeal – like so much Soviet strength in those early days – and committed to battle in the same unskilful way.

The sheer weight of German men and metal forced the Soviet rifle divisions in Feodosia backwards, then drove through the peninsula waist towards Kerch itself. The Germans were protected above by Messerschmitt Bf 109s and their way prepared by screaming dive-bombers. Generaloberst Erich von Manstein's task was also apparently made easier by the inefficiency of the Soviet command, and the constant nagging and wrangling of the STAVKA representative, L. Z. Mekhlis (who was also Deputy People's Commissar for Defence and Head of the Main Political Directorate of the Red Army)

Needless to say, the commanders were among the 86,000 men, including 23,000 wounded, who were evacuated between 15 and 20 May across the Kerch Strait to Taman and Cape Chushka – leaving behind nearly 100,000 men and all the remaining tanks. There was no doubt in Moscow where responsibility for much of the disaster lay. Both Mekhlis and the Front Commissar were dismissed and General Kozlov was reduced in rank.

Manstein could now turn his attention and the enormous weight of artillery and air power at his command to the reduction of the port of Sevastopol. To defend Sevastopol the Soviet Coastal Army had some 106,000 soldiers, sailors and marines, 600 guns including those in the heavy coastal batteries, about 100 mortars, 38 tanks and, in the airfields within their perimeter, 55 aircraft. Manstein now marshalled against them 204,000 men of 11th Army, 670 guns including those of enormous calibre in a siege train which he had assembled, 450 mortars, 720 tanks (at something of a disadvantage in such limited space) and 600 aircraft. Most of those who survived the battle were deafened for some time afterwards and, indeed, suffered from hearing problems for the rest of their lives.

The siege opened with a five-day barrage from every piece of artillery Manstein's experts could bring into action, and reminded some of the older members of the 11th Army staff of Verdun and St Quentin 25 years before. The shaking of the earth caused by the mortars, not only when their bombs landed but also when they were fired, would have registered quite high on the Richter Scale – and the shelling was augmented by the bombs dropped by the Luftwaffe, flying in to support Eleventh Army from bases as far away as Perekop and even Odessa.

The main blow fell on the Kmaytsjly-Belbek sector and heralded a drive by LIV Corps towards the eastern end of North Bay. All through the first half of June there was the most bitter fighting, the Soviets defending their trenches and holes in the ground with an astonishing tenacity, disappearing back into them whenever close action paused, and demonstrating that indestructibility which was to impress – and indeed frighten – the men of the German 6th Army later at Stalingrad.

By the third week of June Manstein was sufficiently worried by the apparent lack of progress that he fed the 46th Division into the ring around Sevastopol, bringing it in from Kerch, and then begged more formations from the 17th Army upon the Donbass.

Black Sea Fleet

But eventually, of course, experience plus guns, mortars and their ammunition won the battle, though the Red Army and the Red Navy performed miracles in reinforcing Sevastopol. Destroyers, minelayers, minesweepers, torpedo-boats, even submarines were used to ferry men, weapons and ammunition into the besieged port, on occasion the ship's officers being told that there was no chance of them all reaching the shore; they should try to get as near as possible before they were sunk so that at least some of their cargo might be able to swim or wade in, with luck carrying some weapons or stores.

All the time the huge mortars and guns of Manstein's siege train hurled their massive shells and bombs into the fortress. The huge 80-cm gun 'schwere Gustav' began firing its 7-ton shells into the fortress from nearly 30 km (over 19 miles) away on 5 June, and systematically destroyed the main forts and the huge 'Maxim Gorky' Battery during the next three weeks. Gradually, ammunition shortages, smashed artillery, complete lack of air cover or support after 28 June – not to speak of such human problems as hunger, thirst and lack of sleep – began to take effect, and the German attacking infantry fought their way into the port.

On the night of 28/29 June the Germans managed at last to cross North Bay under cover of a smoke screen, and the following morning other formations drove in from the Fedyukhin Heights towards Sapun Gora; by the morning of 30 June German troops were fighting inside the town of Sevastopol, taking cover in the ruins of the buildings they had themselves demolished.

During the next three days a Dunkirk-style evacuation was organized, with every craft that could sail coming in from Novorossiisk and the neighbouring Black Sea ports, some even braving the perils of the Kerch Straits and coming down from the Azov ports. It is not known how many servicemen and women, how many civilians, died in the siege of Sevastopol; but it had lasted 250 days since it had first been surrounded by German troops who had driven down into the Crimea. And the last 24 days had been of close hand-to-hand combat and devastating bombardment.

The battle had been by no means without cost to 11th Army, and Generalfeldmarschall von Manstein – awarded his baton with the occupation of Sevastopol and the whole of the Crimea – found in July that he was commanding an army, if not desanguinated, at least decimated. It was not immediately available for the next stage of the Führer's plans, which had to be left to Sixth Army to the north under its ambitious commander, General Friedrich Paulus.

He knew exactly where his fame and, he hoped, his fortune were to be made, and his eyes were firmly fixed upon it: Stalingrad.

MP38 sub-machine gun

Often wrongly described as a 'Schmeisser', the German MP38 and its derivatives were designed and produced by Erma. A tough and reliable SMG, the MP38 fired 9-mm Parabellum ammunition from a 32-round box magazine at a cyclic rate of 500 rounds per minute.

Street by Street

Soviet troops advance through a marsh during the botched Soviet counter-attack on the Kerch peninsula. Mekhlis's incompetence lost the Red Army 176,000 men, 3,500 guns and 350 tanks. He was demoted to corps commissar.

The Germans now occupied the entire Crimea. Sevastopol had been cut off by land since the first German attack in December 1941 and relied on the Black Sea Fleet for its supplies. Von Manstein's 11th Army prepared to storm the fortress.

Von Manstein's siege train included the largest gun ever built: the 80-cm 'schwere Gustav' which fired 7 ton armour-piercing projectiles or 5-ton high explosive shells. Sevastopol's mighty concrete forts were pulverised.

Sailors of the Black Sea Fleet
Armed to the teeth, three matelots pose for the camera. The naval personnel fought hard in defence of their base and as the end approached some battery garrisons blew themselves and their guns to pieces rather than surrender.

Schwere Gustav: fort killer
It took 2,000 men 6 weeks to prepare Gustav for firing at Sevastopol. The leviathan fired just 48 rounds but all with cataclysmic effect. Nine rounds were fired into Severnaya Bay, through the water, 100 ft of sea-bed and into a supposedly invulnerable Soviet magazine.

The flotilla leader Tashkent was the last surface ship to enter Sevastopol, bringing in ammunition and taking off the wounded, 22-26 June. After that, entry was by submarine only: 78 sorties brought in 4,000 tons of ammunition before the end.

By 30 June, much of the fortress had fallen and the defenders were being ground down in bitter street fighting. Two submarines were sent to evacuate the senior commanders by Stalin's personal order but the rest of the garrison was doomed.

The last pockets of resistance were crushed on the twenty-seventh day of von Manstein's assault. Here, the swastika is unfurled over the fallen city and the first stage of the German summer offensive has ended in decisive victory.

GAZALA AND TOBRUK: The Desert Fox in action

26 May 1942: Rommel leads the Afrika Korps forward to smash the 8th Army and drive it back to Egypt.

Erwin Rommel had first made his name in a daring infantry raid on the Italian front in October 1917, and the same audacity that enabled him to raid deep behind established positions marked his operations once he became a Panzer officer. His part in the Fall of France in 1940 was again characterized by a deep Panzer raid into the French rear at Avesnes and the subsequent dash to the Channel coast. By 1941 he was in North Africa carrying out a series of armoured operations that constantly defeated numerically superior British and Commonwealth forces which were unable to adapt to the tactics of tank warfare as carried out by Rommel.

By May 1942 Rommel had rapidly learned that armoured warfare in the desert entailed using a new set of 'rules'. In the wide open spaces of the unpopulated desert, mobility and firepower took on new meanings. In the desert there was always a flank to be turned, and positional warfare became increasingly meaningless as mobile forces could turn up from any point of the compass.

In May 1942 Rommel was ready to begin what was to become one of the classic examples of this particular approach to warfare. In that month he had to hand a total of 561 tanks (333 German and 228 Italian) ready to take on a superior British force which had over 900 tanks and numbers of new anti-tank guns. But Rommel did have several advantages. One was that the British tank force was scattered in small packets, and another was that the Luftwaffe had a local numerical superiority that was to serve Rommel well in the days ahead. The British were emplaced in a long defensive line south of Gazala, well protected by massive minefields and located mainly in well-defended 'boxes'. They were expecting Rommel to attack and were not disappointed.

Rommel's attack plan was simple and typical of his methods. Using the relatively immobile Italian infantry to pin the British in their defensive line, he moved his main striking forces south. These were made up of the crack Italian Ariete Division, a unit that Rommel was later to state never let him down, and the bulk of the Afrika Korps made up of the 15th and 23rd Panzer Divisions and the 90th Light Division. These moved south around the end of the British defence lines and then moved north as the Italian Trieste Division carried out a frontal attack on the southern portion of the line. Within a few hours Rommel's forces were well to the rear of the static British lines and began to move towards the Knightsbridge Box, an area which became the focal point of the Gazala battle.

Armoured counter attack

As soon as the British became aware of Rommel's move they started a protracted series of armoured counter-attacks against the attackers. But while the German and Italian units were operating as cohesive formations under central control, the British tank attacks were made by fragmented units operating under various higher tactical controls. Many of these counter-attacks were made in the traditional British cavalry manner by lines of tanks simply charging towards the Germans, who destroyed them by a combination of tank gun and anti-tank gun fire, including numbers of 37-mm and 88-mm (3.46-in) anti-aircraft towed weapons that accompanied the Panzers into action. These fragmented attacks, including some which had numbers of the new 75-mm (2.95-in) gun-armed Grant tanks recently arrived in the theatre did manage some successes, and gradually Rommel's forces diminished in numbers and effectiveness as supplies of ammunition and fuel were expended. Rommel himself saved this situation by leading a supply column straight through the British minefields and lines on the night of 29 May. He was able to do this mainly because the minefields were not covered by defensive fire and thus Rommel was able to bring forward the fuel to keep his units in motion.

The Gazala battles went on for two weeks in series of attacks and counter-attacks that gradually threatened to bring both sides to a complete standstill from sheer exhaustion. As a general rule the Germans and Italians were able to keep the overall initiative, as they were able to keep switching the point they wished to attack and were always able to move out to the south when things went against them. The British and Commonwealth troops generally remained static or else fell back towards their main supply bases in the El Adem and Tobruk

One that got away
A South African soldier who escaped from Tobruk is interviewed by a British officer. Many units in the Tobruk garrison fought a successful battle but there was no leadership to co-ordinate the defence. The 8th Army made no effective attempt to interrupt Rommel's attack.

A question of command

Rommel's attack began on 26 May, concentrating on the southern flank of the British line. The British knew the attack was coming but failed to concentrate, and brigades were beaten one by one by the massed German armour.

Valentines lie burning after Rommel penetrated the 8th Army's centre. He was in fact surrounded but gambled that British brigades would move at their familiar, torpid pace. He was right and defeated Ritchie's counter-attack on 5 June.

On 11 June Rommel was still outnumbered 200:150 in tanks but yet again he fielded his armour together, where it mattered. By the end of 12 June German observers watched the surviving British armour fall back behind the Knightsbridge Box.

areas. From time to time frontal attacks were made against the main line south of Gazala. By mid-June Rommel's supply line was in a precarious state, to the extent that his armoured units were keeping going on captured supplies alone. The Grants, when encountered, were a particular headache for the Germans, who were able to destroy them only by the use of their 88-mm anti-aircraft guns, although the 37-mm anti-aircraft guns were only marginally less effective.

On 20 June the Germans were approaching the perimeter of the Tobruk defences. Tobruk is one of the few ports on the North African coastline, and with this port under German control the Afrika Korps would not have to depend on supply lines reaching back as far west as Tripoli. As usual the British and Commonwealth troops fought doggedly, but they were operating from static defensive positions, and once the Germans were through the perimeter in true Blitzkrieg fashion they were able to roll up the line and take the port along with 30,000 prisoners and masses of supplies and equipment. They were able to put the latter two to good use in the campaigning days ahead.

The fall of Tobruk had a dreadful effect on Allied morale, but the Gazala/Tobruk battles had one long-

term outcome that Rommel could not foresee. With a great success and a new promotion behind him, he carried on his advance to the east, only to come up against the defence lines carefully emplaced at Alam Halfa, south of El Alamein. There the Afrika Korps was finally halted in a battle that the overextended German armoured units were unable to carry. To the south was the Quattara Depression where tanks could not venture. This time there could be no armoured sweep round an open flank, and Rommel could not break through with his depleted numbers. Thus July 1942 saw the beginning of the end for the Afrika Korps.

German soldiers examine an abandoned Matilda
At regimental level British armour fought with a new-found professionalism, but senior commanders reacted too slowly and failed to co-ordinate their actions. Rommel led from the front, relying on his fingertip feel for the battle to keep him one step ahead all the time.

Rommel's air force: Messerschmitt Bf 109s
The air battle above Gazala and Tobruk involved evenly matched numbers of planes with the Germans enjoying a slight qualitative advantage. These Bf 109s display the typical German mottled desert colour scheme and wear white Mediterranean theatre bands.

Afrika Korps military police 1942

This Oberfeldwebel (Sgt Major) wears standard tropical uniform and the distinctive *Feldgendarmerie* metal gorget. Soldiers and military police are not always the best of friends, German troops nicknamed the MPs 'chained dogs' after their badge of office.

On June 13 Rommel's surviving armour triumphed again and Ritchie ordered Knightsbridge to be abandoned. XIII Corps was now in dire danger of being cut off from Tobruk so it too retreated. A series of fierce rearguard actions followed.

Tobruk was now exposed to German attack. It had a strong garrison but the defences had been neglected and Major-General Klopper surrendered after just 48 hours fighting. 30,000 bewildered and angry men were captured, including 19,000 British soldiers.

Auchinleck sacked Ritchie but Rommel still managed to drive the British back to Egypt. The vital port facilities of Tobruk were now able to supply the Afrika Korps and British fortunes in the desert had reached their nadir.

BATTLE OF MIDWAY: Decision in the Pacific

4 June 1942: The Imperial Japanese Navy tries to lure the Americans into a colossal ambush at Midway.

Like Admiral Jellicoe's Grand Fleet in World War I, the Imperial Japanese navy was nurtured on the concept of the 'great decisive battle', and Admiral Isoroku Yamamoto devised the 'MI' operation to bring this about. Landings were first to be undertaken in the Aleutians, drawing American strength north in counter-attack. Once this was committed, the strategic US outpost of Midway Island was to be taken. Only 1850 km (1,150 miles) from Hawaii it would pose a threat that Admiral Chester Nimitz, commander-in-chief Pacific, could not ignore. His weakened fleet would be thrown into the island's recovery but would be 'bushwhacked' by the Japanese in full strength. The plan was flawed both by its complexity and by its instigators not realizing that the Americans could largely divine their intentions by decoding of radio intercepts.

American carrier strength was currently at a low ebb. Of the four decks in the Pacific only USS *Enterprise* and *Hornet* of Vice Admiral William Halsey's Task Force 16 were at Pearl Harbor (recently returned from launching Dolittle's famous B-25 raid on Tokyo). USS *Yorktown* arrived with bomb damage from the Coral Sea on 27 May but was docked and repaired sufficiently for action in a remarkable three days. The newly-repaired USS *Saratoga* was still on the western seaboard and was never to arrive in time.

The Japanese committed 162 ships to 'MI' organized in 13 separate groups. Of these, aircraft from the carriers *Junyo* and *Ryujo* began their attack on Attu in the Aleutians on 3 June, but the Americans were not drawn. Planned Japanese reconnaissance by both flying-boat and submarine in the Midway area had failed, but American aircraft from the island located elements of the enemy invasion force in the forenoon of 4 June while they were yet nearly 1125 km (700 miles) distant to the west. Still unsighted was the Japanese spearhead, Vice Admiral Chuichi Nagumo's seasoned carrier group less the two decks unavailable following the Coral Sea action. Some 480 km (300 miles) astern of these was the main battle fleet, with Yamamoto himself in the battleship *Yamato*, ready to fall upon the Americans once they were committed. As a catalyst, the Midway Operation Force was advancing some 965 km (600 miles) to the south.

Ambush the ambushers

Enterprise and *Hornet* (commanded by Rear Admiral Raymond Spruance in the absence of an indisposed Halsey) were in company with Rear Admiral Frank Fletcher's *Yorktown* (a potentially problematical division of responsibility) and waiting, unsuspected, in a position about 565 km (350 miles) north-east of the island. Yamamoto, the would-be ambusher, was about to be ambushed in turn.

At 0430 on 4 June Nagumo launched the first strike of 72 bombers and 36 fighters against the island. He was about 385 km (240 miles) from target and continued to close at high speed.

As a powerful defensive screen of fighters circled above to take care of a return attack from Midway, nearly 100 aircraft were armed with AP bombs and torpedoes to deal with the American ships as they approached.

At 0530 Nagumo's force was sighted by a Midway-based Consolidated PBY and the island's whole air complement was scrambled. With the Japanese carriers now pinpointed, Spruance moved in. Between 0630 and 0700 the enemy aircraft succeeded in damaging the island's facilities against a stout defence but signalled that a second strike would be required. Already, however, Nagumo found himself with 67 aircraft lost or damaged, the whereabouts of American carriers (if any) yet unknown, and the remaining four decks involved in the operation widely dispersed in the complexity of Yamamoto's plan. Any unease that Nagumo may have experienced was relieved somewhat by the total lack of success enjoyed by those Midway-based aircraft that had attacked him. Their strength, however, convinced him of the wisdom of a follow-up strike against the island and, in the continuing absence of reports of any American fleet movement, the remaining aircraft aboard were ordered to be rearmed with blast bombs, and were struck below for the purpose.

At 0800, however, Spruance and Fletcher had launched a 151-aircraft strike. This was still en route when, at last, a Japanese reconnaissance floatplane found the Americans. Its signal provoked something akin to panic at Nagumo's end, with the aircraft aboard having to be rearmed yet again. Despite this the Japanese fighter cover was highly effective. While many of *Hornet*'s aircraft failed to find the target, a combined attack by 41 Douglas TBDs at 1018 lost 35 aircraft. It did, however, bring down the fighters to sea level so that the following 49 dive-bombers had it all their own way. *Akagi*, *Kaga* and *Soryu*, closely grouped, took two, four and three

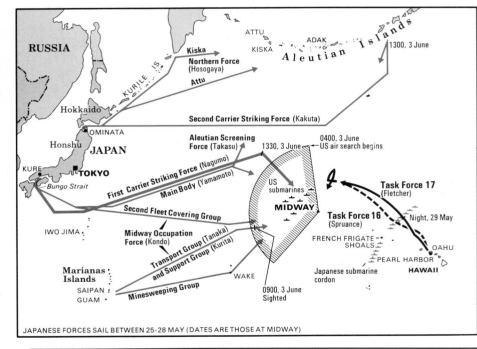

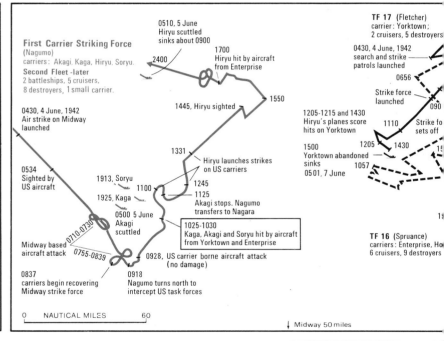

JAPANESE FORCES SAIL BETWEEN 25-28 MAY (DATES ARE THOSE AT MIDWAY)

0   NAUTICAL MILES   60   ↓ Midway 50 miles

Four out of four

Admiral Yamamoto sailed for Midway in the world's most powerful battleship, Yamato. After six months of nonstop victory the Japanese were over-confident, their plan involving the intricate manoeuvring of widely dispersed forces.

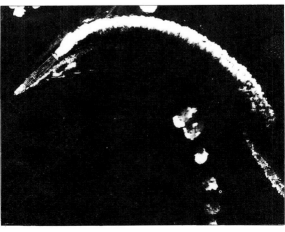

Approaching Midway, the Japanese were bombed by a force of B-17s from 20,000 ft. Here one of the carriers applies full helm to dodge the sticks of bombs. No hits were scored and the carriers flew off their first airstrike on Midway at 04.30, 4 June.

While the Japanese carriers were re-fuelling and re-arming their planes they were bounced by 151 US Navy aircraft. The torpedo-bombers drew down the fighters leaving the Dauntless dive-bombers free to sink three out of four Japanese carriers.

TBF-1 Avenger from Midway

Intended to join *Hornet's* air group, several Avengers were still on Midway Island when the Japanese attacked. Six of them joined the air strike launched from the island that was massacred by Japanese fighters and naval gunfire. They were all lost and scored no hits.

heavy bomb hits respectively. Littered with fuelled aircraft and two sets of munitions, all were soon fiercely ablaze and out of the action, later to sink. *Hiryu* was distant from the remainder and escaped for the moment, launching dive-bombers in return. These found *Yorktown* as she was recovering her own victorious aircraft and, though roughly handled by her fighter screen, hit her three times. Ablaze, she came to a halt about 1220 but then managed to yet again get under way. Only 200 km (125 miles) now separated the forces, and a second *Hiryu* strike put two torpedoes into her at about 1445. Abandoned, she refused to sink and was taken in tow.

The last strike

Again *Enterprise* and *Hornet* sent off their weary, surviving aircrews. Forty Douglas SBDs found *Hiryu* about the same business. Four bombs removed most of her forward flight deck and four near misses shook the hull. Completely gutted, she was later scuttled.

Only the eventual loss of the *Yorktown*, to submarine torpedoes while still in tow, marred the completeness of the American victory.

Eleven battleships had been present but the action hinged on, and was decided completely by, aircraft-carriers. The over-confident Japanese had been halted. Within six months of Pearl Harbor four of the six culprit carriers were on the bottom of the Pacific, and the enemy had been obliged to abandon his plans to isolate Australia.

Left: Admiral Yamamoto's masterplan
Yamamoto's plan was to launch a diversionary attack in the Aleutians to draw off American forces. His main force would then attack Midway, and as the Americans hurried out from Pearl Harbor he would ambush them with his four fleet carriers backed by the biggest battleships in the Pacific: *Yamato, Nagato* and *Mutsu*.

Above: *Yorktown* after *Hiryu's* first strike
After midday on 4 June **Yorktown** lay dead in the water battered and burning. But first-class damage control had her back in action before a second Japanese air strike arrived and scored the two fatal torpedo hits.

Hiryu *had escaped the American air strike and her planes caught* Yorktown *as she recovered her aircraft. Here* Yorktown *darkens the sky with her anti-aircraft barrage while a Japanese bomber roars past. Hit by three bombs,* Yorktown *was crippled.*

Excellent damage control enabled Yorktown *to make 20 kts by 1445 but a second strike from* Hiryu *slammed in two more torpedoes and, listing ominously, she had to be abandoned. A Japanese submarine sank her the next day.*

Enterprise *and* Hornet *dispatched another strike which found* Hiryu *sheltered by two battleships, four cruisers and several destroyers. It availed her nothing. Japan's carrier force had received a mortal blow.*

FORGOTTEN SACRIFICE: The Arctic Convoys

June 1941: The hard-pressed Royal Navy receives a new and perilous task, convoying vital war supplies to the USSR.

Hitler's ill-advised assault on the USSR in June 1941 gave the beleaguered British an unlikely and problematical ally. Supplies were needed urgently and had to come by sea, adding to the responsibilities of the already sorely-stretched Royal Navy, and only the Soviet Arctic ports could be considered for shipments. Dependent upon the season this demanded a 10- to 15-day passage for convoys, the route flanked to the eastward by a German-occupied Norway. Winter pack ice forced their track closer towards this hostile coast, with near four months of unbroken darkness and deep gloom affording some cover but at the expense of weather conditions of unrelenting vileness. With the ice sheet retreating in summer the route could be more distant, but was in permanent daylight and open to virtual round-the-clock attack.

Where the North Atlantic convoys were threatened predominantly by submarines and those in the Mediterranean by surface forces and aircraft, the Arctic run was menaced by all these forms and the escort system organized accordingly. This soon developed the form of an immediate escort, usually of corvettes and anti-submarine trawlers/whalers in the early days; a close cover of free-manoeuvring cruisers with destroyer escort which could rapidly reinforce the convoy on demand; and a distant cover of Home Fleet heavy units to guard against forays by the substantial naval forces built up by the enemy in northern Norway.

On 21 August 1941 the first, unnumbered seven-ship convoy sailed from Iceland for Archangel, arriving without incident 10 days later. This was shortly after the invasion of the USSR, and was a political gesture as much as experiment. The PQ/QP convoy cycle commenced soon after, the inability of the enemy to interfere allowing escort strength to drop to as little as a cruiser and a pair of destroyers.

With the coming of the dark period the cycle was accelerated, so that by early February 1942 12 north-bound PQs totalling 93 ships had been passed, with the loss of only one ship to a U-boat. With lengthening daylight in March 1942 things livened up with the passing PQ12 and QP8 narrowly avoiding interception by the newly-arrived battleship KMS *Tirpitz* and her destroyers.

Only three weeks later the enemy achieved something like co-ordination, and PQ13 lost five ships: two to the very effective Junkers Ju 88 torpedo bomber, two to U-boats and one to a marauding destroyer force. In tackling the latter, the now usual close cover was unfortunate to lose the cruiser HMS *Trinidad* to one of her own rogue torpedoes. Two U-boats were sunk, one rammed by one of the ocean minesweepers that gave such yeoman service.

U-boats: the invisible menace
As the Arctic convoys gathered pace in 1941, the German navy detached submarines from the main campaign in the Atlantic to Norway. Here they could operate with the support of the Luftwaffe. The tables were turned from 1944 when bigger convoys included escort carriers.

Right: A convoy passes through 'Arctic fog'
The Soviets never accepted the difficulties involved in sailing the Arctic route and loudly complained about 'British cowardice'. Admiral Pound was driven to ask the Soviet ambassador how he would like to command the Royal Navy.

The convoy routes to Murmansk
Summer was the more dangerous time for the convoys as the 24-hour daylight left them open to air attack. On the other hand the ice retreated, allowing the ships to sail farther away from the Luftwaffe airfields in Norway. The weather conditions in winter were indescribable but restricted German air and surface ship activity.

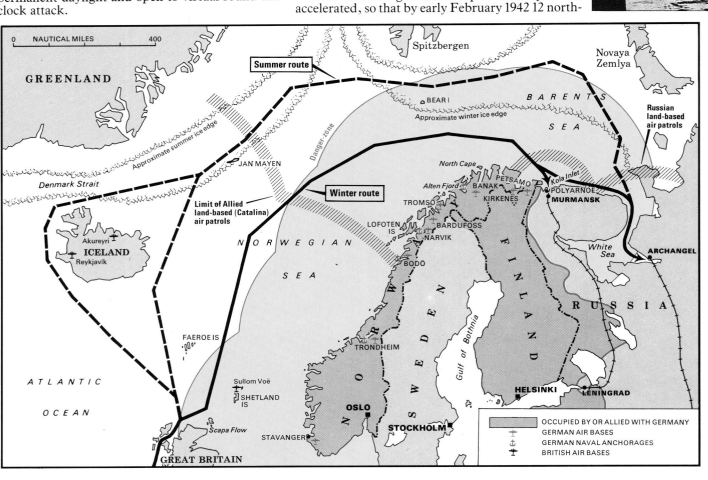

In the land of the midnight sun

Scraping the edge of the Arctic pack ice, the first convoys sailed for Murmansk in August 1941 and only the appalling weather conditions restricted their efforts during the autumn. The perpetual daylight left the ships horribly exposed to air attack.

During the winter, a time of almost constant darkness, the Germans concentrated U-boats, aircraft and surface warships in Norway. In March 1942, convoy PQ12 was heavily attacked by the Luftwaffe.

Admiral Hipper: *one of the German surface warships which lurked in Norwegian fjords, ready to pounce on the convoys. Their presence forced the Allies to provide powerful surface escort including battleships of the Home Fleet as distant cover.*

Unpredictable weather reduced to mere chance planned interceptions by both sides. Sixteen of PQ14's 24 ships were obliged to return because of ice conditions, but Ju 88s out of Kirkenes sank two of the empty QP10.

Over 260 Luftwaffe aircraft and over 30 U-boats were by now available, and both remaining 'pocket battleships' had been moved north. Despite the daylight lengthening ominously, politics demanded the running of PQ 16 in May. It suffered seven losses, six of them to aircraft.

Where is the Tirpitz?

By the end of June, when PQ17 sailed, German surface forces in the north had been reinforced by the battleship *Tirpitz*, a heavy cruiser and all remaining serviceable destroyers. By 1 July eight U-boats were concentrating on the convoy, which was also under continuous aerial surveillance. Only on 4 July, however, did the attack develop and the Admiralty ordered the convoy to scatter, firmly believing that the *Tirpitz* was out. As it happened she did not sail until the next day and then returned almost immediately. This, however, did not help the convoy which lost 23 out of its 34 ships to aircraft and submarine as, singly or in small groups, they struggled the last 1300 km (810 miles) virtually un-escorted.

Not until September 1942 did the next convoy run, in the form of PQ18. Its 40 ships enjoyed a for-midable escort that, at last, included an escort carrier. The enemy mounted a major effort but, though mass air attack sank 10 ships and U-boats a further three, the price was the loss of three U-boats and 27 aircraft.

Subsequently northbound convoys were recoded JW, starting at JW51. This much delayed operation ran in two parts. Neither suffered loss but the cruiser and the destroyer close cover of JW51B fought a spirited defensive action against superior enemy surface forces on the last day of 1942.

Between February and November 1943 no convoys ran as all escorts were diverted to the Atlantic route, where the U-boat offensive had reached its peak. Then, within the space of nine weeks, a total of 106 ships passed north in six operations for the loss of only three ships.

From spring 1944 the convoys doubled in size and were accompanied by one, or even two, escort carriers. The aircraft from these made short work of shadowers while ever less-experienced U-boat commanders found themselves pitted against 20 destroyers and a battle-hardened support group before being able to penetrate as far as the corvettes of the close escort itself. Not surprisingly, the convoys ran to the close of hostilities with small inconvenience other than from the eternal, remorseless weather.

In all, 1,526 ship movements were involved in 77 convoys to and from north Russia, 98 ships being lost. Overall success was due to the dedication and perseverance of both merchantmen and escorts.

Blohm und Voss Bv 138 flying boat

Known to the Luftwaffe as 'the flying clog', this five-man reconnaissance aircraft shadowed the Arctic convoys and vectored in U-boats and air strikes.

A German aerial photograph of PQ17, the ill-fated convoy ordered to scatter in July 1942. Dispersal was ordered in the belief that Tirpitz *had put to sea. The four Allied cruisers could not have lasted long against the German battleship.*

A U-boat noses through the wreckage of a freighter belonging to PQ17. US merchantmen raised large American flags on 4 July as a gesture of defiance. 23 ships were lost, taking down their crews, 400 tanks, 200 planes and 4,000 lorries.

The next convoy did not sail until September with the onset of bad weather. None sailed between February and November 1943 as the Battle of the Atlantic reached its crisis. Thereafter the convoys resumed and defeated the German attack.

DISASTER AT DIEPPE: No Second Front

Dawn, 19 August 1942: the biggest cross-Channel raid begins on the town of Dieppe. But the Germans are ready and waiting.

Operation 'Jubilee', the raid on Dieppe, was the biggest operation of its type carried out during World War II. Ten major military units took part – the larger part of them Canadian. Casualties were heavy, only one formation succeeded in taking its objective, but the operation did succeed in answering a vital question which had been plaguing the Allied planners since Dunkirk, when it had first been realized that in order to defeat Hitler and all for which he stood, an invasion of the French coast would have to be undertaken. The question was: would it be possible to capture a French port during the first days of the invasion?

The attempt to capture Dieppe itself was made by six battalions and an armoured regiment of the 2nd Canadian Division, landing at Puys, Pourville and on the Dieppe beaches between these villages. But on each side of this coastal stretch were batteries of coastal defence guns which could blow out of the water any ships seen approaching the shore, and to deal with this problem two British Commandos were landed – No. 4 on the west to destroy the batteries at Vesterival-sur-Mer and Varengeville, and No. 3 on the east to destroy those at Berneval.

Canadian landings

8 August 1942, 252 craft left four English south coast ports, the nine infantry landing ships carrying men of the Essex Scottish and Royal Hamilton Light Infantry to land on the beaches in front of Dieppe Casino; of the South Saskatchewan Regiment and of the Queen's Own Cameron Highlanders of Canada to land at Pourville; and of the Royal Regiment of Canada to land at Puys. The 14th Canadian Army Tank Battalion and the Fusiliers Mont-Royal would land in support of the Dieppe assault, while the Royal Marine 'A' Commando would assist in the capture of headlands which dominated the exposed beaches.

By 0335 on 19 August the convoys were off their objectives, the men in their landing craft and an apparently unobserved approach to the shore was in progress. Then a burst of fire on the far left flank revealed that No. 3 Commando had run into enemy shipping off Berneval and within minutes the whole length of the enemy defences was alert.

Nevertheless, on the right flank the troops of No. 4 Commando were carrying out a copybook attack. They landed on time, were well ashore and approaching their main target from two directions by 0540, had destroyed a nest of machine-guns by 0607 and at 0630 assaulted the main battery. The charges were placed, the guns blown up and No. 4 Commando was back aboard their craft and on their way home by 0730. At the eastern end, No. 3 Commando had emerged from the fight with the enemy ships badly scattered and only one troop of 17 men and three officers was ashore on time. But they so harassed their target, the Goebbels Battery, with sniper and Bren gun fire that the guns never opened up on the main assault taking place around Dieppe. They also were successfully withdrawn.

But between these two Commando assaults, total disaster had fallen upon the Canadians. Whether the Germans had prior intelligence of Operation 'Jubilee' or not (and there is some evidence that they did), they had obviously anticipated an attempted landing on the Dieppe beaches and had prepared meticulously for it.

Concealed heavy machine-guns swept the approaches and then the barbed wire entanglements which ranged along the beaches between the sea and the promenade, and when the desperate survivors of the first landing dived for hollows in the sand and shingle, mortar bombs landed among them with a precision which spoke of careful preparation. Snipers coolly picked off anyone showing leadership, to such an extent that no commanding officer, few company commanders and fewer senior NCOs survived the morning, and the battle became a series of desperate actions by individuals – most of whom were killed as soon as their purpose was seen – or small groups, quickly isolated.

Caught on the beaches

The attack on Dieppe itself foundered in the shallows and died on the beach. The Essex Scottish and Royal Hamiltons met such a weight of fire that it was a wonder that any of them reached even the prison-camps, let alone returned home. Tank landing craft attempting to get in to give support were blasted as

Hawker Typhoon

Ultimately a very successful fighter bomber, the Typhoon first saw action over Dieppe. The results were inauspicious with two aircraft lost when they were attacked in error by Canadian Spitfires. The whole Allied air effort was poorly co-ordinated and failed to provide much help for the ground troops.

'A reconnaissance in force' (Winston Churchill)

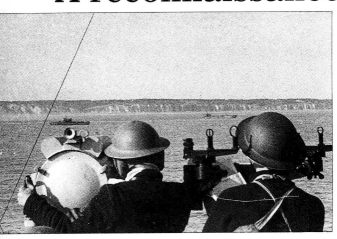

In the early hours of 19 August, some 6,000 troops including 4,900 Canadians began to attack the port of Dieppe. The town and surrounding cliffs were heavily fortified and the beach defences were not suppressed by the air and naval bombardment.

Part of the anti-tank company of the German 571st Regiment deployed in Dieppe itself where the six Canadian battalions were landed. The German guns were preregistered on the beach which was also swept by concealed machine-gun nests.

The infantry were supported by the Calgary Regiment of Churchill tanks. But the first wave of armour was late, their CO was killed as soon as his vehicle landed, and the tanks found all entries into the town were blocked.

Left: Inspecting their handiwork
German officers examine the interior of a wrecked landing craft. There is some evidence that the Germans were forewarned of the Dieppe assault, but the attack lost the element of surprise anyway when 3 Commando's landing craft ran into a German coastal convoy.

Right: Here died the Calgary Regiment
27 Churchill tanks landed on the beach and 12 were knocked out before they had travelled more than a few yards. The others found themselves unable to break into the town and were picked off one by one.

they emerged from the smoke, and their tanks hit as soon as the ramps went down. Nevertheless, 27 tanks did reach the shore and six ploughed through the wire to reach the promenade. One climbed the steps of the Casino, and three moved along the promenade blazing away at enemy posts until they ran out of ammunition: in the end all were wrecked and most of their crews were killed.

Last attack

In ignorance of the true situation, the force commander sent in the reserves of Fusiliers Mont-Royal and Royal Marines: but it was to no avail and these men were virtually thrown away. By 0900 the true situation had been realized and an attempt was made to withdraw. The naval craft raced in and out, desperately trying to lift men off the beaches, but the sacrifices they made were poorly rewarded: when by early afternoon on 19 August the ships finally withdrew to make their sorry way home, they left behind 215 Canadian officers and 3,164 men, 279 Royal Navy or Commando officers and 726 British other ranks.

But they also brought back the answer to that vital question. It was No! If a port was necessary in the first days of the great invasion, then the Allies must take one with them.

302nd German Infantry Division
Although a second-line formation, the 302nd Division defending the Dieppe sector had fortified its position well and the mile-long beach was completely covered by interlocking fields of fire. The 571st Regiment occupied the town itself with a battalion in reserve 5 miles to the south-west.

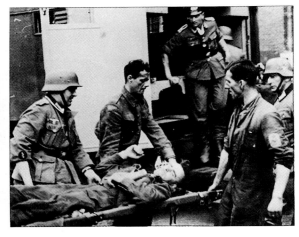

How so large a raiding force was to be extracted in broad daylight from under the noses of the Germans had not been thought through. Pinned on the beach by heavy fire, few men could be brought off and the survivors were captured.

The British contingent included army Commandos and Royal Marines. The initial Commando attacks went well, Major Peter Young and 19 men taking out a German battery defended by 200 troops, but 'A' Commando was shattered on the beach.

One Royal Marine, pinned down on the main beach, described Dieppe as 'the biggest cock-up since the Somme'. As the bewildered troops were herded into captivity, a new battle began amongst the staff to unload responsibility for the disaster.

DRIVE FOR THE VOLGA

One year after the invasion of the Soviet Union, the German army launches its great summer offensive to win the war.

On 28 June 1942 the great Summer Offensive of the Wehrmacht opened with Generaloberst Hermann Hoth's 4th Panzer Army sweeping forward to the north of Kursk, while Generaloberst Friedrich Paulus' 6th Army, which included 11 infantry divisions and a panzer corps of its own, drove parallel with them to the south of the city. Their first objective was the Don bend, but 160 km (100 miles) beyond lay the prize of Stalingrad and control of the lower Volga and its oil traffic to the industrial centres of the USSR.

Two days later, Army Group A under Generalfeldmarschall Siegmund List burst over the Donets bend and drove south east towards Proletarskaya, the Caucasus and the oil centres themselves, Maikop, Grozny and Baku.

It seemed at first that the days of easy victory had returned, for whatever Soviet forces were encountered they were swept away with almost contemptuous ease. For the first time in many months the ground favoured the large-scale, sweeping advances, hundreds of miles of open rolling corn and steppe grass offering perfect country for the massed armour of both Hoth's and Paulus' legions; indeed to those who watched the huge motorized squares with panzers forming the frames and soft transport and artillery crashing along inside, it seemed that the day of the modern Roman legions had dawned. Their advance was visible from miles away – smoke from burning villages and dust-clouds as the heavy vehicles crunched their way over the fields signalling the implacable progress of a perfectly functioning war machine.

Hoth's panzers were at Voronezh by 5 July,

throwing both the local Red Army command and STAVKA into turmoil as they tried to foresee which way – north towards Moscow again or south towards the oil – this huge offensive would turn. General Nikolai Vatutin was hurriedly ordered to form a new 'Voronezh Front' and was so successful in herding together the remnants of the Red Army divisions swept away to the north by the Panzer army in those first few days that Generalfeldmarschall Fedor von Bock, commanding the whole Army Group South, proposed to swing both Hoth's panzers and part of Paulus' infantry left to deal with Vatutin before driving on towards the main objectives.

'The Russian is finished'

But excitement had gripped the German High Command. Von Bock was summarily dismissed, Paulus was entrusted wholly with the advance and capture of Stalingrad while Hoth's panzers, instead of leading Paulus' divisions, were to swing south east, drive down between the Donets and the Don to 'assist in the early passage of the lower Don'. At this time the oil was still the major objective, Stalingrad merely another Soviet city to be despoiled in due course and one not likely to give the Wehrmacht a great deal of trouble.

Hitler was in a happier frame of mind than he had been for months. 'The Russian is finished!' he announced on 20 July, and even the generally overcautious Generaloberst Franz Halder agreed. 'I must admit, it looks like it.'

It continued to do so for a few weeks yet. The only problems posed in the south were those of traffic control, for both Generaloberst Ewald von Kleist's and Hoth's panzers arrived at the Donets crossing at the same time. A certain amount of acrimony resulted, especially as Kleist saw not the slightest reason for the change in plans or for the introduction of a rival panzer commander into the theatre of his own 1st Panzer Army. To demonstrate his own virtuosity, he accelerated the pace of his advance once across the river, captured Proletarskaya on 29 July, and by 9 August was at Maikop, with another column guarding his left flank at Stavropol. The great prizes of Grozny, Batumi and Baku seemed within grasp.

But for Paulus, matters were not going quite so well. In the 6th Army's progress down the Donets/Don corridor there was little problem for his panzer corps (under General Gustav von Weitersheim) driving alongside Hoth's Corps; but of course the 11 infantry divisions, many of whose formations were on foot, found it difficult to keep up and even to remain in touch. By the time they had reached Chernyevskaya on the River Chir in the Don bend they were all well strung out, and only the lack of a well-organized Red Army block allowed them to close up to the huge river itself.

Nevertheless, there was some fighting in the bend, and Paulus became more and more convinced that without Hoth's support he would not be able to get 6th Army across the Don in sufficient strength to take Stalingrad 'on the march' – which had been his original ambition. As Hoth's panzers were doing little but annoying Kleist, OKH (the Army High Command, responsible since December 1941 for control of operations on the Eastern Front but under Hitler's direct control) agreed that Panzer Army should now hook around to the north east and drive along the south bank of the Don. But unexpected resistance along the River Aksay delayed them, so that from 10 to 19 August Paulus' army waited in the bend, its artillery massed and ready for the great attack.

The plan was straightforward and conventional. Weitersheim's XIV Panzer Corps would form the northern flank, three of Hoth's panzer divisions and two motorized divisions would form the southern flank, while nine infantry divisions would fill the centre. They were all across the Don within 24 hours and, to the delight of every German headquarters organization between Stalingrad and Berlin, Weitersheim's panzers reported that they had reached the banks of the Volga across the northern suburbs of Stalingrad by the evening of 23 August. It was only a narrow penetration, but support was driving through to bolster the advance, Hoth's panzers were slowly forcing their way through from the south (though they still had some way to go) and it seemed that only one more heavy blow would secure triumph.

On the night of 23/24 August Stalingrad was subjected to an air raid reminiscent of the heaviest London blitz. The bulk of the bombs dropped were incendiary, and the wooden section of the city – most of the workers' shopping and housing blocks – burned in a holocaust as spectacular as the destruction of the London docks. By morning the pyre rose high into the air, acres of Stalingrad suburbs had been reduced to charred ashes and it was evident to the thoroughly satisfied German observers that only the main factories and stone-built offices remained for the attention of the German artillery.

But during the next few days something else became evident: the Soviet determination to fight every step of the way.

The '88' in action on the road to Stalingrad
Bugbear of Allied tank crews, the dreaded 8.8-cm gun serves here as additional field artillery against the retreating Soviets. Unknown to these men, the Red Army's massive reorganisation is under way and it is becoming a far more dangerous opponent.

'Not a step backward'

German armour races towards Voronezh as Hoth's 4th Panzer Army breaks through the Soviet lines, July 1942. The Soviets had captured the German plans but Stalin clung to his belief that the main attack would fall on Moscow.

Luftwaffe anti-aircraft gunners scan the sky for opposition, but the advancing German formations suffered little interference from the air. 300 miles to the north, Soviet divisions were force-marching from Tula to reinforce the southern defences.

The 6th Army was left to advance on Stalingrad alone as major units including XL Panzer Corps were stripped off to join the southern thrust. The Germans hoped to surround a large section of the Red Army between the Don and Donets.

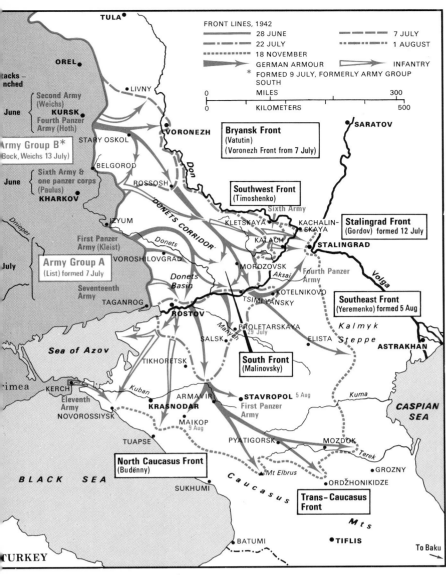

The southern front, June-August 1942
The German plan was to break through over the Don and take the Donets crossings with their armour, encircling vast Soviet forces in the Donets Basin. Now fighting far more effectively than in 1941, the Red Army retreated and just managed to halt the German penetration of the Caucasus.

Left: In the foothills of the Caucasus
As the Germans advanced towards the Caucasus they entered a land of minority peoples who had evinced no enthusiasm for Stalin. While the Red Army held back the Germans, Beria and the NKVD orchestrated a wave of terror against the Kalmyks and other unfortunate inhabitants in the path of the German advance.

On the banks of the Volga
A German machine-gunner presides over a peaceful Volga. The city of Stalingrad was expected to fall like all the others and the 6th Army looked forward to wintering in the captured city. In fact, 180,000 civilians were busily fortifying the place and the Red Army was preparing to stand and fight.

But despite the pace of the German advance, they seemed to be fighting a new enemy. The Soviets fought rearguard actions with unaccustomed professionalism and withdrew in good order. For the German infantryman, the strain began to tell.

Oil tanks blaze at Kuban as Army Group 'A' penetrates deep into the Caucasus. But a reorganised Soviet defence blocked further advances as Stalin issued his 'Not a step backward' order on 28 July.

On 23 August elements of the 79th Panzer Grenadier Regiment reached Spartanovka, a northern suburb of Stalingrad. Air attacks burned much of the wooden housing. The battle for Stalingrad had begun.

Crusade in the East: An MG34 machine-gun team on the steppe. The first snows of 1942 signalled the failure of the German Army's second attempt to defeat the Red Army in a blitzkrieg campaign. The soldiers were now condemned to another devastating Russian winter. But no-one, from the front-line infantry to Hitler's staff, anticipated the scale of the coming Soviet counter-attack at Stalingrad.

BATTLE OF GUADALCANAL: All for an Airfield

7 August 1942: 19,000 US Marines land on the island of Guadalcanal in the USA's first counter-offensive in the Pacific.

In 1942 the Solomon Islands suddenly became a key strategic position in the developing war in the South Pacific. In Japanese hands they would threaten the supply routes between the USA and Australia, in Allied hands they would form first a shield for the build-up of Allied strength in Australia, second an essential springboard for an Allied offensive to drive the Japanese back to their own islands.

By May the Japanese had already installed a sizeable garrison at the magnificent anchorage of Tulagi on the small Florida Island at the eastern end of the Solomons, and at the end of that month they began ferrying troops across the Nggela Channel to the larger island of Guadalcanal. Soon reports were reaching MacArthur from the team of Australian 'coastwatchers' that the Japanese were constructing an airfield near Lunga Point and the village of Kukum, and the danger of Japanese bombers being able to operate from there against Allied shipping, and even against the Australian mainland, became obvious.

On 7 August, somewhat to the surprise of all concerned, a force of 19,000 US Marines under Major General Alexander Vandegrift was landed successfully at both Lunga Point and Tulagi, and by the evening the Marines had chased the 2,200 Japanese construction workers off into the jungle, while 36 hours later the 1,500 Japanese soldiers at Tulagi had also been eliminated. By 8 August the airfield was being completed by US engineers and had been rechristened Henderson Field, and by 20 August the first Grumman F4F Wildcat fighters and Douglas SBD Dauntless dive-bombers had landed.

But before that, of course, the Japanese had reacted. The Battle of Savo Island had severely weakened Allied naval strength, and the withdrawal of Rear Admiral Richmond Turner's force had left the Marines very short of materials with which to build strong defences; fortunately, there was quite a lot of Japanese material around, and in the next two weeks it was put to good use.

This was proved on 18 August when a Japanese force of some 6,000 troops commanded by Colonel Ichiki, who was under the impression that only 2,000 US Marines had been landed, attacked Henderson Field and ran into a deadly storm of fire which quickly wiped his command from the face of the earth. Thereafter, Japanese attacks were a trifle less reckless, but the Imperial command never seemed able accurately to foresee the US Marines' strength on the island.

Every battle of the 'Slot', from each phase of the Battle of the Eastern Solomons, through the Battles of Cape Esperance and the Santa Cruz Islands to the last engagements which the Japanese called the Naval Battle of Guadalcanal, were fought to take more Japanese troops to the island in order to regain control of Henderson Field. The Tokyo Express had brought in another 8,000 men by 13 September – and over 1,200 of them were killed that night on Bloody Ridge.

A month later, after Cape Esperance, the Japanese strength had risen to 22,000 troops on the island – but there were now 23,000 marines with another 4,500 on Tulagi, for it was far easier for the Allies to reinforce from Australia than for the Japanese from their own homeland, or even from Luzon. Bombardment of Henderson Field by the heavy guns of two Japanese battlecruisers set fire to fuel stocks, destroyed over half the aircraft there and so thoroughly ploughed up the field that the bombers had to return to Australia for a time. But the land attack on the field was beaten off yet again at the end of October with Japanese losses running into thousands, while the Marines, fighting from well-sited and well-dug defensive positions and gaining experience with every hour, lost only a few hundred. American medical teams were now saving a large proportion of the wounded and most of the sick.

On the night of 14/15 November, when seven of

US Marine

65,000 strong in 1941, the USMC grew to 450,000 by the end of the war. Guadalcanal was the first of a series of Pacific island battles which established the Marines as one of the USA's toughest combat units. The two-piece camouflage suit shown here did not appear until mid-1943 after the one-piece tropical 'frog suit' had proved too heavy and uncomfortable.

From the Halls of Montezuma

A pall of smoke rises from Tenambogo as American air strikes pound Tulagi and the surrounding islands, 7 August 1942. The small Japanese garrison on Tulagi was overwhelmed and 19,000 men established on Guadalcanal.

Landing craft at Lunga Point on 8 August, the day the Marines overran the airfield. That night, the Japanese navy defeated an Allied cruiser squadron at Savo Island but stopped short of an assault on the defenceless transports.

As the US Marines established their positions on Guadalcanal the Japanese garrison badly underestimated the size of the American force. Colonel Ichiki led a regimental-sized force into a hopeless attack which failed with heavy losses.

the transports Rear Admiral Raizo Tanaka was trying to bring down the Slot were sunk, only 4,000 of the 11,000 Japanese troops sent to Guadalcanal arrived, and as they went into action the Americans abandoned the defensive which they had held so successfully for nearly four months and went over to the offensive. During the last days of the month the Marines enlarged their perimeter so that in the early days of December there was space for the 25th Infantry Division, the 2nd Marine Division and the 'Americal' Division – XIV Corps under Patch – to come in and relieve Vandegrift's gallant but now tired 1st Marines. Quickly Patch organized for a drive out, to clear the Japanese from the island.

But by now Imperial Japanese Headquarters was beginning to count the cost. Since 7 August losses totalled 65 naval craft and more than 800 aircraft; as for men, the calculations were difficult to make. It was apparent that while there were over 50,000 American troops on Guadalcanal, well supplied and well fed, whatever number of survivors of Lieutenant General Harukichi Hyakutake's 17th Army remained were on one-third of normal rations and so weakened by hunger and disease that a new offensive was beyond them.

On 4 January 1943 the reality was accepted in Tokyo and the orders went out. Between 1 and 9 February destroyers of the Tokyo Express came back to Guadalcanal for the last time, and successfully evacuated 11,000 men – whose rearguard had tenaciously kept back the American advance for the required time, and who left only their dead on the beaches.

Leatherneck armour
A column of US Marine Corps M3 light tanks picks its way through the tropical forest on Guadalcanal. Armed with a 37-mm gun and up to four machine-guns, the M3 enjoyed considerable success against an opponent lacking modern armour and short of large-calibre anti-tank guns.

Left: Victory in sight – US Marines west of the Matanikao
In December 1942 the US Marines drove the Japanese 17th Army over the river Matanikao and westwards along the northern coast of Guadalcanal. The Japanese accepted that they had no chance of a land victory and fell back steadily towards Cape Esperance and evacuation.

Surprise, surprise
Major-General Vandegrift's 1st Marine Division was hastily organized and had little experience of combined operations but it achieved complete surprise when it landed in August. It fought for the rest of the year on Guadalcanal until relieved in December by the 2nd Marine Division, and the US Army's 25th and 'Americal' Divisions.

The Japanese garrison, reinforced by sea, launched its fiercest assault on the 12-14 September. At 'Bloody Ridge' to the south west of Henderson Field they were finally beaten off with some 1,200 casualties, having got within 1,000 yards of the airstrip.

Allied landing craft disgorge supplies onto Guadalcanal in the shadow of a Japanese transport driven ashore and wrecked by US aircraft. Seldom have naval and ground battles been so closely interdependent as in the Solomons campaign.

After three months defending the airstrip, the Marines were able to go over to the offensive in November. The Japanese 17th Army withdrew north-west along the coast and was finally taken off the island after a textbook rearguard action in January.

SOLOMONS: The Sea Battles

As the troops slug it out on Guadalcanal, powerful naval forces converge on what becomes known as 'Iron Bottom Sound'.

USS *South Dakota* under torpedo attack
Manoeuvring hard to avoid the lethal attentions of a Nakajima B5N 'Kate', the brand-new battleship *South Dakota* fights back with 5-in aircraft guns. She was the only American warship to carry proximity fuzed shells at Santa Cruz and claimed 26 Japanese aircraft shot down.

The American landings on Guadalcanal marked the first stage in a long Pacific struggle. The Marine landings were soon to come under pressure from the sea, as the Japanese navy threw its weight behind attempts to thwart the invasion. The virtual annihilation of an Allied cruiser force off Savo Island showed up American inexperience, and Japanese mastery of night fighting at sea. Fortunately for the landing ships, Vice Admiral Gunichi Mikawa's powerful cruisers left the scene for fear of being found by the American carrier force on the next day. The four cruisers which sank to the bottom of 'Iron Bottom Sound' were the first of many vessels to be lost in these crowded waters.

Although the Japanese controlled the Slot (the passage down the centre of the Solomons chain) by

USS *South Dakota*

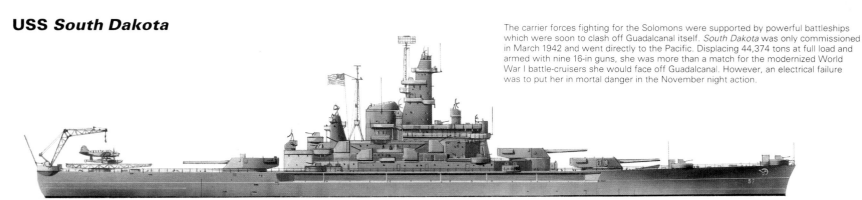

The carrier forces fighting for the Solomons were supported by powerful battleships which were soon to clash off Guadalcanal itself. *South Dakota* was only commissioned in March 1942 and went directly to the Pacific. Displacing 44,374 tons at full load and armed with nine 16-in guns, she was more than a match for the modernized World War I battle-cruisers she would face off Guadalcanal. However, an electrical failure was to put her in mortal danger in the November night action.

night, American air power commanded it by day. The campaign became a series of moves and counter-moves, with the Japanese sending resupply convoys racing down the Slot in what became known as the 'Tokyo Express' with the Americans attacking them during the day from the air. The Imperial navy tried to get the American carriers within striking range of a combined fleet force under the command of Vice Admiral Chuichi Nagumo of Pearl Harbor fame. In the battle of the Eastern Solomons (22-25 August 1942), on 23 August, the Japanese light carrier *Ryujo* was sunk while USS *Enterprise* was put out of action. Later, USS *Saratoga* was torpedoed and sidelined for months, while on 14 September the submarine *I-19* torpedoed USS *Wasp*. The ship exploded after fires raged out of control all day. Meanwhile, the Japanese were pressing their convoys forward in support of their starving troops on Guadalcanal. A convoy was attacked by Rear Admiral Norman Scott's force of two heavy cruisers, two light cruisers and destroyers off Cape Esperance on the night of 11/12 October. Scott was not aware of the Japanese distant escort of three

heavy cruisers, but the Japanese were just as surprised when contact was made. In a confused night action the Americans got the better of the Japanese, but at the cost of allowing the convoy through.

Battleship Bombardment

The Japanese upped the stakes considerably two nights later, when the Marine positions around Henderson Field on Guadalcanal were hammered by the heavy fire of the battleships *Kirishima* and *Hiei*, the only US Navy challenge being made by four PT boats. The next night heavy cruisers moved down the coast, lobbing 752 203-mm (8-in) shells into the Marine positions. Without more naval support Major General Alexander Vandegrift's command would not be able to beat the Japanese. Fortunately, the fire-eating Vice Admiral William Halsey had taken command in the South West Pacific, and he saw his duty to support the Marines, even if it meant risking his carriers. This is what Admiral Isoroku Yamamoto and the combined fleet expected, and Yamamoto decided to move his own carriers south to finish off American naval power in the

Pacific. On 25 October US aircraft spotted a Japanese force of three carriers, with a fourth on its way down the Slot. After a typical carrier battle off the Santa Cruz Islands (the main combatants never setting eyes upon each other), the Japanese light carrier *Zuiho* had been sunk and the large carrier *Zuikaku* damaged. On the American side USS *Hornet* was abandoned after a torpedo strike, and the long suffering *Enterprise* was hit. Damage was slight, however, and she was operational within hours. The Japanese were convinced that they had sunk her and the *Hornet*, together with a battleship and a number of escorts. They knew about the *Hornet*, because they had come across the abandoned hulk burning fiercely. The ship which had launched the first strike against the Japanese homeland was eventually put down by Japanese torpedoes early on the morning of 27 October.

Tactically, the Japanese had won a victory. Strategically, the Americans had delayed the enemy enough so that, when the final combined assault on Guadalcanal came, the Marines and Navy had a chance to win.

The Battle of Santa Cruz

The destroyer USS O'Brien is struck by a torpedo from a Japanese submarine as she screens the damaged carrier Hornet. *A 'Val' dive-bomber smashed into* Hornet *at 09.15, 26 October 1942.*

The battle had begun when a pair of Dauntless dive-bombers located the Japanese carrier Zuiho at 07.00 and slapped two 500-lb bombs into her stern, setting her ablaze. As usual, the Japanese navy was

operating several scattered squadrons and although Zuiho was doomed, the big fleet carriers Zuikaku and Shokaku launched air strikes of their own.

© Richard Natkiel, 1986

	MAIN US AND
	JAPANESE AIR STRIKES

0   NAUTICAL MILES   150

Damaged Zuiho and Shokaku

Zuikaku

1230   1500

1000   0930 Shokaku hit   Zuikaku   Junyo

0700   0105, 27 Oct,
2 battleships,   0740   destroyer hit
carrier   5 cruisers,   Zuiho hit
Junyo,   12 destroyers
2 destroyers   2000
(Kakuta)
0400   0920
Chikuma   Carrier
hit   Group*
Advance Force   (Nagumo)
(Kondo)   0400   Striking
0800   0915, Hornet hit, sinks later
STEWART IS   Force   1015, Enterprise hit
0730   0400
Vanguard
Group†   1830   carriers
Overall commander of   (Abe)   Enterprise
Japanese fleet –Adm Kondo   0400   2300   and Hornet

1400
SANTA CRUZ   Task Forces 16 and 17 (Kinkaid)
IS   2 carriers, 1 battleship, 6 cruisers,
*3 carriers, 1 cruiser, 8 destroyers   14 destroyers
†2 battleships, 4 cruisers, 7 destroyers   (1012, destroyer Porter torpedoed)

The Santa Cruz action: 26 October
The battle occurred because Japanese naval forces were sent to
support their army's supreme effort to eject the US Marines from
Henderson Field. The plan was for the Japanese carriers to land
aircraft on the airstrip the moment it was overrun.

Left: Hornet lies blazing
A torpedo strike by Japanese carrier aircraft left *Hornet* a blazing
wreck too dangerous to approach but the stubborn flat top refused to
die. Even after the retreating Americans pumped eight torpedoes and
400 shells into her, she remained defiantly afloat.

Hornet after the first attack
Hornet's list is evident during the early afternoon of 26 October.
Enterprise avoided sharing her fate by darting into a convenient rain
squall when the Japanese air strike arrived in the morning.

Hornet, *already crippled by dive-bombers, now
sustained mortal damage from Nakajima B5N
'Kate' torpedo-bombers. Racing low over the water,
the 'Kates' dodged the American Wildcat fighters
and suffered few losses from AA fire.*

The Japanese fleet carrier Shokaku *seen above was
struck by four 1,000-lb bombs in rapid succession
during an American air strike, which struck the
Japanese fleet at the same time as USS* Hornet
received her first damage.

Shokaku *limped away from Santa Cruz, but
although the Japanese had sunk* Hornet *for the loss
of the smaller* Zuiho, *their veteran aircrew had
suffered nearly 50 per cent casualties and 250
machines had been lost.*

EL ALAMEIN: Montgomery's Victory

23 October 1942: Under the inspired leadership of Lt. General Montgomery, the 8th Army hits back at the Afrika Korps.

The front line at El Alamein was blocked at the northern end by the sea and at the southern end by the Qattara Depression. There was thus no open flank for the attacker to swing around as had happened at all previous desert battles, and as a result no alternative to a frontal assault, similar to those of World War I.

At 2100 on 23 October 1942, the artillery of General Sir Bernard Montgomery's 8th Army opened with a barrage unparalleled in North Africa, and under it the Australian, New Zealand, Scottish and South African infantry of XXX Corps advanced, followed immediately by thousands of engineers clearing 7.3-m (24-ft) wide paths through mine-marshes in places extending for 2750 m (3,000 yards). Through these paths the armour of X Corps was intended to pass before fanning out in front of the infantry to protect them from attack by Generalfeldmarschall Erwin Rommel's Panzer divisions.

By dawn on 24 October the infantry had in most cases reached their objectives, but traffic jams and accidents had held up the armour which, when daylight came, was directly under fire from German artillery. As a result for nearly eight days a grim battle was fought in the vast dust-bowl between the coast and the Miteiya Ridge, the Australians in the north fighting a series of 'crumbling' battles, in the centre on Kidney Ridge the men of the 2nd Battalion the Rifle Brigade fought the famous 'Snipe' action, and the New Zealanders edged their way up and over Miteiya Ridge itself. Meanwhile, Montgomery reconsidered his plans, regrouped his armour – including the 7th Armoured Division, brought up from XIII Corps area in the south – and prepared a further armoured thrust.

Operation Supercharge

At 0105 on the morning of 2 November Operation 'Supercharge' was launched. Once again a shattering bombardment opened across the width of the advance, and once again the infantry marched forward with minefield clearance teams immediately behind, their objective the line of the Rahman Track. Close behind the infantry advance came their own support armour, whose task was to thrust forward in the darkness up and over the Aqqaqir Ridge, while behind them the 1st Armoured Division was to crash out through the gap they had made and destroy the Axis forces beyond. Speed and exact timing were essential.

Unfortunately one armoured brigade delayed the main thrust for a quarter of an hour; as the main assault climbed the Aqqaqir Ridge the sun rose behind them, and they moved dramatically from shadow at the foot to full daylight at the crest. Here they met the massed fire of all the remaining German anti-tank guns: in less than 30 minutes 75 of the 94

Messerschmitt Bf 110E

This Bf 110 was based at Berca in late 1942 and carries a MK 101 30-mm cannon for anti-tank action. The British also employed cannon-armed aircraft to attack the thinner top armour of tanks, equipping Hawker Hurricanes with twin 40-mm guns. With both armies dependent on lorry-borne fuel, water and ammunition, control of the air was vital.

The Desert Air Force
An RAF Kittyhawk takes off to attack the Axis supply lines. Montgomery appreciated the importance of the air battle, pitching his headquarters next to that of the Desert Air Force. By the time of El Alamein, the British enjoyed a 5:3 numerical superiority in the air.

Valentine tank

Although the 8th Army's 1,000 tanks included 250 new American Shermans, the Valentine infantry tanks saw heavy action at El Alamein. Unlike the Matilda, the Valentine was able to take larger guns and most 2-pdr armed vehicles now mounted 6-pdr guns. Some were later fitted with 75-mm weapons.

"It will be a killing match" Lt. General Bernard Law Montgomery

Rommel's advance from Gazala had been exhausting, but Panzer Armee Afrika only needed one more victory to break deep into Egypt and overrun the Suez Canal. The odds were against him, but that had never stopped him before.

Montgomery's attack was more akin to the set-piece assaults of World War I than the earlier mobile battles in the desert. A tightly controlled barrage by 450 field guns would precede a carefully planned infantry attack to break into the German defences.

A clip from the British wartime film, 'Desert Victory' celebrates the eventual success of the infantry assault which began at 22.00 on 23 October. Four divisions of XXX Corps attacked, penetrating deep into the enemy defences.

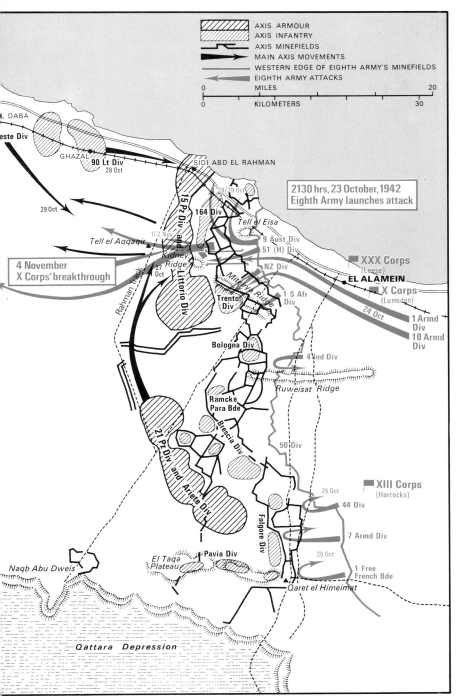

AXIS ARMOUR
AXIS INFANTRY
AXIS MINEFIELDS
MAIN AXIS MOVEMENTS
WESTERN EDGE OF EIGHTH ARMY'S MINEFIELDS
EIGHTH ARMY ATTACKS

MILES 0 ... 20
KILOMETERS 0 ... 30

DABA
GHAZAL
90 Lt Div 28 Oct
...este Div
SIDI ABD EL RAHMAN
29 Oct
15 Pz Div and
164 Div
Tell el Eisa
28/29 Oct
1/2 Nov
Tell el Aqqaqir
Kidney Ridge
9 Aust Div
51 (H) Div
27 Oct
4 November
X Corps' breakthrough
Littorio Div
Trento Div
Miteiriya Ridge
NZ Div
XXX Corps (Leese)
EL ALAMEIN
X Corps (Lumsden)
1 S Afr Div
24 Oct
1 Armd Div
10 Armd Div
Rahman Track
Bologna Div
4rnd Div
Ruweisat Ridge
21 Pz Div and Ariete Div
Ramcke Para Bde
Brescia Div
50 Div
Folgore Div
25 Oct
XIII Corps (Horrocks)
44 Div
El Taqa Plateau
Pavia Div
7 Armd Div
Naqb Abu Dweis
25 Oct
1 Free French Bde
Qaret el Himeimat
Qattara Depression

2130 hrs, 23 October, 1942
Eighth Army launches attack

25-pdr field gun in action
25-pdrs provided the bulk of British field artillery. Until Alamein the 8th Army had usually failed to concentrate its artillery but this time the artillery was co-ordinated masterfully. Over a million rounds were fired during the course of the battle.

Desert Victory
Unlike the fluid desert battles which preceded it, the front at Alamein was restricted by the sea to the north and the impassable Qattara Depression to the south. Set piece battles have always been the British army's *forte* and Rommel had no chance to display his genius for improvisation in a mobile battle.

tanks had been wrecked, over half the crews killed or wounded.

But Rommel was having major troubles of his own. Since the last days of October he had realized that his German-Italian Panzer Army was being ground down by sheer weight and volume of fire, and he had made plans to disengage them and pull back. But as he began to put these plans into action, an order from Hitler arrived forbidding the slightest retreat and ending 'As to your troops, you can show them no other road than that to victory or death!'

If he could neither retreat nor stay where he was,

then he must order an advance – in the hope that fortune might favour him as she had in the past and his thrust might hit a weak spot. But there was no weak spot in Montgomery's deployment, and during the rest of the morning and the afternoon of 2 November the Panzer divisions threw themselves against the solid wall of 8th Army artillery, and by the evening had only 35 tanks left between them. This was the action in which the strength of the famous Deutsche Afrika Korps was finally broken.

It was also the day when the Panzer Army defences at El Alamein were first punctured, albeit

by but a small force. During the previous night armoured cars of the Royal Dragoons had found their way out of the south-west corner of the salient that had been punched into the original Axis defence line, and threaded their way through and into the rear areas of the defending formations, shooting up quite a number of them on their way.

The Great Break-out

Their signals convinced Montgomery that the way was open for the great break-out, so during the next 48 hours the main armoured weight of the 8th Army was re-grouped. By dawn on 4 November the Argyll and Sutherland Highlanders had penetrated through south of Tel el Aqqaqir to find that the expected DAK defences had gone, that Rommel had decided to disobey his Führer and that the whole Panzer Army was withdrawing – leaving behind a few stragglers, some wrecked artillery and tanks, areas of uncleared mines and a large number of booby-traps.

The Battle of El Alamein was over, and all that remained was to organize an effective pursuit.

British armour was supposed to pass through the gaps created by the infantry to terminally unzip the Axis position. Unfortunately the tanks failed to press ahead and when they finally emerged, German tanks and guns blocked any further advance.

Rommel knew he was beaten by 2 November and began a masterly rearguard action. But his losses had been catastrophic – this tangled heap of Italian armour bears witness to the heroic last stand of Ariete Division, which was annihilated.

An armoured car brings in some of the 30,000 prisoners taken at Alamein. Montgomery's pre-battle predictions about the length of the battle and the number of Allied casualties (13,500) were both proved correct.

NIGHTMARE AT STALINGRAD

September 1942: The German 6th Army hammers its way into Stalingrad. But its flanks are guarded only by a thin screen of Rumanian and Italian troops.

After careful preparation the first heavy and concentrated attack on Stalingrad by the German 6th Army took place between 14 and 22 September 1942, with the attackers in control of the air above and with a three-to-one advantage in manpower. During these nine days of bitter action Generaloberst Friedrich Paulus' infantry cleared the bend of the River Tsaritsa and reached the Volga, captured Stalingrad's Number 1 Railway Station, forced General Vasili Chuikov to change his 62nd Army headquarters position and brought German artillery close enough to the main landing stage severely to jeopardize the nightly passage of ammunition and stores from the main dumps on the east of the river.

Both sides were then so prostrated by exhaustion

This was revealed on 19 November – after six different offensives by the 6th Army against Stalingrad defenders, who by then were confined to the area around the Krasni Oktyabr and the Barrikady factories along some 8 km (5 miles) of the river bank, and after such a Calvary of fighting one tortured soul wrote in his diary, 'when night arrives, one of those scorching howling bleeding nights, the dogs plunge into the Volga and swim desperately to gain the other bank. Animals flee this hell; the hardest stones cannot bear it for long; only men endure.'

At dawn on 19 November a thunderous barrage opened to the north from 2,000 guns and Katyusha batteries, and all who heard it sensed that a new phase of the battle was about to begin. Later in the morning another bombardment crashed out, this time in the south – and the 6th Army staff officers suddenly became acutely conscious of the weakness of their flanks. These were held by Rumanian armies whose soldiers and commanders were not so

dedicated to the destruction of Soviet Russia as themselves – nor so well armed, for the bulk of their weapons and vehicles had been captured in France two years before.

Three days later, the staff officers knew that their fears had been well-founded. Along 80 km (50 miles) in the north and 50 km (31 miles) in the south, Zhukov's shock armies had broken the Rumanian front into shards, driven all before them back over the Chir, captured intact the vital supply bridge at Kalach – and encircled Paulus and the remaining quarter of a million soldiers of the 6th Army. Now the besiegers were themselves besieged.

At first, of course, in both Berlin and Stalingrad the view was taken that an army of such size constituted a positive tactical advantage when behind enemy lines. Its reinforcement and supply was just a problem to be solved, and in the meantime the Red Army was faced with the difficulties of maintaining their encirclement and in doing so employing hundreds of thousands of men and guns which could not be put to use elsewhere.

Operation Winter Storm

Generalfeldmarschall Erich von Manstein, whose 11th Army had been incorporated into a new Army Group Don between Army Groups B in the Don/Volga theatre and A down in the Caucasus, was given the task of correcting the predicament which had arisen as a result of Zhukov's counter-offensive. At first he felt that his best course would be to tempt the Soviet armies westward away from Stalingrad, thus taking some of the pressure off the 6th Army and allowing Paulus room and time to organize a break-out to meet a drive up from the south by some Panzer divisions from Generaloberst Hermann Hoth's 4th Panzer Army; but Operation Wintergewitter (Winter Storm) launched on 21 December from the Don on each side of Kotelnikov, was solidly blocked on the Myshkova by the 2nd Guards

Ilyushin Il-2 Sturmovik ground-attack aircraft

As the 6th Army's onslaught was heavily supported by Ju 87 Stuka dive-bombers, the Red Army depended on the Il-2. Carrying bombs, rockets, hollow-charge anti-tank bombs and cannon, the Il-2 was a powerful strike aircraft and over 36,000 were built during the war.

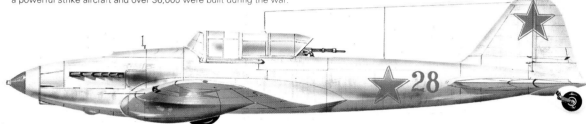

that for a few days a sullen silence fell upon the area, punctuated only by sporadic machine-gun fire and mortar bursts; but quite soon the battle amid the ruins began again, and what seemed to some observers a battle of attrition recommenced, in which the side with the larger numbers would win.

But those observers were wrong. German losses were far in excess of Soviet losses, and indeed there was a different purpose and mentality controlling each side. Berlin was already proclaiming the capture of Stalingrad, and to Hitler's eyes no loss of life could compensate for his own loss of face if it were not quickly confirmed; Paulus must have as many men as could be shipped to him and he must feed them into the cauldron without scruple. But Marshal Georgi Zhukov had a different view; he had plans for the employment of the armies being formed on the east side of the Volga, and they did not include immolation in the devastated city, no matter what the men of the desperate 62nd Army might be suffering. He would feed in just enough men to keep the defence of Stalingrad alive – and dangerous to the besiegers – but the mass of men and arms accumulating under his command had a more strategic purpose.

Verdun on the Volga

The 6th Army found Stalingrad heavily fortified: of the 500,000 inhabitants, some 180,000 had been labouring under Red Army supervision to turn their city into a fortress.

As the fine autumn gave way to the first chill of the approaching winter, the 6th Army had captured most of the city. The Red Army clung desperately to its surviving positions on the west bank of the Volga.

A Red Army counter-attack under way in early November. The Soviet defences were anchored on two large factory complexes which were ideal for sustaining a protracted defence.

Army – and there seemed little inclination by 6th Army commanders to order a break-out.

Then on 25 December Zhukov launched yet another attack, drove Hoth's army back beyond its starting point around Kotelnikov and the German forces to the north well back beyond both the Chir and the Aksay – and suddenly the distances separating the two German fronts were too great for supplies to get through to Paulus by land, while Luftwaffe Generaloberst Wolfram von Richthofen was becoming more and more gloomy about the prospects of air support as the weather closed in. Paulus and his army were evidently in some danger. Could it be that Stalingrad was not quite so firmly in German hands as the Berlin propaganda machine had said?

As 1943 dawned the German 6th Army began desperately to protect itself with dense fortifications around an area some 50 km (31 miles) from east to west and 30 km (19 miles) from north to south. They were surrounded by 10 Soviet armies, and although some Red Army formations were guarding the distant borders against possible German relief columns, the main energies and attentions were directed against the pocket. On 8 January General Konstantin Rokossovsky, who had been given the task of destroying the 6th Army, sent in a proposal for its surrender, and when this was rejected began the last phase of the Battle of Stalingrad with a bombardment from thousands of guns and mortars, augmented by attacks by the bombers and ground-attack aircraft of the 16th Soviet Air Army.

By 17 January the area in German hands had been halved, by the 21st the last German airfield at Gumrak had been captured and the battle was being fought out again in the concrete tombs of Stalingrad – but with the roles reversed. By this time the 6th Army had been depleted by over 160,000 casualties of one category or another.

The last act was played out as January ended and February began. On 31 January the shell of the Central Department Store was captured and Paulus and his staff surrendered – unconsoled by the fact that Hitler had promoted Paulus to field marshal two days before; and on 2 February the remainder of the army laid down its arms. More than half the 300,000 men trapped in Stalingrad had been killed by the time of the surrender. A fortunate few, some 35,000, had been evacuated by air, but the surviving 90,000 men were herded to Siberia on foot. Many died on the march from cold and starvation, and the rest were condemned to a slow death in the mines and work camps. Many of those still alive in 1945 were never released, and only about 5,000 of the doomed army ever returned.

Left: Holding back the tide: German machine-gunners in action
An MG 34 team prepares to face the inevitable Soviet counter-attack after the ruins of another building fall to the 6th Army. The weather, and the fates have not yet turned against Paulus's soldiers but time is running out.

Towards the Volga. October 1942
German Panzergrenadiers gather themselves for their last desperate effort to storm the city in October. Shattered buildings changed hands repeatedly as the Soviets continued to counter-attack whenever an important position was overrun.

Krasni Oktyabr: the defiant fortress
This major factory complex was the cornerstone of 62nd Army's defences and was the scene of a meat-grinder of a battle. Both sides relied heavily on close air support: here Soviet Il-2 Sturmoviks fly over the factory to strike the German positions on the perimeter.

Factory workers hand over new KV-1 heavy tanks to the re-forming Soviet armoured corps. The USSR's industrial production was now rapidly increasing so the Red Army, unlike the German army, had a substantial number of divisions in reserve.

On 19 November the Red Army broke through on both flanks and surrounded Stalingrad. Relief efforts failed and the 6th Army made no attempt to break out. Food ran out and by January the Germans had eaten 39,000 of their horses.

Paulus surrendered on 31 January 1943. It was the turning point of the war in the east, removing any possibility of a German victory. For the men of the 6th Army it meant death: of the 90,000 men captured only 5,000 were ever to return home.

KASSERINE: The Desert Fox Strikes Back

The Afrika Korps seems doomed by 1943, but Rommel launches his desert veterans against the inexperienced Americans.

By the beginning of 1943 the situation of the Axis forces in North Africa appeared far stronger than could have been foreseen two months before when the Battle of El Alamein had begun. Having starved Generalfeldmarschall Erwin Rommel of troops when victory seemed in sight, Hitler now poured men and *matériel* into the 'Tunisian Bridgehead', apparently in the hope that the Anglo-American forces which had been put ashore in Operation 'Torch' could be held there almost indefinitely. Generaloberst Jürgen von Arnim had nearly 100,000 men and a considerable force of armour at his disposal in the 5th Panzer Army, and although the line he had to defend stretched some 480 km (300 miles) from the Mediterranean down past Gafsa, his opponents had to man the same length – and feed their armies along much longer lines of communication.

Moreover, the Allied armies were divided into three not particularly co-operative groups. In the northern sector the British 1st Army was massed, its obvious purpose a drive to Bizerta, Tunis and Cape Bon. To its south lay the French, poorly armed as yet, not very well trained, still resentful of the British attacks on Mers el Kébir two years before. And to their south lay the Americans – eager and confident, but woefully inexperienced.

During the last weeks of 1942, von Arnim had moved to strengthen his defences by driving the French out of the Pichon Pass, about 120 km (75 miles) south of Tunis and one of the key points along the Eastern Dorsale, the range of mountains which dominates the Tunisian coastal plain. During January he struck again at the French, driving them out of both the Fondouk and Pont du Fahs defiles, and on the last days of the month he drove them from Faid. The key southern passes of the Eastern Dorsale were now at his command.

Meanwhile to the south Rommel had completed his withdrawal from El Alamein across Egypt and Libya, his rearguards now occupying the Mareth Line and awaiting the arrival of General Sir Bernard Montgomery's 8th Army. Rommel could see quite clearly that if he did nothing to prevent it he would soon be squeezed between his new adversaries, the Americans of the US II Corps, and his old ones from Egypt. Swift action might solve the problem, and on 4 February 1943 he suggested that von Arnim's thrusts should be continued past Faid and on down to Sbeitla, while he drove west for Gafsa, on towards Fériana and perhaps, if he could destroy the inexperienced Americans, on to Tebéssa and perhaps even to the coast at Bône, thereby splitting the Allied forces irrevocably.

Operation 'Frühlingswind' (spring breeze) opened on 14 February with an expert hook around from Faid to Sidi Bou Zid, which annihilated a US tank battalion, destroyed 44 Shermans, 26 guns and a mass of transport, and isolated 2,000 men on hilltops. Though Rommel was not yet threatening Gafsa, the US general there ordered its evacuation, and that night in heavy rain French and US troops, Arab and French families all mixed together fled in disarray towards Fériana – where the panic engulfed base troops who promptly destroyed papers and materials before joining the exodus north towards Kasserine.

American counter-attack

In an effort to stop the rot the commander of the US 1st Armored Division, Major General Orlando Ward, mounted a counter-attack from Sbeitla – and of 58 Shermans he launched into battle only four emerged, taking his losses in two days to 98 tanks, 29 guns and 57 half-tracks.

Meanwhile Rommel had taken Gafsa and reached Fériana, where he found wholesale flight and panic, botched attempts to destroy fuel and stores from which his men joyfully salvaged enough to help them well on their way, and sufficient evidence of inexperience and tactical inadequacy to convince him that a bold stroke now would take him at least to Tebéssa. Prospects had not been too bright for him since the heady days of the advance to El Alamein. After a brief conference with his superiors on 18 February he regrouped and prepared for a drive north towards Le Kef, sending the divisions of his old Afrika Korps through Kasserine and Sbiba, holding his 10th Panzer Division back to exploit whichever route promised the better possibilities.

But by now the British 6th Armoured Division and the US 34th Infantry Division were streaming south to block the gaps torn in the Allied line, and General Sir Harold Alexander, shocked by the confusion he found on visiting the US II Corps headquarters, took command. He issued one simple instruction – there was to be no further withdrawal beyond the passes of the Western Dorsale; Sbiba and Kasserine were to be held.

As the newly-arrived forces took up their blocking positions the panic subsided, the fleeing columns were channelled into safety and reorganized, and the arrows showing the German advances slowed and then remained stationary. By 22 February Rommel knew that he must call off the attack as too many Allied reinforcements were flooding down into the line against him, and they were being handled with a much firmer and surer touch.

Operation 'Frühlingswind' was over. It had cost the Allies close to 10,000 men against 2,000 Axis casualties, and it had frightened every Allied HQ in North Africa.

'Spring Breeze'
Operation 'Spring Breeze' was deliberately aimed at the US Army II Corps, and Rommel and von Arnim briefly hoped to split the US forces from the British V Corps to the north. Rommel had but 50 tanks left in the Deutsches Afrika Korps as 21st Panzer had been detached to von Arnim's command. But as the assault developed, Rommel had, for one last time, the whole armoured strength of the Axis forces in Africa under his control. He had little fuel and ammunition in reserve but the opportunity was too good to miss.

(map labels)

Brit V Corps · Corps boundary · Fr XIX Corps · 26 Armd Bde · US 9 Div · THALA · Corps boundary · TEBÉSSA · 19 Feb · US 1 Armd Div · Dj Hamra · DAK · Dj Chambi · EL ABIOD · BOU CHEBKA · 18 Feb · US II Corps · ALGERIA · TUNISIA · THÉLEPTE · FÉRIANA · 17 Feb · BIR EL HAFEY · 14 Feb · GAFSA · 15 Feb · EL GUETTAR · LE KEF · 19 Feb · British 6 Armd Div · 1 Gds Bde · MAKTAR · OUSSELTIA · US 34 Div · PICHON · KAIROUAN · To Sousse · SBIBA · Dj Semmama · EL AIOUAN · 21/22 Feb · 10 Pz Div · 19/22 Feb · 21 Pz Div · Hatab · KASSERINE · 18 Feb · SIDI BOU ZID · 14 Feb · Dj Lessouda · Dj Ksaira · FAID · 17 February Arnim moves 10 Pz Div north, returns it to Kasserine 19 Feb · 10 Pz Div · 21 Pz Div · SENED · MAKNASSY · To Sfax · Afrika Korps Det (DAK) · To Gabes · To Tunis · To Bône · To Constantine · FONDOUK · DORSALE · EASTERN · WESTERN

14 February 0400 hrs Arnim attacks (Op 'Frühlingswind')

15 February Rommel attacks (Op 'Morgenluft')

— FRONT LINE 14 FEB 1943
← GERMAN ATTACKS 14/22 FEB
◄ INITIAL ALLIED COUNTERATTACKS

0 MILES 50
0 KILOMETERS 80

Learning from the Master

A half-track emerges from the cavernous hold of an American LST during Operation 'Torch', the Allied landings in Morocco and Algeria. The Afrika Korps was now engaged in a two-front struggle that could have only one end.

US troops press forward from Algeria into Tunisia, confident, well-equipped but actually as unprepared for Rommel as the British had been in Cyrenaica two years before. In December, General von Arnim drove the French from the southern passes.

Although Axis power in North Africa had now shrunk to a bridgehead in Tunisia, Hitler released substantial reinforcements and shipped them to Tunis. Rommel hoped he could defeat his enemies in detail and stave off the inevitable.

Left: Cutting edge of the Afrika Korps
German armour was, as so often, outnumbered at Kasserine. This Panzer IV mounts a 7.5-cm L/48 gun and the crew members have attached spare track wherever they can along the hull front. 10th Panzer Division included a company of Tiger tanks which were immune to most Allied anti-tank guns.

German motorcycle reconnaissance
German reconnaissance units had swiftly identified the weaknesses in the French positions along the passes, enabling von Arnim to overrun the vital defensive positions along the border.

B-25 Mitchell medium bomber
Although the Luftwaffe sustained an aggressive defence of eastern Algeria, the Allied ground troops were now supported by a powerful bomber force which steadily reduced the German rear area to a shambles.

German armour suddenly switched westward to pounce on US II Corps at 04.00 on St Valentine's day. Faid fell immediately and while von Arnim's command pressed on to Kasserine, Rommel swept around the south of the American position.

American armour was lured to destruction the same way British tanks had been before Alamein. The US 1st Armored Division lost 54 out of 58 tanks trying to counter-attack. Panic reigned at II Corps headquarters as defeat turned into rout.

It could not last. Rommel had to call off the attack on 20 February, as the 8th Army appeared along the Mareth front. By inflicting a sharp defeat on a complacent US Army he had gained a little time before the final battle for Tunisia.

KHARKOV: Manstein's Masterpiece

As the last survivors of the 6th Army hold out in the ruins of Stalingrad, the Red Army stands poised to attack all along the line.

The destruction of the German 6th Army in the frozen hell of Stalingrad during January and February 1943 was followed by an ambitious Soviet offensive intended to force the Germans back on all fronts. It was in some ways a repeat of the winter offensive 12 months earlier; a multi-front assault which lacked clear strategic objectives. In formulating his plans, Stalin overestimated the Red Army's capabilities and underestimated the German army's powers of recovery.

The Soviet offensive was to begin with a massive assault into the Ukraine. Three fronts (the Voronezh, South West and South Fronts) were involved. The first was aimed for Kharkov, Kursk and Oboyan. General Nikolai Vatutin's South West Front planned to outflank German forces in the Donbas and pin them against the Sea of Azov. Meanwhile the South Front would advance west along the coast in the direction of Mariupol. The South West Front opened its offensive on 29 January 1943, four armies and a 'Front Mobile Group' under Lieutenant General Popov smashing their way forward. By 2 February, when the Voronezh Front launched its attack to the north, the 3rd Guards Tank Army was already over the Donets east of Voroshilovgrad. General Golikov's Vorenezh Front enjoyed similar success, its flank armies (40th, 69th and 3rd Tank Armies) advancing on a line Kursk – Belgorod – Kharkov.

Kharkov was the fourth largest city in the USSR and a major prize. The rapidity of the Soviet advance threatened to cut off II SS Panzer Corps and Army Detachment Lanz, as well as to sever communications between Army Group Centre and the southern German units. On 15 February II SS Panzer Corps evacuated the city rather than face encirclement, and a 160-km (100-mile) gap yawned in the German front line.

The Red Army was now poised to capture the Dniepr crossings at Zaporozhye which would cut off the German supply lines to Army Group 'Don'. Vatutin and Golikov were elated at the prospect, while German commanders were wondering when the apparently inexorable Soviet advance could be halted. But for the Soviet troops on the ground the pressure was telling: their rapid advance had burned out many Soviet formations and divisions were down to a few thousand men. Half the tank strength of the South West Front was out of action as a result partly of battle damage, but mainly of mechanical wear and tear. However, the decision was made to continue the offensive: the spring thaw would come soon and would force a temporary halt in operations as the hard, frozen soil turned to liquid mud.

The Soviet winter offensive January-March 1943
Stalin's great winter offensive was underway even as the last pitiful remnants of the German 6th Army fought on at Stalingrad. The victory on the Volga had imbued the Soviets with fresh confidence and revealed the growing disparity between the German army and the Red Army. The winter offensive recaptured most of the territory lost in 1942.

'Das Reich' returns to Kharkov, March 1943
Grinning members of the 2nd SS Panzer Division 'Das Reich' ride on a StuG III 7.5-cm assault gun during the recapture of Kharkov. The snow is thawing but the vehicle still carries widened tracks to reduce ground pressure and improve mobility over snow.

From the Don to the Donets

This time the Germans were prepared for the appalling conditions of the Russian winter, but the beginning of 1943 saw the Wehrmacht hard pressed to hold its ground. In the back of everyones' mind was the ghastly fate of the 6th Army.

The Red Army had the reserves and the equipment to launch a major winter offensive but Stalin insisted on attacking a very broad front indeed. From Kursk to the Black Sea, the Soviets hurled themselves at the lightly held German front line.

Hitler's insistence on holding ground stemmed from his experiences in World War I, but this time his commanders persuaded him to relent. The Germans fell back, abandoning Kharkov on 15 February, fighting a series of rearguard actions.

It may not have been obvious to the exhausted Soviet troops as they advanced westwards against stiffening German resistance, but their enemies were willingly giving up ground. Generalfeldmarschall Erich von Manstein persuaded Hitler that mindless adherence to World War I defensive tactics would doom his men to another Stalingrad. By trading ground for time, he planned a counterstroke which would regain most of the lost territory and destroy the advancing Soviet forces.

The Soviet commanders were well served by their intelligence officers, and reconnaissance aircraft observed large concentrations of German armour around Krasnograd and major troop movements near Dnepropetrovsk. Unfortunately the conviction that the Germans were still in retreat led to the assumption that this was simply another rearguard on its way west.

Von Manstein struck on 20 February. SS Panzer troops attacked from Krasnograd while XL Panzer Corps raced north to strike Popov's 'mobile group' of four corps, which had just 25 tanks between them. For several days Soviet units were ordered to continue their offensive until the grim reality of their position filtered through to their senior commanders. Even then many units received no instructions to fall back and were encircled by the Germans. By the end of the month von Manstein's forces had broken through to the Donets.

Retreat across the snowfields

The flat, wintry landscape was ideal for an armoured offensive and left the retreating Soviets horribly exposed. Visible at up to 20 km (12 miles), Soviet columns could be engaged with artillery as they hurried east. And given the fact that very few tanks had fuel or ammunition, the Soviet formations were unable to resist armoured attack. Many units panicked under the strain and fled with little semblance of military order. Kharkov was recaptured on 15 March and the front stabilized as the spring thaw imposed its stodgy grip on operations.

Von Manstein's counter-attack remains a model example of defensive mechanized warfare. The Germans did not resist the Soviet steamroller, but retreated swiftly until they could mass sufficient forces for a counterstroke and their enemies had outrun their supplies of fuel and ammunition. When the attack was launched, tank commanders were not hampered by rigid instructions from the rear but were allowed to use their *Fingerspitzengefuhl* (fingertip feeling). Bold use of initiative allowed the German forces to react swiftly to changing circumstances and outmanoeuvre larger but more unwieldy Soviet formations. Von Manstein was sufficiently confident of success to begin planning the summer campaign several days before beginning the counter-attack: thus the Battle of Kursk was already taking shape.

The recapture of Kharkov
II SS Panzer Corps abandoned Kharkov on 15 February to avoid encirclement but von Manstein's counter-attack recaptured the city a month later. Here SS troops wearing thick winter clothing advance into the city centre.

Co-ordinating the defence: a German command post on the move. Both sides knew that the coming spring thaw would bring a temporary halt to operations as the frozen soil dissolved into mud. Stalin urged his commanders on, despite their heavy losses.

The Germans suffered nearly a million casualties during the winter of 1942/3, the Soviets many more. Despite the odds, von Manstein launched his counter-offensive on 20 February and soon drove back the depleted Soviet spearheads.

SS troops re-enter Kharkov on the Ides of March, the crowning achievement of von Manstein's counter-attack. The Red Army had recaptured most of the territory lost in 1942 but underestimated the German army's defensive strength.

KURSK: Turning point in the East

July 1943: The German army launches its last great offensive in the East. But German intentions are telegraphed well in advance.

There was no doubt where the main German blow for 1943 would fall. The fighting of the previous spring had left an outward bulge (salient) in the Red Army lines around Kursk and this was to be the next German objective. Again, in 1943 there was to be a change from previous years in that this time the German blow was anticipated. Although the German staff planned as meticulously as ever, it could not disguise the forthcoming operation, so the Red Army was ideally placed to plan its response.

The Soviets planned for the forthcoming blow by moving nearly three-quarters of their available armour into the Kursk salient. Together with the armour went nearly all their artillery and numerous infantry divisions. Much of this investment went not into a forward disposition but into a powerful reserve in the rear ready for a counter-offensive, as the Red Army was already thinking of a huge advance westwards. In the front lines of the Kursk salient whole Soviet armies were deployed, and opposing them were almost equally powerful forces.

The German attackers were disposed in two large army groups. To the north of the salient was Army Group Centre based on Generaloberst Walter Model's 9th Army with no fewer than three Panzer corps. To the south was Army Group South based on Generaloberst Hermann Hoth's 4th Panzer Army with some of the finest of the available Panzer divisions. In all some 17 Panzer divisions stood ready to fall on the Red Army around Kursk. They were equipped with the latest Tiger and Panther tanks, and in fact the operation was actually delayed until the Panthers were ready, for much was expected of them. They would also be joined by the new Elefant assault gun with its 88-mm (3.46-in) armament.

The Red Army prepared very thoroughly for the assault. No fewer than 20,000 guns of all kinds were massed ready for the German attack, and at the front huge defensive lines equipped with anti-tank weapons of all kinds stood ready. The defensive belts were tens of kilometres deep, with adequate reserves of all forms at the ready. Strongpoints and interconnecting fire plans abounded, and huge minefields were laid.

Partisan movement

The Red Army had one advantage the Germans lacked. Deep in the German rear, partisan bands constantly watched German activities and reported back to Red Army headquarters. Any move the Germans made was relayed back and countermoves were arranged accordingly. Thus it was that as the German forces massed for the attack during the early hours of 5 July 1943, a storm of Soviet artillery fell among them to disrupt and disorganize at a critical moment. The attack had to be postponed for 90 minutes, but eventually it went in to be met by a veritable hail of fire.

Anti-tank barrage

For once attackers and defenders were evenly matched. In numerical terms there was little to choose between the two, but the Germans did have a qualitative advantage with their new tanks; however this was more theoretical than practical, for the tanks ran directly into a wall of anti-tank fire that stopped them dead in their tracks. Red Army tank-killer squads then ran all over them and destroyed them by placing explosive charges in their exhausts or by their fuel tanks. The Elefant assault guns fared particularly badly (nearly all were lost) as they had no defensive machine-guns, and at such close ranges were virtually sitting ducks for the attentions of the tank-killing squads. The Tigers and Panthers managed little better. Many of the prematurely deployed Panthers either broke down or proved to have serious 'bugs' in their systems, and were thus rather

One to the Germans: a burning T-34
For both sides, it was not so much the loss of tanks that mattered, but the casualties among skilled tank crew. Wounded Soviet tank men were treated separately from other casualties and were rushed back into action as soon as they were fit again.

less than effective. As ever, the Tigers survived well but could make little headway against the massed anti-tank guns. By the end of the day the defences of the salient were almost everywhere intact.

By 12 July the time was right for the counter-stroke. It started on the southern flank of the salient when the remaining forces of the 4th Panzer Army massed for another advance. As they moved forward they ran straight into the massed armour of the Soviet 5th Guards Tank Army. It was the greatest tank battle in history as well over 1,500 tanks met head-on in a mighty clash of armour. A huge dust cloud developed in which the tanks of both sides milled and jostled, but this time it was the turn of the Red Army to come out on top. Their tanks and crews were fresh and had not had to endure over a week of hard combat before they reached the battle, as had been the case for the Germans. Also their T-34s were backed up by new armoured vehicles like the SU-85 self-propelled gun, in action for the first time with an 85-mm (3.34-in) high-velocity gun mounted in an armoured superstructure on a T-34 hull and used as a very effective tank-killer. Another Red Army surprise was the first appearance of the SU-152 Zvierboy (animal hunter), a KV chassis mounting a 152-mm (6-in) howitzer that was able to shatter German tanks by shell power alone.

By the evening of 12 July the Soviets were in possession of the battlefield as the Germans fell back to the rear to avoid annihilation. The 4th Panzer Army had been virtually destroyed and what was intended

The old magic fails

Men from 2nd SS Panzer Division 'Das Reich' question a Soviet prisoner. German commanders became aware the Soviets knew what was coming, but Hitler insisted on sticking to the plan. Many senior officers dreaded the outcome.

For once, Stalin had heeded his officers and called off the Soviet summer offensive. The Soviet reserves poured into the Kursk salient ready to repulse the coming German onslaught. Then the Red Army would mount an offensive of its own.

The mighty Tiger heavy tanks formed the vanguard of German armoured attacks, behind them came the lighter Panzer IIIs and IVs. Formations of up to 200 machines manoeuvred in dense masses on the open steppe. It remains the greatest tank battle in history.

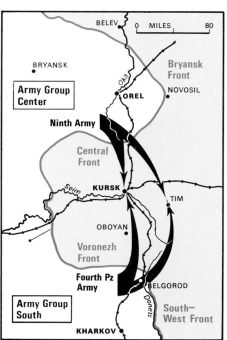

Operation 'Citadel': pinching out the Kursk Salient
On the map it looked so simple, but two armies can read a map. The German army prepared to come on in the same old way, albeit with heavier tanks and better aircraft. The Soviets planned to let the Germans wear themselves down against concentrated defences then launch their own offensive.

The beginning of the end: retreating from Kursk
The Führer's elite warriors, 1st SS Panzer Division 'Leibstandarte Adolf Hitler' showing the strain. The SS Panzer Corps suffered catastrophic losses and were finally beaten in a massive tank battle on the southern flank on 12 July. They were driven back over their start line during the following week.

Left: Sturmoviks of the Voronezh Front attack 4th Panzer Army
The Soviets built numerous dummy airfields in the salient which absorbed most of the Lutfwaffe's fury. When the ground battle began, the bulk of Soviet aircraft had survived and pounced on the German armoured columns.

Inside a German command post
It had already dawned on the German front-line soldiers that they were attacking a well-equipped, numerically superior enemy in prepared positions. Despite the odds they launched themselves forward with all their customary elan and tactical skill.

to be yet another breakthrough had turned into yet another major German defeat. It was time for the counter-attack, and it duly followed the German withdrawal. Under a huge barrage by over 3,000 artillery pieces the Red Army fell upon the Germans on both flanks of the Kursk salient. Within days it had ceased to exist as the walls of the salient were pushed outward. The battle raged not only on the ground but in the air as well. The Soviet air forces were able to gain a mastery of the air which they used to full effect. As the Germans fell back they were constantly harassed by hordes of Ilyushin I1-2 and other strike aircraft.

The long retreat begins

The Kursk fighting did not finally die down until late August, but by that time the Germans had been pushed rearward far beyond their original start points. Their long retreat to Germany had finally begun, and although they were later to regroup and regain local initiatives, their ultimate defeat was already well under way. The Germans were not beaten at Kursk by the Soviet armed forces alone. They were also beaten by the latent energy of the ordinary Soviet people who worked long shifts under desperate conditions for many months in order to arm, clothe and feed the front-line Red Army soldiers, and without them the Soviet armed forces would have been powerless. They provided the energy that finally overcame the power of the German Reich.

The Elefant tank destroyer

Great hopes were pinned on this heavily armoured vehicle armed with an 8.8-cm gun. Unfortunately it lacked any defensive machine-guns and was horribly vulnerable to infantry tank-killing squads. Like the whole offensive, the Elefant's operational debut was an unqualified disaster.

The Red Army's plan depended on countless batteries of anti-tank guns. Firing volleys at individual German tanks they tore the guts out of the Panzer divisions, critically weakening them before the Soviets unleashed their own armour.

The Germans came on in the same old style and their armour suffered heavy losses. On 12 July the Soviet tank armies counter-attacked, these KV-1 heavy tanks soon regaining the lost positions and driving the Germans over their start line.

This is the end: the catastrophic losses irrevocably shifted the balance of power in the East and the German army could no longer hold back the Red Army. Hitler could continue to plot, but the 1,000-year Reich perished on the steppe near Kursk.

TARGET FOR TONIGHT:
The night battles over Germany

March 1943: RAF Bomber Command launches a sustained bombing campaign against German cities.

Shortly after the 'Torch' landings in North Africa during November 1942, the British and American leaders conferred at Casablanca to determine the future course of the war. One result was a directive, put before Air Chief Marshal Sir Arthur Harris, setting out his bombing priorities, which were 'the progressive destruction . . . of the German military, industrial and economic system, and the undermining of the morale of the German people to a point where their capacity for armed resistance is fatally weakened'. To begin to achieve this objective RAF Bomber Command was now fairly well-equipped, possessing on 4 March 1943 a total of 18 Avro Lancaster squadrons, 11 of Handley Page Halifaxes, six of Short Stirlings and 15 of Vickers Wellingtons, all operational at night, for a total of 321 Lancasters, 220 Halifaxes, 141 Stirlings and 268 Wellingtons.

The first manifestation of the great night bombing offensive that now broke over Germany and lasted until the end of the war was what came to be known as the Battle of the Ruhr. This started on the night of 5/6 March 1943 with a raid by 442 aircraft against Essen, the first full-scale operation in which the navigation and bombing aid 'Oboe' was used successfully.

Six weeks later Bomber Command carried out one of its most famous raids of all time, the attack (Operation 'Chastise') on 16/17 May by 19 Lancasters of No. 617 Squadron, led by Wing Commander Guy Gibson, against the Möhne, Eder, Sorpe and Schwelme dams, whose hydro-electric stations supplied power to the industrial Ruhr. Dropping special 4196-kg (9,250-lb) 'bouncing' mines, the Lancasters breached the Möhne and Eder dams for the loss of eight aircraft; Gibson survived to be awarded the Victoria Cross for his leadership on the raid.

The Battle of the Ruhr continued until June, and was considered highly successful for the widespread damage caused, being made possible principally on account of the radio aids available which were efficient at the relatively short ranges involved in flights to the Ruhr.

As new Lancaster and Halifax squadrons continued to join Bomber Command, Harris now determined on the destruction of a single vital city in Germany and on the night of 24/25 July launched 791 heavy bombers against Hamburg, the first of four massive raids on the city in 10 days (Operation 'Gomorrah'), carried out in concert with the heavy bombers of the USAAF which attacked the city during daylight hours. Hamburg was chosen not only on account of its importance as an industrial city but for the manner in which the great port could be distinguished on H_2S radar, a blind bombing and navigation aid that had been in use by Bomber Command for some six months. ('Oboe' could not be used because of Hamburg's distance from the UK). Vital ingredient in the raids on Hamburg was the first significant use of 'Window', vast clouds of tinfoil strips dropped by the bombers to saturate enemy radar screens with spurious signals. In the four Bomber Command raids 2,630 bombers attacked Hamburg, dropping 8,621 tons of bombs which destroyed more than 6,000 acres of the port, killed more than 41,800 inhabitants and injured over 37,000. The loss of 87 aircraft represented less than three per cent of the aircraft despatched and was well within sustainable limits.

RAF Bombers 1943-44

Avro Lancaster
The Lancaster was the mainstay of Bomber Command's squadrons from 1943. Illustrated here is the most famous Lancaster of them all: Wing Commander Guy Gibson's aircraft from No. 617 Squadron which led the 'bouncing bomb' attack on the Ruhr dams in May 1943.

De Havilland Mosquito B Mk IX
The targets were struck first and marked with incendiary bombs by special squadrons of Pathfinders. The Mosquito was an ideal aircraft for the task as its phenomenal performance made it virtually immune to German night-fighters. The aircraft illustrated flew with No.105 Squadron in 1944.

Handley Page Halifax B Mk II
Although the Lancaster eventually equipped many more squadrons, the Halifax remained as important aircraft to Bomber Command. Over 6,000 Halifaxes were produced in a multitude of versions. This aircraft flew with No.78 Squadron.

Striking at the heart of the Reich

Daylight bomber attacks on Germany at the start of the war had proved disastrous and the RAF began to use the cover of darkness. The Armstrong Whitworth Whitley was widely used by Bomber Command in its first night raids on Germany.

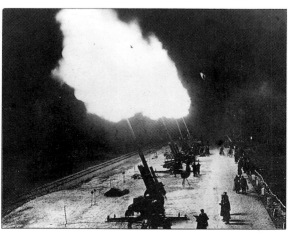

Reichsmarschall Goering placed his faith in searchlights and heavy AA batteries, boasting that no bomber would be able to attack Germany. But attack they did and the Luftwaffe soon evolved a network of radar stations and night-fighters.

By early 1943 Bomber Command had acquired better aircraft and new navigation aids, making it a formidable striking force. Here, an Avro Lancaster is silhouetted over Hamburg in January. Six months later the city was burned to the ground.

The morning after. Berlin 1944
The German capital was subjected to 16 concentrated raids between November 1943 and March 1944 but the great distance to the target and strength of the defences eventually forced Bomber Command to abandon this battle: 587 aircraft and 3,640 men had been lost over Berlin.

The devastating Battle of Hamburg encouraged Harris to open his last great setpiece assault, this time on Berlin itself (although numerous other targets continued to be attacked before, during and after the attacks on the German capital). On the night of 18/19 November 1943 Bomber Command sent 444 bombers, of which 402 attacked the city, losing nine aircraft, while a simultaneous attack was carried out by 325 bombers on Mannheim, the first occasion on which two heavy raids were launched on a single night.

The offensive against Berlin continued through the winter of 1943-4, almost invariably in bad weather but, despite the employment of Bomber Command's specialist Pathfinder Group, No. 8, commanded by Air Commodore D.C.T. Bennett, and the use of sophisticated marking and radio countermeasures techniques, the concentration of damage and accuracy of bombing fell far short of expectations. A total of 16 major raids was launched before the 'battle' ended on 24/25 March 1944, involving 9,111 bomber sorties. The raids cost the command a total of 587 aircraft and more than 3,500 aircrew killed or missing, an unsustainable loss rate

of 6.4 per cent. The damage and casualties inflicted were considerably less than at Hamburg, and the Battle of Berlin failed in its purpose of breaking the spirit of the German people.

One other major raid was launched by Bomber Command at this time (before it was switched to attacks in support of the coming Normandy landings), 795 four-engine bombers being sent to Nuremberg on 30/31 March 1944. On account of inaccurate weather forecasting, inefficient pathfinding and poor raid planning, the bomber stream disintegrated and suffered heavily from German nightfighter attacks; more than 100 bombers were lost. Worse, Nuremberg was scarcely hit by the bombers.

During the final eight months of the war, Bomber Command returned to Germany in greater strength than ever (it ended the war with 56 Lancaster squadrons, 17 of Halifaxes and 18 of de Havilland Mosquitoes, for a total of 2,370 aircraft). Its last target priority was the German oil industry, an industry so completely devastated that it was to be the chronic lack of aviation fuel that finally grounded the once-formidable Luftwaffe.

'Bombs Away!'
Pressing the button on an Avro Lancaster's bombsight releases the bombload and marks the halfway point of a mission. The raids deep into Germany meant many long hours in the air with an lapse in concentration likely to be fatal.

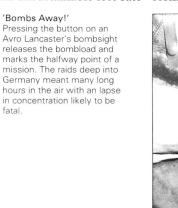

Bombing through the clouds Accurate bombing was not easy. In the early years of the campaign it was common for only one crew in 10 to drop their bombs within 5 miles of the target. But by 1943 navigational aids allowed the bombers to find large cities and even attack through cloud.

Luftwaffe night fighters

Junkers Ju 88G-6b
The ubiquitous Ju 88 made a highly effective night-fighter. This aircraft carries *schräge Musik*, upward-firing cannon which enabled it to approach the British bombers from below and inflict fatal damage without warning.

Heinkel He 219 Uhu (Owl)
The later years of the Luftwaffe were notable for the appearance of some magnificent aircraft which never realised their true potential, thanks to political infighting. The He 219 was the best night fighter of the war with outstanding performance, heavy cannon armament and even ejector seats. Fortunately for the RAF, only modest numbers were deployed.

Halifaxes on their way to attack one of the synthetic oil plants in Germany's industrial heartland, the Ruhr valley. It proved very difficult to target specific sectors and industry, but much easier to torch whole cities.

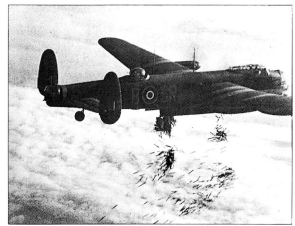

During the winter of 1943/44, Bomber Command suffered heavy losses despite equipment like 'Airborne Cigar' (ABC) carried by this Lancaster. ABC jammed signals between the German night-fighters and their ground control.

By the last weeks of the war, Bomber Command had thoroughly pounded every major population centre in Germany. The nightly battles over the Reich had forced the Germans to devote major resources to home defence: it was a vital contribution to victory.

THE SCHWEINFURT RAIDS: Battle over Germany

August 1943: Over 300 B-17 Flying Fortresses raid Schweinfurt, centre of the German ball-bearing industry. They are unescorted and the Luftwaffe is waiting.

The original plan to cripple the vital German ball-bearing industry centred on Schweinfurt was called Operation 'Juggler'. It called for the despatch of 150 Boeing B-17Fs of the 4th CBW (Heavy) to bomb the big Messerschmitt factory at Regensburg-Prüfening and then to fly on to bases in North Africa, taking off shortly before the 240 B-17Fs of the 1st CBW which were to attack Schweinfurt. British and American Supermarine Spitfires and Republic P-47s would provide penetration cover as far as Brussels for the Regensburg raid, thereby attracting the great majority of enemy fighters into the air too soon to interfere seriously with the main raid on Schweinfurt by forcing them to land and refuel at the critical time as the main force pushed through.

From the outset of the raids, which were launched on 17 August, bad weather destroyed these carefully laid plans. Thick fog over the 4th CBW's bases delayed the Regensburg raiders, but eventually they were ordered off to ensure their arrival over the African bases in daylight. However, being based further inland in the UK, where the fog persisted longer, the 1st CBW was unable to take off until three-and-a-half hours later, by which time the covering fighters were themselves on the ground refuelling. Furthermore the 4th CBW had attracted the undivided attention of the German defences, losing 24 B-17s (from the 94th, 95th, 96th, 100th, 385th, 388th and 390th Bomb Groups) of the 146 aircraft that crossed the enemy coast.

Enemy Coast Ahead

By the time the 1st CBW reached the Belgian coast the enemy fighters had re-armed and refuelled and were again on the alert; and fighters that had been called from distant sectors of the Reich earlier in the day were now concentrated in the very areas to be covered by the Schweinfurt raiders. As 230 B-17Fs of the 91st, 92nd, 303rd, 305th, 306th, 351st, 379th, 381st and 384th Bomb Groups entered Belgian skies the leading box of 60 bombers was assaulted by successive waves of fighters from JG 26, followed by elements of JG2, JG 3 and I/JG 5. Before the target was reached and bombed at 1457, this one box had lost 21 aircraft, and seven others had turned for home without bombing. In all, the target was struck by 183 B-17s despite the persistent attempts by the fighters. By the time the 1st CBW arrived back over its bases it had lost 36 aircraft together with 371 crew members; 19 other B-17s were withdrawn from the combat-ready list for lengthy repairs.

Subsequent reconnaissance disclosed that only two of the five vital ball-bearing plants had been significantly damaged (the VKF and KGF facilities); post-war intelligence showed that bearing production was reduced by only 21 per cent, and then for not more than three weeks. Indicative of American realization that the raid had failed in its aim was reflected in the absence of any Distinguished Unit Citations among the 1st CBW's groups; by contrast, every one of the 4th CBW's groups that had bombed Regensburg won a DUC.

As combat reports were studied it became all too clear that with the current level of German ability and determination to resist the deep penetration raids, the unescorted daylight raid plan was failing. An immediate outcome was accelerated delivery of the B-17G with increased forward gun armament (in a chin turret); in the longer term the range of the American escort fighters (the Republic P-47 and Lockheed P-38) was progressively increased by the use of larger droptanks, until eventually these two types were joined by the superlative North American P-51D.

Unknown to the Americans at the time, the 17 August raid on Schweinfurt prompted the Germans to start dispersing the ball-bearing industry throughout Germany. A second heavy raid was launched on 14 October by 420 B-17s and Consolidated B-24s. Once again bad weather interfered and prevented the B-24 element from assembling with the B-17s, and it was accordingly ordered to fly a diversionary feint over the North Sea. Thus it was that no more than 291 B-17s eventually set out for Schweinfurt, the leading 1st Division flying an almost direct route to the target, and the following 3rd Division following a dogleg route in an attempt to confuse the enemy as to its eventual target. The former therefore took the brunt of the German fighter reaction, the 305th Bomb Group, for instance, losing 14 of its 17 aircraft. Once more 60 American bombers were lost to the Luftwaffe, the majority of them to the pilots of I Jagdkorps. Ironically, on this occasion the bombing results were judged to be excellent – against an industrial target that had largely been moved elsewhere. Even the claims by the American B-17 gunners to have destroyed 288 enemy fighters had eventually to be confirmed as no more than 53.

Schweinfurt re-visited

The American 1st Division again raided Schweinfurt on 24 February 1944 when 238 B-17Fs and B-17Gs, this time with long-range fighter escort, took off for the long flight over Germany, losing only 11 of their number. The RAF now took a hand, and on the same night 663 Handley Page Halifaxes and Avro Lancasters dropped 2,000 tons of bombs. And on the night of 30/31 March 1944, during the disastrous RAF raid on Nuremberg, more than 100 Halifax and Lancaster crews dropped about 400 tons of bombs in the Schweinfurt area, believing it to be Nuremberg. Further attacks by the 8th Air Force B-17s and B-24s were flown by day on 21 July and 9 October 1944 against Schweinfurt, and the last

Warming up a Flying Fortress. February 1944
After the attack in August, Schweinfurt was raided again in October with the loss of another 60 bombers. The third strike was launched the following February, this time with long range fighter escort which succeeded in keeping the German fighters away. Only 11 bombers were lost although (unknown to the USAAF) the ball bearing industry had now been dispersed all over Germany.

Fight for a Factory

17 August: B-17s of the 381st Bomb Group which formed part of the 230-strong second wave head off. The first wave was to attack Regensburg then fly on to North Africa, diverting the German fighters from the second wave at Schweinfurt.

The first wave (4th CBW) was delayed by fog over its airfields and the P-47 fighters which were to have escorted it as far as Belgium were forced to land and refuel, leaving the Fortresses to battle through the German fighters alone.

24 of 4th CBW's 146 B-17s were shot down during the attack but most of the bombers managed to retain their defensive formation and flew all the way to North Africa. Meanwhile, 1st CBW was heading into Germany to its destruction.

raid, by medium bombers of the US 9th Air Force, took place in April 1945.

While the martyrdom of Schweinfurt assumed the proportions of an American bombing epic, it served well to demonstrate the characteristic flaws in the whole Allied strategic bombing plan: that no decisive result would be achieved through bombing without comprehensively accurate intelligence about the enemy's ability to disperse his vital war targets, and without prior winning of air superiority in the enemy's air space.

Boeing B-17

Bristling with defensive machine-guns, the B-17 Flying Fortress received its name in 1935 when the first prototype flew and it was confidently believed that bombers could beat off defending fighters alone. This B-17F is shown in the colours of the 91st Bomb Group which took part in the disastrous raid on 17 August.

Vapour trails over the Reich
The spectacular contrails left in the wake of the bomber stream made the mass daylight raids a stunning sight but were an unwelcome advertisement from the crews' point of view. No amount of dashing leather flying kit could keep out the icy chill of 20,000 ft and frostbite was a real hazard, particularly to the waist gunners who stood by open hatches. As each attacking fighter was fired on by a multitude of Air Force gunners, the US kill claims sometimes exceeded the entire fighter strength of the Luftwaffe. This, and an exaggerated belief in the effects of the bombing, encouraged the USAAF to press on despite the heavy losses over Schweinfurt.

Messerschmitt Bf 110

The Bf 110 *Zerstörer* (destroyer) had come badly unstuck during the Battle of Britain. But it survived as a fighter-bomber and was in its element against unescorted heavy bombers until the arrival of long range Thunderbolts and Mustangs in 1944 banished it to night operations.

The timing of the American attack had broken down, allowing the German fighters to refuel and re-arm before the B-17s of 4th CBW appeared over the Reich. Here Messerschmitt Bf 109s armed with air-to-air rockets are prepared for action.

The tight defensive formations of the bomber groups disintegrated under determined Luftwaffe attack; the leading 60-strong group lost 28 aircraft before it reached the target. Nevertheless, 183 B-17s reached and bombed Schweinfurt.

Landing took a final toll of American lives as 2 crippled B-17s crashed at Manston. The raid inflicted trifling damage on German industrial capacity and the target was to be attacked again with equally futile results the following year.

OPERATION HUSKY: The invasion of Sicily

With North Africa in Allied hands the invasion of Sicily is a necessary preliminary to an attack on mainland Italy.

Armstrong Whitworth Albemarle

A failed British bomber design, the Albemarle was pressed into service as a transport aircraft. This is a Mk V of 297 Squadron RAF which towed some of the ill-fated gliders during the landing on Sicily. Note the 'invasion stripes' which would regularly adorn Allied aircraft from now on.

Throughout the morning of 9 July 1943 the invasion fleets steamed past Malta, those carrying the US 7th Army under command of Lieutenant General George Patton on the west of the island, those carrying the British 8th Army under General Sir Bernard Montgomery on the east. Some 2,500 ships and landing craft escorted or were carrying 160,000 men, 14,000 vehicles, 600 tanks and 1,800 guns in what was to that date the largest amphibious operation in history.

Upon reaching the shores of Sicily the armies would storm open beaches, and in order to occupy the entire island they must defeat an enemy force of nearly 300,000, of whom 40,000 were German veterans of the 15th Panzergrenadier Division and the 'Hermann Goering' Panzer Division.

On crowded airfields in Tunisia, the engines of 109 American Douglas C-47s and 35 British Armstrong Whitworth Albemarles were warming up and their crews climbing aboard, while behind each plane was linked a Waco or Horsa glider packed with the 1,500 officers and men of the British 1st Airlanding Brigade. Just before 1900 the aircraft began to take off into clear evening air. But by the time they were approaching Malta for their assembly and turning point the sky had darkened, they were into the gale centre and the winds were driving the planes off course and buffeting the gliders.

Two hours after the British airborne forces had taken off, another 222 C-47s filled with 3,400 American paratroops had taken off from Tunisian airfields, soon to find themselves in the same chaos and disorder as that which was engulfing the British brigade. Nearly 40 of the tows of the combined force wisely turned back, but only 54 of the British gliders landed in Sicily, the rest going down into the sea with the cargoes drowned; the American paratroops were dropped into Sicily, but only some 200 were anywhere near their objectives, and for some hours their commander, Major General James Gavin, was under the impression that he had been dropped into mainland Italy.

The Italian units along the stretch between Cape Passero and Syracuse had decided that no-one in their senses would attempt a seaborne landing in such weather and had relaxed their attention once the Allied aircraft had flown off, so the first waves of the British assault landed without opposition and swept over the coastal defences almost before their presence was noticed. Belatedly, a few inland artillery units opened fire on the invasion beaches, to be blanketed immediately with shells from one or more of the six battleships (*Nelson, Rodney, Warspite, Valiant, Howe* and *King George V*) which had accompanied the force for just this purpose.

Shortly after dawn on 10 July advanced units of the British 5th Division were approaching Cassibile and by 0800 the town was in their hands, the whole of the British XIII Corps was coming ashore to the south of the division while the 51st (Highland) Division and the 1st Canadian Division of XXX Corps, with Royal Marine Commandos on their western flank, were ashore around the corner of Cape Passero, between the point and Pozzallo.

Farther to the west, the US 7th Army had not been quite so fortunate. The coastal defenders had not been asleep along their stretch and the ships and landing craft came under fire from almost the moment of their arrival. Again, fire from the heavy naval guns soon obliterated most of the opposition (much to Patton's astonishment and delight, as he had placed little reliance upon naval assurances) but the pier at Gela which would have been very useful for a quick build-up was blown to pieces by demolition charges as two Ranger battalions were actually sailing for it, and by 0430 Italian and German aircraft were over the crowded beaches to sink two transports in an awkward position.

Airborne landings

But by mid-morning all the forward formations of the 8th and 7th Armies were ashore and probing inland, and the latter was suddenly to receive an unexpected bonus. If their airborne colleagues were not in exactly the right positions, they had coagulated during darkness into 20 or 30 independent groups and were creating chaos in the country just behind the landing beaches, cutting communications, ambushing lone cars, lorries or even small convoys, attacking crossroad guardposts and on one occasion holding up an entire Italian mobile regiment which had been sent to find out what was happening at Gela.

At the other end of the invasion beaches, however, the tiny part of the British airborne force, just

Il Duce's reluctant warriors
German suspicions of Italian intentions were confirmed early in the campaign for Sicily and General Hube was dispatched to the island with the HQ of XIV Panzer Corps to take command of the island's defence. Italian privates surrendered while their officers plotted to overthrow Mussolini.

The race to Messina

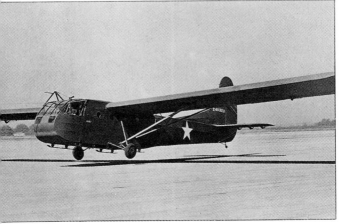

The amphibious landings were supplemented by a massive air landing involving parachutists and glider-borne troops. Unfortunately many of the gliders like this Waco CG-4 dropped short and crashed into the sea, drowning their occupants.

The landings took place on 26 beaches along 150 miles of Sicily's south-eastern coast. Only half-hearted resistance was expected from the Italians; the strength of the opposition would depend on how many German troops were posted to the island.

The American airlanding was as unsuccessful as the British, with the troops scattered over a wide area and their commander beginning to suspect he had been dropped in mainland Italy by mistake.

British troops come ashore
Montgomery's 8th Army which landed in Sicily comprised four infantry divisions with two in reserve plus three armoured brigades. The fighting resembled the last stages in Tunisia and the 8th Army was to suffer 9,000 casualties as it pressed slowly north.

Seapower in action: HMS *Nelson*
Six battleships led the shore bombardment group of a naval task force comprising 182 warships and 126 landing craft. Three large convoys of men and equipment sailed from Egypt, Tunisia and the UK, rendezvousing off Malta before heading for Sicily.

100 men who had been landed in the correct place, assumed the task of the entire 1,500-strong brigade and had rushed and taken the Ponte Grande over the River Cavadonna just south of Syracuse. By mid-afternoon they were in desperate straits. At 1530 a massed assault overran the survivors, but eight managed to escape and, as the British had removed all the demolition charges while in possession of the bridge, the Italian marines had now to try to emplace some more. Two of the escaping eight therefore took position half way up an overlooking hill and from there sniped at every movement on the bridge, while the remaining six, stumbling with exhaustion, made their way south towards Cassibile. Five km (three miles) along the road they met a mobile column from the 5th Division. They led this column back to the bridge, which fell immediately into British hands again, and by 1700 the column was driving into Syracuse itself.

By the end of the first day the British therefore held the coastal strip from Pozzallo around to Syracuse, a vital port that was in their hands and sufficiently undamaged for immediate use, while the US 7th Army held nearly 65 km (40 miles) of beach between Scoglitti and Licata. Inland, scattered bands of British and American airborne troops were loose over the southern half of the island, successfully spreading alarm and confusion.

Within 10 days Canadian units had reached Enna in the centre of the island, and two days later Patton's troops had not only reached the north coast but had turned west and occupied Palermo, taking prisoner thousands of Italian soldiers who were more than happy to stop fighting, and being welcomed everywhere by delighted Sicilians to whom quite a number of the American soldiers were related. Very soon it became evident that the bulk of the inhabitants of the Italian mainland felt the same way.

Paratroops of XI Air Corps
As the Allies prepared to attack, the Germans combined the 7th Air Division (re-designated 1st Parachute Division) with the newly formed 2nd Parachute Division to form a strategic reserve of 30,000 elite troops. They would be the cornerstone of the German defence of Italy.

LSTs disgorge their cargoes onto the beach at Licata. Montgomery planned to advance straight up the eastern coast towards Messina to block the retreat of the garrison over the straits and into Italy, but it was not to be.

The Germans decided to evacuate Sicily rather than attempt a last-ditch stand. Tough formations including paratroops fought a vigorous rearguard action as they fell back on Messina.

Patton's men reached Palermo after a lightning strike across the island but the German decision to evacuate prevented any encirclement. Battering against the German rearguards on Sicily gave a foretaste of the Italian campaign.

THE BATTLE OF THE ATLANTIC

The most critical battle of the war takes place not on the European mainland but across thousands of miles of ocean.

Successful prosecution of the war in Europe depended absolutely upon a steady flow of supplies being maintained by convoyed merchantmen plying between the New and Old Worlds. The primary weapon employed by the Germans in their attempts to strangle this flow was the U-boat and the submarine supremo, Admiral Karl Doenitz, well understood his priorities. Even before his appointment in 1935 he had developed and proved group ('wolfpack') tactics, and went on to define the types of boat best suited to near and distant operations as well as the number required to beat a fully-organized convoy system. Even after the Anglo-German Naval Agreement of 1935 had allowed the Germans quite generous limits to submarine construction, the grandiose Z-Plan for surface vessel construction prevented their realization. As a result in September 1939, in place of the 300 boats considered necessary, only 56 were complete, of which only 22 were of types capable of ocean service. For a time, losses exceeded commissionings so that, in February 1941, only 22 operational boats remained.

International Law

An unrestricted sinking policy was, Doenitz considered, legally justified with merchantmen escorted, armed and given instructions to ram on opportunity. The declared war zone first extended to 20° West, about 800 km (500 miles) west of Ireland. Initially pickings were rich as merchantmen returned individually to the UK, while the major routes from the UK to Halifax and Sydney, Nova Scotia saw convoys escorted through only 15° longitude from either end for lack of suitable escorts. Small numbers at this time prevented the U-boats from attacking in packs, but surface raiders were proving a real threat so that great efforts had to be made to cover convoys with older battleships. All too often only a solitary Armed Merchant Cruiser (AMC) was available but, fortunately, the *Jervis Bay* convoy (HX84) was to be a solitary incident.

With the fall of France in June 1940 Doenitz could operate his boats from Biscay ports, shortening transit times and effectively increasing numbers on station. Convoys were, therefore, routed north of Ireland while the increasing availability of long-range maritime aircraft encouraged U-boats to work farther westward. To this time total Allied losses had been a containable 630,000 grt (gross registered tons), but already the 'aces' were beginning to emerge, Hartmann's *U-37* returning on 9 June 1940 with a 43,000 grt bag from a 26-day cruise.

The low, plunging platform of a submarine's tower offers a very restricted horizon, but Doenitz's pleas for regular air searches fell largely on deaf ears, while his hopes of an improvement in locating convoys, potentially possible with the availability of

Italian boats based on Bordeaux after July 1940, were dashed – the boats were of unsuitable design and national temperaments clashed.

In January 1941 Doenitz gained control of I/KG40, a Luftwaffe wing equipped with the Focke-Wulf Fw 200 Condor and based at Bordeaux-Mérignac. These long-range aircraft could not only sink stragglers but report convoys to available submarines. Initially their navigation could be up to 130 km (80 miles) in error, resulting in poor concentrations, but by using them as orbiting beacons on which bearings could be taken the problem was met.

The first successful group attacks on Atlantic convoys occurred in September 1940, both SC2 and HX72 experiencing concentrations of six U-boats and losing a total of 17 ships of nearly 100,000 grt. Assaults were made at night and surfaced, exploiting the U-boats' small profile and favourable surface speed, while rendering the escorts' Asdic (sonar) useless. Despite Doenitz having written of it before

U-635 takes her final dive
Caught by a Sunderland of No. 422 Squadron, RAF, the U-boat is successfully depth-charged. Aircraft and airborne radar sharply reduced the potential of the U-boats whose underwater performance was far inferior to their surface capabilities. Some boats took the council of despair and shipped extra anti-aircraft guns, determined to fight it out.

the war, the British had no plans to counter the tactic and U-boat commanders such as Kretschmer, Schepke, Prien and Kuhnke began to make their names. The escorts' initial response was in powerful illuminants such as 'Snowflake', but the real answer by night lay in the radars that began to become available early in 1941. Further escorts were also being supplemented by more aircraft, while high frequency direction-finding (Huff Duff) sets in the escorts turned Doenitz's reliance on regular radio transmissions from his boats into a weapon that was used against them.

It was a dour struggle, with 1941 seeing the loss of 496 Allied merchantmen of 2.42 million grt in the North Atlantic, a total eclipsed by 1,006 ships of 5.47 million grt in 1942. Half a million gross tons per month would have put in sight Doenitz's objective of destroying shipping faster than it could be replaced. He was frustrated by the enormous Allied programmes of emergency construction of standard types, Liberty, Ocean, Fort, etc, and by the German

high command's repeated use of his boats for less-productive 'side-shows'.

Despite some notable setbacks, most convoys still managed to cross with little incident. During 1941 close cover became possible for the whole crossing, not least because of the crucial expansion of the Royal Canadian Navy. Further, even as the Allied escorts added to their experience, the Germans began to lose theirs with the gradual destruction of their 'aces'. A sustained air offensive against transiting U-boats in the Bay of Biscay produced an excellent return, the Germans buying increased protection by the development of the *Schnorkel* (snort), but in forcing them to remain submerged this expedient greatly reduced their performance. Having contacted a convoy, submarines were now also likely to find an escort carrier providing local air cover to keep them down, while cruising escort groups quickly reinforced the close escort at the onset of any threat.

The U-boat with a high, sustained underwater performance was, therefore, developed as a matter of the highest priority, but was to enter service too late.

March 1943 saw 500,000 grt lost but, from this point, the U-boat offensive went into decline. Between May and August alone, though 98 new boats were commissioned, 123 were lost; each represented a trained crew perished or prisoner. Despite the submarine loss rate and every effort to disrupt the assembly programme by bombing, total strength remained at well over 400 from mid-1943 until the end of hostilities. But their North Atlantic success rate declined dramatically: 463 ships of 2.59 million grt in 1943 but only 132 of 0.77 million grt in 1944, a period which saw the build-up to the Normandy invasion.

The victory in the Battle of the Atlantic was, arguably, the single most important of the war and cost the Allies some 12 million grt, over half their mercantile losses for the complete conflict.

The five-year battle

The lessons of 1917 were forgotten by the Royal Navy between the wars and largely ignored by the Kriegsmarine, which had only 22 ocean-going U-boats in service in 1939. But once at sea, the German submarines rapidly gained the upper hand.

Convoys were instituted but few escorts were available and the British were unprepared for the German tactic of night-time surface attacks, although the German Admiral Doenitz had published articles on the subject before the war.

In the absence of aircraft-carriers, some merchantmen were equipped with Hurricane fighters to protect convoys against German aircraft. The Hurricanes only shot down half a dozen Fw 200 Condors but drove many others away.

Short Sunderland

Nicknamed 'The Flying Porcupine' by German pilots, this magnificent aerial leviathan was equally feared by U-boat crews. The masts along the fuselage are for its radar, and its depth charges are carried internally. RAF Coastal Command began the war just four years old and starved of funds, but it expanded rapidly to play a vital part in the Atlantic victory.

Fw 200 Condor

Originally a 26-seat fast airliner, the Condor ranged far over the Atlantic searching for convoys and vectoring in the U-boats. They carried a bomb and cannon armament to attack shipping themselves: five Condors, 1,000 miles from their Bordeaux base attacked a convoy in February 1941 and sank five ships.

'River' class frigate

Displacing 1,320 tons and armed with a 4-in gun, 'Hedgehog' and 200 depth charges, the 'River' class were dedicated escort vessels introduced after the limitations of the 'Flower' class had been revealed. 138 'River' class frigates were built during 1942-44, 70 of them in Canadian shipyards.

U-boat *U-106*

Long-range ocean raiders with a complement of 48 men, the Type IXs were steadily developed throughout the war. Carrying 22 torpedoes and a 10.5-cm gun, they had a range of 15,000 miles. *U-106* fought off the American coast, in the Caribbean and off West Africa before she was bombed and sunk off north-west Spain in August 1943.

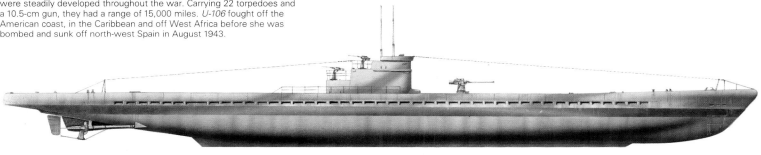

In 1942 the U-boats had a second 'Happy Time', easily finding targets silhouetted by the bright lights of the US east coast. A general blackout would have cut losses, but was delayed for six months due to opposition from the tourist trade.

The pendulum of technological superiority eventually swung inexorably in favour of the Allies during 1943. By that year the German high command knew that a U-boat was unlikely to survive more than three or four patrols.

Radar, aircraft, improved underwater weapons and the dedication of the Allied navies gained the upper hand, although their opponents fought with bravery and determination to the end of the war. The Royal and Merchant Navies lost over 80,000 men.

SALERNO: Balanced on a Knife Edge

September 1943: The Allies are poised to invade Italy. Restricted by the range of their fighters, the landings have to be at Salerno.

By the completion of the campaign in Sicily during August 1943, the main political and tactical decisions about the next step had been taken. The mainland of Italy would be invaded, and the operation would take place in three phases: Operation 'Baytown', whereby the bulk of General Sir Bernard Montgomery's 8th Army would cross the Straits of Messina on to the toe of Italy; Operation 'Slapstick' by which the rest of the 8th Army would land at Taranto on the eastern side of the Italian peninsula; and Operation 'Avalanche' which would put the US 5th Army, consisting of the British X Corps and the US VI Corps (under command of Lieutenant General Mark Clark), ashore in the Gulf of Salerno between Amalfi in the north and Paestum in the south. The British corps would land on the left flank (to the north of the River Sele) and the US corps to the south.

The question which exercised all minds, of course, was the possible strength of the opposition, especially to 'Avalanche'. Would the Italians resist? Would the Germans pull back rapidly to northern Italy if their partners surrendered? Or would every step of the way up the long peninsula be a bitter fight?

Italian Armistice

The first question was answered as the 'Avalanche' convoys carrying the assault forces were actually at sea. Italy had capitulated and in the south Italian formations were abandoning their positions, often throwing away their arms and uniforms, and hurrying home. Moreover, reports from 8th Army units which had crossed from Messina some days before seemed to indicate a rapid German withdrawal; hopes were high on board the transports that theirs would be an unopposed landing, followed by swift penetration inland, easy link-up with 8th Army troops and the occupation of Naples within a matter of hours.

For a short time it looked as though all this would occur. The first ashore, at 0310 on the morning of 9 September 1943, were three US Ranger battalions on the far left flank at Maiori, who met no opposition and within half an hour were marching westwards towards Amalfi, eastwards towards Salerno and north to seize the Chiunzi Pass on the overlooking mountains. On their right British army Commandos landed at Vietri sul Mare and hooked right to enter Salerno, but half an hour later when Royal Marine Commandos landed on the Salerno beaches they hit strong German opposition and needed support waves and all their courage and expertise to expand their beachhead to give them a tenuous hold in the city itself. The Royal Marines were the first to get a taste of the furies to come.

Junkers Ju 88 of KG54 Geschwader 'Totenkopf'

The German army in Italy had little air support available in 1943, which led to some critics like Liddell Hart arguing that the Allied landings could have been farther north. KG54 was withdrawn to Bergamo after Allied attacks on German airfields in southern Italy.

An LST ramp delivers part of the American armoured regiment landed on 9 September at Salerno.
The landings illustrated the classic problem of amphibious warfare: the defenders could concentrate troops opposite the beach-head faster than the attackers could get men and equipment ashore. It was no easy matter to transfer ashore the incredible amounts of kit, ammunition and supplies demanded by four divisions.

B-25 Mitchell medium bomber

Based in Sicily, powerful fleets of twin-engined bombers attacked German communications throughout the battle for Salerno. With road and rail links blocked and limited largely to nocturnal movement, it was exceedingly difficult for the Germans to concentrate their armour for an effective counter-stroke.

A Near Run Thing

'Red' Beach at Salerno on 9 September 1943: opposition to the southern flank of the landing was negligible and American troops pressed inland. Farther to the north, the British forces met some resistance from a line of strongpoints.

Luftwaffe gunners prepare to defend their position against the heavy Allied air attacks in support of the landings. Both sides were well aware that the assault on mainland Italy had to be within fighter range of the Allied air bases on Sicily.

The German plan was to hold the beach lightly, wait until they were sure where the main beach-head was, then counter-attack with massed armour. Here, a British PIAT anti-tank rocket team engages enemy armour probing its position.

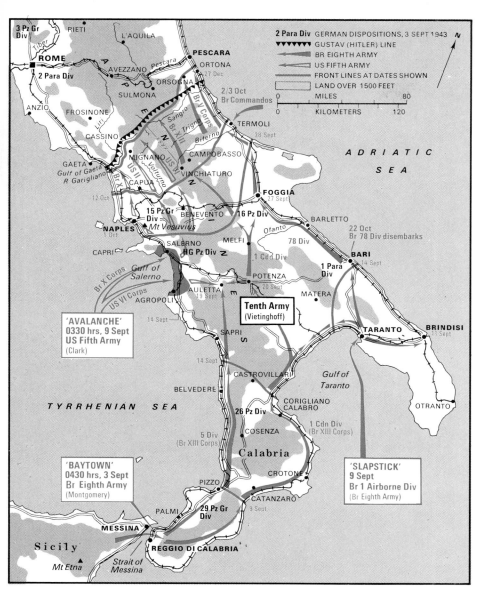

SS men interrogate an Italian officer
Once an Allied invasion of Italy was under way, Italians raced to distance themselves from Mussolini and the Fascist state. The Germans were ready for this defection and rapidly disarmed the Italian army. Assuming control of the country, they prepared to halt the Allied advance towards Germany.

The Soft Underbelly
Italy had been described as the 'soft underbelly' of the Axis, but mountainous terrain defended by the German army is anything but soft. Montgomery's 8th Army was delayed by aggressive German battlegroups in Calabria and extensive mining and demolitions. The Salerno landing force was attacking exactly where predicted and could only trust to massive naval and air power to help beat off the inevitable onslaught.

To their right, the brigades of the British 46th and 56th Divisions came ashore with some difficulty but were soon moving on the southern outskirts of Salerno and the Montecorvino airfield beyond – a vital objective as Salerno was beyond extended air coverage from the Sicilian airfields. The few German tanks which were met were obliterated by naval gunfire.

To the south of the River Sele the two US divisions (36th and 45th) had reached the shore quite easily, but then came under fierce German heavy machine-gun and mortar fire. For a while chaos reigned, but there was no way off the beaches now and gradually order was restored and the companies began to fight their way forward.

By the end of the first day they had reached the line of the railroad and in places beyond it, and the Germans in front seemed to have withdrawn. So to Clark all seemed to be going well: on both sides of the Sele his formations were ashore, the only ominous factor being an 11.25-km (7-mile) gap which

existed between them as neither of the inner flanks had reached the river.

Generaloberst Heinrich von Vietinghoff-Scheel, commanding the German 10th Army in southern Italy, had been intent upon withdrawing all his forces from the foot of Italy when first the British 8th and then the US 5th armies had invaded; and it was obvious that if the Salerno beach-head expanded rapidly many of his forces would be trapped to the south. As soon as he could, therefore, he massed his forces and sent them first to seal in and then to obliterate the beach-head – and as he had three Panzer divisions, two Panzergrenadier divisions, and control of the only airfield in the vicinity (at Montecorvino) he came close to success. By 11 September the fighting along the lengths of both fronts was bitter in the extreme, only naval gunfire protecting the British and US infantry from the Panzers; and on the morning of 13 September Vietinghoff realized the existence of the gap at the Sele rivermouth. This he interpreted as a deliberate splitting of the Allied

force preparatory to evacuation, and redoubled his efforts to obliterate his opponents.

The fighting in both areas increased to Thermopylean proportions, the Allied troops desperate to hold on but with only light weapons against Panzer divisions, their naval artillery support being gradually withdrawn as the ships ran out of ammunition. Their only hope of reinforcement for the moment seemed to be from the air, and that night 1,300 men of the US 82nd Airborne Division dropped in near Paestum and were quickly in action; and now Allied heavy bombers were switched from distant targets to pound the approaches to the beach-heads.

Beach-head secured

Then on 14 September the British 7th Armoured Division joined the northern beach-head, the last regiments of the US 45th Division joined the southern beach-head, and during that night another 2,100 paratroops of the 82nd Airborne Division were successfully dropped in. The beach-heads were safe.

To their south, slowly but implacably, the 8th Army was coming closer. On 17 September Vietinghoff asked for and received permission to call off his attacks and to retire to defensive positions farther north. The battle for Salerno was over. It had cost the Germans some 3,500 men, the Allies close to 9,000: but by early October the Allies held southern Italy from Naples across the Termoli.

By the end of 9 September, two Panzer and two Panzer Grenadier divisions were racing towards Salerno ready to drive the Allies into the sea. The beach-head was held by four infantry divisions with a smattering of armour support.

A Sherman of the Royal Tank Regiment ferries an infantry section through Salerno. The major German assault was delivered on 13 September, their troops buoyed up by the (false) news that the Allies were on the verge of evacuation.

Men of 2/6 Queens pass a brewed-up Panzer IV outside Salerno. The counter-attack failed although it did inflict heavy losses on the Allied troops in the beach-head. The Germans withdrew to prepare their defences across Italy.

BLOODY TARAWA: Battle for the Gilberts

Girded by a coral reef, the tiny atoll of Tarawa looks like paradise in the Pacific. But its coral rock is honeycombed with tunnels manned by 5,000 Japanese.

The American advance on Japan from 1943 to 1945 was to follow two major axes, that through the Solomons, New Guinea and the Philippines being paralleled by another through the myriad atolls of Micronesia. Of the latter, the Marshalls were strategically the most important, but had been steadily fortified since the commencement of a Japanese mandate following World War I. As little was known about the Marshalls and, indeed, to protect the rear of the advance, the Gilbert Islands to the south-eastward had first to be secured. Thorough air reconnaissance showed that the islands of Tarawa (with an airfield) and Makin (with a seaplane base but suitable for an airfield) were the key points. Both islands were, therefore, assaulted simultaneously on 20 November 1943.

Diversionary attack

In support was Vice Admiral Raymond Spruance's recently constituted 5th Fleet, whose five modern battleships covered six fleet and five light carriers, with 700 aircraft. These were largely diversionary but had the effect of drawing the main Japanese fleet forward from its base at Truk in the Carolines to Eniwetok in the Marshalls. Though now only 1125 km (700 miles) from Makin, and including six battleships in its strength, this fleet was of little practical use as its carriers had been obliged to return to Japan to work up with new air complements following the detachment of their aircraft for the defence of Rabaul. Only the Pearl Harbor veteran *Zuikaku* remained, and she with only a scratch air group aboard. The Japanese C-in-C was thus unable to attack, and sent half of his available 18 submarines south to pick off targets of opportunity.

The capture of Makin

Makin was known to be lightly held but, as significant Japanese air bases existed at Mili and Jaluit, less than an hour's flying time distant, almost disproportionately large forces were used to secure the island rapidly and start construction of an airfield.

Few true amphibious ships of any consequence were available and troops went ashore at the western end of the island in LCVPs lowered from attack transports and LVTs (amphibious tractors) from the two available LSTs. As they ran in, a 20-minute aerial bombardment by carrier aircraft was followed by a pounding from some old battleships, together with cruisers and destroyers. It was fortunate that there was negligible resistance for the water over the skirting reef was far more shallow than had been expected and, in the face of mounting congestion, the transports had to move close-in to speed things up. At about 1000, when the beach-head was reported as

secured, a second assault was being carried out from the lagoon side of the island, one of many that fringed the atoll like an irregular necklace.

Again the assault was on a small scale, further LCTs being followed by tank-laden LCMs from one of the only two LSDs available in the theatre. Only 800 Japanese were ashore, less than half of them combat troops. Their skilful and stubborn resistance, however, kept 6,500 marines at bay for three days until there came the classic signal 'Makin taken'.

Where Makin is a skinny tongue of coral only some 13 km (8 miles) in length, Tarawa, some 120 km (75 miles) distant, is even smaller, its area measured in only acres and nowhere more than 3 m (10 ft) above sea level. The island was almost totally covered by its airfield, which was defended by

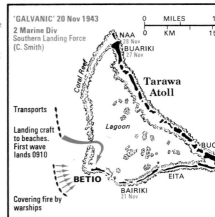

Target Tarawa
The tiny size of the idyllic atoll made it difficult to assault but equally difficult to defend. The Japanese had little chance of mounting a successful counter-attack on the American beach-head.

Across the lagoon

Landing boats and assault barges brought the Marines to within 500 yards of the shore but the coral bottom prevented the craft going any closer. The Marines had to wade towards the atoll under sustained fire from the Japanese defenders.

The first wave established a beach-head but all attempts to advance across the atoll were stopped dead. The Japanese had dug in deep to survive the preliminary bombardment and their bunkers were difficult to spot.

US Marines press forward towards the Japanese airfield which is shrouded in smoke from naval bombardment. The tiny size of the atoll prevented the US Navy providing much support from its heavy guns.

Right: Tarawa viewed from the air
The coral surrounding Tarawa stands out clearly. It was a severe natural obstacle, no boat could cross the last 500 yards and the Marines had no choice but to wade in and hope they could suppress most of the defensive fire.

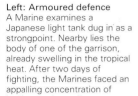

Left: Armoured defence
A Marine examines a Japanese light tank dug in as a strongpoint. Nearby lies the body of one of the garrison, already swelling in the tropical heat. After two days of fighting, the Marines faced an appalling concentration of bodies on the atoll.

On the gunline
Admiral Hill and his staff observe the bombardment from the battleship USS *Maryland*. It seemed impossible for anything to survive the awesome firepower of the Navy gunline off Tarawa, but the Japanese had dug well and dug deep.

nearly 5,000 seasoned troops, well dug in. Here the Americans, in an operation similar to that at Makin, put ashore only 5,000 marines who, with their LVTs, suffered dreadfully as they floundered over the ragged coral heads which extended up to 500 m (550 yards) offshore. Many drowned through the weight of their equipment as they were wounded or simply fell over. It took another three days of hand-to-hand fighting to secure the island, with the opposing side too closely engaged for warships to have a lot of influence beyond destroyers pounding enemy base areas. By the end of 23 November no Japanese remained alive, and the airfield was operating under new ownership. Tarawa was to be the yardstick for many landings to come and much was learned. Of the enemy, only 150 had been captured alive, while the Americans had suffered about 3,400

casualties, including 990 dead.

The success of the American operations was due largely to the inability of the Japanese to strike effectively at the naval support groups upon which so much depended. US carrier-based air strikes suppressed the meagre enemy air strength but, even so, a comparatively minor counter-attack on the evening of the first day succeeded in putting a torpedo into the light carrier USS *Independence*, which survived but had to be withdrawn. The larger carriers were just beginning to mount radar-equipped night-fighter patrols, in good time to defeat the new Japanese tactic of nocturnal torpedo bomber attacks using markers placed by reconnaissance floatplanes.

Worse, the rather protracted events ashore obliged the fleet to dally longer than had been anticipated and, after 22 November, the enemy's sub-

marines began to arrive. While four of the eight were sunk (a catastrophic loss) one (*I-175*) torpedoed the escort carrier USS *Liscombe Bay* early on the 24th. The result cruelly exposed the relaxed standards adopted as an expediency to produce the CVEs in large numbers.

The torpedo struck amidships and splinters penetrated the unprotected bulkheads of the bomb stowage. In a catastrophic explosion the entire after end of the little carrier was destroyed, the flight deck then collapsing. So great was the force of the blast that the old battleship USS *New Mexico*, a mile away, was showered with fragments. Two-thirds of the carrier's 900-odd crew lost their lives.

Left: Fire control
A Marine squad leader directs the fire of his men against a Japanese strongpoint. The Japanese defensive positions were carefully sited to provide mutually supporting fire which inflicted heavy losses on the Marines as they fought their way forward.

The beaches. 23 November 1943
An M4 Sherman and a cluster of Marines who failed to make it ashore. The sight of dead Marines bobbing up and down in the surf was seared into the minds of many men who fought on Tarawa. It was a scene destined to be repeated all the way across the Pacific.

Marines surge around one of the Japanese strongpoints which had to be taken out with grenades and flamethrowers. The battle for Tarawa was to last for about 60 hours of non-stop, close-quarter fighting.

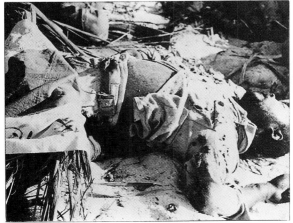

The garrison was destroyed, suffering 97 per cent casualties. Those who were captured were mainly too badly wounded to resist and some of them subsequently committed suicide rather than endure the dishonour of captivity.

Knocked-out LVTs litter the beach after the island finally fell. The fanatical Japanese resistance forced the US fleet to remain close by Tarawa for a day too long, allowing the Japanese submarines to attack the carrier force.

NORTH CAPE:
The sinking of the *Scharnhorst*

Boxing Day 1943: As the arctic twilight gives way to winter darkness, *Scharnhorst* is suddenly illuminated by star shell.

Broken during the long daylight of summer, the Arctic convoy cycle of 1943 resumed in the November with two convoys passing in each direction without loss. On 19 December, however, Admiral Karl Doenitz gave a commitment to Hitler that the next convoy would be attacked by U-boats in conjunction with the battlecruiser KMS *Scharnhorst*, the last fully-operational heavy unit remaining in northern Norway.

It was British practice to sail convoys from each end to cross in the zone of greatest hazard simultaneously, so that a single group of the hard-pressed Home Fleet could cover both. Thus the next northbound convoy, the 19-strong JW55B left Loch Ewe on 20 December, the 22 ships of the reciprocal RA55A departing Kola Inlet three days later. Each was given a close escort but with good intelligence as to *Scharnhorst*'s intentions the heavy distant cover was split, with the commander-in-chief (Admiral Sir Bruce Fraser) with the battleship HMS *Duke of York* accompanied by the cruiser *Jamaica* and four destroyers, and a separate force of three cruisers, HMS *Belfast* (Vice-Admiral R.L. Burnett), *Sheffield* and *Norfolk*. This latter group was reinforced by four destroyers from the escort of RA55A once it was apparent that this convoy had passed the danger zone.

The northbound convoy was dogged by German reconnaissance aircraft but with conditions very poor for an already-weakened Luftwaffe strength only one air attack was mounted, while a U-boat group was unable to make contact. *Scharnhorst* departed Altenfjord, hard by the North Cape, at 1900 on Christmas Day accompanied by five large destroyers of the 4th Flotilla. The usual flag officer, Rear Admiral Oscar Kummetz, was on leave and had been replaced by Rear Admiral Erich Bey, who headed confidently northward with his destroyers spread ahead on a line of search. Under orders he pressed on apparently heedless of his destroyers which, labouring in a heavy sea from their port quarter, fell back. By 0800 on 26 December they had lost visual contact.

At this critical juncture *Scharnhorst* was cutting across the bows of JW55B and some 80 km (50 miles) ahead of it. With the latter's progress reported by Hansen's *U-601*, Bey had good reason to anticipate a successful intercept. What he did not know was that Burnett's group was closing him rapidly from the north-eastward, while *Duke of York* was steering east to cut off his retreat.

Radar contact established

At 0815 Burnett made an eight-point turn to starboard to steer about north-west to close the convoy across a considerable beam sea. At 0840, with the first hint of what passes for winter dawn in these latitudes, *Belfast* established radar contact at 22850 m (25,000 yards).

Radar was to play a crucial role in the subsequent action and, at this point, the unsuspecting Bey was between Burnett and his charges, now only 50 km (31 miles) distant. The cruisers closed as rapidly as conditions permitted and *Scharnhorst* was sighted by *Sheffield* at 0921, the range being 11900 m (13,000 yards). Only the 203-mm (8-in) guns of *Norfolk* were able to engage and got off a few salvoes in the fitful glimmer of starshell. *Scharnhorst* pulled away rapidly but was hit twice, one shell putting her gunnery radar out of action.

With the larger German much the faster in the conditions, Burnett anticipated that she would loop around to attack the convoy from the north-eastward. He acted boldly on this assumption and neatly intercepted again at 1221, dead on cue. There followed a fierce 20-minute exchange of fire which

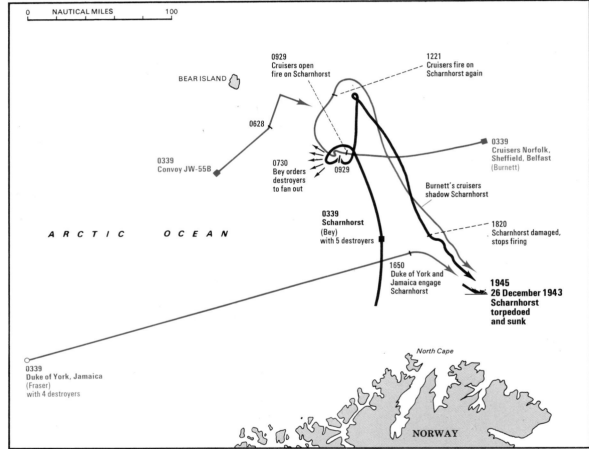

Map key:
- 0929 Cruisers open fire on Scharnhorst
- 1221 Cruisers fire on Scharnhorst again
- BEAR ISLAND
- 0628
- 0339 Convoy JW-55B
- 0730 Bey orders destroyers to fan out
- 0929
- 0339 Cruisers Norfolk, Sheffield, Belfast (Burnett)
- Burnett's cruisers shadow Scharnhorst
- 0339 Scharnhorst (Bey) with 5 destroyers
- 1820 Scharnhorst damaged, stops firing
- ARCTIC OCEAN
- 1650 Duke of York and Jamaica engage Scharnhorst
- 1945 26 December 1943 Scharnhorst torpedoed and sunk
- North Cape
- 0339 Duke of York, Jamaica (Fraser) with 4 destroyers
- NORWAY
- 0 NAUTICAL MILES 100

Left: *Scharnhorst*'s last voyage
In September 1943 the *Tirpitz* had been badly damaged by an audacious attack made by 'X' type mini-submarines. *Scharnhorst* was left to sortie alone against the convoy JW55B. German naval signals were being monitored and de-coded at Bletchley so the Royal Navy had ample warning of *Scharnhorst*'s intentions.

Battle in the Arctic Sea

Scharnhorst *races along the French coast during the famous 'Channel dash' which returned her and her sister* Gneisnau *to Germany.* Scharnhorst *joined the mighty* Tirpitz, *lurking in Norwegian fjords waiting to pounce on the British convoys to the USSR.*

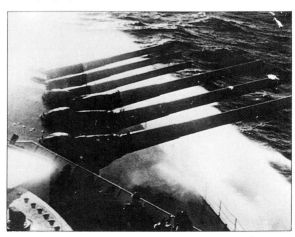

Scharnhorst *sailed on Christmas Day to attack convoy JW-55B but Enigma decrypts betrayed the German intentions to the Royal Navy. Admiral Sir Bruce Fraser planned to ambush the* Scharnhorst *and end her raiding career.*

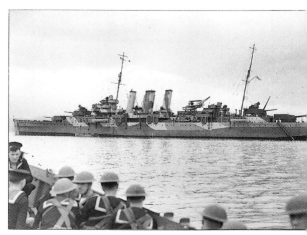

The heavy cruiser Norfolk *accompanied by the light cruisers* Sheffield *and* Belfast *provided close cover for the convoy. Before dawn on 26 December their radar systems detected the approaching German battlecruiser.*

Duke of York *fires a 14-in broadside*
At North Cape, Duke of York *fired on* Scharnhorst *for one and a half hours as the German battlecruiser plunged through the heavy seas seeking to escape. At 6.20 a 14-in shell slowed her down, allowing the destroyers to catch up and torpedo her.*

Left: The Pride of Hitler's Navy
Scharnhorst and her sister Gneisenau had sunk the British aircraft carrier HMS Glorious during the Norwegian campaign in 1940. Their Atlantic forays could not be sustained but her appearance back in Norway in 1942 was a source of deep anxiety to the Admiralty.

KMS *Scharnhorst*: Hitler's ocean raider

Displacing 38,900 tons at full load and armed with nine 11-in guns, *Scharnhorst* was designed as a commerce raiding battlecruiser. She and her sister *Gneisenau* raided the Atlantic convoys during 1940-1 but she was left to go to Norway alone after *Gneisenau* was crippled in an RAF raid on Kiel in November 1942.

damaged both *Norfolk* and *Sheffield* before Bey was again persuaded to retire. *Scharnhorst* steered something east of south, as if for home. As, unwittingly, she was making straight for Fraser's group, Burnett adopted the classic track-and-report role.

At 1418 Bey radioed to his lost destroyers, actually now about 110 km (68 miles) away to the north-west, to return. *Scharnhorst*, now totally alone, seemed not to appreciate the significance of Burnett's radio signals and at 1617 duly appeared on the *Duke of York*'s radar plot at nearly 36575 m (40,000 yards).

Caught by surprise

The trap had been perfectly sprung. At 1650 *Belfast* illuminated the German by starshell from astern, *Duke of York* and *Jamaica* opening fire at 10975 m (12,000 yards) from her starboard beam. *Scharnhorst* was totally surprised and swung to the north, but was headed eastward by a probe from Burnett. Fraser paralleled the German, who again began to draw ahead. *Duke of York* could, however, bring to bear six 356-mm (14-in) guns to *Scharnhorst*'s three 280-mm (11-in) guns and the latter began to take punishment, with A turret knocked out and underwater damage which began to slow her. At 1824 Fraser checked fire to give his straining destroyers a chance. The four S-class ships, including the Norwegian-flag *Stord*, split into half divisions and, in a chaotic attack from both sides, probably managed four torpedo hits, with only HMS *Saumarez* suffering damage in return.

At 1900 Fraser again opened fire on the now-limping *Scharnhorst*. At only 9600 m (10,500 yards) their trajectories were too flat to allow the shells to cause lethal damage, but the target rapidly became little more than a wreck whose fires glowed through the pall of smoke that surrounded her. Burnett's destroyers, *Belfast* and *Jamaica* all attacked on opportunity with torpedoes, and *Scharnhorst* sank at about 1945, only 36 of her crew being rescued from the bitter, dark waters. She had absorbed possibly 11 torpedo and over a dozen heavy-calibre shell hits.

By contrast Fraser's flagship had incurred no damage, beyond both masts being pierced by 280-mm shells, and had disposed of the major threat to the Arctic convoys, leaving the way clear to releasing units of the Home Fleet to reinforce the Eastern Fleet.

A view from HMS Belfast: *the cruisers opened fire on* Scharnhorst *and the battleship turned away after a brief exchange of fire. She was after the convoy, not a cruiser squadron although Admiral Doenitz would later criticise Bey for not sinking them.*

Deft manoeuvering by Burnett enabled him to intercept Scharnhorst *again and drive her south, into the path of Fraser's battleship HMS* Duke of York. *At 4.50 pm, guided by radar, the British battleship opened fire from 12,000 yards.*

Duke of York, *the cruiser* Jamaica *and four destroyers took nearly three hours to batter* Scharnhorst *into silence. Surrounded by smoke, no-one saw her go down.* Duke of York, *seen here tying up on her return, received only minor damage.*

137

BIG WEEK: Striking at the heart of the Reich

February 1943: Landings in France demand air superiority so the Allied bombers attack German fighter factories in a sustained offensive.

Throughout 1943 the US strategic bomber forces had been developing their daylight offensive with pinpoint attacks against Germany's war-making industries. Some successes had been achieved, but the primary lesson of the 1943 campaign for the daylight bombers remained the inescapable fact that the strength of the German fighter arm was too great to allow the US 8th and 15th Air Forces to maintain a sustained campaign. The advent of long-range escort fighters, such as the North American P-51 Mustang, had alleviated the situation, but the New Year's Day message to USAAF commanders in Europe issued by General H. H. Arnold, commanding general of the US Army Air Forces, made the point forcibly: 'It is a conceded fact that Overlord and Anvil [the proposed Allied landings in northern and southern France] will not be possible unless the German Air Force is destroyed. Therefore my personal message to you – this is a *must* – is to destroy the enemy air force wherever you find them, in the air, on the ground, and in the factories.'

European commanders were all too aware of the problem, and by November 1943 Operation 'Argument' had been developed as an Anglo-American scheme to address the situation. This was to be a short but sharp round-the-clock offensive against the German fighter arm: the bombers would strike Germany's fighter production centres, causing decisive damage and in the process tempting up current German fighter assets to be destroyed in large-scale battles with the Allied fighters escorting the bombers. For some months there was no adequate weather 'window' for the offensive, whose purposes were defined on 14 February 1944 as the destruction of the German fighter arm and the industries on which it depended, followed by attacks on the German V-1 launch sites in France and the Low Countries, and by attacks on Berlin.

The right weather finally arrived late in February, and on the night of 19/20 February RAF Bomber Command got the ball rolling with the despatch of 823 four-engined bombers against Leipzig. The fact that the German night-fighter arm was still in good fettle was attested by the loss of 78 bombers. On the following morning the Americans joined the fray, despatching 1,008 Boeing B-17s and Consolidated B-24s against Leipzig, Poznan, Tütow, Gotha, Brunswick, Halberstadt and Oschersleben and a

number of smaller targets. The 8th Air Force's bomber fleet was escorted by no fewer than 661 fighters (17 US groups and 16 British squadrons) found by the US VIII and IX Fighter Commands and RAF Fighter Command, the Mustangs being supplemented by Lockheed P-38s and Republic P-47s all fitted with drop tanks to give them an operational radius of 800 km (500 miles) or more.

Generalleutnant Josef Schmid's I Jagdkorps responded in modest strength, launching 362 sorties to meet the 941 bombers that were credited with attacks. The Americans lost 21 bombers, and the Germans suffered 62 aircraft shot down and another 18 damaged: it was a good start for the American side of what was to become generally known as 'The Big Week'.

Bomber Command returns

It was now the RAF's turn again, and on the night of 20/21 February Air Chief Marshal Sir Arthur Harris despatched 598 bombers against Stuttgart, suffering 11 losses. The following morning another US bomber fleet began to rise from Major General James Doolittle's 8th Air Force bases in England: 861 four-engined bombers were launched against Brunswick and the airfields or bases at Diepholz, Rheine, Werl, Gütersloh, Münster-Handorf and Achmer. American losses were 16 aircraft, while Generaloberst Hans-Jürgen Stumpff's Luftflotte Reich lost 33 fighters of its subordinate formations (I and II Jagdkorps plus the 7.Fliegerdivision). For the next three nights RAF Bomber Command launched only minor operations, in the form of nuisance raids by de Havilland Mosquito twin-engined bombers and minelaying sorties by four-engined aircraft, and the weight of the offensive thus fell on the American forces.

On 22 February the 8th Air Force was joined by Major General Nathan Twining's 15th Air Force from bases in Italy, and the Americans planned a medium effort against the major Messerschmitt production centre at Regensburg and the ball-bearing factories at Schweinfurt, supported by smaller efforts against Oschersleben, Halberstadt, Aschersleben, Bernburg and Gotha. In the event part of the 8th Air Force's effort was curtailed, and of 446 bombers despatched some 41 were lost, while the 529 American fighters scored 59 German fighters

The 24-hour battle
An Avro Lancaster of RAF Bomber Command takes off for Germany. With the British attacking during the night and the USAAF bombing by day, the German defences were stretched to the limit.

Polka dot air force
The 8th Air Force's raids involved formations of bombers several hundred strong. These aerial armadas were marshalled over England by specially painted B-24s which returned to base once the formation was assembled and on its way to Germany.

'In the air, on the ground and in the factories'

The American daylight raids on Germany during 1943 had led to severe bomber losses because no Allied fighter had the range to escort them all the way. The arrival of the North American Mustang in October signalled a dramatic change.

RAF Bomber Command opened the offensive on the night of 19/20 February. The following morning, over 1,000 American bombers raided Germany escorted by 661 fighters. In the ensuing air battle, 62 German fighters were shot down.

Behind their fighter screen the bombers relied on tight formations for safety. Their machine-guns could cover all angles of attack. It was the damaged aircraft, like this B-24 on three engines and unable to keep formation, that were in trouble.

Messerschmitt Bf 109K

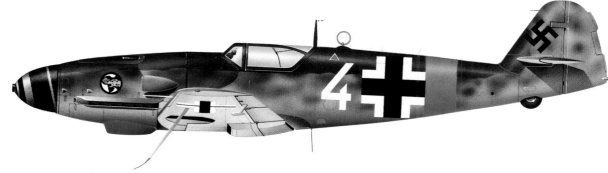

Despite the Allied bomber raids, German fighter production continued to increase, month by month until 1945. The Bf 109K was the ultimate production version of this veteran fighter, seen here with the green band denoting its Defence of the Reich role. Although aircraft continued to be delivered to the squadrons, the Luftwaffe's strength eventually began to fail as experienced pilots were killed or injured.

shot down and another 14 damaged.

The weather intervened on 23 February to cause a respite, and on this day Generalfeldmarschall Erhard Milch returned from an inspection tour of aircraft production centres to report that 'The situation of our leading production centres is highly strained, not to use a stronger word.' Milch had anticipated a production rate of 2,000 aircraft per week for February but now conceded that 800 was a more likely figure. Operations resumed on 24 February. The 15th Air Force launched 87 bombers against the Daimler-Benz aero engine factory at Steyr: Generalmajor Huth's 7.Fliegerdivision responded with vigour and shot down 17 of the bombers. The 8th Air Force sent out 809 four-engined bombers against Schweinfurt, Gotha and Poznan: again the defences responded in strength, some 48 bombers being shot down. However, the initial part of the attack had been targeted on Schweinfurt and Gotha to the south, drawing the bulk of German fighter strength in that direction and so permitting the northern force to hit Poznan, Tütow and Kreising against minimal opposition.

RAF Bomber Command returned to the fray on the night of 24/25 February, attacking Schweinfurt with 733 four-engined bombers, of which 33 were lost. And on the following morning the final American raid of 'The Big Week' was committed: the 15th Air Force raided the Messerschmitt works at Regensburg while the 8th Air Force also tackled Regensburg as well as targets at Augsburg and Furth. Huth was faced with the problem of two bomber streams converging on Regensburg, and

B-17 Flying Fortresses
Impeccable formation keeping by B-17s of the 381st Bomb Group. Leaving the surface of the aircraft polished rather than painted gave the bombers a little extra airspeed, and camouflage was of little relevance when part of a 1,000 bomber raid.

decided to pitch his major strength against the southern stream: 33 of the 15th Air Force's 179 unescorted bombers were shot down. The 8th Air Force had supplied an escort for its 738 bombers, but though the Germans succeeded in downing 39 bombers, this was a smaller proportion of the overall strength.

Casualties compared

The 8th and 15th Air Forces had launched some 3,300 bomber sorties, losing 226 bombers. In addition 28 fighters of the VIII, IX and XV Fighter Commands had been lost. But on the other side of the coin the Germans had lost some 290 fighters (plus another 90 damaged) and, perhaps more importantly, large numbers of their dwindling supply of experienced pilots. Ultimately fighter production was not too severely affected, for decentralization of production was already under way and was accelerated by the formation of a Jägerstab (fighter staff) under Dr Otto Saur on 1 March 1944: this removed fighter production from the Reichsluftfahrtministerium, which had emphasized offensive warfare and thus gave priority to bomber production, to Dr Albert Speer's production organization. But while the Allied fighter forces were growing in strength and capability, the German fighter arm had suffered a mortal blow to its skilled manpower.

North American P-51B Mustang

The long-ranged Mustang finally tipped the scales against the Luftwaffe. This aircraft belonged to the 357th Fighter Group of the 8th Air Force which escorted a bomber formation all the way to Berlin and back in March 1944.

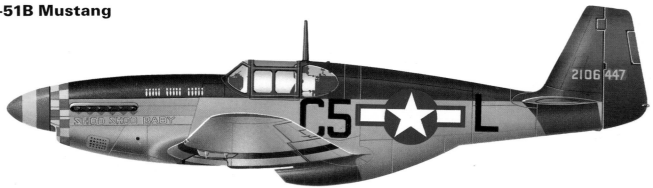

The 15th Air Force, based in Italy, attacked Germany on 22 February and again two days later. Targets included the Messerschmitt factory at Regensburg, the aero-engine plant at Steyr and the ball-bearing factories at Schweinfurt.

Responding aggressively to each attack on the Reich, the Luftwaffe suffered mounting losses of both fighter planes and irreplaceable trained pilots. The Allied air forces suffered too, but with their numerical superiority losses could be made good.

The intensive raids of 'Big Week' actually inflicted much less damage on German fighter production than had been hoped since industrial plant had been dispersed all over the Reich. But the Luftwaffe's fighter arm would take months to recover.

Marines of the Soviet Baltic Fleet prepare to go ashore. As the Red Army unleashed its greatest offensive in the summer of 1944, the Baltic Fleet conducted a series of amphibious raids. The collapse of the German Army Group Centre left their northern forces isolated. They held out in the Baltic Republics until the end of the war. These Soviet Marines are well armed with a combination of PPSh41 sub-machine guns, SVT40 self-loading rifles and a Degtyarov light machine-gun.

CASSINO: Battle for the Monastery

January 1944: The Allied advance on Rome is blocked by the town of Cassino in the Liri valley.

From the east to the west coasts of Italy the Germans built the Gustav Line. Using some of the most powerful defensive features that nature could supply the Germans constructed a long line of defensive positions, both man-made and enhanced-natural, that created a major obstacle to the Allied armies driving north through Italy in the winter of 1943/4.

In only one place was there even a remote chance of breaking the line, and that was at Cassino in the Liri valley. Even here the town was protected by an artifically swollen river and numerous fortified positions, and overlooked by what became known as Monastery Hill with its Benedictine monastery forming a natural observation post to cover the country for many miles around. Such was the strength of the Gustav Line that even this best chance of Allied success was a veritable fortress for the defence.

If the strength of the Gustav Line were not enough, the Allies had to attack in the middle of the Italian winter. Winter in central Italy is a season of rains, cold and poor visibility, so the Allies had also to contend with the elements. Additionally, they were hampered by a long supply line that extended across a large number of river crossings over which supplies had to be moved on Bailey or improvised bridging. The Italian campaign was both an engineer's and an infantryman's campaign.

Frontal attack fails

The first battle took place over a month during January and February 1944. It was very much a frontal attack and it soon stalled. The Allies found themselves attempting to advance directly into a well organized and stubborn defence. A direct frontal attack across the Liri by an American force in brigade strength turned into a major military disaster, and even when they managed to cross elsewhere the Allies found themselves faced with an almost sheer climb to the crest of Monte Cassino.

The Gustav Line was held by a variety of formations including two Panzer divisions. These Panzers could do little to influence the fighting directly for the terrain was just as hostile to them as it was to the Allies, so the tanks were frequently used as pillboxes, often dug into strong buildings to provide added protection. The Germans also used a new ploy in the form of simplified Panther tank turrets set into steel boxes dug into specially chosen defensive positions. Most of these were inland from Cassino, up in the mountains, but where they were situated the Allies soon learned that there was no way by which they could make any headway. At no point where there was one of these dug-in turrets could the Allies break through at any stage of the battle. Prominent in the German defence of Cassino was the

Five Stubborn Months

After an abortive American attack in January, the Cassino position was attacked on 15 February. New Zealand infantry managed to get into the town for a few hours before being ejected by a vigorous German counterattack supported by armour.

The second attack was preceded by a massive barrage and 455 bombers levelled the Benedictine monastery. 4th Indian Division failed to make any real progress, suffering heavy losses from hidden machine-gun posts on Monastery Hill.

A view from in front of Cassino graphically demonstrates the importance of Monte Cassino. Both sides had agreed with the Vatican not to attack this international religious centre. This is one of the last views of the monastery before it was destroyed.

Left: After the storm
The pulverised monastery after the Germans evacuated it, May 1944. General Freyberg's request for the airstrike remains controversial but 4th Indian Division which assaulted it on 15 February was sure it contained German artillery observers if not actual weapon positions.

Above: Shermans in town
Only with armour in close support and with ferocious artillery preparation could the Allies force their way into the town. Here, an M4 Sherman advances over the remains of part of Cassino with the German-held hills in the background.

For you the war is over
German airborne troops captured during the unsuccessful assault on Cassino on 15 February. The German paratroops retain their distinctive helmets and camouflage smocks although their jumping days are over. Their gallant and skillful defence of Monte Cassino was an incredible achievement.

Luftwaffe's 1st Parachute Division, devoid of parachutes since the invasion of Crete and fighting as infantry.

It was these paratroops who were in the thick of the fighting during the 2nd Battle which opened in mid-February. This started with an attack on the monastery itself, which was utterly destroyed by precision bombing. Unfortunately for the Allies this proved to be a major mistake, for all it achieved was to turn the monastery from a strong position into an impregnable fortress. The German paratroops promptly moved into the debris, which they found to be an ideal defensive position, and there they remained. The rest of the battle evolved into a fierce round of infantry attacks met with strong defensive fire, and even hand-to-hand fighting in some areas. What advances were made were later lost in the usual German counterattacks.

There followed a lull, mainly imposed by the weather which changed from bad to worse, preventing any operations. The 3rd Battle started on March 15 with a major aerial attack on the town of Cassino itself. In this bombing attack every structure in the town was either demolished or damaged in some way, and the waiting attackers believed that no-one could be left alive in the inferno. But as is often the case enough defenders did survive, and these also lived through the artillery bombardment that followed the bombers. They managed to put up their usual spirited defence and delayed the bulk of the Allied attacks apart from one small operation in

which a feature known as Castle Hill was taken. This hill was directly under Monastery Hill, and throughout that night the Germans made several attempts to retake the hill together with the old castle on the summit. In some of the most ferocious combat of all the Cassino actions the Germans were held off, but at a fearful cost.

Tanks in the town

This 3rd Battle was noteworthy as it was the first time the Allies had attempted to use tanks. The Shermans and Stuarts of the 2nd New Zealand Division managed to find a way through the rubble of the town itself and started to climb towards the summit. They could not get far without infantry support and had to turn back, but at last a foothold on Monte Cassino ridge had been made. Farther inland the Goumiers of General Alphonse Juin's French Corps were making steady but unspectacular progress through the mountains using time-honoured tactics and mule-carried supplies.

The 3rd Battle eventually came to a halt after only a week. Once again the defence had held, mainly because by that time it had been strengthened to the point where 23 German divisions faced 28 Allied divisions, a ratio very much in favour of the defence. The only way the Allies could really force their way through was to mass an attacking force at one point and ram their way through. Thus the pattern for the 4th Battle was set. The Allies rearranged their forces to obtain a local superiority, and when the attack

started in early May it was made by several divisions in place of the brigade-sized grouping that had been used earlier.

By the time the attacks started the winter weather was long past and the infantry moved forward into the dust of an Italian summer. As usual the attack got under way with fire from massed artillery, over 1,600 guns in all, and as usual the Germans fought back as stubbornly as ever. But this time the Allies were attacking in overwhelming strength. In the mountains the French broke through the defences, and at Cassino itself the Polish II Corps surged forward to take the monastery. With the monastery taken the whole of the Gustav Line had been penetrated, for the old military adage that a mountain line is turned once it is penetrated at any point held just as true for the Gustav Line as for any other. With the Cassino ridge in Allied hands the way through to Rome was cleared. From 19 May onwards the Allies could once more resume their advance north and Rome was duly taken in early June.

The battles for Cassino had lasted for five months. When it was over the town of Cassino resembled one of the villages on the Western Front of World War I. Whole areas around the town were shattered and the monastery itself was a heap of ruins. Between them the Allies and the Germans had suffered over 50,000 casualties, many of whom were never found; the British alone lost over 4,000 men 'missing'.

A mortar team in action amongst the rubble of Monte Cassino. German paratroops immediately occupied the ruined Abbey and turned it into a fortress. They were to hold it tenaciously against fearsome odds for another three months.

The Allied army attacking the Gustav Line included units from nearly every nation at war with Germany. Here, Polish troops of 3rd Carpathian Division storm Hill 393 during the final attack in mid-May 1944.

Outflanked by Juin's French troops to the south and by the Poles to the north, the German defenders withdrew from the tortured rubble of Monte Cassino on 16 May. Eluding encirclement, the defenders withdrew to the 'Hitler Line', 10 miles to the west.

'A STRANDED WHALE': The Anzio Landings

The Italian campaign seemed deadlocked so the Allies launched another amphibious landing at Anzio, 20 miles south-east of Rome.

By January 1944 the Allied armies in Italy had closed up to the Gustav Line, Monte Cassino looming menacingly over Lieutenant General Mark Clark's US 5th Army and the British 8th Army (now under Lieutenant General Sir Oliver Leese) edging its way along the Adriatic coast towards Ortona. Rome, which had seemed so easily within reach three months before, was still beyond grasp, and the succession of frontal attacks which had been necessary to push the Allied armies this far up the Italian peninsula were taking their toll not only of men but also of morale.

Something new was necessary, and Winston Churchill felt he knew what: a hook by sea around the enemy defences, the hurling ashore of a fierce assault force which would rampage across the enemy lines of communication and supply. In order to pin down as large a proportion of the German army as possible, both the 5th and 8th Armies would mount wide attacks on the main defences of the Gustav Line and, if surprise could be achieved and time given for the really powerful force to be landed, this latter could break out rapidly and smash its way clean across the western half of the peninsula.

On the afternoon of 21 January 1943 243 ships of all sizes sailed from the Bay of Naples and under clear skies made for the beaches on each side of Anzio and neighbouring Nettuno. Allied aircraft had pounded German airfields for days before and did so still, keeping the Luftwaffe on the ground, while naval bombardments kept Generalfeldmarschall Albert Kesselring's attention and those of his subordinate commanders elsewhere. By midnight the first ships were off the beaches, the landing craft were loaded and moved off and, to everybody's astonishment, there was no sign of opposition anywhere. By the evening of 22 January, 90 per cent of the assault force – some 45,000 men and 3,000 vehicles – were ashore, the British units on the left already holding the line of the River Moletta, and the American units on the right holding the line of

Above: Clinging to the coast
DUKW amphibious transports run the gauntlet of German artillery as they deliver supplies to the beleaguered troops at Anzio. The landing achieved complete surprise but the vacillating Allied commanders failed to exploit it.

Operation 'Shingle'
The Anzio assault force was commanded by Major General Lucas who was subsequently criticised for his caution and lack of drive. But Clark and Alexander failed to provide any firm leadership, ordering Lucas to 'advance on the Alban Hills'. The assault force, although powerful, would have been hard pressed to penetrate close to Rome and still defend the beach-head.

Left: German withdrawal
An *Elefant* assault gun blown up and abandoned by the Germans on their final retreat from Anzio. The fierce German attacks on the beach-head cost them dearly. Despite the lack of overall direction, the landings did play their part in the attrition battle.

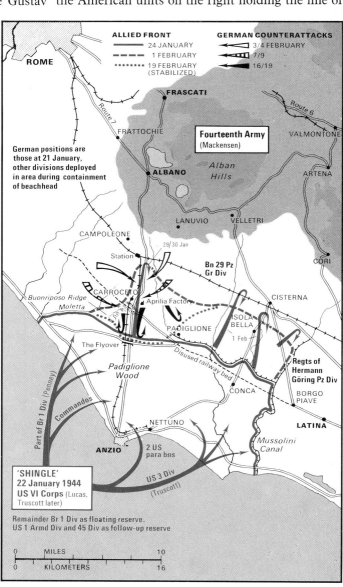

Half measures and half victories

Castelforte, which was finally captured by Free French troops in May, was typical of the defensive positions blocking the Allied advance north. It was hoped that an amphibious landing could cut the German line of communications.

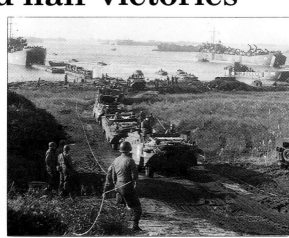

The landings at Anzio, 22 January 1944. Their attention diverted by frontal attacks in the south and coastal barrages by Allied warships, the Germans were caught by surprise with no troops in position to contest the landing.

M4 Sherman tanks rumble on to the beach at Anzio, their thin armour bolstered by sections of track. The beach-head was steadily reinforced but there was little effort to push inland or even to occupy the best defensive ground.

the Mussolini Canal. Hardly a man had been lost – and those had been casualties of mines or accidents – hardly a hostile shot had been heard. To those poised and ready for the break-out it seemed that first the Alban Hills and then Rome – at least – were theirs for the taking.

Unfortunately they were commanded by the wrong men. Clark, commanding the 5th Army from which the force had been taken, was still cautious after the bitterness of the Salerno battle, and Major General John P. Lucas, commanding the Anzio assault force, VI Corps, was neither enthusiastic about the project nor, it seems, anything else. Of his 54th birthday that month he wrote 'I am afraid I feel every year of it!' This was no man to direct an operation which depended upon imagination, eagerness and a willingness to take risks.

The result was that when the forward units had reached their first objectives they were told not to advance further but to await 'consolidation' – which certainly took place. By 28 January 70,000 men were in the beach-head, together with 27,000 tons of stores, 508 guns and 237 tanks – but no orders to move out and begin the 'rampage' had been issued: no orders in fact to do anything but await enemy attack.

Lost opportunity

Against so expert and imaginative an enemy as Kesselring and the men under his command, this was courting disaster. The landing had taken the German command completely by surprise and shock overwhelmed them for a few hours. But though surprise remained, the shock gave way to professional contempt for the lamentable waste of opportunity the Allied commanders were exhibiting. Very quickly Panzer and Panzergrenadier divisions were moving into place to put a band of steel around the Anzio beach-head.

Within a week eight German divisions had taken position and their artillery was shelling the entire area. This artillery eventually included 'Anzio Annie', the pair of 280-mm K5 E railway guns which hurled 255-kg (562-lb) shells into Anzio from

US soldiers captured in the fighting at Anzio are paraded in Rome
It had been a long time since the German army could parade a haul of prisoners before the camera. Here the column of POWs is marched past the monument to Victor Emmanuel II. Note the soldier on the right making the only protest possible in the circumstances.

the Alban Hills, 32 km (20 miles) away! At first Kesselring's intention was to destroy the beach-head entirely, but if the Allied commanders were unable to break out they did possess the means and the determination to remain where they were. Fierce battles of thrust and counterthrust were fought, at one moment a German penetration seemed likely to reach the beaches and cut the beach-head in two: but a desperate counter-attack halted the drive and during the next few days it was thrown back to its starting-point.

Even though both sides soon accepted the reality of the stalemate, the bitter fighting went on day after day, and the weather made conditions worse. Some-

thing of a lull began in early March – though the killing went on with little pause – and through the rest of that month, all of April and most of May a grim war of attrition was fought out, reminiscent of battles on the Western Front in 1917. Then in May the Allies launched their big offensive on the Gustav Line, Monte Cassino was taken by Polish troops on 17 May and on 25 May, four months after the original Anzio landings, patrols met up north of Terracina.

In no way can the story be presented as an Allied success. Churchill probably summed it up best: 'We thought we had hurled a wild cat ashore. All we got was a stranded whale!'

Panthers in Italy
The most sustained effort to push the Allies back into the sea began on 3 February. On the 16th LXXVI Panzer Corps locked horns with the US 45th Division: the Germans' two Panzergrenadier and one Panzer division included a battalion each of Panther and Tiger tanks.

Another bridge down
The German withdrawal from the battle area was marked by their customarily thorough destruction of communications. At the same time, mines and booby traps were laid in profusion for the benefit of any eager pursuing forces.

While the Allied commanders hesitated, unsure of whether to attack the Alban Hills or stay and await attack, the German 14th Army made up their minds for them. Excellent staff work rapidly concentrated troops for a counter-attack.

From 3 to 19 February, the Germans attacked vigorously but failed to penetrate much more than a mile into the beach-head. The Allied troops were powerfully assisted by their artillery and naval gunnery.

After the German attack failed to drive the defenders into the sea, the fighting degenerated into positional warfare more akin to 1917 than 1944. The Allies finally prised open the Gustav Line and broke through to the beach-head at the end of May.

IMPHAL AND KOHIMA: Victory of the Forgotten Army

Japanese troops cross the River Chindwin on elephants at the start of their 'U-Go' offensive. At the end of this bitter battle, half the Japanese soldiers who attacked were dead and every tank and gun brought over the Chindwin stayed there.

March 1944: On the grounds that attack is often the best form of defence, the Japanese 15th Army attacks in Burma.

The events which led to the battle for Kohima began on the night of 7 March 1944 when Lieutenant General Renya Mutaguchi, commanding the Japanese 15th Army, launched Operation 'U', throwing his divisions across the Chindwin river in an attack somewhat grandiloquently dubbed 'The March on Delhi'. The first stage of this was to be the isolation and then capture of the vast stores and administration centre which the British had built up at Imphal.

Diversionary attacks were launched to the south of Imphal, but apart from the main assault on the depot the most important step was the move by the 31st Division under Lieutenant General Sato, which crossed the Chindwin on 15 March and drove towards the small settlement of Kohima with its Naga village, its *maidan* on which the detachment of Assam Rifles drilled, its reinforcement camp in which soldiers returning from leave or hospital awaited their next move forward, its District Commissioner's bungalow with its terraced garden and tennis court, and its vital tactical position commanding the only road along which British reinforcements and supplies could reach Imphal from the railheads in Manipur.

Hasty British defence

They found facing them a hastily-organized defence perimeter manned at that moment by some 1,500 men, mostly of the 4th Royal West Kents augmented by men of the Assam Rifles (streaming back from forward positions where they had been both observing and attempting to delay Sato's advance) and the faithful, tenacious and extraordinarily courageous Naga villagers. One vital British formation of which the first Japanese arrivals remained for some time in ignorance, however, was a battery of 94-mm (3.7-in) howitzers sited on the reverse slope of a hill at Jotsoma 3.2 km (2 miles) to the west of Kohima, manned by Indian gunners of the 161st Indian Brigade.

Within hours of arrival the men of the Japanese 58th Regiment were giving proof of their ferocity, and the Royal West Kents of their stubbornness. The Japanese swept around Kohima from the Naga village to Jail Hill and on the night of 6 April, strengthened as more of their compatriots arrived, succeeded in taking two more of the features inside the defence perimeter, known as D.I.S. and F.S.D. But their attacking units were annihilated on the next morning by the counter-attack of the Royal West

Royal Garwhal rifles patrol forward
The Japanese 15th Army fought and died with ferocious courage allied to bestial cruelty. To defeat such fanatical opposition was a great achievement for British and Commonwealth forces. Even when gravely weakened by malnutrition and disease, the Japanese rearguards were dangerous men to pursue.

Kents.

However, by now more and more of Sato's 12,000 infantry and their gunners were coming up, and he himself was confident of success within 48 hours, though seven days later this confidence was waning. On the night of 13 April massed attacks by wave after wave of cheering assault troops foundered on the rock of the stubborn infantry defence, aided by astonishingly accurate fire from the howitzers at Jotsoma. These broke up Japanese formations as soon as they assembled, accompanied the waves all the way forward to the defences, and harried the survivors as soon as they were ordered back.

And on the following day reinforcements for the hard-pressed British got through to Jotsoma and began planning to blast their way through the last 3.2 km (2 miles). This was to prove appallingly difficult and a necessary delay of 24 hours almost fatal, for during that night the Japanese blasted F.S.D. with every shell and mortar bomb their weapons could fire: the perimeter began to disintegrate, and the F.S.D. position and neighbouring Kukri Piquet were lost.

Private soldier 14th Army

Fighting in the most appalling terrain and climate against a savage and ruthless enemy, the soldiers of the 14th Army endured the toughest campaign of the war. Initially dressed in the Khaki drill uniform worn in the Middle East, by 1943 British and Commonwealth troops wore a jungle green uniform of cellular material. Webbing was often daubed with black patches to improve camouflage.

The battle for Burma

Although the Japanese were on the defensive in Burma, Lt. General Mutaguchi recognised that defensive positions in the jungle could be penetrated so he elected to attack and spoil the offensive the British were no doubt planning.

Japanese troops attacked on exactly the same ground their opponents had selected for their offensive. The British commander, Lt. General Slim, brilliantly co-ordinated a fighting withdrawal to Imphal while holding in the Arakan.

The 14th Army had seen many withdrawals but this one was different. The Japanese faced tough rearguard actions punctuated with vicious counter-attacks. One Japanese commander recognised the change and tried to stop the attack.

Left: Mahrattas attacking a Japanese position
Indian troops contributed the bulk of British and Commonwealth manpower in the Burma campaign and at one point they provided three-quarters of the strength of 14th Army. By 1944 most Indian troops wore jungle green uniforms and British helmets or berets had displaced slouch hats and puggrees.

Rocket firing Hurricanes at a forward airstrip in Burma
In a suitably flat jungle clearing, ground crew load 60lb rockets on to Hawker Hurricanes. The Japanese air force had been defeated in Burma allowing British ground forces to be re-supplied by air. The Japanese lines of communication were badly disrupted by air attack and their ammunition and even food supply broke down completely.

Left: The West Yorkshires at Kohima
US-built M3 Lee tanks in close support of an infantry attack. The 37-mm gun in the turret tracks to the left while the sponson mounted 75-mm gun sweeps forward and right, thus covering all arcs except the right rear. This all-round firepower was particularly valuable in the close terrain of Burma.

But at 0800 on 18 April, the British at Jotsoma and the surrounding area replied with a devastating bombardment of the same kind and under its protection the relief of the original garrison was carried out.

The battle was by no means over. On the British side brigades of the 2nd Division were pouring down the road from Dimapur, while on the Japanese side more and more of Sato's 31st Division were being deployed, and as there was physically not enough room in the Kohima area for two whole divisions to operate, encircling moves were attempted by both sides through the appallingly difficult country around Kohima. This was such that a rate of movement of 1.6 km (1 mile) per day against no enemy opposition came to be accepted as the norm, and when on 27 April rain began falling with a weight and ferocity which none of the troops on either side had ever experienced before, movement became almost impossible and diarrhoea and dysentery took an even greater toll than bullets and shrapnel.

And all the time, on the central Kohima Ridge, the kernel of the battle was being fought. The Dur-hams fought off an attack on Garrison Hill which cost Sato such high casualties that he ordered a cessation of night attacks, and he sent a caustic signal to Mutaguchi complaining of the time the latter was taking to capture Imphal, and also of the total lack of support or supplies coming through to him at Kohima.

Towards the Bungalow

By the end of April the 2nd Dorsetshires had begun fighting their way into Kohima towards the District Commissioner's bungalow, and reached the edge of the tennis court. This now became the scene of an almost Pyrrhic conflict.

The opposing forces were separated by less than 22 m (25 yards), but the Japanese had got there earlier and, great diggers always, had burrowed deep into the terrace which rose at the far end, and also under a big water-tank which dominated the area. No-one could move across the open area in daylight, and Dimapur stores were astonished by the continual demands for gym shoes for night patrolling! But though these proved effective, the battle dragged on with ever-increasing ferocity and it was not until the middle of May, when a single tank managed the tortuous route up the District Commissioner's drive and began blasting the Japanese bunkers, that the British could claim even 'the first set'.

By the end of May Sato knew that he could not take Kohima, and further sacrifice was pointless. After an angry exchange of signals with Mutaguchi, in one of which he pointed out that since crossing the Chindwin his force had received not a single bullet, nor grain of rice, let alone any reinforcements, he sent off his last angry jibe ('The tactical ability of 15th Army Staff lies below that of cadets.'), closed down his radio and ordered his men to retire.

This the Japanese soldiers reluctantly did, desperately fighting off the clutches of the now all-encircling British and firing off the last of their mortar bombs and shells. And the story of their agonizing walk back to the Chindwin, living on grass and roots, their clothing and boots in tatters, using canes or their broken rifles as crutches, is an epic of endurance and courage which no soldier will ever decry, certainly not the equally valorous men who fought them.

Kohima was first attacked on 4 April, and for the next two weeks the battle continued by night and day. The fighting was at close quarters with fanatical Japanese assaults meeting stubborn British and Indian resistance.

Indian troops bring forward a mountain gun in one of the isolated 'boxes' at Imphal. On 10 April, when the situation at Kohima was critical, Slim planned his counter-attack: British forces were to strike eastward from Kohima and Imphal.

On 1 June the remnants of the Japanese 31st Division withdrew from Kohima. Here, Imphal-based Indian soldiers celebrate the meeting between 2nd and 5th Divisions, opening the Imphal road. The Japanese defeat was complete.

D-DAY: The Normandy Landings

6 June 1944: The largest amphibious invasion force ever assembled attacks Hitler's 'Atlantic Wall' at Normandy.

In the spring of 1944 Hitler knew that the war would be decided in France. To a conference of senior generals at Berchtesgaden he observed: 'The whole outcome of the war depends on each man fighting in the West, and that means the fate of the Reich itself.' Casualties on the Eastern Front were then far exceeding Germany's ability to find replacements, and the Reich's industrial centres were under increasingly effective attack from Allied bombers. However, if the Allied invasion of France were to fail, Germany might have the breathing space to counterattack the Soviets and deploy the advanced submarines and 'V' weapons which Hitler hoped would regain him the initiative.

Allied deception plan

The German high command was convinced that the Allied landing would take place in the Pas de Calais area: this was nearer both to the British ports and the German frontier than any other stretch of coastline. That the Germans continued to believe this even after the Normandy landings had begun was primarily due to an exceptionally well orchestrated misinformation campaign. Whereas the real invasion armies assembled in great secrecy all along the south coast, the air waves above Kent hummed with the radio traffic of the non-existent '1st US Army Group'. Fake ammunition dumps, dummy positions and the presence of the famed Lieutenant General George Patton all added to the effect.

The exact timing of the Allied invasion depended on correct meteorological conditions: above all, a low tide at dawn which would expose the underwater defences laid along the beaches. This dictated either 17 May or 5 or 6 June 1944, and in the end General Dwight Eisenhower ordered the attack for 5 June, but had to postpone for 24 hours as a result of poor weather conditions.

The invasion was spearheaded by the largest airborne assault yet undertaken: nearly 20,000 men landed by parachute or glider. The American 82nd and 101st Airborne Divisions dropped to seize vital ground inland from 'Utah' beach while the British 6th Airborne Division was dropped to capture the crossings over the River Orne and Caen Canal on the eastern flank of the invasion beaches.

Assault from the air

The airborne landings were chaotic: the Americans were scattered over a wide area and in the early hours of the morning small groups of paratroopers fought a series of confused actions. The vital crossroads at St. Mère Eglise was taken, but the two US divisions failed to link up and remained badly split up until 7 June. The British landing was more successful and took most of its objectives before dawn.

The landings from the sea began at 0630 on the beach codenamed 'Utah'. Preceded by a heavy air and naval bombardment, the American troops swept ashore 1830 m (2,000 yards) away from their intended beach and met the lightest opposition of all five invasion beaches. The surprised defenders were quickly overcome and the remainder of the day was spent in bringing supplies and men ashore while the leading elements began to push inland to reach the American paratroops.

At 'Omaha' the American landing was hampered by a choppy sea and was opposed by the German 352nd Division, which made a determined effort to throw the invaders back into the sea. By nightfall Major General Leonard Gerow's V Corps was still only clinging to the beach, cut off from 'Utah' by flooded estuaries and from the British 'Gold' beach by the German-held fishing port of Port-en-Bessin. This was finally taken by the Royal Marines on 8 June.

In the Allied centre the landings at 'Gold' faced similar problems with the surf but encountered much lighter opposition, and by midday the British 50th Division was pressing inland. Bayeux was lib-

Their job done
US Army glider pilots heading back to England two days after the landings. The airborne assault was designed to prevent the Germans reinforcing their units along the coast. On the day, the three airborne divisions and the intensive air onslaught prevented any concerted counter-attack.

Right: The floating city
Photographed from a captured German trench, the awesome scale of the amphibious assault becomes apparent. Barrage balloons float overhead providing passive protection from a Luftwaffe that was scarcely given a chance to intervene thanks to the power of the Allied air forces.

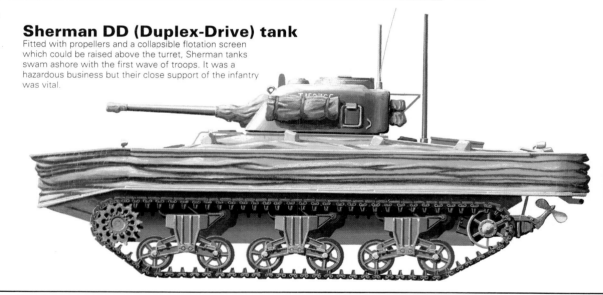

Sherman DD (Duplex-Drive) tank
Fitted with propellers and a collapsible flotation screen which could be raised above the turret, Sherman tanks swam ashore with the first wave of troops. It was a hazardous business but their close support of the infantry was vital.

Fair stood the wind for France

The timing of the landing was dictated by the tides. The Allies had to land at low tide when the German beach defences would be exposed to view. Good weather was also critical both for the amphibious assault and the air landings.

US paratroopers, part of a 20,000-strong airborne force, assemble by their crash-landed gliders. The two American airborne divisions were widely scattered on landing but fortunately were not counter-attacked by the Germans.

The vast invasion fleet sailed across the Channel, 4,000 landing craft and countless larger vessels. They were protected from German interference by over 1,200 Royal and US Navy warships and the complete superiority of the Allied air forces.

erated on 8 June and was spared the battering which was needed to free most other towns in Normandy. On 'Juno' the Canadians were 9.6 km (6 miles) inland by the end of the day although short of the very ambitious objectives set for them. Their attempts to move on the next day were frustrated by a savage counter-attack by the SS Panzer Division 'Hitler Jugend'.

The easternmost landing at 'Sword' beach was strongly opposed. The troops encountered far more obstacles and fortifications than they had been led to expect, mainly because their briefing photographs were nearly a year out of date. They were the only Allied forces to face a major German counter-attack on 6 June, when the 21st Panzer Division launched a vigorous assault at the gap between British and Canadian forces. However, the Panzers were beaten off and the leading troops were within 4.8 km (3 miles) of Caen.

On 7 June Allied attacks all along the coast linked the five invasion beaches to form an 80-km (50-mile) front which no subsequent German attack seriously

threatened to breach. Generalfeldmarschall Erwin Rommel, commanding Army Group 'B', had been proved right: the armoured reserve was held back too far and too late to defeat the invasion, and Hitler's inflexible grip on operational planning had

effectively paralysed the German response to the landings. Some 156,000 troops landed on D-Day, and at a cost of 9,000 casualties they had fatally wounded the Third Reich.

Mulberry harbour
Dieppe proved the difficulty of capturing an intact port so the Allies decided to take one with them: 74 blockships were sunk off the coast followed by 213 ferroconcrete caissons to create an artificial harbour with piers.

British 2nd Army landed on three beaches along a 25-mile front. To their front the British 6th Airborne Division achieved remarkable success, taking the Orne crossings and knocking out the Merville battery.

German prisoners on Utah beach where the US forces quickly overran the defenders and were able to press inland to relieve the airborne troops. The other US landing at Omaha beach met with stiff resistance and came perilously close to defeat.

By the evening the 3rd (Canadian) Division was 7 miles inland, 50th Division within 2 miles of Bayeux and 3rd Division had linked up with 6th Airborne. The race began to reinforce the beach-head before the Germans could concentrate.

THE GREAT MARIANAS TURKEY SHOOT

19 June 1944: The Japanese navy fights to defend the Mariana Islands in what is destined to be the last of the great carrier battles of the Pacific war.

On 15 June 1944 (just nine days after the Normandy landings) a 535-ship American invasion force hit Saipan in the Marianas, following a nine-day passage from the Marshalls. This major step in the leap-frogging reconquest of the central Pacific was possible only through the massive concentration of air power that could be applied by the US carrier fleet.

The operation provoked the powerful response from the Japanese that the Americans had been seeking. Almost all remaining enemy surface strength had been regrouped, as the 1st Mobile Fleet, around five fleet and four light carriers, over-all command being exercised by Vice Admiral Jisaburo Ozawa, successor to Nagumo in command of the Imperial navy's strike force. Ozawa's 430 carrier aircraft were to be supplemented by 540 more based on a ring of island airstrips so that, if the Americans could be brought to battle within this perimeter, his aircraft would enjoy an effectively doubled range, refuelling at either end and attacking the invaders on either leg of the return trip.

In every respect except enhanced range, however, the Japanese were inferior. Task Force 58 (overall command by 5th Fleet under Admiral Raymond Spruance, but tactically controlled by Vice Admiral Marc Mitscher) could dispose seven fleet and eight light carriers, with 900 aircraft and aircrew of superior training, backed by escort carriers with replacements.

Tactically, any action was necessarily influenced by the facts that Spruance was tied to the defence of Saipan, and that the easterly trade winds allowed the Japanese to launch their aircraft while proceeding toward the island while the Americans would be obliged to reverse course. Spruance, cannily, had reduced the odds by a week's war of attrition against Ozawa's shore-based aircraft and airstrips.

Leaving the Philippines on 15 June the Japanese fleet progressed steadily, but its position was accurately reported by US submarines. But, in turn, Ozawa's longer-ranged aircraft had found Spruance. TF58 was operating in four fast-carrier groups, spaced on 20-km (12.5-mile) centres, protected some 24 km (15 miles) to the west by Vice Admiral Willis Lee's surface battle group (including seven battleships) disposed as an AA barrier.

On the morning of 19 June TF58 was still occupied with softening-up the islands when, at 0830 (and still not sighted) Ozawa launched a 69-aircraft strike from 480-km (300-mile) range, its aircraft being ordered to attack and refuel ashore before returning. Fortunately, Lee detected them by radar at 240 km (150 miles), allowing time to scramble a large force of Grumman F6F Hellcats which destroyed 45 attackers for the loss of one of their own.

For this sacrifice the Japanese near-missed three ships and hit the battleship USS *South Dakota* with one bomb.

Just half an hour behind the first enemy wave came a second and more powerful wave, comprising 110 aircraft. The Americans, fully prepared in depth, cut down a further 79, for which frightful price a further near-miss was conceded. The recent introduction of proximity-fuzed ammunition greatly boosted the effectiveness of the American AA fire.

While Ozawa was still beyond Mitscher's aircraft range, he was still attended by submarines. At 0910 the *Taiho* was hit by a single torpedo from USS *Albacore*, and three hours later the Pearl Harbor veteran, *Shokaku*, was rocked by four from USS *Cavalla*. Neither carrier seemed in danger of sinking, but at 1510 and 1530 respectively they were destroyed by massive explosions caused by fuel vapour leaking from ruptured lines.

Ozawa's third strike of 42 aircraft was launched at 1000 and bypassed Lee's gunline but, in seeking to attack from the north, missed Mitscher almost completely and achieved nothing for the loss of seven aircraft. A fourth, and last, force of 82 aircraft left Ozawa's decks at 1130. Most again never found their target but only nine returned, 49 being shot down by Hellcats over Guam or written-off trying to land on its churned airstrips.

Incredibly, the Japanese admiral seemed unaware of the scale of his losses and believed inflatedly optimistic reports from his returning pilots. With barely 100 aircraft aboard, but still not pinpointed by American reconnaissance aircraft, Ozawa pulled back to the westward to refuel overnight and resume the battle on the following morning. He was, in fact, already beaten, having sustained on 19 June a total of 346 lost aircraft against 30 American losses. Scarce wonder that the latter termed it the 'Great Mariana Turkey Shoot'.

From 1430 Mitscher had steamed in the opposite direction in order to recover his own aircraft, and only at 2000 did Spruance allow three of his four carrier groups to turn westward in pursuit of the

The Battle of the Philippine Sea

The islands of Saipan, Guam and Tinian were vital for Japan. In American hands they would be a springboard for an assault on the Philippines or the homeland. US Marines landed on Saipan on 15 June, triggering the Japanese naval counter-attack.

The Japanese carrier fleet launched its first strike against the US Task Force on 19 June. Vice Admiral Ozawa, the Japanese commander, had not been told that most of the shore-based aircraft he thought were supporting him had been destroyed.

US Navy Task Force 58 was able to keep some 300 fighters in the air all day: a shield which few Japanese aircraft could penetrate. Those which did met a withering barrage of AA fire using proximity-fuzed shells.

Japanese. Save for his reluctance to retire and concede defeat Ozawa would have got clear but finally, at 1540 on 20 June, he was discovered at a daunting 445-km (275-mile) range by a Grumman TBF Avenger from USS *Enterprise*. It was late in the day but Mitscher, grabbing his only chance, had 210 aircraft aloft in 10 minutes, following them at high speed to reduce the length of their return flight as far as possible.

The strike came in hard and, despite 20 losses to a withering AA barrage, put two torpedoes into the carrier *Hiyo* (which like the others, exploded and sank), hit the final Pearl Harbor survivor, *Zuikaku*, and the light carrier *Chiyoda* with bombs, and mortally injured two fleet oilers. The 85-strong fighter cover meanwhile downed an estimated 65 Japanese in their defence.

With dry tanks and overtaken by darkness, 80 American aircraft had to ditch short of their carriers although many of the crews were rescued by flying boats the next day. Controversy will continue to rage over whether the cautious Spruance and Mitscher should have taken a chance on Saipan and gone all-out for Ozawa's annihilation. The latter, although thoroughly beaten by virtue of inferior aircrew, had fought an excellent tactical battle. Nevertheless, the American victory in the Philippine Sea marked the final destruction of Japanese naval airpower.

Aboard the *Enterprise*
The US carriers did not locate their opponents until mid-afternoon. They were at maximum range so the American aircraft would have to find, and land on their carriers at night. Ditchings and bad landings accounted for more US losses than Japanese fire.

First wave at Saipan
The Japanese were kept guessing as to the next US objective until 14 June. The attack on Saipan was preceded by airstrikes on many other potential targets misleading the Japanese who initially sent their fleet to Biak Island.

F6F Hellcats: the victors
The strength of the US fighter force above the Task Force cut each Japanese attack to pieces. Ozawa could not believe the scale of the losses and assumed many of his aircraft which had not returned had landed on Saipan. All were at the bottom of the sea and Japanese naval aviation had received a mortal blow.

Although striking first, the Japanese aircraft failed to inflict significant damage. But returning Japanese pilots claimed to have sunk several American carriers and Ozawa launched further attacks.

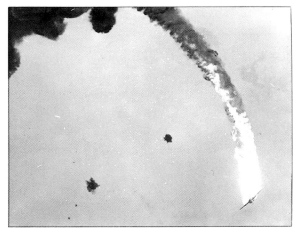

Each Japanese strike was ripped apart by the massed Hellcats, the inexperienced Japanese pilots proving easy prey. During the afternoon, US submarines attacked the Japanese carriers, sinking Taiho *and* Shokaku.

The Americans finally launched a strike of their own at dusk which sank the carrier Hiyo *and damaged two others. But the strike was at extreme range and 80 US planes had to ditch, out of fuel, on the way home.*

THE DESTRUCTION OF ARMY GROUP CENTRE

June 1944: Three years after the German invasion of the USSR, the Soviets launch their greatest offensive of the war.

On 22 June 1944, three years to the day after Barbarossa had been launched, the great Soviet summer offensive opened. From Velikiye Luki in the north around a huge arc to Kovel below the Pripet Marshes, the artillery of four Red Army fronts – 15 armies – crashed out, while the aircraft of four air armies flew overhead, and the infantry and tanks – increased over normal establishment by more than 60 per cent – moved out of their concentration areas into the attack. Their objective – to obliterate the German Army Group Centre which consisted of three infantry armies and one Panzer army under Generalfeldmarschall Ernst Busch (altogether over a million men with 1,000 panzers and 1,400 aircraft), smash through them and all their defences and force back the Finnish and German armies to the north, and the Hungarian, Romanian and German armies to the south.

This was the onslaught which would clear the invader from the soil of Mother Russia.

Within a week the three main bastions of the German defences had been first cut off, then captured – Vitebsk in the north by converging attacks from one army of General I.Kh. Bagramyan's 1st Baltic Front above and one of General I.D. Chernyakovsky's 3rd Belorussian Front below; Mogilev by two armies of General G.F. Zakharov's 2nd Belorussian Front; and Bobruisk by the armies of Marshal K.K. Rokossovsky's 1st Belorussian Front, which moved massively but secretly over countless small rivers and lakes at night, then attacked out of marshy ground that their opponents had considered impassable. Parts of two Panzer corps were cut off and bombed into disintegration, and then Rokossovsky's armies took Bobruisk with 24,000 prisoners.

By 4 July both Zakharov's men and Chernyakovsky's had driven forward nearly 240 km (150 miles) leaving only one pocket of German resistance behind (it surrendered on 11 July); Rokossovsky's 28th Army was approaching Pinsk – and except in the north around Daugavpils (Dvinsk) the Germans were back over the old pre-war Soviet-Polish border.

The momentum never flagged. Everywhere the Germans were in full retreat, though they turned and struck back ferociously at times. Nevertheless, armies of the 1st Baltic Front forced the Dvina and took Polotsk within days; Chernyakovsky's and Zakharov's armies – having already cut off 105,000 Germans as they crossed the Beresina – drove for Vilnyus and Bialystok, taking the latter at the end of the month and causing Generaloberst Heinz Guderian, the newly appointed Chief of the General Staff to note caustically in his diary, 'Army Group Centre has now ceased to exist.'

Immediately north, Chernyakovsky's right flank drove on from Vilnyus to Kaunas in Lithuania and

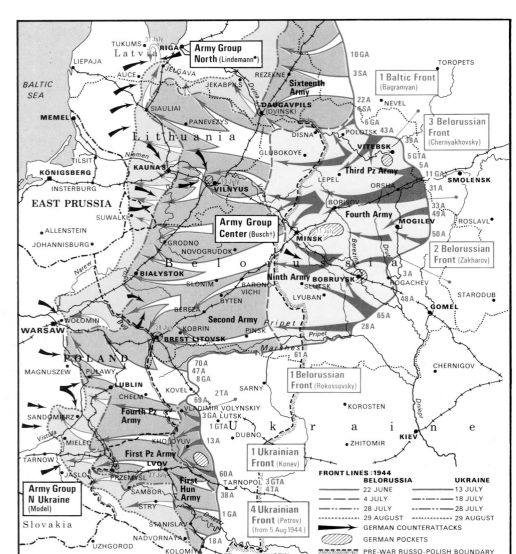

On to Berlin! Army Group 'Centre' was overwhelmed by an offensive of staggering proportions. The co-ordination of this five-Front offensive revealed the new power and confidence of a Red Army which was now unstoppable.

Partisans
Despite a savage counter-insurgency campaign conducted by the most barbaric of the SS units, the German rear areas were subjected to concerted attack by the powerful Soviet partisan movement.

400 miles to go

When the Soviet summer offensive opened, the incredible scale of the operation was known only to Stalin and his five most senior officers. The attack would eventually involve five Soviet Fronts and some six million soldiers on both sides.

The Red Army's decisive campaign opened with major offensives in the south and in the north-west. German reserves were to be drawn to the flanks then the main core of the Soviet thrust would smash the German centre.

The attack on Army Group Centre opened on 22 June, and in one week the Germans lost 130,000 men killed and 66,000 taken prisoner. Soviet losses were staggering but they had the longer purse: burned out units were replaced with fresh formations.

by the end of August had reached the borders of East Prussia, while farther north Bagramyan's Baltic Front armies crossed into both Latvia and Lithuania, and sent an armoured raid up to the Gulf of Riga. Brest-Litovsk fell to Rokossovsky on 28 July and soon afterwards his forces had reached the Bug north of Warsaw, while on his left General V.I. Chuikov's 8th Guards Army had stormed out of Kovel in mid-July, captured Lublin and reached the Vistula, which they crossed on 2 August.

Marshal I. Koniev's armies on the Ukrainian Front had not been embroiled at the start of the offensive, but on 13 July they drove forwards against very strong resistance from Army Group North Ukraine (for this was where the Wehrmacht had expected the Soviet onslaught) and it was not until two more tank armies had been brought up from reserve on 16 July, and this tremendous weight of men and

fire-power began to tell, that the defences cracked. Forty thousand Germans were surrounded near Brody, Rokossovsky's right-hand army drove straight to the Vistula, crossed it and formed a bridgehead at Sandomir, one tank army flanked Lwow to the north and another was thrown into a direct assault which captured the city on 27 July; Przemysl fell, then Mielec at one end of the front and Nadvornaya at the southern end.

By the end of August the Carpathians had been reached along their main length, the Polish border was behind the Red Army positions which had now closed up to the old borders with Czechoslovakia and with Hungary. In two months the Soviet troops had advanced 725 km (450 miles) – at great cost but also inflicting enormous losses on their enemies – and now the time had come again to reorganize the supply lines for the next advance on this front.

Army Group North
With the capture of Tukums on the Gulf of Riga on 31 July, Army Group North was completely cut off. A counter-attack by 5th and 14th Panzer Divisions opened a 25-mile corridor on 21 August but it could not be held for ever. The Baltic republics were doomed.

Waiting for the T-34s
German anti-tank gunners, hastily deployed, await the next wave of Soviet armour. The ferocious pace of the Soviet attack left five major pockets of Axis forces surrounded. This time, German armour did not come to the rescue and all of them were overrun.

SS men in action
Knowing they could expect no mercy from the Soviets, trapped SS troops frequently fought to the end but with little aerial re-supply those forces which were surrounded at Vitebsk, Bobruisk, Brody, Vilno and Brest-Litovsk were unable to offer protracted resistance.

Tank riding infantry
Soviet tactics had improved but the infantry support for Soviet armour usually had to ride on the tanks themselves. Nevertheless, they had a substantial numerical advantage: some 11,000 tanks spearheaded the offensive with 85,000 guns and heavy mortars plus 10,000 aircraft. Germany had lost the industrial battle and was now paying the price.

IS-II heavy tank

The strength of Soviet heavy industry had grown enormously during 1943. Not only did the Germans face superior numbers of T-34s, but the Red Army was now able to field heavier armour such as the IS-II, the first tank to mount a 122-mm gun. Its thick armour was impervious to most anti-tank weapons. In early 1944 they tended to be used as command tanks leading battalions of about 20 T-34s, but by the end of the summer they were operating in whole battalions.

Steamrollered on the ground, the Germans also lost control of the air. The forces surrounded at Bobruisk were pounded into submission by the 16th Air Army. With few AA guns left and no air support, defence against Soviet bombing was impossible.

For five weeks, no attempt to stabilize the front succeeded and the German army was in full retreat. The Soviets liberated a devastated and depopulated countryside. Several units overran trains loaded with children, ready for deportation to Germany.

A posed picture celebrates the greatest Soviet victory of the war in the east. Of the 70 German divisions facing 1st, 2nd, 3rd Belorussian and 1st Baltic Fronts, 60 had been eliminated. The Red Army was now within 400 miles of Berlin.

NORMANDY BREAKOUT

The Normandy *bocage* favoured German infantry defenders more than Allied armour. Even so, a breakout had to be achieved.

At the end of June 1944 there were many seriously worried men in Whitehall and Washington, men whose whole attention had been concentrated for months (in some cases years) upon the successful liberation of Europe from Hitler's domination, and who now suspected that their plans were going awry. On 6 June the Allied armies had stormed ashore in Normandy as part of the greatest amphibious operation in the history of warfare, and during those first, heady days had secured such apparent success as to raise the hopes and banish all doubts. Now the hopes were lower, the doubts back and growing.

But there was an exception among these downcast Allied leaders, the man in command of the formations actually engaged in the fighting. General Sir Bernard Montgomery, whose rocklike confidence provided balm to those who believed in him and was a source of deep annoyance to the many who did not. The believers were right. As early as 11 June Montgomery had stated that his objective was to draw the greatest possible weight of enemy forces on to the eastern end of the bridgehead, i.e. towards Dempsey's forces aimed at Caen, thus weakening the opposition in front of Bradley's forces until the time came when they could break out, first to occupy the whole of the Cotentin peninsula, then to cross the Selune river just south of Avranches and release the recently formed US 3rd Army, under the flamboyant Lieutenant General George Patton, to flood out to the west and take the whole of Brittany and the vital ports of Brest, Lorient and St Nazaire.

Patton's position before 1 August had been somewhat equivocal, for the US VIII Corps under Major General Troy Middleton was really a part of Patton's 3rd Army but had been loaned to Bradley's 1st Army for the invasion. This was the corps on the western flank of 'Cobra' which had swept down the Cotentin coast to take Avranches and cross the Selune, and on 28 July Bradley had asked Patton to assume responsibility for VIII Corps area as 'Deputy Army Commander', despite the fact that Patton was not supposed to be in Europe and was officially commander of the 3rd Army.

Liberation of Brittany

But at noon on 1 August all this changed. Patton was now in undisputed command of four corps (VIII, XIII, XV and XX) containing eight infantry and four armoured divisions, under operation orders issued before D-Day, and confirmed by Montgomery on 27 July and by Bradley that morning: his first and prime task was to liberate Brittany and its vital ports as quickly as possible.

Instructing the armoured divisions of Middleton's VIII Corps to race straight for Brest, Vannes and Lorient without worrying about their flanks or anything except their speed, he turned away from the Atlantic and directed his attention eastward to the gap between Chartres and Orléans, over 160 km (100 miles) away, beyond which lay the Seine; on the Seine lay Paris, and Patton, an ardent Francophile, purposed to be the first Allied commander to reach the French capital.

By now XV Corps under Major General Haislip was forming just south of the Avranches gap in order to hold enemy pressure off the hinge of Middleton's corps and in theory to protect its left flank, but as the divisions came up, either by accident or design they faced east, away from Brittany and towards the heart of France.

Race to Le Mans

Haislip's XV Corps moved first, on 5 August, and by 8 August was not only across the Mayenne but had reached Le Mans 65 km (40 miles) on; Walker moved on 7 August, took Angers on 11 August and raced forward to cover Haislip's flank towards the Chartres/Orléans gap, moving at 25 to 32 km (16 to 20 miles) per day.

But there now occurred a slight check on the onward rush. Other eyes than Montgomery's and Patton's were watching strategic developments, and whatever the Wehrmacht generals might prescribe, Hitler was still in command. His eyes were on that narrow gap between Mortain and Avranches through which all Patton's supplies must be fed. On 4 August four Panzer divisions of General Paul Hausser's 7th Army struck eastwards through Mortain and was 11.3 km (7 miles) on towards Avranches before it was stopped as Bradley, now commanding the 12th Army Group, sensed the danger and threw in two corps from the US 1st Army.

There was bitter fighting, but Avranches remained inviolate. But now two German armies and a Panzergruppe (nearly 100,000 men) were concentrated west of a line running south from Falaise to

German sniper
The Allied advance was often bogged down by the desperate resistance of a handful of German troops. A few well concealed snipers could mean that it took hours, and many casualties, to clear a French village.

Poor Bloody Infantry
For all the Allies' industrial superiority and the vast logistic effort in Normandy, each advance was won by hard infantry fighting. Three months of battle for Normandy cost 21st Army group 83,000 casualties.

Breakout and pursuit

Montgomery planned to draw the German mobile reserve towards the British front by attacking towards Caen. Once the German strength was committed to the western end of the Normandy bridgehead, Bradley's army group could break out.

Allied airpower largely restricted German vehicle movement to the hours of darkness. However, the Germans had concentrated enough armour and anti-tank guns along the British front to make any breakout battle very costly indeed.

From 17 to 20 July, the British attacked towards Caen with three armoured divisions. But although the defences were pounded by heavy bombers, enough defenders remained to block the attack, knocking out over 200 British tanks.

Alençon, while Dempsey's British and Canadians were a few miles north of Falaise and Haislip's tanks were at Le Mans. It needed no great imagination to see what would happen if they were to meet, and Montgomery was playing it cool when he said 'If we can close the gap completely, we shall have put the enemy in the most awkward predicament.'

The Falaise Gap was not closed with total effectiveness, though the destruction of German equipment and their loss of some 60,000 men was a severe blow; but Haislip's XV Corps did not reach Argentan on 13 August and could probably have gone on to Falaise had not demarcation lines and poor liaison prevented it.

To the south of them Walker's XX Corps had by the 16th reached Chartres, while by another feat of organization Patton had fed in his fourth corps (XII Corps under Major General Manton S. Eddy) even farther out on the right flank to take Orléans. Some 485 km (300 miles) now separated the farthest-flung divisions of Patton's 3rd Army (Middleton's men at Brest and Eddy's at Orléans) and the gap was to widen even further. Haislip's men left Dreux on 16 August and reached Mantes-Gassicourt on 19 August, Walker's XX Corps left Chartres on 16 August to reach Melun and Fontainebleu on 20 August (thus XV and XX Corps cut the Seine both above and below Paris almost simultaneously) and Eddy's XII Corps drove into Sens from Orléans on the afternoon of 21 August.

In 21 days, therefore, Patton's 3rd Army had advanced eastward from Avranches 320 km (200 miles) to the Seine, and westward 240 km (150 miles) to Brest. The Americans had liberated some 116550 km^2 (45,000 square miles) of France, and played a significant part in the destruction of the immense German forces trapped in the Falaise pocket.

This was a considerable military achievement by any standards and, in terms of logistics, a classic.

Above: The liberation of Caen
The heavy bomber raid on Caen remains one of the most controversial actions of the Normandy campaign. Here a British armoured car halts in front of a gigantic bomb crater in the remains of the town.

British armour east of the Orne
Festooned with local camouflage, British Cromwell tanks await the order to advance. Attacking on a narrow front during Operation 'Goodwood', the British armoured forces were unable to break through German defences sited in great depth.

Master of the skies
The destruction of the German army was a striking demonstration of the power of aircraft on the battlefield. Here an RAF Mustang in distinctive 'invasion stripes' passes above a French village with an armoured column moving along the road.

Churchill tank

Continuing the 'infantry tank' tradition, the Churchill was a slow but well protected tank armed with a 6-pdr gun. All Allied armour was outclassed by the superb Panther and Tiger tanks fielded by the Germans, but whereas the Allies could quickly replace tanks lost in 'Goodwood' the Germans could not.

US forces overran north-west France, capturing the Allies' first major port, Cherbourg. Now they were released to plunge south and westwards, behind the German forces in Normandy. Forbidden to retreat by Hitler, the German army was in serious trouble.

The German army in Normandy was soon almost surrounded, its only avenue of retreat the 'Falaise Gap'. All movement along the narrow roads was severely hampered by flights of rocket-firing Typhoons and other ground-attack aircraft.

Hitler's insistence on not giving up ground meant the destruction of the German forces in Normandy. As the Soviet summer offensive went into top gear the fall of France had now become inevitable. The next battle would be for the Reich itself.

DEATH OF A CITY: The Warsaw Rising

With the Red Army's guns audible in the distance, the Polish underground rises against the apparently retreating Germans.

During July 1944 the Red Army had swept forward through Belorussia, at times advancing a remarkable 40 km (25 miles) per day. By the end of the month Brest-Litovsk was in their hands, to the south of Warsaw they had crossed the Vistula between Magnuszew and Pulawy, and to the northeast they were fighting for the town of Wolomin, less than 16 km (10 miles) away. On the evening of 31 July rumours swept Poland's capital that Soviet units were already fighting in the suburbs around Praga on the eastern side of the Vistula.

The Polish Home Army had been in existence as a clandestine force almost since the city had fallen in the late summer of 1939. In Warsaw itself the army consisted of some 38,000 soldiers – 4,000 of them women. But there were arms for only 25 per cent of them, ammunition for a maximum of seven days' fighting, no artillery, no tanks, few vehicles of any sort and, of course, no air force. But they were inspired by the age-old patriotic fire of the Poles, consumed by hatred of the German occupiers – and at this particular moment anxious that when the Soviets entered the city the Poles would be in a position to welcome them as 'master in their own home'. The Polish Home Army and its leaders were loyal to the Polish government in London, not to the Polish communists led from Moscow.

During the third week of July it had seemed that the Germans had decided to evacuate Warsaw. German stores, workshops, military commands, police and army units were all pulled out, only the military

traffic feeding the remaining bridgeheads over the Vistula still remaining in evidence. Then Hitler commanded a halt to retreat, Generaloberst Heinz Guderian was placed in command, German units flooded back, two SS Panzer divisions and a parachute division closed up to the south of the city, and wall posters, street address systems and police patrols all exhorted the Poles to rally to the defence of their capital against the Bolshevik invaders.

Capture of the Old Town

But by this time the decisions had been taken. General Tadeusz Komorowski, codenamed 'Bor', had issued his orders, and at 1700 on 1 August the Polish Home Army in Warsaw struck against the Nazis. An element of surprise helped them, as did the fact that some of the German units and patrols were still in the process of establishing themselves. During that night the Old Town, the City Centre, Powisle along the river between the Poniatowski and Kierbedzia Bridges, Zoliborz in the north, and Mokotow, Sielce and Czerniakow in the south, were all taken over by the Poles while large areas between became the scene of heavy fighting.

For the next two days the battles in the streets continued, though German strongpoints proved impregnable to the light infantry weapons (and rapidly decreasing stock of ammunition) which were all the Poles had – though they were buoyed up all the time by the sound of heavy fighting only a few miles away on the other side of the river. They were sure they could hold out until the Red Army arrived.

Then on 3 August the sounds of battle faded, on 4 August they stopped altogether and the Red air force disappeared from the skies above Warsaw. The Polish Home Army realized it was on its own.

Both Winston Churchill and Franklin D. Roose-

In the Old Town. August 1944
A German infantryman watches from the rubble of a building as a Hetzer tank destroyer enters the street. The Poles had enough small arms for about a quarter of their initial strength, and the shortage of anti-tank weapons was even more desperate.

Hetzer tank destroyer

Mounting an anti-tank gun with limited traverse on an obsolete tank chassis produced a mobile, armoured, anti-tank platform which was much cheaper than a tank. The Germans were one of the first armies to deploy tank destroyers: the Hetzer was a 75-mm PaK 39 gun on the chassis of the old Panzer 38(T).

velt were appalled. Urgent representations to Stalin were at first ignored, then countered with the announcement that as the Poles had not consulted him about their revolt he could take no responsibility for it; anyway, after the enormous efforts of the Red Army throughout July in reaching the Vistula, it was now so exhausted that it could mount no more attacks until rested and resupplied. He also refused permission for American or British aircraft to land on Soviet soil should they attempt to drop ammunition or food into Warsaw and then lack the fuel to return to the Allied lines. It was quite evident that Stalin did not wish any Poles but his own nominees to be 'masters in their own home'.

It is a tribute to Polish valour and endurance that they held out for so long. Hitler's fury at the Polish revolt was such that he ordered the extermination of all of them and the destruction of Warsaw, then handed the execution of his commands to Reichs-

'Power-seeking criminals' — Joseph Stalin, 22 August 1944

The Polish underground army had grown steadily since 1940 despite the iron hand of German authority. The Jews were confined in a walled-off ghetto and knew early liberation was the only way to avoid the Nazi genocide programme.

The rising began when the Soviet army was nearing Warsaw after weeks of intense fighting but had already abandoned plans to take the city 'on the march' now that German reinforcements had begun to assemble. The Poles were unaware of this.

Loyal to the government in exile based in London, the Home Army wanted to establish a non-communist government in Warsaw before the capital was liberated by the Red Army. The German reaction to the rising was unbelievably savage.

Left: Sturmgeschütz assault guns
With metal plates mounted on their sides to protect them against infantry anti-tank rockets, two assault guns lead a German attack on a Polish strongpoint. Against such odds it is remarkable that the Poles managed to hold out for two months.

Right: 'Goliath' cable-steered tanks
Packed with explosive, these remote-controlled tracked bombs were an ingenious weapon for fighting in built-up areas. The German assault on Warsaw combined the latest technology with medieval barbarity.

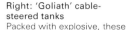

Left: Another pocket falls
As the Germans overran each position any prisoners were usually shot or driven in front of the tanks for the next assault. Wounded were doused in petrol and burned alive. The survivors retreated, using the sewers as their main communication route.

Right: Deporting the survivors
Deportation or immediate extinction in the gas chambers awaited the survivors of the battle for Warsaw. The Soviet attack towards the city came too late and their bridgehead over the Vistula, which included pro-communist Polish troops, was overrun.

führer-SS Heinrich Himmler. Reinforcements were rushed to the city by road and rail – police, infantry, a brigade of criminals especially recruited from jails, two brigades of Soviet troops who had defected to the Nazis, all under SS Gruppenführer Erich von dem Bach-Zelewski, an expert in fighting partisan movements.

Aided by tanks, cannon, flamethrowers and Luftwaffe dive-bombers, the Germans inevitably beat the Poles back from their positions. For some time the Poles kept communications going through the sewers, their spirits cast down by the lack of outside help but their determination kept alive by reports reaching them of German atrocities committed all around them. Prisoners were shot; doctors, nurses and civilians in the hospitals murdered; the wounded soaked in petrol and burned alive. Until 16 September no help came to them at all from the Red Army, sitting but 16 km away to the east. On that day Soviet aircraft appeared above the city and dropped food and arms: but 'dropped' was literally true, for no parachutes were used so most of the weapons were smashed on landing. It was perhaps the cruellest – certainly the most cynical – of Stalin's reactions to the Polish attempt to preserve some form of democracy.

After two months an armistice was agreed on 2 October and the Home Army laid down its weapons. It is estimated that some 150,000 Poles died during the Rising and German losses are given as 26,000. When the survivors had been marched away and the city completely evacuated, von dem Bach-Zelewski's units began their systematic destruction, blowing up or burning whole areas, removing any valuables worth taking to the Reich.

When it was complete they turned their faces eastwards again, where the Red Army was now ready to recommence its advance towards Berlin.

Women members of the Jewish resistance
The anti-semitic policies of the pre-war Polish government were nothing compared to the 'final solution' engineered by the Nazis. The Jewish underground had nothing to lose by 1944 and as the battle progressed, the whole Polish resistance fought with the courage of despair.

Hitler appointed SS Gruppenführer von dem Bach-Zelewski to crush Warsaw. He unleashed a brigade of ex-convicts and Kaminski's SS brigade of 6,000 Russian POWs whose psychopathic hatred of Poles was given full rein.

Stalin refused to order an attack on Warsaw to help the Home Army. He denied the use of Soviet airfields to Allied aircraft so the few supplies the Poles received came from Allied bombers based in Italy. Defeat became inevitable.

After two months of butchery, the Home Army surrendered. Half its 30,000 men and women were dead and many of the survivors would perish in the concentration camps. Some 200,000 of Warsaw's one million citizens had died.

LEYTE GULF: Final Victory

As US forces landed in the Philippines the Japanese navy launched a last desperate attack to stave off the inevitable.

Just four months after the Japanese reverse at the Philippine Sea the Americans staged a massive landing at Leyte, the first move in the reconquest of the Philippine islands themselves. At the head of the US battlefleet, now restyled the 3rd Fleet, Admiral William Halsey had replaced Admiral Raymond Spruance. His carrier force, still under Vice Admiral Marc Mitscher, had expanded further to nine large and eight light carriers, with nearly 1,200 aircraft.

The Japanese contingency plan, 'SHO-1', included only four carriers which by then were so short of aircrews that a total of fewer than 120 aircraft could be embarked. Anticipating that any enemy counter would have to rely on land-based airpower, the American carrier groups had conducted a three-week attritional campaign so that less than 200 Japanese land-based aircraft were left to oppose the landings, which took place between 17 and 20 October 1944 in Leyte Gulf.

Because of the wide dispersion of the oil-starved Japanese fleet, when 'SHO-1' was initiated on 17 October it involved widespread movements. Halsey's main force, covering the landing zone, was to be lured away to the north by Vice Admiral Jisaburo Ozawa's four carriers (the Northern Force, other-

wise the Mobile Force, Strike Force) offered as deliberate bait. Duly uncovered, the Gulf was to be attacked at dawn on 25 October simultaneously by two powerful surface battle groups and the transports annihilated. The Central Force (Force 'A' of the 1st Strike Force, 5th Fleet) under Vice Admiral Takeo Kurita would exit via the San Bernardino Strait and attack from the north, while the Southern Force (unwisely divided in two parts under Vice Admirals Shoji Nishimura and Kiyohide Shima as Force 'C' of the 1st Strike Force and 2nd Strike Force of the 5th Fleet) would approach from the south via the Surigao Strait.

Again the far-ranging American submarines struck first. Approaching the Philippines from the west on 23 October, Kurita's powerful Central Force, which included five battleships and 10 heavy cruisers, suffered three cruisers torpedoed, two of which sank. Early on 24 October aircraft from Mitscher's carriers (TF38), operating in four groups to the east of the islands, also located the Southern Force.

With all available Japanese air power engaging TF38 (sinking the light carrier USS *Princeton*), Kurita was without cover as his group crossed the Sibuyan Sea in the centre of the islands. Five separate US air strikes thus inflicted considerable damage, including the sinking of the super-battleship *Musashi*, but Kurita, though delayed by seven important hours, ploughed doggedly toward San Bernardino.

The Southern Force, with two battleships and four cruisers, was tracked across the Sulu Sea. As its approach was obviously going to be through Surigao Strait, Vice Admiral Thomas Kinkaid aimed to block it here with his 7th Fleet, the fire-support force for the US landings.

Halsey should similarly have corked Kurita in the San Bernardino Strait, but his interest was elsewhere. Ozawa, after several attempts to advertise his presence to the north, was finally 'discovered' at 1540 on 24 October: four carriers, two hybrid battleship/carriers and three cruisers. Halsey, understandably, took the bait whole. Though Kurita was in no way beaten, air strikes against him suddenly stopped as Halsey moved north, taking with him even Vice Admiral Willis Lee's fast battleship force.

Modernized dreadnought
Launched in March 1914, *Fuso* was modernized during 1930-33, receiving new machinery and 2,500 tons more armour. Accompanied by another old battleship, *Yamashiro*, she formed the backbone of Nishimura's squadron at Leyte Gulf. She was sunk by two torpedoes from US destroyers on 25 October.

Leviathan in danger
Kurita's squadron included the two greatest battleships ever built, *Yamato* and *Musashi*. The latter took enormous punishment from US aircraft as Kurita pressed doggedly across the Sibuyan Sea. Struck by 17 bombs and 10-19 torpedoes in successive strikes, *Musashi* dropped behind and eventually foundered.

'Mogami' class heavy cruiser
The four magnificent warships of the *'Mogami'* class formed the 7th Cruiser Squadron previously commanded by Kurita when he was a rear-admiral. Two were lost at Leyte: *Mogami* herself was crippled in the Surigao Strait night action and sent to the bottom by an airstrike the next day. *Suzuya* was sunk in the action off Samar.

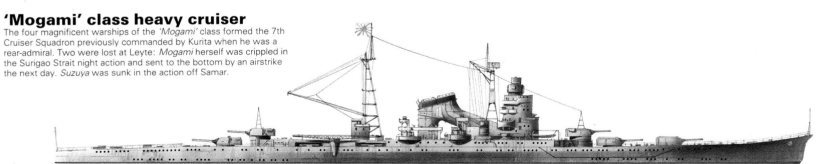

'There are such things as miracles' — Vice-Admiral Kurita

The Japanese plan was to lure the American aircraft-carriers away from the landing beaches by using their own carriers including converted battleships like Ise *as a decoy. Then the US landings would be attacked by two squadrons of Japanese battleships, one from the north and one from the south. The US Navy did not know just how few aircraft remained in the Japanese carriers.*

The weaker southern squadron was attacked by destroyers in the Surigao Strait in the early hours of 25 October. Fuso *was torpedoed and sunk, and* Yamashiro *ran into six American battleships and was torn apart. Here USS* West Virginia *opens fire on her in what was destined to be the last battleship versus battleship action in history.*

Against the near-toothless Ozawa were pitted 64 warships and nearly 800 aircraft, but the San Bernardino Strait had been left wide open.

Halsey pinpointed Ozawa as early as 0200 on the fateful 25 October, at which point Kurita was just three hours short of the San Bernardino Strait and Nishimura was barging up the Surigao Strait.

Nishimura and Shima, though aware of the delay to Kurita's timetable, strove to adhere to their own, running blindly at overwhelming opposition to reach Leyte Gulf by dawn on 25 October. With adequate time to prepare, Kinkaid placed Rear Admiral Jesse Oldendorf's six veteran battleships and eight cruisers across the northern end of the strait. To even reach them the Japanese would need to navigate the length of the waterway, first harried by 39 PT boats and then by three destroyer divisions. From 2236 on 24 October the torpedo boats attacked, mostly singly but all without success in the face of powerful defensive fire. By 0230 on 25 October, in the narrows between Leyte and Dinagat, the destroyers were taking over. Both of Nishimura's battleships were torpedoed, *Fuso* breaking in two. Already hit by two torpedoes *Yamashiro*, now supported by only a cruiser and a destroyer, ran into Oldendorf at 0353 and was effectively obliterated. Although the other two units and Shima's small force managed to get back down the strait to temporary safety, the southern jaw of the Japanese pincer had been destroyed.

Battle in the San Bernardino Strait

Not so the northern: even as Shima stumbled back out of the Surigao Strait at about 0530 on 25 October, Kurita came out of the San Bernardino Strait behind schedule and puzzled by lack of any opposition. By great good fortune three rear-echelon groups of escort carriers lay to the east of Samar, between him and the beaches and, though geared to a support role he could, together with shore strips, put up a goodly number of aircraft. From 0630 these little carriers were involved in a very confused action, coming even under 460-mm (18.1-in) shell fire from the *Yamato*. They were stoutly fought and magnificently defended by their destroyers and escort destroyers. Kurita, already rather demoralized by events, with no air cover and believing himself to be under attack from at least one of Mitscher's main carrier groups, turned back. For the loss of an escort carrier and three smaller ships, the Americans sank three Japanese heavy cruisers and almost certainly saved the whole Leyte operation.

USS *Pennsylvania* and USS *Colorado* lead the way into the Lingayen Gulf
The Japanese defeat at Leyte Gulf destroyed the Imperial Navy as a fighting force. The subsequent American operations would be hampered by suicide pilots in *kamikaze* strikes, but the Japanese surface fleet could no longer offer serious resistance.

Halsey, meanwhile, despite receiving desperate pleas for assistance, stayed to finish off Ozawa's carriers with six separate air strikes, the last of which was not launched until 1710. At 1100 he had ordered back one carrier group and Lee's battleships to plug the San Bernardino Strait. They arrived at 0100 on 26 October, some three hours after Kurita had retreated through the strait after the battle off Samar. It could easily have been a disaster.

The final gamble of 'SHO-1' had not paid off, the Japanese losing four carriers, three battleships and 10 cruisers – and their last trained aircrews. From this point on, the US Navy was never seriously threatened by the Imperial Navy.

Escort carrier, USS *Sangamon*
Sangamon was one of four converted fleet oilers which formed part of the escort carrier force off Samar. Her sisterships *Suwannee* and *Santee* were among the first to be damaged by deliberate suicide bombing attacks. *Santee* was also damaged by a torpedo from the Japanese submarine *I-56* but all the 'Sangamon' class survived Leyte and were back in action by early 1945.

Ozawa's carrier decoy force worked perfectly, luring the aggressive Admiral Halsey away, leaving the San Bernardino Strait, through which Kurita's battleships had to pass, undefended. Ise was one of the few major units of Ozawa's force to escape.

Kurita's battleships suffered casualties but they pressed on. All that remained between them and the beaches was a force of escort carriers, but Kurita overestimated the opposition and turned around. Here USS St Lô takes a hit from a Kamikaze.

US carrier aircraft followed up the retreating Japanese. This heavy cruiser is under attack from Hellcats from USS Hancock and was sunk two hours later. Kurita's precipitate retreat had thrown away the last chance of a Japanese naval victory.

OPERATION MARKET GARDEN: The Battle for Arnhem

17 September 1944: The Allies stage the greatest airborne assault of the war to capture vital bridges on the road to Germany.

During the morning of Sunday 17 September 1944 the inhabitants of south-east England witnessed the assembly in the skies above them of the greatest airborne armada of all time. From 22 airfields stretching from Dorset to Lincolnshire over 1,500 aircraft climbed into the air, and as the fighter and bomber units sped away on their protection or distraction tasks Douglas C-47 Dakota transports and Short Stirling bombers converted for troop-carrying, some of them towing a total of 478 gliders packed with men or vehicles, formed up for their journeys over the North Sea to the Netherlands.

One stream made for their dropping zone at Eindhoven; these held the men and equipment of the US 101st Airborne Division (commanded by Major General Maxwell Taylor). The second, larger stream, flew as far as the small town of s'Hertogenbosch where the stream split into two. The larger part carried the US 82nd Airborne Division (Major General James Gavin) towards the area between Grave and Nijmegen, while the smaller part carried the Air Landing Brigade and one Parachute Brigade of the British 1st Airborne Division (commanded by Major General Robert Urquhart) to the division's landing grounds 16 km (10 miles) to the west of the town of Arnhem and its vital bridge over the Neder Rijn.

The bridge and four other bridges to the south at Nijmegen, Grave, Veghel and Eindhoven were the objectives for these airborne forces, for farther to the south (along the line of the Meuse-Escaut Canal) waited the forward troops of the British 2nd Army, poised to hurl themselves forward along the Eindhoven-Arnhem road and across all the canals and rivers between, outflanking the main German defences of the Siegfried Line and thus forming, in the words of their commander-in-chief, Field Marshal Sir Bernard Montgomery, 'a springboard for a powerful full-blooded thrust to the heart of Germany'.

The bridge at Arnhem was the tip of that springboard, the *Ultima Thule* of Operation 'Market Garden'.

What Allied planners had not appreciated was that the Germans were using the area to rest first-line divisions. So in addition to miscellaneous local forces organized as the 85th Division the lightly armed paratroops would come up against the 9th and 10th SS Panzer Divisions of SS-Gruppenführer Willi Bittrich's II SS Panzer Corps – and the headquarters of Generalfeldmarschall Walter Model's Army Group 'B' to take operational command.

Twelve converted British bombers and six American Dakotas carried the Pathfinder company that dropped first, and within its time schedule the company's work was completed; as the 149 Dakotas carrying the men of 1st Parachute Brigade arrived over Dropping Zone X the flares were all burning and the marking tapes laid out, as they were for Landing Zones S and Z where the 254 Airspeed Horsa and 38 giant General Aircraft Hamilcar gliders of the Air Landing Brigade and Urquhart's headquarters were released from their tows, first to drop with stomach-wrenching acceleration then to level off and skim silently to their destinations. From the entire force only five gliders had been hit or the tows cut during the journeys, and only 35 aircraft lost – many of these after they had dropped their parachutists or slipped their tows. As a loss rate of 30 per cent had been predicted the omens looked good at first for 'Market Garden'.

Heading for the bridge

Nevertheless the first troop movements were slow to begin. It was 1530 on that fine Sunday afternoon before Lieutenant Colonel John Frost had assembled the men of his 2nd Parachute Battalion and led them off on their 13-km (8-mile) march to the Arnhem Bridge.

Frost's battalion reached Oosterbeek, a small town halfway to Arnhem, and Frost was about to detach one company to capture and cross the railway bridge over the Neder Rijn (to storm the southern end of the main bridge while the rest of the battalion took the northern end) when a loud explosion revealed that they were too late and that the rail bridge had been blown.

This was a serious setback, but the British paratroops pressed on after first brushing aside resistance by German armoured cars and snipers inside Oosterbeek town; but it was dark by the time Frost and his men reached Arnhem Bridge.

Meanwhile Urquhart was facing another severe difficulty: his signal sets were not working. So in order to find out what was happening, Urquhart set out after his paratroops by Jeep.

He found Frost's HQ close to the Rhine bank, then turned back and towards the sound of battle near Oosterbek. There Urquhart found Lieutenant Colonel Fitch's 3rd Battalion (heavily engaged with young German troops who had been rushed down to block them and who fought with fanatical zeal) and also found the commander of 1st Parachute Brigade, Brigadier Gerald Lathbury. By now it was dark and it was evident that German Panzer units were coming into position between 3rd Battalion and Arnhem, as they were also between Lieutenant Colonel Dobie's 1st Parachute Battalion working its way along the railway running into Arnhem from the west.

Paratroopers in action in Oosterbeek
Armed with pistols and Sten sub-machine guns, British paratroops probe the limits of their position. The bulk of the British forces were hemmed in at Oosterbeek, unable to assist 2 Para's epic defence of the bridge at Arnhem.

Into a hornets' nest

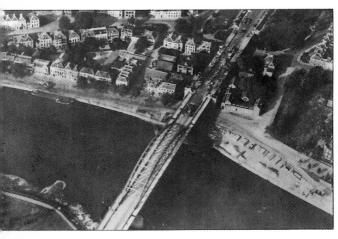

Arnhem bridge, seen shortly after 2 Para was overrun, was the last bridge in the series. If all three could be taken in one giant bound, the German industrial heartland would be open. But the plan depended on an optimistic timetable.

While US 82nd and 101st Airborne divisions took Eindhoven and Grave, the British made an alarming discovery. Some POWs came from 9th and 10th SS Panzer divisions. They had landed on top of a refitting Panzer Corps!

2 Para reached the bridge at Arnhem but was cut off from the rest of the brigade. 1 and 3 Para were pinned down at Oosterbeek. A German assault over the bridge was beaten off but the lightly equipped paratroopers soon ran short of ammunition.

But by now the pattern of the battle had been formed; powerful and efficient German units were being fed into the gap between Frost's men at the bridge and all possible reinforcements – and even when the 4th Parachute Brigade under Brigadier John Hackett arrived on the Monday afternoon it could only fight its way forward to join the remnants of 1st and 3rd Battalions, blocked around Oosterbeek and the small farms and houses to the west. Throughout the next two days the separate battles raged with ever-increasing ferocity, the advantage moving to the Germans as a result of dwindling numbers on the British side (and dwindling ammunition too, for to the near-despair of the men fighting in constricting areas the RAF's supply aircraft were dropping the vital canisters in zones already occupied by the enemy).

By Wednesday night it was all over at the bridge. Frost had been wounded during the late afternoon, the Germans had shelled into chaos every building the paratroops had occupied, and now their Panzers moved inexorably across the bridge; German infantry closed in and took the few fit survivors prisoner, carrying away and treating the wounded with care and courtesy.

Spirits were raised briefly on the afternoon of Friday, 22 September, when the Polish 1st Airborne Brigade under its gallant General Stanislaw Sosabowski was dropped just south of the river, but the ferries had been destroyed and every attempt by the Poles to go to the rescue of the British came under withering fire from both banks; in the end only about 50 Poles got across. And the ordeal of the 1st Airborne Division had still another three days to run.

The men had been told that they would be relieved certainly within four days, perhaps in two; in the event they were on their own for nine days. Three battalions of the 43rd Division at last reached the southern bank of the river on Sunday afternoon, and some men of the 5th Dorsets crossed to bring help and reassurance to the exhausted, famished, desperate paratroops still holding on, and during the following afternoon their evacuation was organized.

That night XXX Corps artillery put down a devastating curtain of fire all around the perimeter, the glider pilots of the Air Landing Brigade taped out an escape route and, when darkness had fallen, guided their dazed and staggering comrades down to the bank where British and Canadian engineers

waited in assault boats which had somehow been rushed up from Nijmegen.

Operation 'Market Garden' had been a good idea. It was defeated by lack of information of enemy dispositions around Arnhem, by bad luck with weather which had contributed to XXX Corps' delay, and mistaken planning which had dropped 1st Airborne Division too far from its objective.

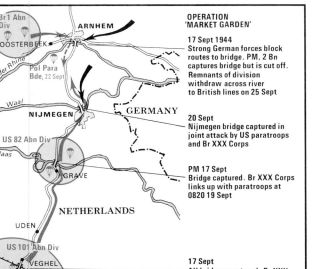

OPERATION 'MARKET GARDEN'

17 Sept 1944 Strong German forces block routes to bridge. PM, 2 Bn captures bridge but is cut off. Remnants of division withdraw across river to British lines on 25 Sept.

20 Sept Nijmegen bridge captured in joint attack by US paratroops and Br XXX Corps

PM 17 Sept Bridge captured. Br XXX Corps links up with paratroops at 0820 19 Sept.

17 Sept All bridges captured. Br XXX Corps links up with paratroops PM 18 Sept

ALLIED AIRBORNE LANDINGS AT MIDDAY 17 SEPT 1944
MAIN GERMAN COUNTERATTACKS

Three bridges The British XXX Corps had to advance on a one road frontage to link up with the airborne forces, against German defences which were well sited and stubbornly held. But if it came off, Allied troops would be poised to attack Germany's industrial heartland, the Ruhr.

Oosterbeek, 18 September Two British army cameramen of the Parachute Brigade share some food with a Dutch girl. The Dutch underground later smuggled many British soldiers back to the Allied lines after the failure of Market Garden.

Left: Holding on Hampered by radio sets which did not work and the absence of tactical air support, the paratroops could only hang on to their positions and hope XXX Corps managed to break through.

17 September: the British landings Paratroops descend onto the Drop Zone with gliders crash-landed in the foreground. Glider landings entailed considerable risk but were the only way of providing lightly armed airborne soldiers with anti-tank guns, jeeps and heavy supplies.

German troops at Arnhem The local Dutch SS battalions offered light resistance but the German opposition was soon stiffened by the Panzer troops. Worse still, Arnhem turned out to be the headquarters of Field Marshal Model who reacted with his usual vigour, improvising a defence until reinforcements could arrive.

The British Parachute Brigade HQ in a state of all round defence as 'Market Garden' falters. 82nd Airborne made a heroic assault over the Waal to capture Nijmegen on 20 September but time was running out.

As German pressure increased it became obvious that the British forces had to be evacuated. On 25 September Horrocks ordered Urquhart to fall back and some 2,500 men were extracted under cover of a ferocious barrage from XXX Corps artillery.

British paratroopers are marched into captivity. Ordered to hold for up to four days, they had clung to their positions for nine. Whether Arnhem could have worked or whether it was over-ambitious remains the subject of vigorous debate.

RETURN TO THE PHILIPPINES

Having defeated the Japanese navy at Leyte Gulf, American forces can now begin the liberation of the Philippines.

After the great carrier battle of the Marianas, American forces went on to complete the capture of Saipan, thereby providing an important base for subsequent B-29 attacks on Japan. They landed on Guam on 21 July, and on Tinian four days later. The final capture of Guam on 10 August marked the end of the American campaign in the Central Pacific and the end of organized Japanese carrier warfare. The *Hiyo* had been sunk by air action, and the *Taiho* and *Shokaku* had been sunk by US submarines, while no fewer than 1,223 Japanese naval aircraft had been destroyed in the two-month campaign.

Four further Japanese carriers, the *Zuikaku*, *Chitose*, *Chiyoda* and *Zuiho*, went to the bottom during the battles of Leyte Gulf. On 30 November, only 11 days after her commissioning, the huge ex-battleship aircraft-carrier *Shinano* (68,060 tons) was sunk by the submarine USS *Archerfish* in Tokyo Bay. Before the end of the year the carriers *Unryu*, *Shinyo*, *Taiyo*, *Chuyo* and *Unyo* had been sunk and the *Junyo* was permanently crippled. During the same period the US Navy lost but one carrier, the light carrier *Princeton*.

Although the initial landings on Leyte marked the start of the Philippines campaign, the invasion of the main island, Luzon, did not take place until 9 January 1945, four divisions being put ashore in

Reigning supreme
Seen from the fantail of USS *Essex*, the carriers *Langley* and *Ticonderoga* return to Ulithi atoll after preliminary strikes against the defences on the Philippines. The battleships *Washington, North Carolina* and *South Dakota* follow in their wake. US naval power drove the defenders from the beaches before the American landings.

Lingayen Gulf. Already Task Force 38 had had to contend with a powerful new enemy: atrocious weather. On 18 December a fully-fledged typhoon struck the fleet; three destroyers capsized with the loss of more than 800 men; aircraft tore loose in the carriers, starting fires as they ripped up electric cabling; the *Cowpens*, *Monterey* and *San Jacinto* between them lost 33 aircraft, 19 others were swept off the battleships and cruisers, and the smaller escort carriers lost a further 94. Such losses and the search for survivors in the mountainous seas delayed the ultimate assault on Luzon.

As pre-emptive strikes against Japanese air bases on Formosa were being flown by the carriers of TF 38 in the first week of 1945, the Lingayen Gulf assault force, carried by the US 7th Fleet under Vice Admiral Thomas C. Kinkaid, came under heavy attack as it approached the landing area. The escort carrier *Ommaney Bay* was hit and sunk on 4 January, and the following day the *Manila Bay* was damaged and suffered more than 70 casualties; on 8 January both the *Kitkun Bay* and the *Kadashan Bay* were badly damaged and had to retire from the battle.

South China Sea

On 9 January, as the American forces went ashore in Lingayen Gulf, Admiral William F. Halsey's 3rd Fleet (including TF 38), with eight fleet carriers, five light carriers, two escort carriers, six battleships, 11 cruisers and 61 destroyers, entered the South China Sea, its main task being to locate and destroy the two battleship-carriers, *Hyuga* and *Ise*, and also to prevent the Japanese from sending reinforcements to Luzon. Although the giant carriers were not found, the American carrier aircraft flew wide-ranging strikes over French Indo-China, China proper and Formosa; few targets were found.

Suicide attacks around Luzon continued to increase, the Australian cruiser *Australia* being hit five times. Fighting on the ground grew fiercer and, despite an order from General Yamashita to evacuate Manila, a Japanese admiral organized resistance by 20,000 men in the naval base. Bataan fell on 16 Febuary, and Corregidor (in Manila Bay) on 28 February. By then, however, the bulk of the American carrier forces had moved on to prepare for the invasion of Iwo Jima. Indeed, with the steady but bloody advance through Luzon, and the overrunning or building of airstrips on the island, it now fell to the fighter and fighter-bomber squadrons of the USAAF and US Marine Corps to provide cover over the battlefield, and to the guns of the fleet to create a curtain of fire against the suicide attacks.

On 4 March 1945, after 173 days ashore on Luzon, American forces finally captured the shattered city of Manila, having lost more than 40,000 in dead and wounded, and more than 360 aircraft. Ten days later Iwo Jima also fell to the Americans. The US 10th Army, and the 16 carriers of Task Force 58 in support, were poised for assault on the last stepping stone to Japan: Okinawa.

In the streets of Manila
The Japanese naval personnel who defended the capital had fortified Manila with thoroughness and ingenuity. It took over 3 weeks to overrun them and the city was shattered in the process. On 25 February the last positions fell, and 3 days later the Philippine Commonwealth government was re-established by General MacArthur.

Kamikaze attack off the Philippines
The US fleet was assailed by numerous suicide bombers. Although anti-aircraft guns could usually shoot incoming aircraft to pieces it was not easy to destroy them entirely. With the pilot dead at the controls and the fuel tanks blazing, a kamikaze follows a ballistic trajectory towards its target.

'I shall return'

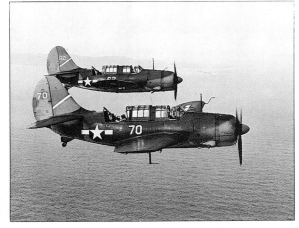

By Christmas day 1944 organized Japanese resistance on the island of Leyte was at an end. American carrier aircraft had already begun to bomb the enemy positions on Mindoro and Luzon.

The Japanese manned ex-American fortifications. This is Fort Drum in Manila Bay: after a naval bombardment, troops climbed on top of the fort from landing craft with scaling ladders. The interior was filled with gasoline and ignited.

Landings began on Luzon on 3 January; in a week, 4 divisions were ashore and pressing towards Clark Field. MacArthur made another landing on the west coast of the Bataan peninsula, preventing the Japanese following his line of retreat in 1942.

Nakajima Ki-84 *Hayate*

Code-named 'Frank' by the Allies, the *Hayate* (gale) was the most effective late war Japanese combat aircraft. Manoeuverable and unusually well armed for a Japanese fighter, large numbers of them were dispatched to the Philippines on the eve of the American landings.

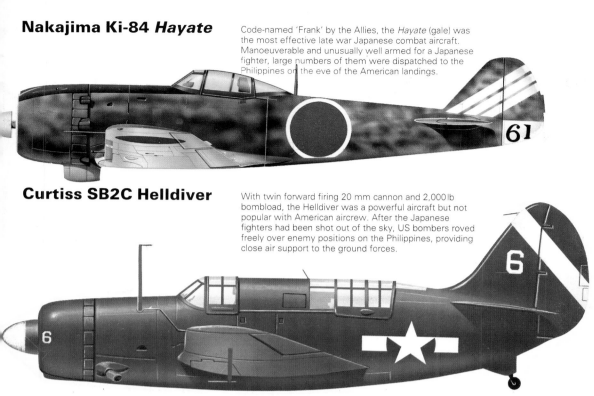

Curtiss SB2C Helldiver

With twin forward firing 20 mm cannon and 2,000 lb bombload, the Helldiver was a powerful aircraft but not popular with American aircrew. After the Japanese fighters had been shot out of the sky, US bombers roved freely over enemy positions on the Philippines, providing close air support to the ground forces.

Heading for Manila
An SB2C Helldiver is hurled into the sky from the deck of USS *Hancock* on 25 November 1944. The softening up attacks which preceded the landings were very effective, inflicting heavy losses on the defending fighters and causing the Japanese army to offer its main defence away from the beaches.

11th Airborne Division was landed near Manila and US troops reached the outskirts of the capital in early February. The Japanese army commander, Yamashita, withdrew his men but Rear-Admiral Iwabuchi organised a desperate defence.

The battle for Luzon continued into March, US forces suffering 40,000 casualties including 10,000 killed. 190,000 of the 250,000 defenders were to die, as their customary ferocity could not make up for the lack of equipment, food and ammunition.

Liberated prisoners of war receive their first square meal in three years. Japanese treatment of the prisoners taken in 1941-2 had been inexcusable. Luckily for the POWs, American troops overran the prisons on the second day of the attack on Manila.

THE LAST BLITZKRIEG:
The Ardennes Offensive

16 December 1944: to the astonishment of the Allies, the Germans launch a major offensive through the Ardennes forest.

By mid-December 1944 the main bulk of the Allied forces was concentrated (as were the attentions of the Allied high command) towards both ends of the battlefront. In the north the Anglo-Canadian armies had at last cleared Antwerp and opened the Scheldt estuary, and the US 1st and 9th Armies were set to close up to the lower Rhine and threaten the vital Roer dams. In the south Lieutenant General George Patton's US 3rd Army, after its spectacular drive across France, was poised to sweep through the equally important Saar region towards the Rhine at Mannheim.

Between the two powerful groupings were strung out some 80,000 American troops along 145 km (90 miles) of front, the bulk of them consisting of Major General Troy Middleton's VIII Corps which had been brought across from Brittany, backed by one armoured division, the 9th, which had but lately arrived in the area and had not yet seen action. They were there because this part of the front, the Ardennes section, was a quiet part, covered in front by the sparsely settled German Schnee Eifel, and behind by the steep wooded hills and foaming trout streams which had always been, despite the events of 1940, regarded as unsuitable country for open warfare.

Wacht am Rhein

They were thus considerably shaken when at 0530 on the morning of 16 December they were suddenly deluged by the heaviest artillery bombardment even the veterans among them had experienced, and when after periods varying from 20 to 90 minutes they peered out into the pre-dawn murk, they found themselves overrun by German shock troops surging forward through their positions, followed closely or soon after by powerful Panzer and Panzer-grenadier units, many of them bearing the jagged double streak of the Waffen-SS.

Even as the fighting in the Falaise Gap was ending, Hitler had announced that by November a force of some 25 divisions must be prepared to launch a huge counter-offensive against the Anglo-American armies; and to the astonishment of the German high command that force had come into existence, conjured from every corner of German life: rear-area administrative echelons, 16-year-old boys, civil servants, small shopkeepers, university students and the scourings of the prisons, all had been swept into the armed services.

Thus had been formed three German armies, and they were by mid-December marshalled under an exemplary cloak of secrecy and subterfuge opposite the US VIII Corps. In the north were poised the units of the 6th SS Panzer Army under SS-Oberstgruppenführer Sepp Dietrich, erstwhile commander of Hitler's personal bodyguard in the street-fighting days and later of the crack 'Liebstandarte Adolf Hitler'. In the middle section of the attack front waited the 5th Panzer Army under the trusted army General Hasso von Manteuffel. And on the southern flank of the attack to form the 'hard shoulder' against any possible northward counter-move by formations of the US 3rd Army was the 7th Army under the dogged but unimaginative General Erich Brandenburger.

Altogether some 200,000 men would take part in Operation 'Wacht am Rhein' (Watch on the Rhine) equipped with more tanks, more artillery and more ammunition than had been granted to any similarly assembled German force for many months past; and in addition to those more or less conventional fighting divisions, there waited in the rear 1,250 paratroops under Oberst von der Heydte, a veteran of Crete, to drop in front of the main assault, seize bridges and crossroads, and attack any headquarter organizations they could find. Moreover, to help them spread alarm and despondency, the famous raiding commander SS-Sturmbannführer Otto Skorzeny commanded a special force of volunteers driving American vehicles and wearing American uniforms, a ploy which would result in their being shot if they fell into Allied hands.

M7 105 mm self-propelled gun
The overcast skies deprived the Allies of close air support making the role of the artillery doubly important. The highly successful M7 was the first fully tracked self-propelled gun introduced by the US army and was widely used by British forces.

Below: Shot as a spy
Sgt Manfred Pernass, aged 23, faces a US firing squad after being captured in American uniform. The US rear areas were raided by English-speaking German troops in Allied uniforms under the command of the redoubtable Otto Skorzeny. After the Malmedy massacre, the US army was not in a forgiving mood to any of Skorzeny's men who surrendered.

Above: Frozen to death
A German officer, injured by American shelling near Mauberge, lies frozen solid. The intensity of the fighting in bitter winter weather was reminiscent of the Eastern Front, as was the behaviour of some of the SS formations.

Panthers in the snow

Hitler's plan appalled his generals, so to ensure obedience the attack was led by the Sixth SS Panzer Army, the first time so large a unit was designated SS. The main striking force was commanded by the Fuhrer's former bodyguard Sepp Dietrich.

Four thinly stretched American divisions were battered by 16 divisions in two Panzer armies. Here, bewildered US prisoners watch a King Tiger tank rumble majestically towards the front.

US resistance stiffened considerably as the news spread that the Germans had massacred American POWs. Although chaos reigned at Eisenhower's headquarters, the frontline American soldiers stubbornly resisted the German assault.

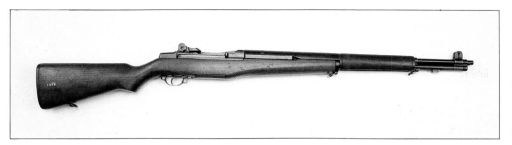

.30 calibre M1 Garand
Adopted by the US Army in 1932, the Garand was the first self-loading rifle to enter military service as a standard weapon. Fed by an 8 round clip it was robust and reliable.

Gewehr 43 7.92 mm rifle
This German self-loading rifle fired full power 7.92 mm rounds but was only in limited service on the western front. A telescopic sight mount was fitted as standard and many were used as sniper rifles.

How are the mighty fallen
Very heavily armoured and carrying an 88mm gun, the King Tiger was the most powerful tank of the war but the best fighting vehicles are useless without fuel. This one was captured on the Stavelot road after German logistic arrangements had broken down and the dejected crew surrendered.

Dinner is served
Despite their supreme commander's unseemly panic, the GIs in the frontline displayed a dogged courage in resisting the onslaught. Hot food was essential but not always possible during the battle; this picture was taken in early January after the Germans were on the retreat.

And it was here that the attentions of both attackers and defenders became concentrated. It was Lieutenant General Omar Bradley's 12th Army Group which caught the offensive in its central section, and at first Bradley wrote it off as merely a spoiling attack to disrupt the 1st Army's threat to the Roer in the north and the 3rd Army's to the Saar in the south; but he soon realized that it was more than that. On 19 December he ordered Lieutenant General Courtney Hodges in the north to swing some of his 1st Army divisions back to hold a flank and then drive down to St Vith, and Patton to do the same in the south and send his crack 4th Armored Division up to relieve Bastogne. Being Patton, of course, he objected, but then suddenly cheered up. 'What the hell,' he said, 'we'll still be killing Krauts!', and with an efficiency which compels the greatest admiration he swung the bulk of his army through 90° in 48 hours.

In the meantime, General Dwight Eisenhower had released his reserves and they sped to the two vital points in every truck and jeep they could find: the 82nd and 101st Airborne Divisions, recently recovered from their battles at Nijmegen and Eindhoven, raced north from Patton's lines, the 101st dropping off to begin its famous stand at Bastogne and the 82nd passing on to St Vith. The battle now was becoming one of mobility, and that game the Americans knew how to play.

Panthers in the snow

As von Manteuffel's spearheads probed farther and farther west (they never crossed the Meuse, though the 11th Panzer Division did reach nearly to Dinant) American tank destroyers and artillery shored up the flanks of the penetration while their infantry fought doggedly forward into the gaps or held on grimly in isolated positions. For most of the time, moreover, they fought without air cover, for the weather favoured the Germans for days on end. But by Christmas Day, after some of the bitterest fighting in Europe, the sting had been drawn from the German onslaught; although von Manteuffel mounted a last desperate attack on Bastogne, it was beaten off and on the following day Patton's tanks arrived to break the siege.

Meanwhile, Field Marshal Montgomery had taken command of the northern flank and in order to 'tidy up the battlefield' he authorized a withdrawal from the St Vith salient, and brought the British 29th Armoured Brigade down on the Americans right flank to hold the deepest penetration. When on the following day the whole of the US 2nd Armored Division came down to join them, Hitler's last offensive in the west was brought to a halt.

It has undoubtedly given the Allied leaders a nasty jolt, and it would be many more days before the Ardennes salient was entirely flattened, but in fact the offensive had used up a great deal of the rapidly-diminishing German war *matériel* and it caused Hitler the loss of manpower which he could better have used on the other side of the Rhine. It had been defeated by the ability of American leadership to deploy guns and armour with supreme efficiency, and by the dogged courage of the American infantryman.

The objective for this surreptitiously assembled force was Antwerp, plus the splitting of the Allied armies threatening the German frontier, the annihilation of the Anglo-Canadian armies and the US 1st and 9th Armies alongside them by starvation as their main supply-port was captured, and an immense morale boost for the German public together with such a shock to the Allies that the consequent bickering between them would wreck their future strategic planning for weeks and possibly months.

Leading elements of the 1st SS Panzer Division under their ruthless commander, Oberst Jochem Peiper, swept through a gap in American lines to Honsfeld in the north, captured a large petrol dump at Bullingen and then caught American troops on the move at Malmedy crossroads before racing on towards Stavelot. Unfortunately for all parties concerned, his men, inured to the bitter fighting on the Eastern Front, shot down 19 American prisoners at Honsfeld, 50 at Bullingen and nearly 100 at Malmedy, a piece of barbarism which defeated itself; when rumour of the massacres swept through the embattled American positions it produced feelings of both fury and desperation and caused even the greenest units, sometimes commanded by only junior NCOs, to fight with a committed ferocity which baulked the important German thrust to the south.

It also spelled the almost immediate death of any of Skorzeny's men discovered at their clandestine tasks.

One of von Manteuffel's spearheads had success similar to Peiper's, but without that ruthlessness, and reached the village of Auw just in front of the vital road junction of St Vith, but here it ran into the tank destroyers and main artillery of an American infantry division which held them, forcing the main drive of von Manteuffel's army southwards into the gap between St Vith and the other vital road junction, Bastogne.

The German plan was to reach the Meuse on the first day but by 20 December they were still 20 miles short. US forces surrounded in Bastogne were relieved on Boxing Day as General Patton's 3rd Army counter-attacked from the south.

Over the Christmas period the skies cleared and the Allied airforces intervened. Field Marshal Montgomery took charge of the northern flank and the fate of the German offensive was now obvious to all except perhaps Hitler himself.

Knocked out Panther tanks litter the battlefield where Hitler expended Germany's last reserve. It was a futile waste of men and resources which, had they not been lost, might have made the invasion of Germany far more difficult.

STRANGLING JAPAN:
The Submarine War in the Pacific

The Japanese Navy conquers a vast maritime empire but US submariners are soon menacing Japan's vital sea lanes.

While prewar Japanese planning for the acquisition of a vast oceanic empire had been meticulous, the subsequent problems of sustaining it with a large merchant marine had been scarcely considered. Japan's whole strategy was, after all, posited on a short period of active hostilities, while commerce protection was a defensive concept and, therefore, not worthy of naval consideration. Even though the USA was known to have a substantial submarine force, Japan went to war with no plans for convoy organization, few anti-submarine escorts and virtually no training.

Like the Japanese, the Americans had defined the primary functions of their submarines as reconnaissance for the surface fleet and attack on enemy warships. Unlike the Japanese, the Americans rapidly grasped the revised nature of the operational situation and went for the commerce. Designed for ocean warfare their boats were large and capable of long, fast passages on the surface. Initially they were slow diving, while their poor submerged endurance and unhandiness was tolerable only because of poorly organized countermeasures. Nevertheless, Far Eastern waters were generally shallow and the enemy was well supplied with depth charges.

Following the progressive loss of the Philippines and the East Indies, US submarines were based on the Australian ports of Fremantle and Brisbane, under Captain John Wilkes, and on Pearl Harbor under the control of Vice Admiral Charles Lockwood. Though sharing broadly similar aims with the Germans, these two commanders did not opt for the close control exercised by Admiral Karl Doenitz, preferring instead to rely on the considerable initiative of individual skippers.

During the period of the great Japanese advances the few US submarines immediately available could do little but slow things down. On 16 December 1941 the 8,660-grt Japanese freighter *Atsutusan Maru* was sunk by the submarine USS *Swordfish*, acquiring the dubious privilege of being the first of several thousand losses. The first enemy warship to

US Navy Submarines

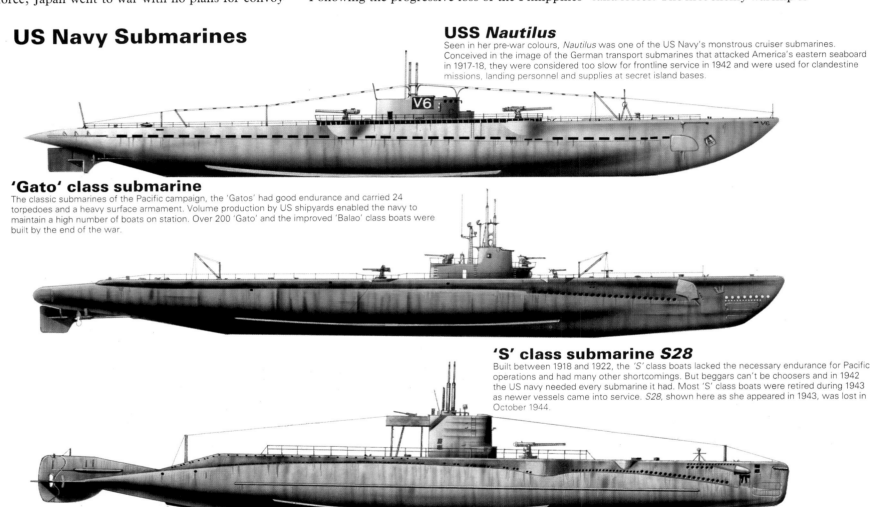

USS *Nautilus*
Seen in her pre-war colours, *Nautilus* was one of the US Navy's monstrous cruiser submarines. Conceived in the image of the German transport submarines that attacked America's eastern seaboard in 1917-18, they were considered too slow for frontline service in 1942 and were used for clandestine missions, landing personnel and supplies at secret island bases.

'Gato' class submarine
The classic submarines of the Pacific campaign, the 'Gatos' had good endurance and carried 24 torpedoes and a heavy surface armament. Volume production by US shipyards enabled the navy to maintain a high number of boats on station. Over 200 'Gato' and the improved 'Balao' class boats were built by the end of the war.

'S' class submarine *S28*
Built between 1918 and 1922, the 'S' class boats lacked the necessary endurance for Pacific operations and had many other shortcomings. But beggars can't be choosers and in 1942 the US navy needed every submarine it had. Most 'S' class boats were retired during 1943 as newer vessels came into service. *S28*, shown here as she appeared in 1943, was lost in October 1944.

Hitting the blind spot

February 1942: USS Trout brings her cargo of gold from the doomed Philippines. In the same month, the US submarines opened their offensive against the Imperial Navy, S-37 sending the destroyer Natsushio to the bottom of the Macassar strait.

In 1942 US submarines sank 84 Japanese ships for a loss of 3 submarines. The following year 308 vessels were sunk for the loss of 15 submarines but the Japanese overestimated the American losses and remained complacent.

The US submarine crews had to endure very long patrols and, until 1943, the bitter disappointment of malfunctioning torpedoes. Radar sets arrived in 1942 enabling submarines to conduct 'blind' night attacks.

be sunk was the destroyer *Natsushio*, which fell victim on 8 February 1942 to the elderly 'pig-boat' *S-37* in the Macassar Strait. Three days later, USS *Shark* became the first submarine to be lost on patrol, in this case off Celebes (Sulawesi).

During the whole of the slow build up of the submarine offensive things were made difficult by defective torpedoes, the percentage of which reached near-crisis point and which resulted in many unsuccessful attacks, often at great risk to the crews. Torpedoes were frequently heard to hit the target without exploding.

The turning point was reached when the exasperated skipper of USS *Tinosa* hit a large stationary tanker with 11 torpedoes, of which only two exploded, the ship surviving. Urgent, belated research exposed the poor design of the firing pistols, but improved weapons (including wakeless, electric torpedoes) did not enter service until late 1943. Poor-quality torpedoes encouraged several skippers to adopt a very bold surface attack using their heavy 127-mm (5-in) deck guns. An important acquisition from August 1942 was the SJ surface radar set which, with a suitable plot, enabled boats to carry out 'blind' night attacks.

War of attrition

Despite their problems, the submarines accounted for 138 Japanese merchantmen by the end of 1942, a total of 600,000 grt. Three boats had been lost, but 33 more had been commissioned. In 1943 the force more than doubled these figures, gaining 56 more boats for the loss of 15. With all sources of captured tonnage now exhausted and with an inadequate new building programme, the enemy showed a net loss in available tonnage of 16 per cent on the year.

Time on station was extended for the American boats by the use of tenders or mobile forward bases, while the beginnings of a Japanese convoy system was met by the formation of 'wolf-packs', usually composed of only three boats and bearing distinctive soubriquets such as Wilkins' Wildcats and Roach's Raiders. Individual 'aces' emerged in skippers such as 'Mush' Morton who, before being sunk in USS *Wahoo* in la Perouse Strait, sank 20 ships of over 60,000 grt. Overall record for tonnage destroyed went to USS *Flasher*, whose 100,000 grt total still compares modestly with those of many U-boats, e.g. *U-35*'s 224 ships of 536,000 grt during World War I and *U-48*'s 53 ships of 318,000 grt in World War II.

By 1944 many of Japan's island garrisons were going unsupplied, and the home country lost half its imports of raw materials. Oil losses were of particular significance, shortages beginning to restrict the movement of the battle fleet itself. Targets by 1945 were becoming ever fewer for the Americans as more submarines competed with marauding carrier aircraft. Two boats after the same target actually collided under water.

Rogue torpedoes were never fully eliminated. One resulted in the loss of Dick O'Kane's USS *Tang* in the Formosa Strait as he sought to add to his score of 24 ships. During 1944/5 112 new boats joined the force, many being employed as lifeguards on the route of the now-continuous bomber streams. Over 600 aviators were thus saved to fly again.

Braving extensive minefields, the submarines spent the final months of the war penetrating even the Inland Sea. By the surrender Japan had lost over 8 million grt, of which 5 million had fallen to the submarines, which had lost 42 of their own number in return. The boats had accounted also for over 200 warships but, where this loss had only reduced the Japanese chances of winning, the destruction of the merchant fleet was a primary factor that contributed to Japan's defeat.

USS *Puffer* in action
Launched in November 1942, *Puffer* was the 56th *'Gato'* class submarine. This picture was taken through her periscope in 1943 when she torpedoed and sank the *'D'Artagnan'*, a captured merchant vessel in Japanese service.

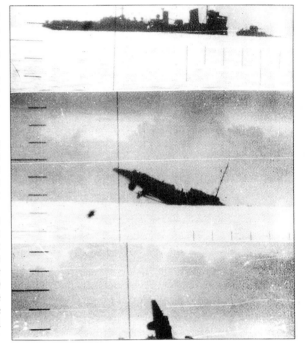

Death of a destroyer
Her bows blown off by a torpedo, an old Japanese destroyer ploughs her way under. Although the submarines inflicted some spectacular casualties on the Japanese navy, it was the steady attrition of merchant vessels that won the war.

Kaibokan Type 'A' escort vessel

The Japanese had neglected to build many escorts before the war, their defensive image not endearing them to the offensively minded Imperial navy. Even when ordered in 1937 these vessels were intended for fishery fleet protection, minesweeping and convoy duty in that order. Displacing 1020 tons at full load they carried 18 depth charges and had excellent endurance.

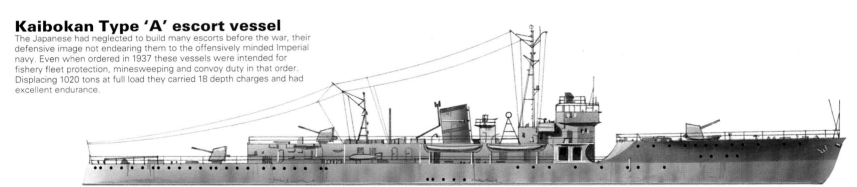

In 1944 US submarines accounted for 548 vessels, totalling nearly 2.5 million grt. The Japanese merchant marine was practically wiped out. Island garrisons were isolated and vital resources needed in Japan failed to arrive. Japanese industry plunged into decline and the Imperial fleet began to feel the effect as fuel supplies dwindled.

By the time this freighter was sunk in June 1945, American boats were penetrating Japanese home waters and the South China Sea was positively alive with submarines. Their iron grip had strangled Japan's maritime lifelines, crushing the life out of the Empire.

STORMING INTO GERMANY:
The battle of the Rhine crossings

March 1945: Allied armies are poised along the banks of the Rhine, the last barrier protecting the Reich itself.

In February 1945 the task for the Canadian army in the north, the British army next to it, the four US armies stretching down to Strasbourg and the French army in the Vosges, was to cross the Roer, Our and Saar rivers and reach the Rhine.

By 21 February, Goch, Cleve and Calcar were in British and Canadian hands, and to the south the US 9th Army could launch Operation 'Grenade' and fling bridges across the Roer opposite Mönchen Gladbach, which they took on 1 March. Five days later Cologne was in American hands and on 7 March, to the astonishment of the Allies and to Hitler's inexpressible fury, the Remagen Bridge over the Rhine had been taken, apparently undamaged, and was in use by the US 1st Army. Fortunately auxiliary bridges were thrown across, both up- and down-stream from Remagen, during the days which followed, so when on 17 March, weakened by bombing, by the attempted German demolitions, by the drumming of thousands of infantry feet and the heavy lurches of overladen vehicles, the whole bridge fell sideways into the Rhine – taking 28 US engineers to their deaths – at least the disaster did not cut off the bridgehead on the east bank from all supplies.

By 24 March over 150,000 more German soldiers found themselves in Allied PoW camps, and a large but unknown number had been killed; by the end of the month the west bank of the Rhine from the Channel to the Swiss border was in Allied hands.

The Allies were thus now only 485 km (300 miles) from Berlin.

On the night of 23 March 1945 Field Marshal Sir Bernard Montgomery's 21st Army Group began crossing under a barrage from all of the artillery weapons that had been assembled. The first troops went across in Buffaloes with numbers of DD Shermans and other special vehicles in train. Air support was so intense that Wesel itself was confidently bombed by RAF Bomber Command when Allied troops were only a few hundred yards away. This not only cleared Wesel of the enemy but prevented the Germans from moving through the town to counter-attack.

The Allies did not have it all their own way. The mud was so bad in places that not even the Buffaloes could make much forward progress, with the result that some of the second assault waves, crossing in boats, came under intense fire and took heavy casualties.

The main assault arrived at about midday when

Across the Rhine by Buffalo
Men of the Dorset Regiment cross the Rhine in their amphibious tracked personnel carrier. Although lightly armoured and petrol driven, the Buffalo series were highly successful. If light resistance was encountered they allowed the attackers to rapidly expand the bridgehead.

the first of the Allied airborne forces came into sight. What became known as the 'armada of the air' flew over the Rhine to disgorge two divisions of parachute troops who seemed at times to make the sky dark with their numbers. They were soon followed by glider tugs that unleashed their charges to land in an area known as the Diersfordter Wald and another known as the Mehr-Hamminkeln. These glider troops did not land unscathed. Despite all efforts of the Allied air forces to neutralize flak sites near the landing points, some guns escaped to concentrate their fire power on the gliders, and about one quarter of all glider pilots involved became casualties in this operation. The numbers that did land safely were such that the airborne forces and the troops that had made the river crossings were able to join up, often well in advance of the anticipated times. By nightfall the Rhine bridgeheads were secure and despite some localized German counter-attacks they were across the river to stay.

American crossings

Attempts to cross by the American armies along the more southern stretches of the Rhine, although mounted by fewer men with smaller resources, were just as successful. One had occurred the day before the 21st Army Group launched the main crossing – south of Mainz between Nierstein and Oppenheim by an assault regiment of the US 5th Division, part of XII Corps of the 3rd Army, under command, needless to say, of Lieutenant-General George S. Patton.

German infantryman 1945
Although facing overwhelming odds, the German army fought with incredible professionalism into the spring of 1945, long after defeat was inevitable. This SS man is armed with a fully automatic 7.92 mm *Sturmgewehr* 44, the ancestor of modern assault rifles.

The last obstacle

Hitler's Ardennes offensive had destroyed the German army's last reserves and the Allied attack over the Rhine received no major counter-attack. But fierce local resistance was still encountered, especially in fortified villages.

A catalogue of human errors led to the bridge at Remagen being captured intact. Hitler was furious and several unfortunate officers were summarily shot 'pour encourager les autres'. However, the main Allied attack was downstream at Wesel.

Southern Germany is good defensive terrain so the main Allied effort was aimed at the North German Plain. On 23 March, 21 Army Group stormed the Rhine at Wesel with two divisions of paratroops landing on the far bank on a 5 mile front.

Arado Ar 234 jet bomber

The bridge at Remagen was subjected to the first all-jet bombing raids in history as Ar 234s swooped out of the low clouds escorted by Messerschmitt Me 262 jet fighters. The single-seat Ar 234s were also used for high speed reconnaissance flights over the UK. With a top speed of 460 mph and a bombload of up to 4,400 lb, the Ar 234 was a formidable machine indeed.

Right: Frankenthal, 26 March 1945
Men of 7th Infantry Regiment, 3rd division arrive on the east bank during the US 7th Army's assault over the Rhine. The subsequent advance towards Saxony dictated the position occupied by US troops in Germany today.

Left: Waiting for the Luftwaffe
The Luftwaffe was ordered to make up for the army's failure to demolish the Remagen bridge and mounted an intensive series of bombing raids. Here, two M3 half tracks armed with quadruple .50 cal machine guns sit in the March drizzle.

Advancing through Munster
US Paratroopers hitch a lift on a British Churchill tank. The turret is festooned with spare track as a defence against the hollow charge anti-tank rockets in widespread use with German infantry. Most German armour was immobilised through lack of fuel.

The divisional commander, Major General Leroy Irwin, made some small protest about the shortness of time he was given for preparation, but in the face of Patton's urgency he sent the first wave of assault boats across the 300 m (1,000 feet) wide river just before midnight, under a brilliant moon and the artillery support of a group which later complained that it could find little in the way of worthwhile targets. The first Americans to land captured seven German soldiers who promptly volunteered to paddle their assault boat back for them, and although later waves ran into sporadic machine-gun fire the regiment was across before midnight and moving towards the east-bank villages, with support regiments flooding across behind them. By the evening of 23 March the entire 5th Division was across the river, a bridgehead formed and awaiting the arrival of an armoured division already on the west bank.

During the next few days crossings were made at Boppard and St Goar, Worms and Mainz, and by the end of the month Darmstadt and Wiesbaden were in US hands and armoured columns were driving for Frankfurt-am-Main and Aschaffenburg beyond; farther south, the French had put an Algerian division across near Germersheim. Now a huge Allied bridgehead could be formed from Bonn down to Mannheim, from which would be launched the last Western offensive designed to meet the Soviets on the Elbe and split Germany in two. The main objective for the US 12th Army Group would be the industrial region of Leipzig and Dresden.

To the north, the Anglo-Canadian 21st Army Group was to drive north towards Hamburg, its left flank (the Canadians) clearing Holland of the enemy and then driving along the coast through Emden and Wilhelmshaven, its right flank (US 9th Army) curving around the Ruhr to meet Lieutenant General Courtney Hodges's 1st Army formations at Lippstadt, thus encircling Generalfeldmarschall Walter Model's Army Group 'B' in the Ruhr. After Hamburg the British would close up to the Elbe down as far as Magdeburg, and send other forces up into Schleswig-Holstein and the Baltic.

There was some argument as to the desirability of 21st Army Group racing for Berlin, but General Dwight D. Eisenhower, solidly supported by Roosevelt, felt that the German capital was in easier reach of the Soviets who – Roosevelt was sure – would prove both co-operative and amenable in regard to post-war European responsibilities.

Stalin would doubtless have been amused had he learned of the arguments.

Meanwhile the US bridgehead to the south continued to expand despite the collapse of the Remagen bridge. Here, the endless column of motor transport pours over one of several pontoon bridges near the remains of the main bridge.

To Montgomery's petulant fury, Eisenhower redirected the Allied advance at Leipzig instead of Berlin and opened a personal communication with Stalin. As a military decision it made sense but it revealed the naivety of the US administration.

German civilians loot a train as Allied troops press on. The war was lost and most German troops, conscious of what was happening in the east, were ready to surrender although handfuls of young volunteers and SS men fought to the last.

THE SANDS OF IWO JIMA

19 February 1945: On the bloodiest day in the history of the United States Marine Corps, two Marine divisions attack the fortress island of Iwo Jima.

By the end of 1944 it had become quite evident to the US commanders in the Pacific that in the near future they would have to mount a large-scale attack on the Japanese island of Iwo Jima.

Three factors made the decision inescapable. First, heavy Boeing B-29 bomber raids on the Japanese mainland, then being mounted from the Marianas, were proving prohibitively expensive as even North American P-51 Mustangs could not escort them on the 4500-km (2,800-mile) round trip, and they thus lacked essential fighter protection over the target area; Iwo Jima lies only 1060 km (660 miles) from Tokyo and possessed two airfields, one of which could take B-29s immediately. Second, even with no further advance towards Japan Iwo Jima was a highly desirable link in the defences of the newly captured Marianas. And thirdly, the island was traditionally a part of the Japanese homeland (it was administered by the Tokyo prefecture), and its fall would thus constitute a severe psycholog-

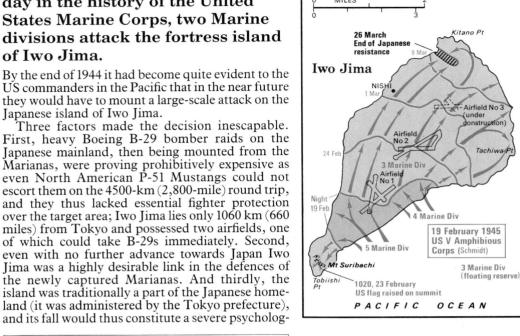

Iwo Jima

19 February 1945
US V Amphibious Corps (Schmidt)

26 March End of Japanese resistance

Kitano Pt
9 Mar
NISHI 1 Mar
Airfield No 3 (under construction)
Airfield No 2
Tachiwa Pt
24 Feb
3 Marine Div Airfield No 1
Night 19 Feb
4 Marine Div
5 Marine Div
Mt Suribachi
Tobiishi Pt
1020, 23 February US flag raised on summit
3 Marine Div (floating reserve)

PACIFIC OCEAN

Fortress Iwo
The tiny island was important primarily because of its airfields. In US hands they would enable fighter aircraft to escort the B-29 bomber raids on Japan. The Japanese were painfully aware of this and their garrison was well equipped and had ample time to prepare its defences.

Right: In the caves
By early March the Japanese positions were divided into indefensible pockets, but the Japanese refused to surrender. Many were entombed in their tunnels as US troops sealed the entrances with high explosive.

0900 hrs, 20 February (D-day+1)
The landings on 19 February cut the island in half, isolating Mount Suribachi (seen here in the background) from the Japanese positions in the north of Iwo Jima. From then on the advance proceeded almost yard by yard as the Marines battled their way forward.

ical blow to the Japanese people. The island must therefore be captured; isolation would not be enough.

Unfortunately for the Americans the Japanese high command possessed just as keen an understanding of strategic realities, and had long appreciated the necessity of denying Iwo Jima to the Americans. One staff officer even went so far as to suggest that as Japanese air and naval strength had suffered an apparently irreversible erosion, serious consideration should be given to a project of sinking the island into the Pacific, or if not the whole island then at least the half which contained the main airfield. Iwo Jima is, after all, only 8 km (5 miles) long, 4 km (2.5 miles) wide at its broadest, and at its tallest point (the summit of Mount Suribachi) only 170 m (550 ft) high.

The suggestion was turned down, but as early as June 1944 the highly regarded Lieutenant General T. Kuribayashi was sent to organize the defence of the island, and given clearly to understand that in case of failure he should not expect to see his family or homeland again; the same stricture applied to the 20,000 veteran reinforcements who followed him to Iwo Jima during the months which followed. As they were provided with heavy and medium artillery, anti-aircraft batteries, heavy and light machine-guns, mortars and tanks, together with relevant ammunition all on an ample scale, their morale was in no way cast down by their predicament.

They therefore set to work with a will, dug their artillery well into the ground, and constructed successive lines of defence across the width of the island

a task in which they were considerably aided by the fact that Iwo Jima is of volcanic origin, so the soft pummice is easily quarried yet still self supporting however deep it is cut. By the following March 4.8 km (3 miles) of tunnelling wound its way under the northern half of the island.

For the defenders this was just as well, because in order to 'soften up' the island before the landing both the US Navy and the USAAF carried out massive bombardments. The US Navy began its assault in November 1944 with fire from the guns of six destroyers and four heavy cruisers which lasted a whole morning and was repeated at regular intervals until February, while on 8 December Consolidated B-24s and North American B-25s began an assault which was to last 72 days before climaxing on the morning of 19 February with an attack by 120 carrierborne planes, dropping napalm along the strip of ground just inland of the proposed landing beaches. From then on the bombardment took the form of a creeping barrage from the massive guns of seven battleships, four heavy cruisers and three light cruisers.

Four hundred and fifty vessels of the US 5th Fleet were offshore at dawn on the morning of 19 February, and around and among them swarmed 482 landing craft of various descriptions bearing the men of eight US Marine battalions; and at 0902 the first wave hit the landing beaches, 5th Marine Division platoons on the left, 4th Marine Division platoons on the right.

For the first 20 minutes it seemed as though the US Navy and the USAAF had done the job for the marines, who met only sporadic and scattered resistance, apparently totally unorganized. Then as

Inch by inch, yard by yard

Heavy bombers attacked Iwo Jima for 72 days before the Marines landed. Here B-24 Liberators pound the Japanese positions on 21 October. The airstrip, which would allow US fighter aircraft to reach Japan, is clearly visible.

US warships bombarded the island at intervals from November onwards, and in the three days preceding the assault the defences were shelled by 7 battleships and 7 cruisers. Iwo Jima has a surface area of only 10 square miles; every inch was covered.

The Marines hit the beach at 0902 while 120 carrier aircraft deluged the defences with napalm and the furious naval bombardment redoubled in intensity. Eight battalions deployed onto Iwo Jima's narrow beach along a frontage of little over a mile.

the marines moved up towards a low sand ridge, concentrated fire from concealed machine-gun and mortar posts opened and a deadly rain of metal swept the 1.6-km (1-mile) strip; the most costly operation in the history of the US Marine Corps had begun.

For a matter of seconds the shock of the sudden deluge of Japanese fire froze the marines where they lay, then training and the realities of the situation galvanized them into action. They could not stay where they were and live; they could not go back, for despite the shot and shell which furrowed the beach behind them LCVs were still swimming in through the surf and waves of supporting companies were flooding ashore and packing the beach-head.

Sheer pressure drove the leading platoons forward out of the maelstrom behind them into and over the nearest Japanese defensive positions, some of which they destroyed, leaving others to their comrades coming up behind; and in less than an hour they had widened the beach-head to 800 m (880 yards). Seven whole marine battalions were ashore with their essential equipment, forward patrols had reached the edge of the main airfield and another was in sight of the western beach.

Beach-head secured

Undoubtedly Kuribayashi had made a fundamental error in allowing that first wave of marines to get ashore, for by the end of the day 30,000 marines and their weapons and stores had been landed, and they were there to stay. Their casualties had been high (that had been expected), but the combination of pressure from behind and desperation had flung the leading elements straight across the neck of the island, isolating Mount Suribachi and its garrison from the main defending force, and placing the southern end of the main airfield firmly in American hands.

The ensuing four days were spent in capturing Mount Suribachi (the most famous photograph in American history, of the flag being raised by a Marine patrol on the summit, was taken on 23 February), and from then on a savage battle of attrition was fought as the marines assaulted the defence lines to the north. Bayonet, rifle, flamethrower and grenade were the weapons with which the fighting was conducted for the next 21 days, for the Japanese defenders were not only fighting from well dug-in positions, but followed the practice of waiting in deep cover until the marines were closed up to within 50 m (55 yards) or less before manning their guns and thus betraying their positions, seemingly to vanish again after a violent spasm of vicious and costly close-quarter battle.

By D+10 many marine formations were down to half strength, and although the 3rd Marine Division had now been put ashore it soon found itself blocked by a positive lattice of defensive positions which constituted the northern half of the island. Complexities of underground bunkers faced them, and mazes of interwoven caves, in one area 915 m (1,000 yards) wide and 200 m (220 yards) deep: 800 pill-boxes, blockhouses and dugouts each held fanatical defenders every one of whom, it was afterwards revealed, had sworn to kill at least 10 marines.

It was not until D+18 that the first marine patrols reached the north-east shore of the island, and then it became possible to partition the area still in Japanese hands into small pieces and gnaw away at each piece until the defence was crushed. But at last it was done. On the night of 25/26 March the last defenders launched a final Banzai charge against their attackers, and the following morning the bodies of the 300 devoted servants of the Emperor who had carried it out littered the ground around the entrance to their last position.

By this time the first B-29s had landed on the island's main airstrip, and by the end of March squadrons of P-51s were flying in to take up their role of escorting the heavy bombers against the Japanese mainland. It all formed a significant step in the defeat of Japan, but it had cost the marines 6,821 killed and three times that number wounded; and of the 23,000 Japanese who had been on the island when the first landings took place, only 216 were ever taken prisoner, most of them badly wounded.

Iwo Jima was less than 25.9 km² (10 sq miles) in area. It had taken 72 days of air bombardment, three days of concentrated naval hammering and 36 days of the most bitter infantry fighting to conquer it.

How long, and at what cost, would it take to conquer the Japanese homelands by the same methods?

Left: 4th Marines go ashore
For the 4th Marine Division this was their fourth amphibious assault in 13 months. The short beach rose to a low ridge and the ground beyond was swept by concealed machine-guns which had survived the US bombardment.

Below: Mount Suribachi
21 February: the sinister hump of Mount Suribachi looms over the US beach-head. The summit was overrun two days later but many Japanese remained in the mountain, holed up in a labyrinth of caves and tunnels.

The landing beach seen from Mount Suribachi
Men and supplies are unloaded on the original invasion beach after the capture of Suribachi. The northern shore in the distance remained in Japanese hands until early March when the perimeter was finally breached.

The 4th Marine Division landed roughly in the centre of the island with the 5th Marine Division on its left flank near Mount Suribachi. As they breasted the low ridge here the Japanese machine-guns opened fire.

The Marines reached the west coast of Iwo Jima on their first day ashore but it took another 35 harrowing days of close-quarter fighting to root out all the defenders. Japanese positions were linked by miles of tunnels.

US Coast Guards help the wounded back to the fleet: US forces sustained some 27,000 casualties including 6,821 dead to capture an island 5 miles long and 2½ miles wide. Of the 23,000 defenders, less than one man in one hundred survived.

BATTLE FOR BERLIN: Nemesis in a T-34

Berlin, April 1945: the Red Army batters its way into the Nazi capital against a motley army of teenagers, pensioners and desperate SS men.

On 1 April 1945 Marshals Georgi Zhukov and Ivan Koniev had arrived in Moscow for a briefing on the subject of the Battle for Berlin. Stalin informed them that the devious and conniving Western Allies were planning a swift Berlin operation with the sole object of capturing the city before the Red Army could arrive – an announcement which, not surprisingly in view of the recent achievements of the Red Army, incensed them both.

They had expected to mount the attack on Berlin in early May, but in these special circumstances they would accelerate all preparations and be ready to move well before the Anglo-Americans could get themselves solidly inside German territory. Which of the two fronts – Zhukov's 1st Belorussian or Koniev's 1st Ukrainian – should have the task, and the honour, of driving straight for Berlin? This was a question to which the wily Georgian left an ambiguous answer by drawing on their planning map a demarcation line between their commands, which ended short of Berlin at Lübben, 30 km (18.6 miles) to the south east.

When the last offensive of the Red Army was launched its aims were to advance to the Elbe and to annihilate all organized German resistance before them, including the capture of Berlin and the reduction of its garrison. For this purpose Zhukov and Koniev had some 1,640,000 men under their command, with 41,600 guns and mortars, 6,300 tanks, and the support of three air armies holding 8,400 aircraft.

To oppose them were seven Panzer and 65 infantry divisions in some sort of order, 100 or so independent battalions, either remnants of obliterated divisions or formed from old men, children, the sick, criminals or the simple-minded, collected together by SS teams sent out from the Chancellery bunkers in which Hitler and his demented entourage were living out their last fantasies, with orders to conjure yet another army from the wreckage of the Thousand Year Reich.

Unorganized and half-trained though they might be, the bulk of the German formations defending Berlin against the Red Army nevertheless fought at first with a blind ferocity and a blistering efficiency which demonstrated yet again that the epitome of high morale in combat is that of the cornered rat – which is the reason he so often escapes.

But there would be no escape for the Germans now.

At dawn on 16 April tremendous artillery and air bombardment opened all along the Oder and Neisse rivers, and out of the Soviet bridgeheads stormed the first waves of shock troops. It took Zhukov's northern thrust two days to smash through some 6.5 km (4 miles) to reach the Seelow Heights, and his southern thrust to advance 13 km (8 miles) – and at that point they had seen no sign of a crack in the German defences despite the casualties on both sides. Koniev's shock troops, however, were not so strongly opposed and they advanced 13 km the first day; so on 18 April Koniev fed in two tank armies and ordered them to fight their way to the north west, into the Berlin suburbs. His right-hand flank brushed Lübben, but only just.

Perhaps inspired by competition, Zhukov now drove his infantry and tank armies forward with ruthless vigour, and by 19 April both his thrusts had advanced 30 km on a front almost 65 km (40 miles) in width, destroying as they did so the bulk of the German 9th Army, immobilized in the path of the attack by lack of fuel. On 21 April General V.I. Chuikov reported that his 8th Guards Army, which he had brought all the way from Stalingrad, was into Berlin's south eastern suburbs.

Koniev, having thrown his own counter into the battle for the capital, now devoted the bulk of his endeavour due westwards towards the Elbe. By 20 April two of his tank armies had reached Luckenwald – thus splitting the German Army Group 'Centre' from Berlin and the defences in the north – and then drove two more armies given him by STAVKA up towards Potsdam where on 25 April they linked up with one of Zhukov's guard tank armies which had come around the north of Berlin. Thus the city, its inhabitants and its 200,000-man garrison were surrounded.

Defender of the Reich
German manpower was all but exhausted by the end of 1944 and the surviving army units were now supplemented with *Volkssturm* units of boys and old men. Half-trained if they were lucky, they fought to defend the German heartland with the same ferocity with which the Soviets had clung to Stalingrad.

Keeping the Red Flag flying
An IS-II tank parks triumphantly in the 'lair of the Fascist Beast' as the Soviet press described Berlin. As resistance collapsed the Red Army embarked on an orgy of rape and murder but since the attackers included men recently freed from the concentration camps this came as no surprise. By the summer a VD epidemic among the troops compelled Zhukov to restore discipline.

Nowhere to hide

Falling back, March 1945. Despite the courage and professionalism of the German army, the Soviet war machine was now unstoppable. Hitler refused to leave Berlin and prepared to fight the final battle.

On 20 April, Hitler's 56th birthday, Soviet artillery fired its first barrage at Berlin and Allied bombers paid the doomed city their last fiery visit. The next day, the first Soviet tanks penetrated NE Berlin.

By 22 April Zhukov's forces were dividing into battle groups: infantry companies with anti-tank guns, engineer flamethrower teams and a tank platoon. The city was surrounded and the troops swarmed forward to stamp out German resistance.

ISU-152 self-propelled gun

Mounting a 152-mm (6-in) gun in a thickly armoured box, the ISU-152 was crudely built, uncomfortable to fight from, and only the command vehicles had radios. It was also mass produced and very difficult to stop. Soviet armour and infantry were not well co-ordinated and in street fighting this led to heavy losses. But with 464,000 men, 1,500 tanks, 12,700 guns and 20,000 *Katyusha* rocket launchers attacking Berlin, lack of tactical finesse was not a problem.

'It is the hour of the strong hearts'
So proclaims the German caption to this picture, exhorting all Germans to fight to the last against the Bolshevik hordes. Many of the men carry *Panzerfaust* anti-tank rockets which were to inflict serious losses on Soviet armour during the battle for Berlin.

T-34s in the vanguard
Several Soviet tank corps were used to isolate Berlin and then to drive vigorously for the Tempelhof airfield which was Hitler's last escape route. The Soviets were not to know that the *Führer* had decided to stay and die in the capital of his '1000-Year Reich'.

Below: the last cartridge
Despite the fearsome odds, few German units disintegrated and most fought on to the bitter end. The formidable discipline and professionalism of the German army was never demonstrated more clearly than in the dying moments of the Nazi regime.

On the same day units of the 5th Guards Army reached the Elbe at Torgau and within minutes were exchanging drinks, hats, buttons and photographs with Americans of the US 1st Army. The scenes of triumphant comradeship and co-operation which followed were repeated up and down the central axis of Germany, as soldiers who had fought westwards from Stalingrad met those who had fought eastwards from Normandy, and during the brief period in which they were allowed to fraternize they learned to recognize each others' qualities. It is a tragedy that friendships made then were not allowed to continue.

On 1 May Chuikov, now well inside the Berlin city centre, was approached by Generaloberst Hans Krebs, the Chief of the German General Staff, with three other officers bearing white flags desirous of negotiating a surrender. With almost unbelievable effrontery, the German general opened the conversation with the remark:

'Today is the First of May, a great holiday for our two nations.'

Considering the outrages carried out in his country by the nationals of the man addressing him,

Chuikov's reply was a model of restraint.

'*We* have a great holiday today. How things are with you over there, it is less easy to say!'

But the first moves towards an official end to hostilities in Europe had been made.

Berlin surrendered unconditionally on 2 May, on 4 May Field Marshal Sir Bernard Montgomery took the surrender of all German forces in the north – and on 7 May the 'Unconditional surrender of Germany to the Western Allies and to Russia' was agreed, the instrument itself signed by General Jodl for the defeated, and Generals Bedell Smith and Suslaparov for the victors, General Sevez also signing for France. The war in Europe was at an end.

Hitler had committed suicide on 30 April, having first married and then poisoned his mistress Eva Braun, made a will leaving the leadership of his country to Admiral Doenitz, spoken briefly to every member of his personal staff – and poisoned his dog. Afterwards, the bodies of all three were burned.

A man of enormous but demonic gifts, he had lifted his country from a position of weakness and chaos to unparalleled power, and then dropped her back into chaos again – all in the space of 12 years.

On 23 April, Koniev attacked from the south with 650 guns per kilometre of front blasting the German defences. Giant self-propelled guns and even 203 mm howitzers fired over open sights at surviving strongpoints. Resistance began to crumble.

3rd Shock Army had issued nine victory banners before the battle intending to plant them on the Reichstag. The first went up at 1425 hours on 30 April although die-hard Germans were still fighting in the cellars.

Just as resistance ceased in the Reichstag, Hitler committed suicide and his successors tried to open negotiations. Organised German units tried to fight their way out until 5 May but their war was over. The Red Army was victorious.

THE ROAD TO MANDALAY: Triumph in Burma

Chasing the Japanese through the Burmese Monsoon is a nightmare, but 14th Army is determined to finish the job.

By the end of August 1944 the exhausted and near-starving remnants of the Japanese 15th Army were making their painful way back from Imphal and Kohima to the relative safety of the land east of the Chindwin. They were followed, not particularly closely, by the men of Lieutenant General Sir William Slim's 14th Army, the pace dictated largely by the appalling conditions now reigning after three months of monsoon. Long stretches of every road or track had been washed away by weeks of continuous and torrential rain; only four-wheel drive jeeps were able to drive through and everything, from guns to food, being carried on mule-back or manhandled through by men who had not worn dry clothing since June.

In September a directive was issued to Admiral Lord Louis Mountbatten, Supreme Allied Commander, South East Asia: the opening sentence read 'Your object is the recapture of all Burma at the earliest date', and when these orders were transmitted to Slim the latter decided that he could best aid this purpose by one simple achievement. He must destroy the Japanese Burma Area Army, now commanded by Lieutenant General Hoyotaro Kimura, reputedly one of Japan's most outstanding military leaders.

The area in which the Japanese could best be brought to battle would be, in Slim's opinion, between the Chindwin and the Irrawaddy rivers, probably in the huge Irrawaddy loop at Myinmu – Sagaing – Mandalay. In pursuit of this plan he sent the 19th Indian Division across the Chindwin at Sittaung to drive through Pinlebu to Indaw, then to turn south along the west bank of the Irrawaddy for Shwebo. To its south the British 2nd and 20th Indian Divisions would cross the Chindwin at Kalewa, then drive south east towards Monywa and then Myinmu beyond. The Japanese would be caught, after a long and difficult retreat, with their backs to the Irrawaddy, here over 1.6 km (1 mile) wide and across which all their supplies and reinforcements must come.

By 4 December the northern prong was moving, and by 15 December the 19th Indian Division's forward units were at Indaw, ready to turn south. At about this time Slim realized that he must change his plans. Kimura would not fight him in the Mandalay bend, after all, and was already pulling his forces back, presumably to make his stand protecting the Yenangyaung oilfields and the vital rice-fields of the Irrawaddy delta.

Japanese troops cross the Chindwin
The Japanese knew a British offensive was coming but were faced with the familiar problem of defending a river line. Although the Irrawaddy is over a mile across, they could not defend every crossing point.

Japanese army signaller
The Japanese forces had to identify the main British thrust if they were to block 14th Army. Unfortunately for them, they were fooled by a series of feint attacks which seized several bridgeheads. The Japanese reserves were flung into premature battle and expended.

Gurkhas and Grants
Gurkhas advance ahead of M3 Grant tanks, probing for the Japanese rearguard. Some Japanese troops lay in wait by the roadside equipped with a percussion-fused aircraft bomb and a brick. Others would leap from trees on to the tanks which fired machine-guns at each other to sweep them off.

Slim's new plan has been claimed as one of the most daring and momentous of the war; it certainly proved spectacularly effective. Reassembling all of IV Corps except for the 19th Indian Division already poised to drive down the west bank of the Irrawaddy from Indaw, Slim transferred it to Kalemyo and directed the leading brigade (the 28th East African) down through Gangaw, Tilin and Pauk towards the Irrawaddy near Pakokku. Behind it was to come the 7th Indian Division, but some idea of the complexities involved can be gained from the fact that between the head and tail of the division as it moved lay 240 km (150 miles) of quite execrable track, upon which had to travel not only the men and transport of the three brigades, but transporters carrying tanks and huge elements of bridging equipment: wherever the final chosen crossing-point, the river would be at least 800 m (880 yards) wide.

Across the Irrawaddy

It was a magnificent feat of engineering, made the more remarkable by the fact that it was done on time, and moreover remained concealed from the Japanese until the last moment.

Slim's main objective was the Japanese centre of communication and supply between Meiktila and Thazi, without which Kimura's army group could not exist; so during January and the first half of February 1945 every effort was made to give the impression that Mandalay was the prime target. Despite the almost incredible difficulties, by 1 February the 14th Army was closed up along 320 km (200 miles) of the river bank and the Japanese had no idea where the main blow would fall.

Small bridgeheads had already been formed across the Irrawaddy in the north at Thabeikkyin and Singu by the 19th Indian and British 2nd Divisions, apparently to threaten Mandalay; the 7th Indian Division arrived at Pauk on 26 January to threaten both Pakokku and Seikpyu, while at the same time the 20th Indian Division drove through Monywa and on to Myinmu. And on 13 and 14 February, after massive artillery and air strikes which took the Japanese completely by surprise, assault brigades were flung across the river at Ngazun just west of Mandalay, and at Nyaungu south west of Pakkoku. As the first seemed larger than the second, Japanese belief that Mandalay was the main target was confirmed – and all reserves were hurried there.

A Tale of two rivers

To defeat the Japanese Burma Area Army, Slim planned to fight between the River Chindwin and the River Irrawaddy but soon realised that the Japanese had withdrawn their main forces behind the Irrawaddy.

Slim's new plan was to cross the Irrawaddy and advance south of Mandalay. 19th Indian Division crossed at Thabeikkyin. Believing this to be the main attack, Japanese troops hurried to the bridgehead and launched fierce counter-attacks.

On 12 February 20th Indian Division crossed at Myinmu, west of Mandalay, triggering a desperate series of Japanese attacks. But it was really another feint; in the meantime, IV Corps advanced quietly down the west bank of the Chindwin.

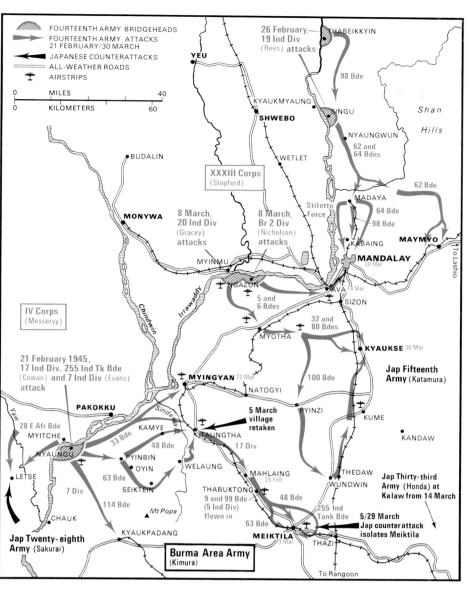

FOURTEENTH ARMY BRIDGEHEADS
FOURTEENTH ARMY ATTACKS
21 FEBRUARY/30 MARCH
JAPANESE COUNTERATTACKS
ALL-WEATHER ROADS
AIRSTRIPS

MILES 40
KILOMETERS 60

Burma liberated
Using his initiative, Maj-General Rees got 19th Indian Division across the Irrawaddy at Thabeikkyin on 11 January. This diverted Japanese attention to north of Mandalay and the planned feint at Myinmu really convinced the Japanese that the main British attack was aimed straight at Mandalay. They had been completely hoodwinked.

Victory in sight
British and Commonwealth forces in Burma were painfully aware that the war against Germany commanded most of British resources and that the decision against Japan would be won in the Pacific by the Americans. But under the exceptional leadership of Lt-Gen. Slim, 14th Army inflicted the greatest defeat the Japanese army ever suffered in a land campaign.

By 18 February a whole new division (the 17th Indian) and a tank brigade had swept through from the borders with India into the Nyaungu bridgehead and three days later it burst out on the road to Meiktila. They were followed by the 7th Indian Division, while the 20th Indian Division to the north gradually built up the battle against the encircling Japanese at Ngazun, who were forced to bring up more strength – thus weakening the defences at Meiktila. At the same time the 19th Indian Division was moving south towards Mandalay from its bridgeheads.

On 4 March, after some of the fiercest fighting of the campaign, the 17th Indian Division took Meiktila, by the following day the whole of the east bank of the Irrawaddy was held by the 14th Army, and Mandalay itself fell on 20 March. Central Burma was now free of Japanese control – though the very many thousands of bodies of dead Japanese soldiers gave evidence not only of their own dedication, but of the ferocity of the battles.

11th Sikhs in pursuit
The Indian army had been reorganised in 1922, famous units becoming battalions within large regiments. The 11th included the old 15th (Ludhiana Sikhs) as its 2nd battalion and the 45th (Rattray's) as its 3rd. By 1945, the Indian army had expanded to 2.5 million men.

Hawker Hurricane Mk IIC

Armed with four 20-mm cannon and fitted with long-range fuel tanks, the Hurricane served very effectively in Burma. The Mandalay campaign depended on air superiority which hampered Japanese strategic movement and allowed British spearheads to press on without worrying about their flanks. Although the forces which captured Meiktila were soon surrounded, aerial re-supply enabled them to fight on until the road was re-opened.

On St Valentine's Day 1945, IV Corps crossed the Irrawaddy at Nyaungu, catching the Japanese completely by surprise. Two mechanized brigades and a tank brigade headed for Meiktila. Two weeks later, the airfield at Thabutkon was overrun.

With the British between the Irrawaddy and the Karen hills, the Japanese 15th and 33rd Armies were trapped. Helped by Chinese withdrawal, the Japanese were able to mount a desperate counter-attack at Meiktila on 18 March.

The Japanese cut the road behind the British forces in Meiktila and all supply had to be brought in by air. But an aggressive defence won time for the full weight of IV Corps to come to their relief. The Japanese army in Burma had been utterly defeated.

OKINAWA: End of an empire

The island of Okinawa is the Allies' penultimate target before the invasion of Japan itself.

In the early hours of 1 April 1945 the US 10th Army, commanded by Lieutenant General Simon Bolivar Buckner, began landing on the island of Okinawa – the main island of the Ryukyu group, 106 km (66 miles) long and between 4.8 and 16.1 km (3 and 10 miles) across. The operation was the largest amphibious assault yet undertaken in the Pacific and involved nearly 550,000 personnel, including 180,000 combat troops. Carrier air strikes in mid-March against the Japanese airfields on Kyushu left the facilities in ruins and destroyed some 500 aircraft, thus ensuring little interference to the landing front from that quarter. Only slight opposition faced the US forces for the first few days, the location of the Japanese garrison remaining a mystery until 5 April when it became clear that the southern half of Okinawa had been painstakingly fortified. Ensconced in a formidable network of bunkers and entrenchments were some 85,000 Japanese troops com-

manded by Lieutenant General Mitsuru Ushijima. Part of the force was made up of fresh conscripts, but the backbone of the defence was the veteran 62nd Division, brought back from China.

Special Sea Attack Force

The infantry battle for Okinawa had barely begun when the Imperial Japanese navy launched its last major operation of the war, a kamikaze mission on the grand scale involving the magnificent battleship *Yamato*. Rejoicing in the title of the 'Special Sea Attack Force', *Yamato* and a destroyer force was dispatched on a one-way voyage to Okinawa where they were to inflict the maximum damage possible before meeting their inevitable destruction. *Yamato* was the largest and mightiest battleship of all time, displacing nearly 70,000 tons at full load; crewed by 2,500 officers and ratings, she was armed with nine 460-mm (18.1-in) guns with a range of 41150 m (45,000 yards) and over 150 anti-aircraft guns. Flying the flag of Vice Admiral Ito, she sailed from the Inland Sea on 6 April accompanied by the light cruiser *Yahagi* and eight destroyers. US submarines spotted the leviathan as she steamed past Kyushu before steering into the East China Sea. Carrier-

borne reconnaissance aircraft located her again on the morning of 7 April and 380 aircraft were launched from Task Force 58. Low clouds and rain squalls proved a slight inconvenience to the aircraft but *Yamato* had no fighter cover and the bombers were able to make their attacks uninterrupted. The giant battleship greeted its deceptively puny attackers with a hail of anti-aircraft fire and manoeuvred to the best of its ability as it began to fight for its life. The US aircraft swarmed around the monstrous bulk, scoring hit after hit, but *Yamato* absorbed them without any apparent effect. But gradually she began to slow and the volume of fire coming up at the bombers noticeably diminished; meanwhile her diminutive consorts had lost all trace of formation, four of the destroyers had been sunk, and *Yahagi* went down at 1400. Half-an-hour later the desperate attempts at counter-flooding could postpone the end no longer and *Yamato* rolled over and sank. Her magazines exploded and a tall column of smoke some 320 km (200 miles) short of Okinawa marked the grave of a proud warship and almost all of her crew.

The heroic failure of this last attempt at surface intervention was followed by a savage series of kami-

Map legend:
- OCCUPIED BY US TENTH ARMY 19 APRIL
- MAIN JAPANESE DEFENSE LINE ('SHURI LINE')
- JAPANESE COUNTERATTACKS 4/5 MAY
- ✈ AIRFIELDS

'ICEBERG' 1 April 1945 US Tenth Army (Buckner)

III Amph Corps (Geiger): 6 Marine Div, 1 Marine Div
XXIV Corps (Hodge): 7 Inf Div, 96 Inf Div

27 Inf Div (Griner) as floating reserve
10/11 April Bn of 27 Div

Jap Thirty-second Army (Ushijima)

21 May Japanese withdraw from 'Shuri Line'
1/2 April Demonstrations by 2 Marine Div

21 June End of Japanese resistance

The last island
With Okinawa as an airbase, the US bombing raids on Japan would be even more effective. Acutely aware of the island's potential as an 'aircraft carrier', the Japanese stationed the veteran 62nd Division on Okinawa and the commander was left in no doubt as to his task.

Coral Ridge
US troops employed every weapon in the American arsenal to assist their assault on Okinawa but whatever the support, the only way to clear a position was for a GI to get in there, rifle in hand. Here a flamethrowing M4 Sherman burns its way forward.

Code of the Warrior

The landings began on 1 April 1945 and the vital airfields all fell on the first day. This is the scene on D-day+2: Yontan airfield on the left is under US control while the amphibious armada delivers more men and supplies to the beaches.

Wary of the awesome American air and naval firepower, the Japanese garrison made little attempt to defend the shore. It was not until the Marines advanced inland that they encountered the main Japanese defences.

At sea, the invasion fleet was the target of a murderous onslaught by kamikaze pilots. Here, USS Enterprise takes another hit. An attempted intervention by the battleship Yamato met with predictable defeat at the hands of US carrier pilots.

Yamato: the last warrior

Yamato was the ultimate battleship in every sense: 70,000 tons of armoured elegance with the heaviest punch afloat. But she belonged to a dying race – as the Japanese navy had demonstrated at Pearl Harbor and to HMS *Prince of Wales* and *Repulse*. Her one-way voyage to Okinawa was a futile and fatalistic gesture.

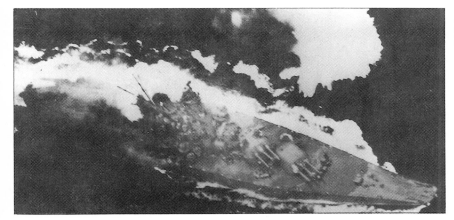

Left: Rocket armed landing craft
Massed rocket barrages delivered incredible quantities of explosive on to a target in the shortest possible time. Mounted in a variety of landing craft they were widely used on Okinawa, blanketing enemy positions with high explosive and preventing any movement by the Japanese.

Above: The last battleship dying
Helm hard over in a vain bid to avoid American torpedoes, the magnificent battleship *Yamato* continues her death ride to Okinawa. Her destruction and the deaths of her 2,700 men availed nothing to the defenders. The greatest *kamikaze* of them all had perished in a futile holocaust.

Right: USS *Bunker Hill*
Although a pitiful gesture of despair, the *kamikazes* posed a major threat to the US Navy which suffered a steady stream of casualties to them. The Japanese even employed purpose-built suicide jet bombers in the futile defence of Okinawa.

kaze air attacks on the US warships off shore, while Ushijima's troops stubbornly contested every yard of their island. On 19 April Buckner essayed a concentrated attack to punch a hole in the Japanese defences but it failed with nearly 1,000 casualties. For the rest of the month and into May the 10th Army battered against the 'Shuri' line in a remorseless routine of colossal bombardments followed by desperate assaults against blockhouses and bunkers cunningly sited and fanatically defended. Although the Americans knew that the casualty rate was running wildly in their favour as the occupants of each position were killed to a man, US casualties were mounting at an alarming rate. By the end of May it seemed a breakthrough might at last be achieved, but the sudden onset of torrential rains bogged down operations for over a week. Taking full advantage of the weather, Ushijima extracted his surviving units from the battle and began to withdraw to the south. An American attempt to break through the Japanese rearguard was repulsed and the

Japanese occupied new positions on the southern tip of Okinawa and prepared to make their last stand.

The 10th Army pushed forward for the last stage of the battle and set about the grisly task of breaking into the Japanese positions. Finally on 17 June the Japanese garrison was divided into three encircled pockets, no longer capable of a coherent defence, and some of the more recent conscripts began to surrender. Buckner broadcast a message to Ushijima urging him to stop the fighting and save the lives of his surviving soldiers, since the end was inevitable. Ironically, Buckner himself was killed on the next day when a Japanese shell blew lethal slivers of coral into him while he inspected the 8th Marines. Ushijima survived him by a week, committing ritual suicide with his chief of staff after sending a last report to Tokyo. 'Our strategy, tactics and equipment were used to the utmost and we fought valiantly . . . but it was nothing before the material might of the enemy.' He was perfectly correct: Japan was doomed.

Japanese prisoners on Okinawa
The draconian warrior code which bound the Japanese soldier to his Emperor led most of the defenders to prefer death to the humiliation of surrender. However, unlike most of the island battles, there were some on Okinawa, mostly the younger conscripts, who surrendered unwounded.

The fighting on Okinawa was a savage, close-quarter affair. The Japanese positions were cunningly sited, well camouflaged and mutually supporting. No major counter-attacks were made but the Japanese often infiltrated between US positions.

By 17 June the Japanese defence was broken and their surviving troops isolated in several small pockets. They refused a summons to surrender. Here, US engineers prepare demolition charges to seal a cave full of enemy troops.

US Marines patrol past some of the Japanese dead. Calculations based on the Okinawa fighting showed the Allies could expect to sustain over a million casualties if they had to invade Japan. Fortunately, they would not have to.

BATTLE FOR THE HOLY CITY: Jerusalem 1948

As British troops completed their thankless task of keeping order in Palestine, the Jewish community declared itself a nation state.

In the spring of 1948 the UK was making ready to withdraw its troops from Palestine, and the rival Arab and Jewish populations prepared for war. The Arabs endeavoured to cut communications between the different Jewish settlements and made a concerted effort to sever the link between Jerusalem and the coast.

The Jewish population of the Holy City was supplied by convoys which had to fight along the Jerusalem road as they wound their tortuous way up into the Judaean hills. By welding steel plates to buses and tractors the Jews manufactured improvised armoured vehicles, but casualties mounted steadily. Knocked-out vehicles were pushed into the roadside to keep the carriageway clear and their rusted hulks remain there to this day, a silent memorial to the sacrifices made to keep the lifeline open.

As the conflict escalated the Haganah launched its first major operation: a brigade-scale attack to clear a corridor to Jerusalem along which the convoys could safely move. At midnight on 5 April 60 trucks loaded with supplies raced up the Jerusalem road while 1,500 Haganah personnel in three battalions battled for control of the surrounding hills. A series of further convoys entered the city in the next two weeks, but by the end of April the Arabs had managed to re-impose the siege.

Arab invasion

The British finally left Palestine on 14 May. In Tel Aviv David Ben-Gurion proclaimed the establishment of the independent Jewish state to be known as Israel. Egypt responded with an air raid on the next day, and Syria, Jordan, Lebanon, Iraq and Egypt all invaded Israel in support of the Palestinian Arabs.

The high ground at Latrun where the ruins of a Crusader castle look down on the coastal plain was captured by the Jews in Operation 'Maccabee' on 16 May, but two days earlier the Egyptian army had crossed the southern frontier and reserves were rushed away from the Jerusalem front to meet the new danger. This enabled the 4th Battalion of the Arab Legion to occupy the Latrun area without opposition, while the main body advanced on Jerusalem, occupying the Mount of Olives on 17 May.

Jewish forces had taken control of most of Jerusalem outside the old city walls except for the easternmost areas. On 18 May the Arab Legion passed through Gethsemane and attacked the Old City, simultaneously mounting an assault into Sheikh Jarrach. Supported by armoured cars, the Legion made a dashing assault on the Damascus Gate before subjecting the Jewish quarter to a concentrated artillery barrage.

The Legion's continued advance into the maze of narrow streets that constituted the Old City was bitterly contested. Molotov cocktails and PIAT guns accounted for several armoured cars, while others were destroyed when the wall of the Notre Dame Monastery was blown up and collapsed on them. The Legion pressed home its attack fearlessly, the units assaulting the monastery on 23 May suffering nearly 50 per cent casualties before they would admit defeat. Their commander, General Sir John Glubb, abandoned the attack on the next day: he had no reserve left and could not afford the Legion's entire strength to be sucked into street fighting.

Meanwhile to the south Arab Legion units supported by Moslem Brotherhood forces advanced from Bethlehem. The Jewish Quarter of the Old City was cut off and the handful of defenders were squeezed into an ever smaller perimeter in desperate house-to-house fighting. With the cellars overflowing with wounded and the ammunition running out, the garrison of the Jewish Quarter could sustain its epic resistance no longer and surrendered to the Arab Legion on 28 May.

The capture of the Jewish Quarter of the Old City was to be the last victory of the Arab Legion. Glubb could not afford to resume the assault on the rest of the Old City. Instead he concentrated on maintaining the blockade and a regular artillery bombardment, hoping to starve the defenders into submission.

Israeli attempts to capture Latrun failed with heavy losses, and the Jerusalem road remained firmly blocked as the deadline to the first United

Surrender in the Old City
Soldiers of the Transjordan Arab Legion take the surrender of Haganah troops cut-off in the Jewish quarter on 28 May. Led by Sir John Glubb, the Arab Legion's gallant assault was in sharp contrast to the half-hearted efforts of some other Arab contingents. But after bitter house-to-house fighting the Haganah perimeter was still holding when the ceasefire came into operation.

Beginning of the battle
A wounded Haganah soldier and his brother shelter in the lee of a British armoured car on 10 February when the Highland Light Infantry intervened to stop a gun battle in Jerusalem: the HLI suffered one dead and one wounded in the action. British attempts to stop the fighting between the rival communities were as unwelcome as they were unsuccessful. Full-scale battles were under way before the last British troops had left.

A State is born

Two RAF men lie dead after attacks by Jewish terrorists in response to an Arab bomb outrage. Caught between two implacable opponents, the British withdrew from Palestine in May 1948.

Riflemen of the Jordanian Arab Legion occupy the historic walls of Jerusalem during their assault which followed the British withdrawal. Jewish troops held most of the city but were cut off from the main Jewish forces.

An Iraqi armoured brigade equipped with British armoured cars heads for Jerusalem. The Arab armies enjoyed numerical superiority but often failed to co-operate with each other. By contrast, the Jews knew that they must stand together or die.

Nations truce approached. Ben-Gurion's solution was an improvised 'Burma road' over rough hillside which successfully linked Israeli-held Beit Susin with the western edge of the Jerusalem defences. The Arab blockade was circumvented and a lifeline to the Holy City finally opened just days before the 28-day truce began on 1 June.

The truce was welcome for all Jewish forces, but none were more grateful than the embattled defenders of Jerusalem. Only a few days' food was left when the ceasefire began and now supply convoys could move into the city without interruption. Despite the best efforts of the UN mediator, Count Bernadotte, the truce was a mere breathing space for both sides and the war resumed in earnest on 9 July. The Israelis made a renewed effort to take Latrun, and on the night of 16/17 July broke through to the north, although further frontal attacks on Latrun were repulsed.

A second UN-sponsored truce came into operation on 18 July and lasted until 15 October. With Latrun effectively bypassed Jerusalem's immediate future was secure: at the end of October Israel won a decisive victory in Galilee, and during the remainder of the year inflicted a series of defeats on Egypt which ended the war.

Sten gun Mk II

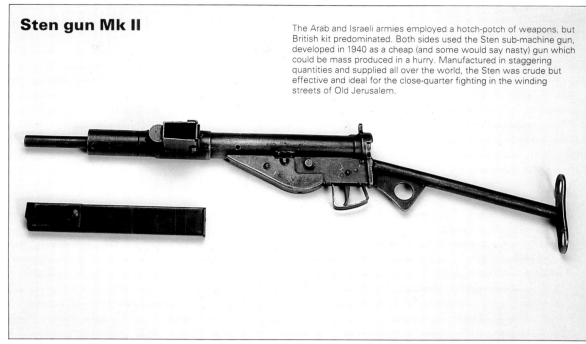

The Arab and Israeli armies employed a hotch-potch of weapons, but British kit predominated. Both sides used the Sten sub-machine gun, developed in 1940 as a cheap (and some would say nasty) gun which could be mass produced in a hurry. Manufactured in staggering quantities and supplied all over the world, the Sten was crude but effective and ideal for the close-quarter fighting in the winding streets of Old Jerusalem.

Left: In the steps of Christ
An Arab armoured car rumbles up the Via Dolorosa, crewmen perched on top clutching Sten guns. In the labyrinth of narrow streets, armoured vehicles proved hopelessly vulnerable to PIAT anti-tank projectiles and 'Molotov' cocktails.

Right: Building the Jewish state
The Arab leaders were determined to extinguish the newly proclaimed state of Israel and massacre its would-be citizens. The local Palestinian population was advised to leave the area to avoid Jewish attacks and leave the job to the Arab regular armies. Cities like Haifa emptied overnight, their inhabitants expecting to return in a matter of weeks in the wake of conquering Arab armies. But the anticipated triumph failed to materialise and, 40 years later, the Palestinians are still waiting.

PLANNED ARAB ATTACK ON ISRAEL
JEWISH TERRITORY, 15 MAY 1948

ISRAELI TERRITORY, 1 JUNE 1948
GAINS TO NOV 1948
" 1 JAN 1949
BOUNDARY OF ISRAEL AT ARMISTICE, JUNE 1949

Lorries with improvised armour ran a gauntlet of Arab attacks to resupply the garrison of Jerusalem. The Arabs drove this truck off the road, poked rifles through the vision slits and shot the driver. His body lies by the burning vehicle.

Jewish forces in the Jewish quarter of the Old City were compelled to surrender on 28 May. However, the Arab Legion had suffered such heavy losses that it could no longer hope to overrun the rest of the Jewish positions.

Arab artillery hammers at Jewish Jerusalem, which came perilously close to being starved out before a new road was improvised over the hills to link the city with the new state of Israel before the UN-sponsored ceasefire came into effect.

SAVING SEOUL: The Inchon landings

September 1950: North Korean forces have overrun all South Korea except a small perimeter at Pusan. Decisive action is needed.

Japan's domination of Korea was brought to an end in 1945. An Allied agreement established the 38th parallel as the dividing line between the northern zone, beyond which Japanese troops would surrender to the Soviets, and the southern zone, which would become an American responsibility. As happened in Europe, the dividing line quickly became a political boundary and North and South Korea found themselves pawns in the Cold War.

By 1947 the problem of the re-unification of Korea had been passed to the United Nations. The establishment of the Republic of Korea was matched by the Soviet creation of the Democratic People's Republic of Korea. The withdrawal of American occupying troops was completed in July 1949, leaving the fledgeling Republic of Korea (ROK) Army to face the North with the help of US advisers.

that arrived could do little to stem the communist tide, and by August the US 8th Army under Major General Walton Walker were defending a perimeter around the port of Pusan, at the extreme south east of the Korean peninsula.

Amphibious Assault

Back in Japan, MacArthur had a plan. The Korean winters are hard, and victory would have to come before November. To that end he proposed to outflank the enemy in an amphibious assault on Inchon, near Seoul. If the 8th Army were to drive up from Pusan, the North Korean armies would be trapped and forced to surrender.

The Joint Chiefs of staff rejected the plan twice. MacArthur needed a Marine Division for the land-

third attempt he persuaded the Joint Chiefs of Staff to back his plan, and Operation Chromite was approved. Admiral Forrest P. Sherman, the Chief of Naval Operations, was the most sceptical. "I wish I had that man's confidence" he said after a long session with MacArthur.

Two weeks before the landing Navy Lieutenant Eugene Clark was secretly put ashore. Working by night and hiding by day, he scouted the approaches and checked enemy defences. Indeed, on the day of the landing he managed to get into a lighthouse and switched on the light, to provide guidance to the first assault ships as they approached the harbour.

A two-day naval bombardment was followed on September 15 by the landings. At 06.30 the 1st Marine Division stormed ashore. The Third Batta-

Heading for 'Blue Beach'
3/5th Marines go ashore at Wolmi Do island, the heavily fortified position which dominated the approaches to the port of Inchon. The Marines landed at 0633 and secured the island by 0800. They could not be reinforced until the next high tide that evening but fortunately the enemy failed to counter-attack.

The Road to Seoul
Soviet supplied T-34 tanks and SU-76 tank destroyers knocked out possibly by air attack. The unsealed vehicles proved horribly vulnerable to the napalm bombs widely used by US fighter-bombers. A bomb landing within 30 yards could douse a tank with enough blazing fuel to incinerate vehicle and crew alike.

A year of northern inspired propaganda, terrorism, and cross-border raids was concluded by a full-scale invasion of the South. The Soviet-trained and equipped communists crossed the border on 25 June 1950. The powerful offensive caught the South by surprise, and in an emergency session the United Nations resolved to help. The Soviet delegation could not veto the measure, because they were boycotting the proceedings.

General Douglas MacArthur, commanding US forces in the Pacific, soon realized that air and naval support would not be enough, and the first American troops were on their way from Japan by June 30. Even so, the three understrength divisions

ing, and almost all of the US Army's general reserve. This was at a time when many in authority thought the slightest sign of weakness would see a Soviet invasion of Europe. Moreover, Inchon itself presented almost insurmountable difficulties. At low tide the approach to the port was a narrow, twisting channel flanked by mile wide mud flats and the landing force would be under the enemy's guns. General Matthew Ridgway considered that it would require perfect timing and a great deal of luck before the "5,000 to 1 gamble" could pay off.

MacArthur persisted. He considered that the very impossibility of the landing would put the enemy off guard, and allow the operation to succeed. At the

MacArthur's last triumph

North Korea invaded the South on 25 June 1950. Hastily deployed US forces were driven back along with the South Korean army until only the extreme south east of the Korean peninsula remained in non-communist hands.

The landings at Inchon on 15 September achieved complete surprise and succeeded despite daunting problems which included lack of maps, one of the largest tidal ranges in the world and the absence of a proper beach.

A minesweeper strikes one of the few mines laid off Inchon: huge stockpiles of Soviet mines were ready on the quay when the Marines landed but fortunately they lacked the proper arming devices.

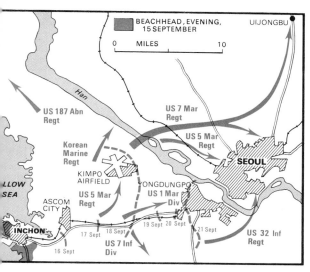

Going for the capital
Against terrific odds the landings at Inchon succeeded at a cost of just 21 dead, 174 wounded and 1 missing. However, whittling out the 20,000 North Korean troops holding Seoul was to be another matter altogether and it took a week of bitter fighting and the destruction of large sectors of the city before the North Koreans retreated.

lion 5th Marines landed on Green Beach, on the island of Wolmi Do. The island, which dominated the port, was secured in 45 minutes. Its artillery emplacements had largely been destroyed by the naval bombardment. The 7th Marine Regiment took advantage of the two hours of high tide to strike across the mudflats at Blue beach. Strategic surprise was complete, and the rest of X Corps, including the 7th Infantry Division together with armour and artillery, landed with little or no opposition.

Tank battle

The next day, 5th Marines took Kimpo Airfield after a short but sharp tank battle. 7th Infantry Division was to head south, to link up with 8th Army forces breaking out of the Pusan perimeter. Unfortunately General Walker's troops were having difficulty, as they had been weakened by the withdrawal of the Marines for the Inchon landings. Not until September 23 did the North Koreans around Pusan begin to withdraw, as a result of the pressure further north.

It was only eight miles from Kimpo to Seoul, but it was very hard going. The North Koreans defended the city tenaciously, and it took more than ten days of fierce house-to-house fighting before the last of the enemy snipers and machine-gunners were flushed from hiding.

Inchon was a bold concept, which had succeeded brilliantly. At the beginning of September the UN forces were fighting to retain a toehold in Korea. By the end of the month they were back at the 38th parallel; vast quantities of materiel had been captured or destroyed, and more than 125,000 Koreans had been captured. Further reverses were to come, especially when MacArthur's headlong pursuit of the North Koreans brought the UN forces into conflict with the Chinese, but for the moment South Korea was safe.

8-inch howitzer in action
MacArthur's first two attempts to engineer an amphibious assault at Inchon were frustrated by the only available forces being diverted to the US forces clinging to the Pusan perimeter. The successful landings coincided with the arrival of fresh troops and the strength of the Pusan garrison increased sharply while their enemies ran out of food and ammunition.

The landings were stunningly successful, and by dawn on 16 September the Marines were pressing on to Kimpo airfield. However, the subsequent battle for Seoul was to be a dour struggle indeed.

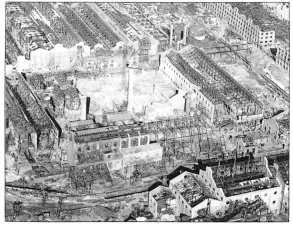

The landings at Inchon were designed to sever the supply line between North Korea and its army in the south. Meanwhile B-29 Superfortresses pounded Northern industrial centres: this is Hungnam after a series of attacks in November.

The Inchon landings were a bold stroke which defeated the North Koreans. Unfortunately, China soon threw off the cloak of neutrality and invaded. Here, US equipment is evacuated in the face of the remorseless Communist advance in December 1950.

OVER THE YALU: The Korean air battles

November 1950: As Chinese troops overrun the US 8th Army in Korea, the first jet air war begins.

Following some months of intermittent border 'incidents' along the 38th Parallel, the artificial boundary separating North and South Korea that had been established by the United Nations, all-out hostilities began on 25 June 1950 when eight North Korean (communist) divisions crossed the border in an attempt to achieve a swift conquest of the Republic of Korea (ROK) and impose reunification of the whole country under a single communist government. The North Koreans had not counted, however, on an immediate decision by the UN to resist their aggression by employing all available Western forces under the command of General Douglas MacArthur.

Few modern American combat aircraft had reached the Far East by mid-1950 and, as USAF Douglas C-54s hurriedly evacuated American citizens from Seoul, the South Korean capital, the only combat aircraft immediately available in the theatre were a small number of obsolescent Lockheed F-80C Shooting Star jet fighters and some North American F-82 Twin Mustang piston-engine fighters. On 27 June, however, occurred the first jet fighter combat by American fighters when four F-80Cs shot down four NKAF Ilyushin II-10s, while elsewhere F-82Gs destroyed three Yakovlev Yak-9s. The inability of the ROK ground forces to defend their own territory was such that the communists made swift progress southwards, Seoul and its airfield at Kimpo falling on 28 June as the South Korean army retreated in disarray.

Heading for the North
Having reached the border between North Korea and China, the F-86 Sabres would fly at 27-33,000ft, just below the usual contrail height where they could see those left by the higher MiGs. When action was joined, the Sabres jettisoned their drop tanks and accelerated to just below the speed of sound. The resulting high stick forces and wide turning circles gave only fleeting opportunities for a quick burst of gun-fire.

On 15 September MacArthur launched a powerful amphibious assault at Inchon, 160 km (100 miles) up the west coast of Korea, gaining (on account of poor communist intelligence) total surprise.

By the end of September scarcely any organized communist forces remained at large south of the 38th Parallel. It was at this moment that General MacArthur made clear his intention to occupy the whole of North Korea, in contrast to the UN's stated objective of simply restoring partition of the two states on the 38th Parallel.

Whatever efforts might have been made by the UN to gainsay MacArthur's hawkish ambitions, the matter was rendered academic when on 1 November 1950 an American F-80C was shot down by Chinese AA guns firing into Korean airspace from across the Yalu river. In another incident the pilots of some UN North American F-51s reported being fired on by Mikoyan-Gurevich MiG-15s which then made off towards Chinese territory.

Chinese intervention

No further pretence at non-intervention was made by the Chinese as, on 3 November, their forces swarmed across the Yalu. An American division was forced hurriedly to retreat to protect its supply lines as the powerful US Navy Carrier Task Force 77 sailed north to launch heavy strikes against the Chinese crossing the Yalu. At first the MiG-15 pilots simply 'trailed their coat' over Korea in efforts to tempt American aircraft into Chinese airspace, but on 8 November a section of four of the communist jets ventured too far and were boxed in by four F-80s; in the first all-jet air combat in history Lieutenant Russell J. Brown, USAF, shot down a MiG-15 which crashed just 185 m (200 yards) inside Korean

The USAF's secret weapon
This unusual view of the Lockheed F-94 Starfire fighter shows the bulbous nose housing the aircraft's radar. This made the F-94 an all-weather interceptor, but the USAF was cautious about exploiting its potential in case its radar fell into enemy hands. This F-94 flew with the night-flying 319th Fighter Interception Squadron.

territory. On the following day a US Navy Grumman F9F Panther pilot from USS *Philippine Sea* also downed a Chinese MiG. On 10 November the Chinese jets shot down a Boeing B-29 heavy bomber. By the end of the month a quarter of a million Chinese troops were in the field in Korea. The war had certainly entered a new phase.

It was realised that with the appearance of the modern Soviet-designed MiG-15, which with transonic performance was far superior to the great majority of aircraft with the UN forces, that the F-80 pilots could not reasonably be expected to match the new enemy fighters. The decision was quickly taken to send to Korea a wing of North American F-86A Sabres, then the latest fighters in service with the USAF, and early in December the 4th Fighter Interceptor Wing, thus equipped, arrived at Kimpo airfield.

The first brushes with enemy jets were inconclusive, but on 22 December eight F-86s fought 15 MiG-15s and shot down six. Further combats were not immediately possible because of the advance by communist forces threatening Kimpo, whence the Sabres were moved southwards out of danger; now based far from the MiGs' patrol areas they were unable to stay long enough to enjoy long patrol sorties. By the same token, however, the communist advance southwards also moved out of range of the MiGs which remained firmly based around Antung beyond the Yalu.

The communist spring offensive of 1951 failed in its objective to overrun South Korea and had all but petered out by the end of May, but nevertheless the Chinese intervention had forced the UN to abandon its original aim of unification of north and south. As both sides now attempted to wring the last ounce of propanganda from the military situation, peace talks aimed at securing a truce opened at Kaesong on 10 July 1951, and dragged on for two years. The hawkish ·MacArthur was replaced by a slightly more conciliatory General Matthew Ridgway, but one of the last operations planned before the change of

Taking the war to the enemy

North Korea invaded the south in June, and for six months the UN forces enjoyed powerful air support unhindered by hostile action. With superior aircraft and better pilots, the US Air Force and Navy made short work of North Korea's elderly Soviet machines.

F-80 Shooting Stars served as fighter-bombers, but the Chinese intervention in November brought Soviet-built MiG-15s over the battlefield. Their superior performance seriously challenged UN dominance in Korea.

The MiG-15s remained based in China where UN aircraft were forbidden to attack them for fear of escalating the conflict. Fortunately the USAF commander, Maj-General Weyland, refused to be cowed and took the war to the enemy.

Shooting Star attack, June 1951
An F-80 streaks towards the target already blanketed in smoke from a previous run. Despite the introduction of jets, fighter-bombers operated much as they had during World War II. Finger four sections of F-80s or F-84s would arrive over the battlefield under control of the joint operations centre on the ground. Forward air controllers operating in light aircraft would mark tactical targets with smoke rockets and the fighter-bombers would bore in and plaster the area with rockets, bombs and napalm.

command was an all-out air offensive against the communists' supply lines which, owing to the vulnerability of the railways, depended almost exclusively on the road network.

Meanwhile development of an improved version of the Sabre, the F-86E, had gone on apace in the USA, and September brought deliveries of this aircraft to the 4th Wing, by now operating from Kimpo. The communists had also increased their force of MiG-15s by activating a second regiment and this was equipped with improved MiG-15bis. At once the tempo of air combat increased, and formations of 80 enemy jets were frequently sighted. One of the war's biggest single combats was fought on 22 October 1951 as eight B-29s, escorted by 55 F-84s and 34 F-86s, were bombing Namsi; suddenly 100 MiGs appeared and boxed-in the escort as 50 others made for the bombers, shooting down three and severely damaging four others. Six MiGs were shot down for the loss of an F-84.

New aircraft deployed

Concerned at the large number of MiGs available to the communists, the USAF now began to withdraw some of the old F-80Cs, replacing them with F-84Es, and a second wing, the 116th, was sent to Korea with F-84s. The night-fighter F-82s of the 347th All-Weather Group were also showing their age (and were of course no match for the MiG-15), and 15 jet all-weather Lockheed F-94s were despatched to the war; this Starfire proved a disappointment as it lacked an adequate anti-icing system. By the end of 1951 F-86Es were replacing F-80Cs with the 51st Fighter-Interceptor Wing and soon the number of MiGs being destroyed started to rise significantly. At that time the 4th Wing's combat record showed a total of 144 MiG-15s destroyed for the loss in combat of 14 Sabres. The MiG pilots themselves were becoming more aggressive and the improved performance of the opposing fighters resulted in numerous combats taking place above 40,000 ft (12190 m). In March 1952 39 enemy jets were destroyed; the following month the tally rose to 44.

Combat information from Korea had long since filtered through to the Sabre's designers and in June and July 1952 yet further improved F-86F Sabres were joining the 51st Wing. At last the Sabre was superior in all respects to the MiG-15bis. By the spring of 1953 there were four wings of F-86s in Korea, and during the last six months of the war these fighters wholly dominated the skies. In May their pilots destroyed 56 enemy jets, and in June no fewer than 77, losing 11 and 23 respectively of their own number.

From an air combat viewpoint the Korean War was interesting in that it was the first major conflict in which large numbers of opposing jet fighters engaged each other. While it is true that there were a number of high-scoring American Sabre pilots (the 31-year-old Joseph McConnell of the 51st Wing heading the list with 16 MiG-15s to his credit), the fleeting nature of those all-jet combats graphically demonstrated that the age of gun-only armament was over. The era of the air-to-air missile was about to dawn.

From its arrival in December 1950, the F-86 Sabre chalked up an impressive kill ratio against the MiG-15. Communist pilots were lost faster than they could be trained and the USAF began to dominate the air battle right up to the Chinese border.

While the Sabres and MiGs battled for the Korean skies, fighter-bombers like these F-84 Thunderjets were once again free to intervene in the land battle. The pioneering use of forward air controllers closely co-ordinated the aircraft with the ground troops.

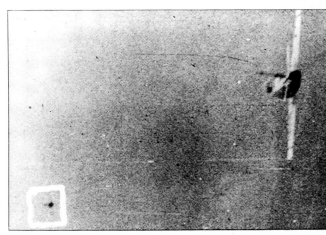

Seen from another Sabre's gun camera, Captain Manuel J. Fernandez shoots down his 13th MiG in May 1953. During that month, 56 MiGs were downed for the loss of 11 Sabres and the Chinese air force had been utterly defeated.

LAST STAND AT DIEN BIEN PHU

March 1954: A French fortress established on the Laotian border is assaulted by 40,000 fanatical Viet Minh.

The decision to take the village of Dien Bien Phu on the Vietnam/Laos border and to occupy it as an 'airhead' was taken by Général Henri Navarre, commander-in-chief of French forces in Indo-China since May 1953, against the strong advice of the man he appointed to control the operation, Général de Division René Cogny.

Two of Cogny's parachute battalions were dropped into the valley from Douglas C-47s on the morning of 20 November 1953, and after a brisk battle there with the surprised Viet Minh troops occupied the village during that afternoon. Three more parachute battalions and a command headquarters were dropped in within four days, and the tasks of lengthening and reinforcing the existing airstrip and digging field defences was going well. In those early days it looked as though Operation 'Castor' could be successful.

But by the beginning of December the basic divergence of view at command level was already indicating problems ahead. A new garrison commander, the elegant cavalry officer Colonel Christian de la Croix de Castries, was dropped in with orders both to turn Dien Bien Phu into a fortress to be held 'without thought of withdrawal', and at the same time to employ at least half his strength in offensive forays. This would not only dominate the valley in which the village lay, but also drive the enemy off at least the lower foothills around and make possible a link up with other French forces across the border in Laos.

There was to be no shortage of men to defend Dien Bien Phu, however flimsy might be their shelters. During the weeks that followed de Castries' strength increased to 10,814 men, the combat battalions consisting of two native T'ai battalions, three of Algerian *tirailleurs* and one of Moroccan, and four Foreign Legion battalions. If the native battalions were not of the highest military competence, the Algerians and Moroccans were to prove themselves of superb quality, while a high percentage of the Foreign Legionnaires had learned their soldiering with the Afrika Korps. The vast majority of the officers were, of course, French.

But already the garrison was suffering casualties. To the astonishment of both Navarre and de Castries, the landing-strip came quickly under fire from Viet Minh 105-mm (4.13-in) guns, and the weight of fire coming into the camp increased ominously as the weeks passed, as did its accuracy. As every tree, shrub or even bush was stripped from the valley floor to provide either fuel or cover for the defence, the entire lay-out of the garrison was revealed to observers on the surrounding hills, and the observers had been there since the first day.

Deploying a recoilless rifle, December 1953
The strategic error in landing a force so deep in hostile territory was compounded by tactical errors at Dien Bien Phu itself. The artillery was concentrated at strongpoint 'Isabelle' where it could not support the vital hilltop posts of 'Gabrielle' and 'Beatrice' 7 km to the north. The trenches seen here are ominously overlooked by high ground within easy artillery range.

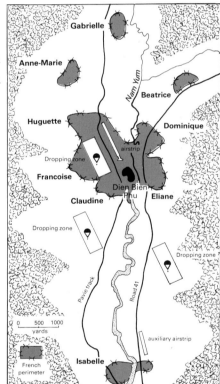

The deathtrap
The French C-in-C occupied Dien Bien Phu to protect northern Laos hoping for (at best) a military stalemate by 1955. But the Viet Minh were far stronger than French headquarters believed and the ensuing debacle sealed the fate of French Indo-China

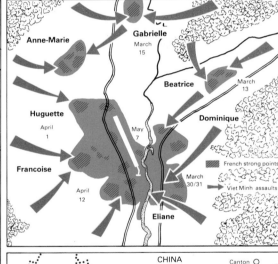

To the last cartridge

December 1953: several weeks after the initial parachute landings, Colonel de Castries (right) assumes command at Dien Bien Phu. The airfield was supposed to be a base for operations in defence of northern Laos.

The position was inspected by most senior officers in Indo-China over the next four months. No-one seems to have worried that the 'fortress' was overlooked by hills or by reports that the Viet Minh had assembled overwhelming numbers of troops.

The battle lasted 57 days but was lost in the first 24 hours when the outposts of 'Gabrielle' and 'Beatrice' were overrun. With these hills in their hands, the Viet Minh overlooked the airstrip. Here, French reinforcements land by parachute on 23 March.

Left: The initial landings
Within a month of the landings, French air force intelligence estimated correctly that over 40,000 Viet Minh troops were assembling around Dien Bien Phu. But the French high command entertained an enormously inflated view of the man-for-man superiority of their men.

Right: The view from a slit trench
Viet Minh artillery pounds the airstrip from its invisible and apparently invulnerable positions in the surrounding hills. As at Verdun, the earth was ground to such a powdery consistency, the troops could no longer dig proper trenches.

Grumman F-8 Bearcat
Although US equipment was widely used by French forces, the USA did not finance the war: American aid amounted to $954,000 while French expenditure topped $11 billion. French air power was defeated at Dien Bien Phu by massed Viet Minh anti-aircraft guns and a mastery of digging and camouflage.

Left: wounded on 23 March
The airstrip was closed five days after this man was hit, so the wounded could not be evacuated. They were crammed into the bunkers where treatment became very difficult as medical supplies ran out.

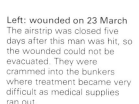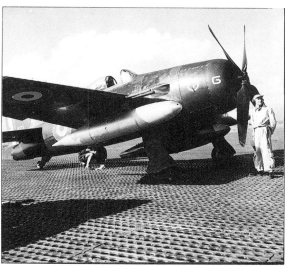

General Vo Nguyen Giap was already assembling a striking force against the French in Dien Bien Phu, far more numerous and far better armed and supplied than the French command had ever dreamed possible. By the beginning of March three Viet Minh infantry divisions comprising 28 battalions were in position with their supporting arms, and also the 351st Heavy Division with 48 105-mm howitzers, 48 75-mm (2.95-in) guns, and the same number of 120-mm (4.72-in) mortars and 75-mm recoilless rifles. Anti-aircraft weapons of every calibre were arriving with each day that passed, and by mid-April the C-119 civilian pilots were refusing to fly over what had become known as 'the chamber-pot'.

The first, stunning blow fell on the French during the evening and night of 13 March 1954. Heavy and accurate fire deluged the entire area, blowing in shelters, smashing trenches and gun positions, setting alight every aircraft except three fortunate Bearcats which scrambled during the first minute of the attack and were then forced by the almost total destruction of the airstrip to fly back to Hanoi. And on the heels of the bombardment came a 'human wave' infantry assault delivered with supreme disregard for casualties, in which the barbed wire defences were blown apart by explosive charges attached to the bodies of the soldiers who flung themselves into them.

By the morning the entire garrison had gained a firm indication of the type of battle which faced

them, and one of their outposts (Beatrice) had fallen irrevocably. There were seven more of these outposts (Dominique, Eliane, Claudine, Françoise, Huguette, Anne-Marie and Gabrielle, all it was said named after de Castries' mistresses), and it soon became obvious that the separate and individual reduction of each outpost was Giap's first objective. As they were located beyond the range of any support except from the central position, and as the heavy artillery there had already been pounded almost into annihilation, this threw their defence entirely upon the individual outpost garrisons, varying between 500 and 2,000 men, each of which would face attacks by whole brigades.

During the next weeks the Viet Minh grip on Dien Bien Phu tightened implacably. Classic siege tactics were followed by Giap's men; trench lines were dug, forward saps run out ever closer to the next objective (on occasion underground to take mines), then one late evening a shattering bombardment would be followed by overwhelming infantry attack by waves of screaming and cheering riflemen.

The garrison was also under new command as the 'parachute Mafia' of battalion commanders had decided between them that de Castries was not the man for the job, and had themselves taken over in a polite, bloodless but uncompromising coup.

The end came on 7 May. Giap had brought up some Soviet-made Katyusha rocket-launchers and these added devastating weight to the bombardment

which crashed down on the evening of 6 May, continued through the night and by morning had reduced the French position to a few hundred square metres around the southern end of the airstrip. At noon, de Castries (still nominal commander) spoke to Cogny by radio and informed him that there were now barely 1,000 men still on their feet; and that afternoon Giap was informed that French firing would cease at 1730.

So ended the battle of Dien Bien Phu. Giap allowed 900 of the worst wounded to be flown out, but the rest made up part of the 9,000 men who started out on what became known as the 'Death March'. None of the wounded who had suffered head, chest or stomach wounds ever came back, and not a very high proportion of even the unwounded. But most of the casualties of the battle lie still where they fell. As Bernard Fall, one of the best historians of the episode has written:

'Most of the French dead are, like royalty, swathed in silk shrouds. Parachute nylon, like courage, was one of the commonest items at Dien Bien Phu, and on both sides.'

A C-47 based at Tan Son Nhut prepares to drop supplies to the beleaguered garrison. Deployed so far from French centres of strength, the men at Dien Bien Phu could not be relieved by ground forces.

Viet Minh artillery pounded the French positions to pieces and proved impervious to French airstrikes. Anti-aircraft guns shot down the supply aircraft and the garrison's ammunition supply dwindled. The survivors surrendered on 7 May.

The Viet Minh treatment of the prisoners was abominable: a 500-mile death march killed more men than any battle of the Indo-China war. Denied any medical treatment, no-one with abdominal, chest or head injuries survived.

185

BATTLE FOR SINAI: Israeli blitzkrieg

29 October 1956: After diverting attention to its border with Jordan, Israel launches a surprise attack on Egyptian forces in Sinai.

After Colonel Gamel Abdel Nasser seized power, Egypt received substantial military aid from the USSR and began to concentrate troops in the Sinai peninsula. Fortifications were constructed and new military roads laid down, pointing like a dagger at the heart of Israel. A joint Egyptian/Syrian military command was created, expanded to include Jordan in 1956. Meanwhile, *fedayeen* terrorists mounted increasingly vicious raids on civilian targets within Israel, many from the Gaza strip where over 200,000 Palestinian refugees were encamped.

The Arab powers were obviously preparing to refight the 1948 war of independence. Israel's solution was a pre-emptive strike on the leading Arab power, Egypt. By destroying Nasser's forces in Sinai, Israel would remove the strongest Arab army from the strategic equation and eliminate the terrorist nest at Gaza. Equally importantly, it would stop the Egyptian naval blockade which prevented Israeli shipping passing through the Straits of Tiran.

In October 1956 the moment was right. Nasser had infuriated France by supporting the FLN campaign in Algeria, and the UK by nationalizing the Suez Canal. The USA was busy with a presidential election and the USSR was stamping out the last embers of Hungarian freedom in Budapest. With the superpowers distracted and assistance promised from an Anglo-French task force, Israel attacked on the evening of 29 October.

Diversionary attack

Arab eyes were on the Jordanian front, where Israel had deployed its crack parachute brigade and attacked the Police Fort at Kalkilya in retaliation for another terrorist incident. Meanwhile in Sinai, Israeli pilots flying World War II surplus North American P-51 Mustangs were swooping low over the desert, cutting Egyptian telephone lines with their propellers and wings. The main body of the 202nd Parachute Brigade left the Jordanian frontier on the morning of 29 October and moved secretly towards Egypt.

At 1700 a battalion of Israeli paratroops jumped from their Douglas C-47 Dakotas to land at the eastern end of the Mitla pass, 70 km (45 miles) from the Suez Canal. At a stroke they had cut Sinai in half and blocked the path of Egyptian reinforcements from the Suez sector. The rest of the brigade under the bellicose Colonel Arik Sharon raced westwards from Israel and, smashing through a motley Egyptian force at Themed, linked up with the paratroops by nightfall on 30 October.

Despite Israeli air attacks, the Egyptian 2nd Brigade advanced from Suez and occupied strong defensive positions at the western end of the Mitla Pass. Sharon recklessly attacked and, although the Egyptians were ejected from the pass and sent hurrying back over the canal, the paratroops incurred over 150 casualties in an operation that had no strategic necessity.

Textbook victory
After Nasser nationalized the Suez Canal, Egyptian forces were redeployed ready to meet any Anglo-French retaliation. The possibility of an Israeli attack was certainly recognized but the Egyptian army was larger and better equipped. However, Nasser failed to appreciate the difficulties in absorbing the new Soviet equipment and expanding the army. Caught unawares, the Egyptian army was beaten in detail, suffering several thousand dead and 6,000 captured.

Israelis in Gaza
The *Fedayeen* strongholds in Gaza were overrun without great difficulty and the demoralized Egyptian garrison surrendered. On 1 November, the Israelis overran El Arish and the Egyptian high command ordered a general retreat from Sinai.

Operation Kadesh

The Palestinian refugees from 1948 remained in camps along the Israeli border where they were recruited into terrorist groups for attacks on Israel. Here, a party of Israelis return from a punitive raid in response to the latest Fedayeen atrocity.

All the Arab states were arming for a re-fight of 1948 but Egypt presented the greatest menace. Israel struck without warning, paratroops seizing the Mitla Pass and armoured columns racing into Sinai to overrun the startled Egyptian units.

The largest concentration of Egyptian forces lay in the north at Abu Agheila near the sprawling refugee camps of the Gaza strip. Abu Agheila was taken after a fierce battle on 31 October and the Gaza strip fell by 2 November.

The second phase of the battle for Sinai took place to the north where the bulk of the Egyptian forces were dug-in at Abu Agheila. The first of three lines of fortifications was stormed on 31 October, but the second attack was postponed to deal with elements of the Egyptian 1st Armoured Brigade: two battalions of T-34 tanks and a company of SU-100 assault guns plus a battalion of motorized infantry. This force was stopped in its tracks by Israeli air attack and chased back to the Suez Canal.

The Israeli 7th Armoured Brigade launched its epic attack on the second Egyptian fortified line at Raefa Dam on the evening of 31 October. The defences included 10 Archer self-propelled anti-tank guns and six 25-pdr guns: every Israeli tank was hit but the assault continued into darkness. Across a battlefield illuminated by brewed up tanks and blazing buildings, the Israeli attack was pressed home with the utmost determination; many tanks ran out of ammunition and the crews were reduced to throwing grenades and firing sub-machine guns from their hatches. The Egyptian defence collapsed.

The remaining part of the Abu Agheila position was attacked unsuccessfully by the 10th Brigade on 1 November but the Egyptians, fearing encirclement, withdrew anyway during the night. The same day, the 'Golani' Brigade attacked Rafah in Gaza and reached El Arish on 2 November. Pressing westwards, it advanced to within 16 km (10 miles) of the Suez Canal and joined up with part of the 202nd Parachute Brigade which had moved up from Mitla. The substantial Egyptian forces in the Gaza strip surrendered, saving Gaza and the sprawling refugee camps from becoming a battlefield.

Advance from Eilat

The third part of the Israeli strategy was put into action on 2 November when the 9th Brigade, a reservist unit, advanced from Eilat down the forbidding desert coast of the Gulf of Aqaba. The advancing troops were ambushed by the camel-mounted Egyptian frontier force but reached the forward line of Egyptian defences at Ras Nasrani on 4 November to find them unoccupied. They attacked the main position at Sharm el Sheikh in conjunction with part of the 202nd Parachute Brigade; the Egyptian air force could no longer intervene in the battle as its bases west of the Canal were being bombed by British and French aircraft. By early morning on 5 November the southernmost tip of the Sinai peninsula was in Israeli hands and the ceasefire demanded by the UN came into force the next day.

Anthony Eden, the British prime minister, vacillated under political pressure and the Anglo-French force did not leave Malta until 1 November. Although troops were finally landed on 5 and 6 November, the British government caved in under international pressure and agreed to a ceasefire at midnight on 6/7 November. For all its potential, the Anglo-French attack played little part in deciding the battle for Sinai which was won by the sheer professionalism of the Israeli soldiers. Commanders led from the front by example, while initiative and enterprise by all ranks enabled the Israelis to run rings around their opponents who never managed to fight a co-ordinated battle.

Above: El Quseima, 30 October
Israeli infantry wait on the heights outside the Egyptian-held town south of Abu Agheila. In their prepared positions the Egyptians offered stubborn resistance but once outflanked and compelled to fight a mobile battle the Egyptian army disintegrated.

Victory celebrations at Rafah, 1 November
On 1 November, Israeli forces stormed Rafah, cutting off all Egyptian troops in the Gaza strip, which surrendered the next day. Note the mixture of British and American equipment worn by these Israelis examining a Soviet gun.

Fortunately, the Egyptian garrison at Gaza surrendered rather than turn the refugee camp into a battleground. Here, Israeli soldiers inspect an Egyptian anti-aircraft gun abandoned on the beach.

An Anglo-French force attacked Egypt on 5 November, but this intervention was highly controversial and world opinion perversely united in favour of Egypt, destroying the UK's credibility as a world power.

Israeli troops return triumphantly from Sinai after their spectacular victory. But they had won only a breathing space: Warsaw Pact weaponry soon flooded into Egypt to replace lost equipment. The struggle was not over.

IA DRANG VALLEY: Taking on the NVA

November 1965: The newly formed 1st Air Cavalry Division challenges the North Vietnamese Army in the Central Highlands of Vietnam.

The war in South East Asia was unlike any previous conflict in which American troops had been engaged. Stepping in to fill a vacuum after the French withdrawal from Indo-China, the initial involvement was low-key, limited to providing material assistance and advice for the government and the army of South Vietnam. The fact that this government was unusually corrupt was beside the point, for these were the days of the Red Peril and the Domino theory. Anything that prevented the god-

Nung mercenary

The Special Forces recruited and led a bewildering variety of indigenous tribesmen, ethnic Chinese and other mercenary troops. Fighting the enemy on his own terms these *contra-guerillas* were highly effective but could not resist the large formations of NVA regulars which appeared in the Highlands during 1965. This man carries a Danish Madsen SMG.

less communist hordes from sweeping through the whole of South East Asia was a Good Thing.

President Kennedy stepped up American aid in the early 1960s and from 1964 US air and naval units took an increasing part in the war. The first ground combat units arrived in early 1965 with the landing of the 9th Marine Brigade at Da Nang, and by the end of year the trickle of American fighting men arriving in-country had become a flood. Among the formations to reach Vietnam that year was the first example of an entirely new kind of airmobile division. Although the airmobile concept was untried, the First Cavalry Division immediately began to set the pace for the rest of the US Army.

A wounded medic of B Company, 2/7th US Cavalry
Hurriedly deployed to Vietnam and deprived of the call-up of reservists, the US Army nevertheless managed to defeat the NVA in the tropical wilderness of the Ia Drang valley. Helicopter evacuation saved the lives of many US wounded while injured NVA men endured an arduous trek over the border.

On the landing zone
The 3rd Brigade of the 1st Cavalry Division landed in company-sized groups from 14 November and immediately ran into trouble. Only the overwhelming American airpower saved some elements from being overrun: they had landed on top of two NVA regiments.

It was the development of the helicopter which made such a unit possible. It had been proposed that large heli-borne formations could make an assault so fast, and could get around the terrain so quickly, that a division thus equipped could control much larger areas of country than previously possible.

The 11th Air Assault Division was established at Fort Benning to test the concept, and the results were so encouraging that the 11th, renamed the 1st Cavalry Division (Airmobile), was moved in its entirety to Vietnam in September 1965.

Their first test came in the Ia Drang valley, near the Cambodian border. The Chu Pong hills were a suspected North Vietnamese Army (NVA) stronghold, and the valley itself was a major staging area for incoming Northern troops. The 'First Team' set up shop at An Khe, and in October 1965 commenced Operation 'Silver Bayonet'. Part of the reason for the Cavalry's presence was an NVA divisional group of three regiments, under General Man, which had mustered for an attack on the Plei Me Special Forces camp.

Finding Charlie

In November, Major-General Harry Kinnard deployed the Third Brigade of his Division. Its task was to sweep the base of the Chu Pong hills. On November 14 the 1st Battalion 7th Cavalry, under the command of Lt. Col Harold Moore, made an assault into a landing zone called LZ X-Ray. 'B' company landed and moved out towards the hills as 'A' company arrived. 'B' Company was soon heavily engaged, and a simultaneous mortar attack on the LZ kept 'A' Company busy. As they in turn moved out, they attacked the rear of the NVA force engaging 'B' company. Meanwhile the remaining two companies had landed and formed a perimeter on the LZ. A two-company assault to relieve a cut-off platoon failed, and by dusk 'A' and 'B' companies were back at the LZ. The lone platoon held off three major attacks through the night, thanks largely to accurate artillery support.

The 1st of the 7th had obviously landed in a major enemy concentration (in fact two complete NVA regiments), so the 2nd Battalion 7th Cavalry landed on LZ Macon seven miles to the north and 1st Battalion 5th Cavalry were delivered to LZ Victor two miles to the south east. After 26 hours 'B' Company's Second Platoon was relieved, but the fighting around X-Ray continued unabated. Tactical airpower and artillery were vital in holding back the NVA attacks, and for the first time large scale B-52 strikes were called in to blast suspected enemy concentrations. 2nd of the 5th were fighting their way from LZ Victor on foot, while 2nd of the 7th reinforcements were flown direct from LZ Macon and came in under fire.

The night of the 15th saw a massive NVA attack which was beaten back with heavy losses, and the morning of the 16th opened with a 'Mad minute' of American fire followed by a heavy artillery barrage. The lack of response indicated that the NVA had withdrawn, and company patrols reported 643 NVA

Guerrilla war no more

The US Army had hoped to save South Vietnam by deploying small units of Special Forces personnel to lead local forces against the Viet Cong. But bases like this near the Cambodian border were soon menaced by regular North Vietnamese troops.

By 1964 the South Vietnamese government was on the brink of defeat with NVA and VC troops occupying large parts of the country and defeating the ARVN units sent against them. Only US regulars could save the Saigon regime.

The 1st Air Cavalry pioneered new airmobile tactics, using the flexibility of massed helicopters to dominate far larger areas than conventional ground troops. Landed in the Ia Drang valley in November, they ran into a major concentration of NVA troops.

bodies with signs that many more had been dragged away. US losses were 79 killed and 121 wounded.

The Communists were not finished, however. Before the NVA regiments finally retreated into Cambodia, 2nd of the 7th were caught in a classic horse-shoe trap while crossing the Ia Drang river. Only three miles from LZ X-Ray the battalion lost 151 dead, 125 wounded and 5 missing, while killing at least 403 NVA.

Ia Drang was the first time the US Army had met NVA regular units in battle, and though outnumbered the Americans inflicted a severe defeat upon the Communists. With an NVA body count in excess of 1,770, the battles in the Ia Drang had stopped an NVA drive to cut South Vietnam in half through the central highlands. It also taught the North Viet-North Vietnamese an important lesson. Taking on the Americans conventionally was not a good idea, and it would be a long time before they would seek to repeat the experience.

Left: B Company, 2/7th Cavalry, 2 years on
The Air Cavalry on a search and destroy mission during early 1968. The policy of limiting tours of duty to six months for officers and a year for other ranks ensured the experience gained at Ia Drang was soon lost although the *esprit* of the Air Cavalry remained and it continued to be one of the most effective units in Vietnam.

'Every time I hear that name, something terrible happens'
An 'Arc Light' strike by B-52 strategic bombers lays waste the jungle along the Cambodian border, December 1966. Bombing from 30,000 ft, where the Viet Cong could neither see nor hear them, the B-52s could inflict awesome damage although accurate targeting remained a problem.

As different elements of the Air Cavalry brigade landed they were attacked without hesitation by North Vietnamese troops who had become used to victory. The firepower of the American troops came as an unexpected shock.

From 14 to 19 November the NVA hurled attack after attack at the American perimeters. But with everything from mortars to B-52 strategic bombers firing in support of the Cavalry, the NVA suffered heavily. US losses included 240 KIA.

The NVA withdrew into 'neutral' Cambodia where US troops were forbidden to follow by an administration determined to limit the war. The US Army had won its first battle in Vietnam but whether it could win the war remained to be seen.

RETURN TO SINAI: Desert Victory

5 June 1967: 15 minutes after the Israeli air force's surprise attack on Arab airfields, the IDF's tanks race into Sinai.

In May 1967 President Nasser deployed 100,000 Egyptian troops and over 1,000 tanks along Israel's south-western frontier. He declared the Straits of Tinan closed to Israeli shipping and publicly proclaimed his leadership of the Arab states aligned against Israel. The Egyptian leader's scheme was to drive Israel into a war in which his vast army with its modern Soviet equipment would triumph. The Israelis would be driven into the sea and Nasser would be master of the Middle East.

Nasser's hubris was rewarded on 5 June with the Israeli air force's surprise attack that annihilated Egypt's aerial armada before breakfast. With the benefit of complete air superiority, Israeli armoured columns thundered across the Egyptian frontier. The plan was to destroy the enemy forces dug in near the border, then race into the Sinai desert and occupy the two passes leading to the Suez Canal. The Egyptians, who seemed to be anticipating a repeat of the 1956 strategy, were not ready to meet a frontal assault so early in the war. Indeed, Egyptian armour was assembling between Kuntilla and Kusseima to strike into Israel.

The fall of Rafah

At 0800, just 15 minutes after the beginning of the airstrike on Egypt, Colonel Gonen's 7th Armoured Brigade broke into Rafah while a parachute brigade with tank support swept around to the south through 'impassable' sand dunes and assaulted the Egyptian fortifications from the rear. Pressing on down the coast road, Israeli armour managed to penetrate as far as El Arish, but an Egyptian counterattack recaptured their position at El Jiradi, isolating the leading Israelis. General Tal reacted with prompt efficiency and the Egyptians were driven out late on 5 June, restoring Israeli communications with El Arish.

General 'Arik' Sharon's division advanced parallel to Tal's forces in a rough line between Nitzana and Ismailia. Once again the Egyptian fortifications were taken after flanking forces advanced over sand dunes assumed to be impassable by the defenders. In a chaotic, bewildering battle, the main Egyptian positions around Abu Agheila were taken by dawn on 6 June after the Arab artillery batteries, providing vital fire support, were silenced by a heliborne battalion of Israeli paratroopers.

While the two Egyptian divisions were engaged by Tal and Sharon's parallel attacks, General Yoffe advanced between the two battlefields across 55 km (35 miles) of soft sand. By the evening of 6 June his tanks were dug in on the Bir Lahfan crossroads ready to block any Egyptian attempt to move forces between the two battles or reinforce them with fresh troops from the west. Yoffe's bold manoeuvre paid off that evening as an Egyptian armoured brigade

Above: Attacking the Golan Heights
Israel remained on the defensive in the north while the bulk of the IDF dealt with the main enemy in Sinai. As the Syrians had lost their air force on the first day of the war they made no offensive moves until Israel finally attacked on 9 June.

Super-Sherman on the road to Damascus
In 48 hours of heavy fighting the Syrian defences on the Golan Heights were overwhelmed, although at Tel Fakhr it was touch and go for some time. With plentiful air support, the IDF broke through and the road to Damascus lay open.

M48 tank

The IDF employed a mixture of British Centurions, French AMX-13s, upgraded Shermans and the American-supplied M48. Armed with a 90-mm gun, this M48 belongs to the 1st battalion of a tank regiment and retains the high cupola which was often removed to lower the vehicle's silhouette.

Suez revisited

Despite the humiliation of 1956, President Nasser continued to lead the Arab states and created a unified command structure to co-ordinate an Arab invasion of Israel. Here, Egyptian commandos parade in Gaza near the Israeli frontier.

Soviet influence in the Middle East increased steadily, providing the Arab armies with an impressive arsenal. Given the events of 1956, the unreadiness of the Egyptian forces to face a surprise attack from Israel was astonishing.

Infantry half-tracks follow Israeli tanks across the Sinai desert. Outflanking enemy prepared positions, the Israelis routed the Egyptian armour and advanced rapidly on the Mitla Pass. Complete dominance in the air had already been won.

from Ismailia ran straight into his position and was bloodily repulsed.

Egyptian propaganda continued to announce stunning Arab victories but the truth quickly began to filter through. Many senior Egyptian officers, recognizing which way the wind was blowing, abandoned their posts and fled towards the Suez Canal. Others presented themselves to the Israelis, equipped with suitcases of perfume and women's underwear. After the war, Nasser vented his rage against his army leaders, court martialling many officers and driving Field Marshal Amer to suicide.

Tal's forces resumed their blitzkrieg along the northern part of Sinai and were within 16km (10 miles) of the Canal on 7 June. Here they were checked by a tank ambush supported by anti-tank guns and the few surviving Egyptian aircraft. Israeli armour retired and engaged the Egyptian tanks at long range while paratroops with recoilless rifles made a flanking attack in M3 half-tracks and jeeps.

The Israelis broke through to Kantara and by the fourth day of the war they had reached the Suez Canal.

Retreat to Mitla

The Egyptian army in Sinai was now in full retreat and after Tal's forces swung south to storm Bir Gafgafa, the Egyptians were left with no choice but to converge on the Mitla Pass. Yoffe's troops hurried to block this last exit while the Israeli air force remorselessly strafed the long columns moving westwards. Thousands of burning vehicles littered the approaches to the Pass which was eventually reached by nine Israeli tanks under Colonel Shadmi. Unfortunately they had run out of fuel on the way, and four of the tanks arrived under tow by their colleagues. This tiny force then held the Pass until the rest of Yoffe's troops arrived and only a single Egyptian tank managed to break through.

Sharon's southerly advance on Nakhle was en-livened by the capture of the entire equipment of the 125th Armoured Brigade. Its commanding officer, Brigadier Ahmed Abd el Naby, had in fact been captured by Yoffe's division and stated that his orders had simply been to withdraw: nobody had said anything about the tanks! More serious resistance was offered by armoured forces near Nakhle, but in a hectic tank battle, the Israelis triumphed again.

While the entire Egyptian army in Sinai fell apart, Tal's forces advancing west from Bir Gafgafa were attacked by T-55 tanks from Ismailia. The Israeli vanguard was equipped only with French AMX-13 light tanks which had no hope of surviving a hit from a Soviet 100-mm gun. However, they opened fire at 2,750m (3,000 yards) and began a bitter six-hour tank battle which led to the utter destruction of the Arab force. The UN-sponsored cease-fire came into effect at 1830 on 10 June, by which time Nasser's mighty army had been as thoroughly destroyed as his air force.

Wreckage at Mitla Pass
Harried from the air, the Egyptian columns falling back to Mitla were destroyed in a bitter tank action on 8 June and the survivors bombed to oblivion. Note the interesting combination of Soviet armour: a T-34, an SU-100 and several T-54 tanks. Israel captured so many vehicles that her armoured forces ended the war with 190 more tanks than they started with.

Egyptian airstrike
One of the very rare appearances by the Egyptian Air Force in 1967: two MiG-17s strafe Israeli troops near the east bank of the Suez Canal. In Sinai and on the Golan Heights, Israeli air superiority hopelessly disrupted the Arab supply lines.

The Egyptian army sustained over 10,000 casualties in Sinai; another 5,000 troops and 500 officers surrendered. It left behind about 800 tanks, several hundred guns and countless other vehicles. Nasser later admitted the losses represented 80% of the army's military equipment. Israeli losses on the Sinai front were 300 killed and 1,000 wounded and the fact that 23% of the casualties were officers or NCOs bears testimony to the way Israeli units were led from the front.

The scale of the Israeli victory stunned the world. Not only had they crushed Nasser's vaunted army but King Hussein, fooled by Nasser's initial claims of victory, had led Jordan into the war. Despite fierce resistance by the Arab Legion, the holy city of Jerusalem had fallen and the west bank of the Jordan was now in Israeli hands. Having treacherously failed to deliver any of its promised support to Jordan, the Syrian army was in turn utterly routed and the Golan Heights were occupied by the time of the ceasefire. For the first time in her history, Israel could organize a defence in depth. Israel offered to demilitarize Sinai and Golan, and to discuss with Jordan the future of the West Bank, but the Arab leaders, egged on by the USSR, announced their refusal to negotiate at the summit in Khartoum in September. The struggle was set to continue.

Abandoned by their officers, Egyptian troops surrendered in droves. On 7 June, the Mitla and Giddi passes were captured by the Israelis after a hectic tank action, and the Egyptians were trapped much as they had been in 1956.

The surviving Egyptian positions east of the Suez Canal were overrun and on 8 June Israeli troops reached Ismailia and pushed on to Suez. The same day, the west bank of the Jordan was wrested from Jordanian troops.

Egyptian prisoners sit by the Suez Canal. On 9 June the Israelis stormed the Syrian-held Golan Heights and the war was all but over. For the first time in her brief history, Israel had conquered enough territory to be able to fight in depth.

Giap's Gamble: The siege of Khe Sanh

January 1968: The remote American base at Khe Sanh is attacked by overwhelming numbers of NVA.

For much of the Vietnam war, the main supply route to the Viet Cong was down the so-called Ho Chi Minh Trail. This was in reality a complete network of roads and tracks passing through Laos and Cambodia, from where troops and supplies could be infiltrated to almost any point in South Vietnam. Interdiction from the air was difficult, so the Americans tried something else. A chain of strong-points was established south of the Demilitarized Zone (DMZ) athwart the main northern infiltration routes. One of the largest of these was the former Special Forces base at Khe Sanh, just 24 km (15 miles) south of the DMZ and about the same distance from the Cambodian border. The Special Forces compound had moved to the new camp of Lang Vei near by.

Intelligence warnings

From the middle of 1967 intelligence reports indicated an ominous build up of regular North Vietnamese Army (NVA) troops in the area. 20,000 men of the 304th and the 320/A NVA Divisions were close at hand, and the 320th and 324th Divisions were just 25 km away on the trail. All the signs pointed to a major North Vietnamese offensive, whose aim was to eliminate the isolated position at Khe Sanh and the three battalions of Marines who defended it.

General William Westmoreland, commander of the US Military Assistance Command Vietnam,

Target Khe Sanh
Whether the North Vietnamese leaders hoped for another Dien Bien Phu is unlikely to be revealed. After the battle they played down its importance or argued the battle served to draw US reserves away from the cities targeted for attack in the Tet offensive.

AC-47 'Spooky' gunship

'Spooky' struck from the night sky without warning, pouring out up to 18,000 rounds a minute from its 7.62-mm Miniguns while slowly orbiting the target. The effect had to be seen to be believed.

could have evacuated Khe Sanh, but with the full backing of President Johnson he elected to hold the base. This was in spite of the fate of a similar challenge to the Vietnamese almost exactly 14 years previously, at Dien Bien Phu. The Americans were confident they could succeed where the French had failed, and the key to their confidence was a massive application of air power.

Khe Sanh was a relatively small site, with an airstrip and room for about 6,000 men to fight. There were three 105-mm artillery batteries, and one 155-mm battery. In addition, there were several batteries of the very long ranged M107 175-mm gun within 32 km (20 miles) which could provide support. The whole position was heavily fortified, with strong company-sized posts on the high points around. These sites would be needed by the NVA if they were to shell the American positions to maximum effect, as they had done to the French in 1954.

The battle opened on 21 January with a heavy NVA mortar and infantry attack on the fortified position at Hill 861. The outpost beat off the attack, but while it was doing so a mortar, artillery and rocket assault on the main position blew up the 1,500 tons of ammunition in the main dump. The response was a massive application of Marine and Air

Force tactical air power on the surrounding jungle, as well as a pulverizing strike by Boeing B-52 bombers.

The shortage of ammunition could have been crucial, but air supply proved sufficient. Nonetheless, the airstrip was a dangerous place, and any pilot who put down had to run a gauntlet of NVA mortar and artillery fire. Most of the work was done by twin-engined Fairchild C-123s, but the larger Lockheed C-130s made regular air drops.

As January eased into February the battle became a seige. The attacks on the fortified posts were scenes of savage, often hand-to-hand fighting. The Special Forces camp at Lang Vei was overrun by NVA using PT-76 light tanks, the survivors streaming into Khe Sanh. NVA ground attacks eased off by the beginning of February, the main pressure on the base being applied by mortars, rockets and artillery. This barrage was largely answered from the air. The Air Force and Marines managed more than 300 tac-

Support from Camp Carroll
Camp Carroll lay some 15 miles east of Khe Sanh along Highway 9. Here an M107 175-mm self-propelled gun of C battery, 2/94th Artillery Regiment fires on North Vietnamese positions surrounding the Marines.

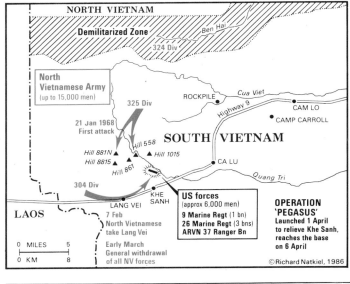

© Richard Natkiel, 1986

Seventy-seven days

The assault began on 21 January with fanatical attacks on Hill 861. These were beaten off but the garrison was then subjected to a ferocious barrage from North Vietnamese artillery concealed in the surrounding jungle.

The nearby Special Forces camp at Lang Vei was overrun on 7 February and the base at Khe Sanh was invested by some 15,000 NVA. Intermittent shelling punctuated by concentrated bombardments became the daily lot of the garrison.

100,000 tons of bombs were dropped around Khe Sanh. In January a special raid by 36 B-52s was ordered after signal intercepts suggested a senior NVA leader was present. It was Giap himself visiting the front, but he narrowly escaped.

tical sorties per day through the entire battle, to which was added an average of 40 jungle-pulverizing B-52 sorties daily.

Sapping forward

In spite of this overwhelming application of airpower, the North Vietnamese continued the siege. They pushed a trench system to within 100 metres of the defences of the perimeter, but the only attack made on the main base perimeter was beaten off on the wire by the 37th ARVN Ranger Battalion. It was not until March, and the 14th anniversary of the opening of the battle for Dien Bien Phu, that the NVA tried again. Unfortunately for them their concentration was noticed and hit by B-52s and the attack was postponed. When they tried again, on the night of 22 March, they became the target for the awesome firepower of 'Spooky'. Even the most hardened of troops would quail before the stream of death hosing from the 20-mm cannon of the Douglas AC-47 gunship, and the North Vietnamese were no exception. Their attack was ripped apart before it had started.

By the end of March it was the Americans who were doing all the attacking. On the night of the 30th a raid by B Company, 1st Battalion, 26th Marines went storming through a Vietnamese assembly area with flamethrowers, satchel charges, grenades and small arms, killing over 150 NVA soldiers before pulling back to the perimeter. The next day the

Army launched its major push to relieve Khe Sanh. The 1st Cavalry Division began Operation 'Pegasus', driving rapidly north towards the besieged Marine post. It was soon clear that the North Vietnamese were withdrawing. By 6 April the Cavalry had arrived. The siege was over.

The Khe Sanh garrison of 6,000 troops had held out against an attacking force six times larger from January to the beginning of April. Over 100,000 tons of bombs were dropped around the perimeter, and hundreds of thousands of artillery shells were fired. American casualties were 199 killed and 1,600

Dodging the next shell
A Marine races for cover as another NVA bombardment begins. Although the garrison received up to 1,000 rounds a day during some periods of the siege, the NVA were hopelessly outgunned from the start, some units suffering over 90 per cent casualties.

wounded. The North Vietnamese probably lost more than 10,000 killed over the same time.

Two months after the end of the siege, the Americans in a change from static to mobile operations decided that the border strongpoints were no longer needed. The base at Khe Sanh was dismantled and abandoned.

US Special Forces

Armed with a captured Soviet AK-47 assault rifle, this member of Special Forces wears few items of issue kit. They operated in small teams commanding large formations of irregular troops: the 800-strong garrison at Lang Vei was led by just 24 Green Berets.

Wreckage on the airstrip
The Marines at Khe Sanh were well posted, and provided with plentiful artillery and overwhelming air support. The situation bore only the most superficial resemblance to Dien Bien Phu but the media fell for it. Walter Cronkite revealed his grasp of military affairs in February when he told a CBS radio audience 'the parallels are there for all to see'. President Johnson had a sand-table model of Khe Sanh built in the White House and anxiously monitored situation reports, having demanded written assurances from the Joint Chiefs of Staff that they believed General Westmoreland could hold Khe Sanh.

The airstrip remained under enemy artillery bombardment and US aircrew developed a number of ingenious methods of minimizing their time on the ground. Unlike Dien Bien Phu, the NVA failed to defeat the aerial re-supply effort.

Planning for the relief of Khe Sanh began on 25 January, but the operation had to be postponed as the full fury of the Tet offensive erupted all over the South. Finally on 1 April, the 1st Air Cavalry Division launched Operation 'Pegasus'.

The first element of 'Pegasus', an ARVN airborne company, reached Khe Sanh on 5 April and the siege was lifted. The full number of NVA casualties will never be known but if North Vietnam expected another Dien Bien Phu it was sadly disappointed.

Battle For An Loc: South Vietnam 1972

Easter 1972: North Vietnam invades the South across their joint border and from the NVA sanctuaries in Cambodia.

On 30 March 1972 120,000 North Vietnamese regulars spearheaded a co-ordinated assault on South Vietnam. In the I Corps Tactical Zone 40,000 troops supported by T-54 tanks and long-range 130-mm guns stormed over the Demilitarized Zone; in the Central Highlands Kontum was besieged; and a third thrust, to the north of Saigon, led to the heaviest fighting since the 1968 Tet offensive. The communists' primary objective was to inflict a humiliating defeat on the South Vietnamese army and demonstrate the failure of Vietnamization. This would compel the USA to negotiate its way out of the Vietnamese quagmire on Hanoi's terms.

Defeat in the north

With low cloud ceilings and anti-aircraft missiles to shield them from South Vietnamese airpower, the NVA assault troops advanced rapidly over the DMZ into I Corps. At first ARVN forces resolutely defended their positions, but a second attack on 27 April broke through to Quang Tri City. The ARVN disintegrated, troops fleeing south abandoning their tanks and guns. Quang Tri was to remain in enemy hands until September and only the essentially political function of the offensive prevented a second battle for Hue.

In III Corps the communist drive was directed at the town of An Loc which was subjected to a heavy bombardment by NVA artillery throughout 12 April. In the early hours of the next morning one communist shell found the ammunition dump and POL (Petrol, Oil, Lubricants) storage area which exploded in a spectacular pyrotechnic display. The NVA ground attack began at 0730 with PT-76 amphibious light tanks and T-54s leading the way. Fortunately for the defenders the tanks outpaced their accompanying infantry and drove into the town on their own, seeming to believe that the town had already fallen. They were caught at close range by South Vietnamese soldiers armed with 66-mm anti-tank rockets (LAWs) and the leading vehicles were immobilized. The others fell back in confusion as Bell AH-1 Cobra gunships subjected the NVA infantry to a hail of 2.75-in rockets. But by the afternoon of 13 April the communists had carried the northern half of An Loc and repulsed a relieving force advancing on the city from the south.

Heavy bombardment

Nightfall brought renewed shelling which seemed to single out the hospital for special attention. By morning An Loc's hospital was a pile of rubble, most of the 300 patients were dead and the town was critically short of medical supplies. With the airfield overrun and helicopter evacuation impossible because of the intense anti-aircraft fire, the plight of

the wounded became pitiful. Field dressings were conspicuous by their absence; the heat and the insanitary conditions within the perimeter did the rest. Wounds festered and cholera broke out later in the week.

Communist shellfire sought out every target of value within An Loc. Aided by spotters on high buildings surrounding the perimeter, the NVA gunners could rapidly bring down fire on ARVN batteries which revealed themselves. Elements of an enemy fifth column were uncovered when six young women were caught with radio transmitters in their bras. Furious ARVN soldiers tied them up in a regular impact area and they were blown to pieces in the next bombardment.

Aerial lifeline

The besieged garrison of An Loc could only sustain its resistance with the aid of aerial resupply, a point not lost on the NVA who brought forth their latest anti-aircraft weapons to frustrate these drops. From 7 to 19 April 300 tons of supplies were dropped. Inevitably some bundles wafted into enemy lines and others generated furious firefights by landing between hostile positions, but these hazardous flights were critically important for the defenders.

By 10 May nearly 25 per cent of the 4,500 ARVN defenders were wounded and after a month of continual action morale was sagging. President Thieu had declared the battle to be a symbol of South Viet-

Just hanging on
Dwarfed by the size of the Browning .50 calibre machine-gun, two ARVN soldiers fire from the roof of an M41 light tank. South Vietnamese tanks fared poorly against the NVA who were well supplied with anti-tank rockets.

The enemy within
While the NVA and Main Force VC units were now able to fight conventional battles against ARVN forces, the rural and urban terrorist campaigns continued. This girl was captured after an exchange of shot with South Vietnamese police.

The writing on the wall

The North Vietnamese invasion began on 30 March 1972. Quang Tri, the South's most northerly province, was overrun. More NVA divisions boiled out of Cambodia to attack An Loc, little over 100 miles north of Saigon.

NVA troops overrun an ARVN position in Quang Tri. The defence crumbled on 27 April and the ensuing retreat became an utter rout. In the III Corps Tactical Zone, An Loc was already under artillery bombardment.

An ARVN Ranger battalion detected the approach of a major force of NVA over the Cambodian border and fell back rapidly to escape encirclement. The city was attacked on 12 April by NVA troops supported by PT-76 light and T-54 medium tanks.

An ARVN Ranger in the Central Highlands
The South Vietnamese troops were as well equipped as their Northern enemies but rarely as well led. Accustomed to massive aerial support and unused to independent operational planning, the ARVN remained in awe of the North Vietnamese who were so willing to die for their cause. President Nixon observed: 'The real problem is that the enemy is willing to sacrifice in order to win, while the South Vietnamese simply aren't willing to pay that much of a price in order to avoid losing.'

AC-119 gunship
AC-119Gs (codenamed 'Shadows') and AC-119Ks (codenamed 'Stingers') were gunship conversions of the Fairchild C-119 transport aircraft fitted with four 7.62-mm (0.3-in) Miniguns or four Miniguns plus two 20-mm Gatlings respectively.

LINEBACKER II: The Christmas Bombing

December 1972: Irked by communist stalling in the Paris peace talks, President Nixon unleashes the USAF's B-52 fleet.

Over North Vietnam, Boeing B-52 operations were long restricted to areas in the southern panhandle where they flew out of range of the MiGs based in the Hanoi-Haiphong area and where SAMs were not initially deployed. This relatively safe situation did not last forever as SAMs were first fired at B-52s on 17 September 1967 during a mission close to the De-Militarized zone on the 17th parallel between North and South Vietnam. However, in this and many subsequent incidents, the heavy bombers foiled North Vietnamese attempts by making full use of their internal electronic countermeasures systems and relying on the effective support of Douglas EB-66 jammers and Republic F-105 'Iron Hand' and 'Wild Weasel' flights. This happy state was not encountered later when B-52s began flying missions over the Red River Delta on 15 April 1972 during 'Linebacker I'. Furthermore, the risks taken by the bomber crews became very high during 'Linebacker II'.

Operation 'Bullet Shot', a systematic build-up of B-52 and support forces to counteract the increased North Vietnamese infiltration in the south, was launched in early February 1972 and over the next

several months the 'Arc Light' force was increased until a peak strength of 206 B-52Ds and B-52Gs was reached in June 1972. Including the aircraft sent on temporary duty from units in the continental USA, three-fourths of these aircraft were based at Andersen AFB on Guam and were assigned to the expanded 43rd Strategic Wing and to the 72nd Strategic Wing [Provisional] while the others were at U-Tapao air base in Thailand with the 307th Strategic Wing and the 310th Strategic Wing [Provisional]. The number of heavy bombers at these two bases had been slightly reduced by 15 December 1972, when senior commanders received notification that President Nixon had authorized the use of B-52s as part of a major air offensive against North Vietnam. The striking power of these aircraft was nevertheless awesome and in the space of 11 days forced Hanoi to curtail its delaying tactics and agree to resume the peace talks in Paris.

Peace through fire superiority

At long last employed in the role for which they had been designed, 129 B-52s (42 B-52Ds from U-Tapao, and 33 B-52Ds and 54 B-52Gs from Andersen) with 39 tactical aircraft providing escort and ECM support, struck airfields at Hoa Lac, Kep, and Phuc Yen, the Kinh No complex and the Yen Vien rail yard, all in the vicinity of Hanoi, during the night of 18 December 1972. Enemy air defences were alert and heavy (SAMs, heavy AAA, and

MiGs); two B-52Gs and one B-52D were shot down, while Staff Sergeant Sam Turner, a B-52D Fire Control Operator (FCO or gunner), destroyed a MiG-21. Additional heavy raids were flown during the next six nights and again every night from 26 through to 29 December, with the last bombs being dropped on the Trai Ca SAM storage area shortly before midnight on 29 December 1972. Thanks to improving tactics and fast dwindling supplies to North Vietnamese SAMs, losses were kept at a reasonable level (three B-52s were lost during the night of the 18th, six during that of the 20th, and two each during the nights of the 21st, 26th and 27th). The overall aircraft loss rate was an acceptable 2.06 per cent and the loss of human lives was lower than had been feared (of the 92 B-52 aircrew members who went down, 14 were killed, 14 were reported missing in action, 31 were rescued, and 33 became POWs and were released in early 1973). Results exceeded the most sanguine expectations, with damage to civilian areas and civilian casualties (1,395 according to Hanoi) kept to a remarkably low level even when targets were struck in the midst of heavily populated areas. The B-52s were credited with the destruction of one-fourth of North Vietnam's petroleum reserves, 80 per cent of its electrical generating capacity, and virtually its entire supply of SAMs. As by then the mining of Haiphong and other harbours had brought shipping to a standstill, and as rail lines into the People's Republic of

Target Hanoi
The Christmas bombing raids on the North Vietnamese capital were the first and last occasions that B-52 Stratofortresses performed the sort of mission they had been designed for. Massed bombers escorted by fighters battled through the world's toughest array of anti-aircraft weapons and interceptors from 18-30 December. The anachronistic spectacle was completed on the first raid when a B-52 used its defensive machine guns to shoot down a MiG-21 interceptor.

Break on through

By prolonging the talks, the North Vietnamese hoped to extract further concessions from a US government anxious to finish American involvement in Vietnam. As a result, the President was prepared to give the Joint Chiefs a free hand at last.

The plan was to attack North Vietnamese industry with massed B-52s. Although the bombers were protected by fighter-bomber strikes and aircraft with more modern ECM, the North Vietnamese air force presented a formidable threat.

Operation Linebacker II began on 18 December and the first of over 1200 Soviet supplied SA-2 Surface-to-Air missiles were fired at the bomber formations. Flying straight and level to improve accuracy the B-52s were a perfect target.

China were effectively interdicted. Hanoi's war making capability was at an end. Sadly the ensuing Paris Agreement did not extract the necessary guarantees to safeguard the future of the Republic of Vietnam, and the sacrifices of Allied personnel soon became fruitless.

The final days

Although the last of the 'Linebacker II' sorties against targets in the Hanoi-Haiphong area was flown by B-52s on 29 December 1972, the war was not yet quite over for their aircrews: missions against targets in the southern part of North Vietnam continued until 15 January 1973: those over South Vietnam until 27 January: those over Laos until 17 April: and those over Cambodia until 15 August 1973. In eight years of 'Arc Light' operations, a total of 26 B-52s had been lost, including two which had collided in flight during the first sortie on 17 June 1965, and two others which had collided south east of Saigon on 7 July 1967. (Among the casualties in this latter accident was Major General William J. Crumm, the commander of the 3rd Air Division at Andersen AFB).

Arc Light
Until Linebacker II, B-52s had been employed on 'Arc Light' strikes over South Vietnam, Laos and Cambodia. Linebacker II did force the North Vietnamese back to the negotiating table but the final treaty was almost identical to the draft hammered out in October. The bombing was intended to demonstrate that Nixon would not hesitate in ordering further air strikes if communist aggression against the South continued after the American withdrawal.

Bombing up a B-52
Flying from Guam involved a round trip of 5,500 miles and B-52s sometimes took off nearly a ton over their structurally safe limit. The standard bomb load consisted of 85 580 lb bombs internally and 24 500 lb bombs on the wing pylons.

Andersen Air Base, Guam
In 1972 there were so many B-52s flying from Guam that some had to be airborne at all times. The extent of the damage they inflicted was wildly exaggerated in the US press. The volume of equipment poured down the Ho Chi Minh Trail in 1973 demonstrated the failure of all the US bombing campaigns to seriously disrupt the North Vietnamese economy as the NVA received no new Soviet or Chinese aid to prepare its final offensive.

US electronic countermeasures reduced SAM hits to about 2 per cent of missiles fired and the North Vietnamese were reduced to firing blind volleys. Most exploded harmlessly: this photo was taken by an RF-101 Voodoo reconnaissance aircraft.

While US public opinion remained neutral, elements of the American media sided openly with the North Vietnamese, damning the bombing raids as 'Stone-Age barbarism'. Pope Paul VI spoke of his anguish at the attacks on 'blessed' Vietnam.

Linebacker II terminated on 30 December: the 'Christmas bombing' had inflicted no permanent damage on North Vietnam but as early as 26 December, the communists were ready to resume negotiations. US involvement in Vietnam was over.

VALLEY OF TEARS: The Battle for Golan

6 October 1973: During the Jewish feast day of Yom Kippur, Syrian and Egyptian forces storm across the border, surprising the Israelis.

On 6 October 1973 five Syrian divisions attacked the Israeli positions on the Golan Heights. They were the Syrian contribution to a joint Syrian/Egyptian plan to wage a limited war which would in President Herzog's words 'turn the clock back to the eve of the Six-Day War in 1967'. While Egyptian forces stormed over the Suez Canal and back into Sinai, Syrian troops were to capture the Golan Heights and threaten Galilee.

Israeli forces defending the 70-km (45-mile) northern front knew they had no ground to fall back on. Even a limited Syrian advance into the Golan Heights would bring Galilee under fire. They were desperately outnumbered: the two Israeli armoured brigades had 170 tanks between them; the three Syrian infantry divisions could muster 130-200 each and the two armoured divisions disposed a total of 500 T-55s and T-62s. When independent Syrian tank brigades are included, the Syrians had some 1,500 tanks in action.

Under cover of an artillery barrage from over 1,000 guns and heavy mortars, the Syrian armour advanced in set-piece battle formation taught to them by their Soviet advisers. Meanwhile, heliborne commandos seized the vital Israeli position on Mount Hermon which had been foolishly neglected despite its splendid view over the battlefield. Fortunately for Israel, Major General Yitzhak Hofi, in charge of Northern Command, had persuaded Moshe Dayan to release the 7th Armoured Brigade held in GHQ reserve and it was deployed in the path of the Syrians in time to meet their onslaught.

Holding the line

Commanded by Colonel Avigdor Ben-Gal, the 7th Armoured Brigade had approximately 100 tanks: American M60s and British Centurions. The Syrian 7th Infantry Division, supported by the 3rd Armoured Division, massed about 500 tanks for the assault between Mas'ada and Kuneitra. The battle lasted without a break from 1400 on Saturday 6 October to Tuesday afternoon and tested the endurance of the tank crews to the very limit. There was no lull in the fighting after darkness fell: both sides had night-fighting equipment and the exhausted tank crews continued to stare, red-eyed, into their sights.

Firing from hull-down positions into their prepared killing ground, the Israelis exacted a heavy toll from the Syrians. Lost positions were rapidly counter-attacked in soldier's battles which turned on the initiative of junior officers. On the Tuesday afternoon the 7th Armoured Brigade launched a last, desperate counter-attack with its remaining 20 tanks, most of them damaged vehicles salvaged by the repair parties and many crewed by wounded

Israeli Paratrooper, 1973

The close co-operation between Israeli infantry and armour was one of the key factors in their success. Fortified positions which defied armoured assault were stormed, often at night, by Israeli infantry. This Para is armed with the FN 7.62 mm machine gun. He wears an assault vest and carries ammunition and water in his chest webbing.

men. As they advanced into the killing ground, now dubbed 'the valley of tears', the Syrians' morale collapsed and they withdrew leaving 500 armoured vehicles behind.

While the 7th Armoured Brigade fought desperately to hold back the Syrians in the northern part of the Golan Heights, the main weight of the attack fell on the 188th Brigade at the south-eastern end of the Tapline Road. The Syrian 5th and 9th Infantry Divisions, supported by large elements of the 1st Armoured Division including 600 tanks, were opposed by just 57 Israeli tanks. Inevitably, the 188th Brigade was destroyed, but its epic fighting retreat held the Syrians back until the morning of 7 October.

During the night of 6/7 October, Lieutenant Gringold led four tanks against the entire Syrian 90th Armoured Brigade and did as much damage as he could before numbers prevailed; 90 per cent of the 188th Brigade's officers and men became casualties. General Hofi gave Major General Dan Laner responsibility for the southern sector and he began by personally directing the columns of Israeli reinforcements crossing the Jordan at the Arik Bridge. Syrian armour had reached Nafekh and overrun General

Abandoned Syrian armour, 13 October
Syrian T-62 main battle tanks caught the wrong side of an anti-tank ditch on the Golan Heights. One has made a spectacularly unsuccessful attempt to negotiate a bridge laid down by an armoured bridge-layer. During the initial attacks, Syrian commandos made gaps in the Israeli wire and minefields but co-ordination broke down as the battle continued.

Rafael Eitan's headquarters.

The Syrian advance was halted on a line running from Kuneitra to within a few miles of the Jordan at Snobar. The Syrians concentrated their divisional supply system around Hushniya ready to resume the offensive but were dismayed to find themselves threatened from the rear. Israeli armoured forces led by Major General Moshe Peled were sweeping north east from the shores of the sea of Galilee and encircling them.

Initially Peled's men were the hammer to Laner's anvil but roles were reversed after the morning of 10 October when Peled's tanks suffered heavy losses attacking the Syrian HQ at Tel Kudne. In a classic battle of encirclement, the Syrian forces in the Hushniya pocket were destroyed utterly and after four days of fighting the Syrians had been pushed back to their own start line. The Golan Heights were choked with over 1,000 wrecked or abandoned vehicles including 867 tanks and the full spectrum of Soviet army equipment from BMPs to BRDM-2s and SAM-6s.

Re-capture of Mount Hermon

The remarkable Israeli victory on the Golan Heights was followed by a judicious counter-attack towards Damascus, and Mount Hermon was retaken by the 'Golani' Brigade. Stung by Syrian President Hafaz el Assad's demands for help, the Egyptians committed their armoured reserve and allowed the Israelis to storm across the Suez Canal and encircle the Egyptian 3rd Army. The USA and USSR pressured for a ceasefire and the war ended on 24 October.

The Day of Atonement

Re-equipped since the debacle of 1967, the Syrian and Egyptian armies launched simultaneous attacks on the Golan Heights and over the Suez Canal. A heavy concentration of SAMs kept the Israeli air force at bay.

Over 1300 Syrian tanks with APCs in close support attacked some 180 Israeli tanks in Golan. The Israelis lacked their customary air support and fought with the river Jordan and Sea of Galilee at their backs.

Although inflicting heavy losses, the Barak and 7th Armoured brigades were driven back. Syrian tanks were within 7km of the Sea of Galilee. But by the evening of 7 October, enough reserves had hurried to the front for the Israelis to plan a counter-attack.

An Israeli Centurion heads for Golan, 6 October
The Arabs attacked on a Jewish feast day for maximum surprise effect but, curiously, this accelerated the deployment of the Israeli reserves. Everybody was at home, civilian transport earmarked for requisition was parked in garages and the roads were already clear.

Above: Israel's armoured bulwark
On 6-7 October, Israel's fate hung on the desperate efforts of two tank brigades to stem the flood of Syrian armour heading straight for Galilee. Although fighting from prepared positions, the Israelis faced horrendous odds and the added danger of Syrian infantry tank-killer teams which infiltrated their lines at night.

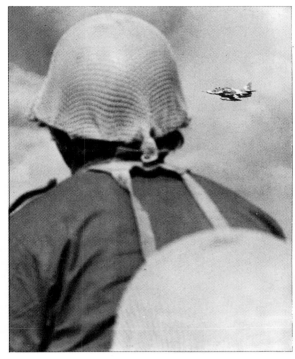

Above: Skyhawk over Golan
Once the Syrian SAM supply dwindled and the Israeli air force had again won air superiority, the Syrian forces were subjected to incessant airstrikes which blocked supplies of food, fuel and ammunition to their frontline troops.

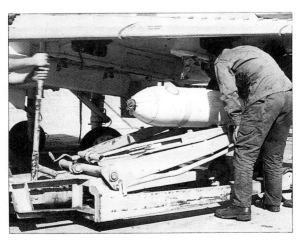

The Israeli counter-attack began on 8 October, grinding forward in bitter fighting towards Gamla Pass. The Israeli air force had by now got the measure of the Arab SAM batteries. Here, an A-4 Skyhawk is prepared for another strike.

Syrian pleas for assistance led the Egyptians to commit their last armoured reserve in Sinai and for Israeli armour to win a third desert tank campaign. Israeli forces crossed the Suez Canal and the Egyptians collapsed.

During 11-13 October Israeli forces overran the original Syrian defences in the Golan Heights. Arab counter-attacks lasted until 24 October but the northern frontline did not move far. Israel was victorious once again.

THIS IS THE END: The Fall of Saigon

1 March 1975: North Vietnam attacks over the old battlefields around Pleiku. It is the beginning of the end for South Vietnam.

After the American withdrawal from Vietnam in 1973, South Vietnam was left to fend for itself. However, under the 'Enhance Plus' scheme immense quantities of military equipment were poured into South Vietnam just before the USA pulled out. In little over six weeks the South Vietnamese air force became the fourth largest in the world. On the ground President Thieu had over a million troops and his forces controlled three-quarters of the country, including 85 per cent of the population.

Unlike the Geneva agreement in 1954, the 1973 treaty allowed the North Vietnamese troops in South Vietnam to stay in the areas they controlled. The CIA estimated that 150,000 NVA were inside the republic in 1973, but they and the remnants of the old Viet Cong guerrilla movement were still licking their wounds after the 1972 offensive. The communists feared that Thieu would overrun many of their areas in the south, organize an election which he would win and then tear up the ceasefire. It would be a return to the dark days of the late 1950s under Diem. On the other hand they were well aware of the shortcomings of the ARVN, which had proved its weakness at offensive operations in the 1971 invasion of Laos and achieved its defensive victories the following year only with lavish American air support.

The communist strategy was thus to mount small-scale attacks during 1974 while enlarging and improving the Ho Chi Minh Trail to provide a firm logistic base for a massive offensive in 1975. An attack that year and an all-out effort in 1976 would hopefully smash South Vietnam's defences and end the 35-year war.

President Nixon's resignation and Congress's reduction in military aid to South Vietnam placed a question mark over American support for their allies. The US withdrawal exposed the absolute dependence of the republic's economy on the American presence. There was no industrial basis for the huge urban populations which had grown in response to a market which had now disappeared, and conditions in the cities worsened rapidly. Soldiers found their wages reduced and Vietnam's endemic corruption plumbed new depths.

The communist General Tran Van Tra lobbied vigorously for a full-scale offensive in 1975 despite opposition from more cautious elements in Hanoi, such as Le Duc Tho. Compromise was reached and Tran was allowed to mount a limited offensive against Route 14, 95 km (60 miles) north of Saigon. The attack began in mid-December, and on 6 January the North Vietnamese flag was flying over Phuoc Binh, the provincial capital.

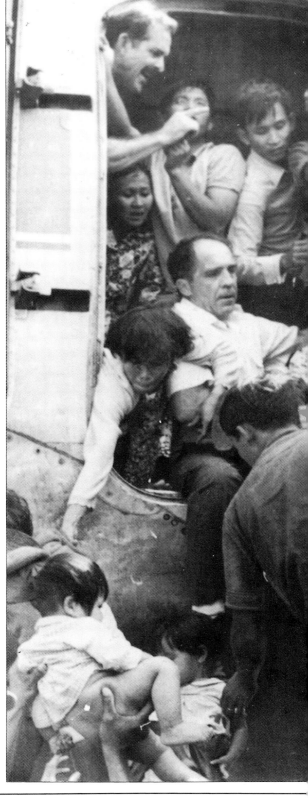

After the battle
A girl cycles past North Vietnamese T-54/55 tanks destroyed at the edge of Tan Son Nhut airbase during the last day of fighting before the South Vietnamese surrender.

The collapse of the South
The rapid disintegration of the Republic of South Vietnam came as a surprise to the North Vietnamese who did not expect to end the war before 1976. The quantities of hardware supplied to the ARVN forces obscured the fundamental weakness of their military machine.

Map labels: SAVANNAKHET, KHE SANH, Demilitarized Zone, QUANG TRI, HUÉ, DA NANG 30 Mar, TAM KY 25 Mar, SOUTH CHINA SEA, QUANG NGAI, LAOS, PAKSE, Central KONTUM, PLEIKU, Highlands, QUI NHON 1 Apr, Ho Chi Minh Trail, SOUTH, TUY HOA 1 Apr, BAN ME THUOT, VIETNAM, 'FISHHOOK', NHA TRANG, DALAT, CAMBODIA, PHUOC BINH, AN LOC, Cam Ranh Bay, TAY NINH, 3 Apr, BIEN HOA, XUAN LOC, LUONG, SAIGON, PHAN THIET, 'PARROT'S BEAK', VUNG TAU, CAN THO, Mekong Delta, Mekong

26 March 1975 Hué falls to Communist forces

30 April 1975 Communist forces enter Saigon

COMMUNIST CONTROLLED AREAS (APPROX) MID-JAN 1975 AND BY 25 MARCH

MILES 0 — 200
KILOMETERS 0 — 300

Ride the Highway west

The North Vietnamese offensive opened in March with an attack on Ban Me Thuot in the Central Highlands. Without American leadership and air support, the ARVN defence collapsed like a house of cards.

The rout became infectious with ARVN troops caught up in a general exodus from the north. The communist atrocities of 1968 had not been forgotten. The US Embassy began preparations for an evacuation of remaining personnel.

The evacuation was postponed by Ambassador Martin who believed the Saigon area could be defended. When it was finally ordered, it was too late: many South Vietnamese employed by the USA were left to their fate.

Escape from Nha Trang
An American civilian pilot struggles against a tide of desperate South Vietnamese fleeing the Communists. This chaotic, heart-rending scene was repeated at every airstrip and port in the South.

The South Vietnamese leaders were stunned by the defeat and further alarmed by the ominous silence from Washington. Meanwhile the Soviet General Victor Kulikov had visited Hanoi with promises of increased support, and the communists scented early victory. Throughout February North Vietnamese troops concentrated in the Central Highlands and struck towards the old battlefields around Pleiku on 1 March. The ARVN deployed their reserves to meet the assault only to find that it was a feint; the real target was Banmethuot, which was surrounded by a second offensive and on 10 March the beleaguered town fell. The South Vietnamese regional commander, Pham Van Phu, piled his family into an aircraft and fled, followed shortly by his demoralized soldiers and their dependents, most of them by road or across country.

The South Vietnamese leadership vacillated, Thieu alternately ordering the abandonment of the northern part of the country then demanding a desperate defence of Hue and Da Nang. He was overtaken by events. The northern ports were engulfed by over a million refugees; the citizens of Hue had not forgotten the bloodbath which attended the brief communist occupation in 1968. The ARVN panicked, and instead of fighting many literally fell over themselves to get on the last plane out.

Coup de grace

In the fantasy world of Saigon politics, the generals were still plotting against each other. Thieu eventually announced his resignation in a television broadcast on 21 April, bitterly attacking America for abandoning his country. The South Vietnamese army briefly redeemed its dismal combat record by a heroic last stand at Xuan Loc, 50 km (32 miles) east of Saigon. But the odds were overwhelming and North Vietnamese columns, spearheaded by T-54 main battle tanks, converged on the capital.

Long range 130-mm guns supplied by the USSR enabled the NVA to shell Tan Son Nhut airbase by 29 April, restricting the American evacuation effort to helicopters only. Ambassador Martin had grossly overestimated the ARVN's defensive capability and ordered the evacuation so late that countless numbers of South Vietnamese who had worked for the USA were left to their fate. In 18 hours a helicopter fleet, mainly Sikorsky H-53s and Boeing Vertol H-46s, evacuated 1,373 Americans and 6,422 Vietnamese to a US fleet off-shore.

Got to get out of this place

Fighter aircraft patrolled the skies to prevent a repeat of the North Vietnamese air strike which hit Tan Son Nhut a few days earlier. In the streets of Saigon frantic mobs fought to get on board the helicopters, ARVN soldiers quietly stripped off their uniforms and looters rampaged through the dying city. Air America Bell UH-1s evacuated a few CIA personnel from several impromptu landing zones, and as the last squad of US Marines boarded a helicopter from the embassy roof the mobs were already ransacking the lower floors. Five hours later, North Vietnamese tanks entered the Presidential Palace and the Vietnam war was over.

To reach the *Blue Ridge*
An ARVN UH-1 helicopter splashes into the sea next to the amphibious command ship USS *Blue Ridge*. The decks were already too crowded for further landings, so pilots had to ditch and be rescued by the ship's boats.

Defenders of the Republic
While their generals plotted against each other, or fled abroad, the South Vietnamese troops offered only patchy resistance. Only at Xuan Loc did ARVN troops fight a successful defensive battle, but by then it was too late.

On April 29 over 1,000 Americans and 6,000 Vietnamese were lifted from Saigon to the US fleet offshore in an 18 hour helicopter operation. The North Vietnamese were already within artillery range of the centre of the capital.

1100 on 30 April: a North Vietnamese T-54 smashes down the gates of the South Vietnamese Presidential Palace. Inside, General Minh led a South Vietnamese delegation which had ousted President Thieu on April 21.

While many ARVN soldiers slipped off their uniforms these Presidential Guards were taken prisoner. The evacuation left masses of paperwork behind which enabled the communists to identify former US employees and agents.

GOOSE GREEN TO TUMBLEDOWN: The Battle for the Falklands

On the 'Great Yomp'
Royal Marines describe a long march as a 'yomp', the Paras call it a 'tab': either way, the advance over East Falklands was an impressive achievement. The unforgiving terrain was hard to move over and offered little cover from enemy fire or observation.

0400, May 21 1982: The first elements of the main British landing force go ashore at San Carlos on East Falkland.

To win in war a commander must employ carefully co-ordinated efforts of all arms. No one arm can succeed if it operates in isolation. However, the repossession of the Falkland Islands in May and June 1982 was essentially an infantry action, albeit heavily dependent on the support of all arms and Services: the 105-mm light guns of the Royal Artillery, the 114-mm (4.5-in) guns of the destroyers and frigates of the Royal Navy, bomb and rocket attacks by BAe Harriers, direct fire support from the armoured vehicles of the reconnaissance troops, mine clearance by the Royal Engineers. Nevertheless it remained up to the infantry, in their classic roles, to close with the enemy, to winkle him out of his positions, and to occupy the ground won.

The first major enemy ground position to be tackled was the garrison of Darwin and Goose Green, some 20 km (12 miles) to the south of the beach-head. This task was given to the 2nd Battalion, The Parachute Regiment (2 Para), who secured the jumping-off point at Camilla Creek from which to launch the attack. A half battery of 29 Commando Regiment Royal Artillery was flown in to support them; not much, but all that could be achieved in the time available. The CO decided to open with a night attack on the hills overlooking the settlements, supported by the half battery and naval gunfire.

2 Para at Goose Green

The attack progressed satisfactorily to start with, but as daylight came on 28 May the full extent of the well-prepared defences, only approachable over entirely open ground, became apparent. With only very limited artillery support, and that from the air prevented by the weather, the achievement of the battalion's objectives was a hard slog. The death of the CO, Lieutenant Colonel H. Jones, personally attacking enemy strongpoints, was an added spur to his men, who used infantry anti-tank weapons very effectively to silence well-established weapon positions. And so, by nightfall, and at a cost of 16 dead and over 30 injured, 2 Para was established on the dominating ground. The night had been spent in preparation for another day's fighting when, at first light, two captured Argentine NCOs were sent forward with an ultimatum. It was only when the reinforced garrison surrendered that the paras realized its size. As well as over 200 Argentines dead on the battlefield, more than 1,000 men came out of Goose Green to surrender.

While this battle was being fought, in order to close with the main enemy garrison around Port Stanley other units of the brigade had begun the

'Great Yomp'. The loss of *Atlantic Conveyor* on 25 May had cost the soldiers a large proportion of their transport helicopter lift (as well as many other important stores), so there was now no other way forward. While 45 Commando Royal Marines marched to Douglas settlement before moving on via Teal Inlet to Mount Kent, 3rd Battalion The Parachute Regiment (3 Para) moved directly to Teal and thence to Estancia Mountain.

Meanwhile, naval Sea King helicopters flew patrols of the SAS right forward by night, and they probed the Argentine forces in the mountains. Then on successive nights, and company by company, 42 Commando RM flew into the landing site they had secured and cleared the enemy from the two main ridges, Mounts Kent and Challenger.

From their positions on Estancia, Kent and Challenger, the three forward infantry units carried out their extensive and detailed patrolling of the enemy positions that were to be their objectives in the main battle which would have to follow if the enemy was to be defeated. It was arduous, cold, dirty and dangerous work, but it paid off when the time came.

Soon after the fall of Goose Green the 5th Infantry Brigade arrived in San Carlos and was tasked with closing up to the enemy on the southern route. In a daring dash by helicopter and any other means of

Honour at stake

After reconnaissance by the SAS and SBS, the main landing took place on 21 May. The amphibious force had been safely landed after an 8,000 mile journey and now began to secure the beach-head.

The first major action occurred a week later as 2 Para attacked Argentine positions at Goose Green, the settlement on the isthmus connecting East Falkland and Lafonia. At some cost, the Paras compelled their opponents to surrender.

With the loss of the vital helicopters aboard the Atlantic Conveyor, *the British troops had to march across East Falkland to the main Argentinian positions in the hills overlooking Port Stanley. By 10 June the British were ready for the decisive battle.*

transport that could be found, 2 Para pushed forward to Bluff Cove, and it was on the final day of the follow-up to this move that two companies of 1st Battalion Welsh Guards were caught in the bombing of the logistic support ship *Sir Galahad* at Fitzroy.

Thus by 10 June the British were firmly established in the mountains 16 km (10 miles) to the west of Port Stanley, the enemy had been cleared from the rest of East Falkland and the final assault on the main Argentine positions could go ahead. This was the classic infantry battle of the war and was carried out in two phases.

In the first phase, making full use of the information gained over the previous nights and days by their observation posts and patrols, 3rd Commando Brigade carried out a co-ordinated three-battalion night attack. In the north 3 Para, in a bitterly contested fight in which Sergeant McKay won the second VC of the war, carried Mount Longdon. To the south of them 45 Commando RM drove the enemy from the particularly rocky and difficult twin

Winning the air battle
Without control of the air above the naval Task Force, the whole operation was doomed to failure. No-one knew quite what to expect from the Sea Harriers which had always been controversial aircraft but they proved to be worth their weight in gold.

San Carlos Water
The landings in the narrow waters between East and West Falkland were necessary as the beaches near Stanley had all been mined and booby-trapped. The ferocious Argentine air attacks on the ships in the Sound were a disagreeable surprise to the Task Force.

Royal Marine Blowpipe launcher, San Carlos
The air defence of the beach-head relied on a mixture of Rapier and man-portable surface to air missiles, the SAMs of the fleet, and massed general purpose machine guns. Although several warships were sunk, most of the Royal Fleet Auxiliaries and merchantmen which carried the supplies escaped intact.

summits of Two Sisters. And southward again 42 Commando, in a brilliantly well-prepared and executed attack, moved right round the flank of Mount Harriet, driving the 300 or so defenders who were not killed or captured *in situ* into British lines to be made prisoners there.

Two nights later, back under command of 3rd Commando Brigade once more, 2 Para conducted a beautifully co-ordinated attack to carry Wireless Ridge, and to watch the sunrise in the heart of the Argentine rear area; while on the main ridge the 5th Infantry Brigade's 2nd Battalion Scots Guards fought their way on to Mount Tumbledown, defeating one of the toughest of the Argentine battalions. This attack was supported by a feint by 1st Battalion Welsh Guards – made up to strength after their losses at Fitzroy by two companies of 40 Commando RM – on the southern flank by the main Stanley road, whence it was believed the Argentines expected the attack to come.

With daylight, 1st Battalion 7th Gurkha Rifles was passing through the Scots Guards to take Mount William when the enemy crumbled and resistance ceased. That night the Argentine garrison surrendered.

An Argentine air strike at San Carlos
An IAI (Israeli Aircraft Industries) Dagger fighter-bomber passes low over a Royal Fleet Auxiliary. The air assault on the Task Force culminated on 25 May, Argentina's national day, with a concentrated strike which sank the destroyer *Coventry* and the freighter, *Atlantic Conveyor*.

Very aggressive infantry patrolling built up an accurate picture of the Argentinian defences so the assault was planned in meticulous detail. Casualty evacuation remained risky with the Argentine air force still very active.

In a series of classic infantry assaults, British forces stormed Mount Longdon, Two Sisters and Mount Harriet. A final night attack on 12 June broke the Argentine defences on Wireless Ridge and Tumbledown, effectively ending the war.

The final assault was supported by naval gunfire, 105 mm guns and light tanks. The surviving defenders streamed away into Stanley in no semblance of military order. At 2100 on 14 June, the Argentine garrison surrendered.

BEKAA VALLEY: Air War over Lebanon

6 June 1982: While world attention is focused on the battle for the Falklands, Israel invades the Lebanon to destroy the PLO.

In the Middle East conflict of 1973 Israel's air force had suffered heavy losses in the first few days of the campaign to the Egyptian and Syrian SAMs, but in the June 1982 invasion of Lebanon by Israeli forces the Syrian missile complex in the Bekaa valley was destroyed without the loss of a single Israeli aircraft.

The Syrian air-defence complex in the Bekaa valley consisted of two SA-2 batteries, two SA-3 batteries and some 15 SA-6 batteries, and had been in position for about 12 months before the Israelis carried out their attack on 9 June. The position of the batteries and their associated equipment had been closely monitored by Israel using RPVs equipped with electro-optical sensors which relayed the data to ground stations in the rear for immediate analysis. It soon became apparent to Israel that with a few exceptions the SAM batteries were static for extended periods and that their exact position could easily be determined.

There were four main parts to the successful attack on the SAM defences in the Bekaa valley: electronic warfare, deception, attack of the SAM sites, and counter-air operations. For the electronic warfare part a number of Boeing 707s, fitted with a variety of electronic warfare equipment, flew well to the rear (out of range of the missiles) and their equipment automatically identified the missile site radars and then jammed them; communications systems, which are essential in any integrated air-defence system, were also jammed.

The second stage was to send over numbers of drones to simulate attacking Israeli aircraft. As these approached the Syrian air-defence networks the radars were activated to track them, and shortly afterwards the Syrian batteries started to launch missiles at the drones.

As soon as the Syrian SAMs started to engage the drones, Israeli air force Phantoms, armed with American-supplied AGM-78 Standard ARMs (anti-radiation missiles) and AGM-45 Shrike ARMs (a weapon also used by the British in the Falklands conflict of 1982) attacked each battery. Before the missile is launched the aircraft carrying the AGM-78, normally a Phantom, receives the hostile

radar signal which is then processed to determine the location and type of target; this information is then passed to the missile which is then launched and homes on to the target. The Standard ARM is a development of a naval surface-to-air missile, and its solid-fuel dual-thrust motor gives it a much longer range than the earlier AGM-45 Shrike, whose parent aircraft has to approach much closer to the target in order to launch the missile. In addition, the AGM-78 has a much larger HE warhead and can therefore inflict more damage on the target.

As soon as the radars of the Syrian SAM batteries had been destroyed, waves of strike aircraft, including McDonnell Douglas Skyhawks and IAI Kfir-C2s, went in and attacked the missile sites with standard iron bombs and cluster-type weapons, the latter being of particular use against the batteries which, with their associated supporting equipment (generators, reloaders and command caravans), tend to be spread out. With these techniques 17 out of the 19 batteries are believed to have been destroyed. It is also probable that the RPVs were in the area of the SAM sites during the attacks to enable the Israeli commanders to the rear to monitor the effectiveness of the attacks closely and to confirm exactly which batteries had ben destroyed and which were only damaged and therefore needed an additional attack.

Airborne command post

To protect its SAM suppression aircraft the Israeli air force employed the Grumman E-2C Hawkeye AEW aircraft as an airborne command post with McDonnell Douglas F-15 and General Dynamics F-16 aircraft flying top cover. The E-2C could detect the Syrian Mikoyan-Gurevich MiG-21 and MiG-23 aircraft as they took off from their bases in Syria, and the Israelis were then able to position their aircraft before the Syrians arrived over Lebanon. Syrian fighters rely heavily on ground control to make a successful interception, and the Boeing 707s jammed the communications links between the fighter and ground stations to such effect that often the Syrian fighters had little idea where the Israeli aircraft were coming from until it was too late.

At a later date several of the more modern SA-8 'Gecko' batteries were destroyed in the Lebanon, and in August and September the same year at least 10 SA-9 'Gaskin' batteries were also destroyed by the Israeli air force.

During the invasion of Lebanon Israel shot down at least 84 Syrian aircraft while their own losses amounted to one RF-4E Phantom reconnaissance aircraft, one A-4 Skyhawk and one Bell AH-1 Cobra anti-tank helicopter.

When the initial reports of the Israeli success in defeating the Syrian SAM defences in the Bekaa valley were disclosed it was widely believed that Israel had invented some new weapons, but this was not the case. Over some time Israel had carefully analysed the situation and used all of its resources to produce a co-ordinated plan that when eventually put into operation worked like clockwork.

Israeli Eagles
The acquisition of the McDonnell-Douglas F-15 Eagle enabled the Israeli air force to retain the technological edge it had enjoyed since 1967. Well trained pilots flying the best machines available and directed by AEW aircraft like the Grumman Hawkeye made an unbeatable combination.

The electronic battlefield

The objective of the Israeli invasion was to destroy the PLO bases in Lebanon from which they raided over the Israeli border. The large Syrian presence in the east of the country meant a bigger clash was inevitable.

Wary of the Israeli's air power, the Syrians deployed numerous SAM batteries in the Bekaa Valley. Unless neutralised, Israeli aircraft would not be able to support their ground forces. Here, an F-4 drops a flare to decoy heat-seeking missiles.

Israeli drones drew Syrian fire. As SAM batteries switched on their radars and launched missiles, they were engaged by Shrike missiles fired from F-4 Phantoms. The Shrikes homed in on Syrian radar transmissions, knocking them out.

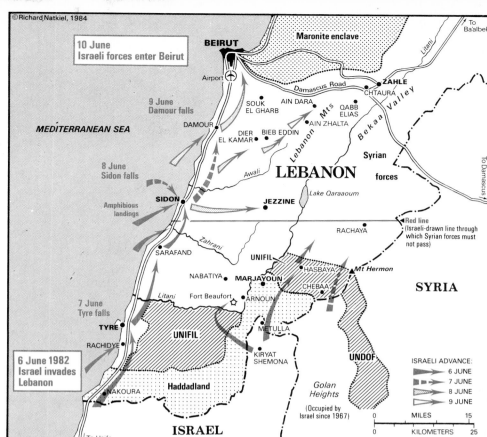

Left: PLO defences
The standard 'Beirut RV': a pick-up truck with twin Soviet 23mm cannon served as an anti-aircraft weapon or as the final arbiter in factional street battles after the Israeli withdrawal.

Right: Lebanon 1982
The invasion was President Begin's solution to the PLO's sporadic terrorist attacks over the northern border. Unfortunately, it embroiled Israel in the Lebanese political quagmire. The PLO bases were overrun and the Syrians defeated but Israel was now committed to holding an indefensible border strip.

Syria on the other hand committed a number of major tactical errors. The worst of these was not moving its SAM batteries very often, so allowing Israel to locate and eventually to destroy them. Logically, as soon as an Israeli RPV had passed overhead any compromised battery should have been moved to a new position and perhaps a decoy battery left in its place. Often far too many radars were operating at once, when in fact only a few were required and subsequently many radars were knocked out by ARMs. Tracking radars were sometimes switched on before the target was even in range to be tracked, so giving away the radars' positions to no purpose.

MiG-23BN 'Flogger F'

Two Syrian air regiments were equipped with this export version of the USSR's MiG-27 'Flogger D'. Inferior to the F-15s and F-16s fielded by the Israelis, they suffered heavy losses. The Flogger F retains the MiG-23MF's powerplant, variable geometry air intakes and GSh-23 twin-barrel gun in a belly pack.

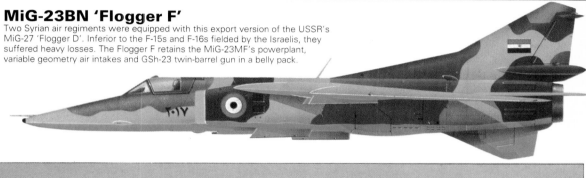

Made in Israel
Produced by Israel Aircraft Industries, the Kfir fighter-bomber flew ground attack missions alongside the F-4 Phantoms during the 1982 invasion of Lebanon. They made extensive use of cluster bombs which were devastatingly effective against the Syrian positions.

Blinded by the loss of their radars, the Syrian SAM batteries were pounded by A-4 Skyhawks and IAI Kfir fighter-bombers. Syrian fighters, which relied on ground control, suffered badly as their communications were jammed by Israeli ECM.

The attack on 9 June destroyed 17 out of 19 SAM batteries. New missiles soon appeared and on 28 July these SA-8s were attacked, 11 Soviet technicians being killed in the process. Here, an F-4 crashes in flames after a hit from an SA-8.

Having dealt with the Syrians, the Israeli air force began the indiscriminate bombing of Beirut into which the PLO had retreated. This, and the massacres at two PLO refugee camps, turned the 1982 invasion into a diplomatic disaster.

INDEX

NOTE: Page numbers set in *italic* type indicate an illustration